Management Control

Theories, Issues and Performance

Second Edition

Edited by

Anthony J. Berry
Jane Broadbent
and
David Otley

palgrave
macmillan

Selection, editorial matter and Chapters 1–6 © Anthony J. Berry,
Jane Broadbent and David Otley 1995
Selection, editorial matter and Chapters 1–5, 7 © Anthony J. Berry,
Jane Broadbent and David Otley 2005
Other chapters © individual contributors 1995, 2005

First edition 1995
Reprinted twice
Second edition 2005

Published by
PALGRAVE MACMILLAN
Houndmills, Basingstoke, Hampshire RG21 6XS and
175 Fifth Avenue, New York, N.Y. 10010
Companies and representatives throughout the world

PALGRAVE MACMILLAN is the global academic imprint of the Palgrave
Macmillan division of St. Martin's Press, LLC and of Palgrave Macmillan Ltd.
Macmillan® is a registered trademark in the United States, United Kingdom
and other countries. Palgrave is a registered trademark in the European
Union and other countries.

ISBN-13: 978–1–4039–3535–9
ISBN-10: 1–4039–3535–1

This book is printed on paper suitable for recycling and made from fully
managed and sustained forest sources.

A catalogue record for this book is available from the British Library.

Library of Congress Cataloging-in-Publication Data
Management control : theories, issues, and performance / [edited] by Anthony J.
    Berry, Jane Broadbent & David Otley.—2nd ed.
       p. cm.
    Includes bibliographical references and index.
    ISBN 1–4039–3535–1
    1. Management. I. Berry, Anthony J. II. Broadbent, Jane. III. Otley, David T.
    HD31.M29196 2005
    658.4′013—dc22   2004063622

10   9   8   7   6   5   4   3   2   1
14   13   12   11   10   09   08   07   06   05

Printed and bound in China

Contents

Preface

Following the publication of two monographs, *New Perspectives in Management Control* (Lowe and Machin, 1983) and *Critical Perspectives in Management Control* (Chua, Lowe and Puxty, 1989), members of the Management Control Association conceived the idea of collaborating to produce a textbook on management control. That book was intended to provide a broader and more flexible text on management control than those available at the time. This second edition reflects this original aim, along with the interests and idiosyncrasies of the various contributors. Part I has been updated and extended to include a new chapter on performance management and the rest of the chapters have been completely revised.

This edition, like the first, is aimed at those attending MBA and specialist masters courses, as well as advanced undergraduate courses. It is also designed to give practising managers a broader understanding of and approach to management control. However it should not be seen as providing the last or the definitive word on management control, but rather as the continuation of current debates. The book accepts that managers are central to the process of managing, but it does not uncritically accept the concept of 'managerialism'. It seeks to provide ideas that will stimulate a wider search for knowledge. It is not a prescriptive and structured course outline, but a resource that can be dipped into on a flexible basis.

The volume consists of two parts, each with a rather different focus. The six chapters of Part I introduce various ideas on management control. The 13 chapters in Part II, each of which is self-standing, can be amalgamated into courses to suit individual preferences.

The aim of Part I is to extend the boundaries of management control by exploring the various approaches to control that have been adopted by those writing on the subject. Chapter 1 examines the domain of organizational control, focusing on systems approaches. Chapter 2 reviews some of the approaches to control that have their roots in organizational literature. In Chapter 3 the way in which organizations and tasks are structured to achieve control is discussed, while Chapter 4 looks at the more detailed procedures that can be used. Chapter 5 explores the context in which control exists. It discusses how organizations are constrained by external forces yet are able to reject or buffer the effect of unwanted changes. Finally Chapter 6 introduces a framework for considering how performance management might be linked to control system design.

It should be stressed that Part I does not seek to prescribe the 'one best way' as we do not believe that this is possible. Thus it merely seeks to show the various dimensions of control that need to be considered by the practising manager, as well as the different ways in which control can be conceived. Our hope is as that, as a broader understanding is achieved, a larger number of possible solutions will emerge.

Part II examines particular control issues that are encountered in different types of organization. While the list of issues addressed is not exhaustive, a broad range of topical and relevant areas is considered.

Chapter 7 examines the general use of one of the most widespread tools of control, accounting. Chapter 8 explores performance management, Chapter 9 looks at control in divisionalized companies and Chapter 10 examines strategy. Chapter 11 reviews literature in which culture is seen as either a means to control or something that affects the possibility of achieving control. Chapter 12 discusses control issues in the context of managing knowledge. Chapter 13 considers the issue of controlling companies that have close relationships with others due to their membership of networks. Chapter 14 looks at the control of supply chains. Chapter 15 investigates control theory in relation to public sector organizations, focusing on schools. This is followed in Chapter 16 by an exploration of the control of risk and the risk of control. Chapter 17 considers the question of ethics and Chapter 18 examines sustainability. In Chapter 19 the editors reflect on the themes raised throughout the book.

Inevitably we will have omitted matters of interest to some readers and included matters of no interest to some. For example we have not explicitly considered the issues of gender and power. The two monographs mentioned earlier cover these important topics and readers are recommended to explore these books to fill in some of the gaps or to delve more deeply into other topics of interest. The comprehensive bibliography at the end of this volume will also facilitate study further. We should stress once more that this revised edition is a work of continuity and development, offering some ideas on organizational control but never pretending to have all the answers. The sheer complexity and uncertainty of human society and the creativity of individuals suggests that we shall never have all the answers to the problems of organization and management control.

In preparing this second edition we have had the support of a great number of people. In particular we have enjoyed the stimulating and critical comments made by many undergraduate and postgraduate students and managers on the first edition. The contributors to this volume are listed separately and our debt to them is obvious. Others who have given background support and assistance, without which we could not have completed this project, include members of the Management Control Association, who commented on chapters at some of their workshop meetings. Lesley Morris has provided secretarial support and coffee. Our thanks go to everyone concerned.

ANTHONY J. BERRY
JANE BROADBENT
DAVID OTLEY

Acknowledgements

The editors and publishers are grateful to the following for permission to reproduce copyright material: The Free Press, a Division of Simon & Schuster Adult Publishing Group, for two diagrams from *Competitive Advantage: Creating and Sustaining Superior Performance* by Michael E. Porter, copyright © 1985, 1998 by Michael E. Porter, all rights reserved; Pearson Education Limited for a diagram from *Strategic Management and Organizational Dynamics*, 2nd edition, by R. D. Stacey, 1996; the editors of *IJBPM* for material from C. Minchington and G. Francis, 'Divisional Objectives and Performance Measures', published in the *International Journal of Business Performance Management*, vol. 2; the editors of *AAAJ* for a table from Laura F. Spira and Michael Page, 'Risk Management: The Reinvention of Internal Control and the Changing Role of Internal Audit', *Accounting, Auditing and Accountability Journal* (1997) vol. 1b; Elsevier for a table reprinted from *Long Range Planning* (1987) vol. 20, no. 5, p. 50, by M. Goold *et al.*, 'Managing Diversity', and a diagram reprinted from *Accounting, Organizations and Society* (1980) vol. 5, no. 2, p. 236, by D. Otley and A. J. Berry, 'Control Organization and Accounting'; Harvard Business School for a diagram from R. Kaplan and D. Norton, 'The Balanced Scorecard . . .', *Harvard Business Review*, 1992; The Brookings Institution, Washington, DC, for material from B. Lev, *Intangibles: Management, Measurement and Reporting*, 2001; de Gruyter for a diagram from M. Alvesson and O. Berg, *Corporate Culture and Organizational Symbolism*, 1992; Basil Blackwell for material from M. Goold and A. Campbell, *Strategies and Styles*, 1987; John Wiley Publishers Inc. for a diagram from E. Schein, *Organizational Culture and Leadership* (1985). Every effort has been made to contact all the copyright-holders, but if any have been inadvertently omitted the publishers will be pleased to make the necessary arrangements as quickly as possible.

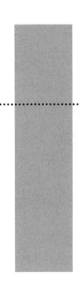

Notes on the contributors

Dila Agrizzi is Lecturer in the Department of Accounting, Management and Finance at the University of Essex, where she teaches Advanced Management Accounting and Issues in Accounting and Management Accounting. Her main research interest relates to management control in the public sector and her current project focuses in particular on the use of Performance Indicators as a control device in the UK National Health Service. She is also interested in the development and usage of costing information in hospitals (which was the subject of her doctoral thesis). Dila worked as accountant in the private sector, before undertaking her PhD studies which were completed in 2003.

Gloria Agyemang is Senior Academic at the University College Worcester, where she leads the public sector management programmes. She has several years' management and teaching experience in universities in the UK and Africa. Her research interests are in the use of finance and accounting technologies within UK government policy for organizational change in the public sector. Currently she is a doctoral student and her thesis examines the effects of Fair Funding and other recent DfES initiatives on management processes within Local Education Authorities.

Amanda Ball is Senior Lecturer in Accounting and Finance at the University of Nottingham. Amanda's current research focuses on the role of systems for accounting and reporting in enabling a transition to a more sustainable future. Amanda is particularly interested in how such systems might develop in public service organizations.

Anthony J. Berry is Professor of Management Control in the Business School of Manchester Metropolitan University, having previously been at Sheffield

Hallam and Manchester Business School. He began his professional life as an aeronautical engineer in the UK and the USA. He has published widely in accounting and management journals. He is editor *Leadership and Organisational Development*. His research interests are management control, risk, consultancy and leadership. He has been a member of the Council of the British Academy of Management and chair of the Management Control Association.

Jane Broadbent is Professor of Accounting and Senior Vice Principal at Royal Holloway, University of London. Initially trained as an accountant in the UK National Health Service she moved to academic life after taking a sociology degree as a mature student. Her research interests focus on the use of accounting as a tool of control in the public services and she has published widely in this area.

Mick Broadbent originally trained as an accountant and is now Professor of Accounting and Associate Dean of the Business School at the University of Hertfordshire. He has published various texts relating to control, performance and the management of financial resources of organizations. His current interest includes the manner in which management accounting and control is embedded within the curricula of university and professional bodies.

Alan F. Coad is Director of Postgraduate Programmes in the Department of Accounting and Finance at the University of Birmingham. As a professionally qualified accountant, he worked at senior levels in both public and private sector organizations. His current research interests include strategic management accounting, inter-organizational cost management, the economics of shared service centres, and institutional perspectives on corporate governance. He is a Council Member and Officer of the Management Control Association.

Paul Collier is Senior Lecturer in Accounting at Aston Business School in Birmingham, where he has been since 1999. Prior to joining Aston, Paul was Head of Training and Development for West Mercia Constabulary, having previously held a number of senior financial and general management positions in manufacturing and service industries and having worked as a consultant in Australia and the UK. Paul has published extensively in relation to police financial and performance management and also in areas of risk and knowledge management. During 2004, Paul was an ESRC AIM (Advanced Institute of Management Research) Public Service Fellow.

John Cullen is Professor of Management Accounting at the University of Sheffield and is a Fellow of the Chartered Institute of Management

Accountants. His main research interests are in the area of supply chain management, supply chain accounting, management control and corporate governance. His research is mainly case-study-based and it has focused on both small and large organizations in both the public and private sectors. The Chartered Institute of Management Accountants funded initial studies and this led to several publications in both academic and practitioner journals and books. Ongoing research projects include a study of reverse logistics in the UK retail sector, value chain and alternative governance structures in community-based business organizations and alternative accountability arrangements arising out of new organizational forms in the NHS.

Christine Helliar is part-time Director of Research at The Institute of Chartered Accountants of Scotland and has recently finished a project on professional ethics. She trained with Ernst & Young in London, qualifying as a chartered accountant. After six years she moved on to investment banking in the City of London and worked for Morgan Stanley, Hong Kong Bank Ltd (part of HSBC) and Citigroup. During her time at Dundee University she undertook, and was awarded, a PhD entitled 'Risk, Derivatives and Management Control'. Professor Helliar has published in a number of different areas, including derivatives and treasury risk management; derivatives and financial reporting; risk; management accounting and control; risk in auditing; finance; and accounting and finance education.

Ken McPhail is Professor of Social and Ethical Accounting at the University of Glasgow. He joined the department in 1996 after completing his PhD at the University of Dundee. Ken's research interests lie principally in the area of accounting and business ethics and he has lectured and published widely, particularly on the confluence of ethics, business education and civil society. His other main research interest is the relationship between religion and business, and he recently edited a special issue of the *Accounting Auditing and Accountability Journal* on 'Theological Perspectives on Accounting'. His current projects include a study of primary schoolchildren's conceptualization of business, charity ethical investment, service-based community learning projects, and business ethics as a built form.

Markus J. Milne is Professor of Accounting in School of Business at the University of Otago, New Zealand. Markus has published extensively in international accounting and business journals on many aspects of social and environmental accounting and reporting. He is currently involved in a three-year research programme on New Zealand Business and Sustainability supported by the Royal Society of New Zealand, and his research interests also closely align with many other interests he has in the outdoors including mountaineering and search and rescue.

Jan Mouritsen is Professor of Management Control at Copenhagen Business School, Denmark. His research is oriented towards understanding the role of management technologies and management control in various organizational and social contexts. He focuses on empirical research and attempts to develop new ways of understanding the role and effects of controls and financial information in organizations and society. He is interested in translations and interpretations made of (numerical) representations (e.g. as in budgets, financial reports, non-financial indicators and profitability analysis) throughout the contexts they help to illuminate. His interests include intellectual capital and knowledge management, technology management, operations management, new accounting and management control. Jan is currently editorial board member of twelve academic journals in the area of accounting, operations management, IT and knowledge management, and management generally.

David Otley is KPMG Peat Marwick Professor of Accounting and Associate Dean at Lancaster Management Schoool, Lancaster University. He has conducted research into the behavioural aspects of accounting and budgetary control systems for over three decades, publishing widely in major international journals. He is currently developing theoretical approaches for the study of the design and use of performance management systems in practice.

Tobias Scheytt is Assistant Professor at the Department of Organization and Learning, School of Management, Innsbruck University. His main research interest lies on the interrelation of management control practices and organizational life. Relating to poststructuralist, critical and systemic approaches to management and organizational issues, his work is particularly focused on the ways in which measurement systems informs modes of organizational perception and knowledge, power relations and culture(s) in organizations.

Willie Seal is Professor of Management Accounting at Birmingham Business School in the University of Birmingham. After graduating from Reading University, he worked in London with Touche Ross, moving to the University of York, where he studied under the guidance of Professors Peacock and Wiseman. After researching and lecturing at universities in Nottingham, Bath and Sheffield, Willie became Professor of Management Accounting at Essex University in 1998. As well as researching and publishing on supply chain management, Willie has focused on the accounting/contracting nexus and financial and performance management in local government. His main current interests are concerned with shared service centres and the role of management accounting in corporate governance.

Kim Soin is Lecturer in the Management Centre, King's College London. Her research interests focus on three areas: first, she is engaged in analysing risk management, regulation and compliance practices in the financial services sector (in particular she focuses on how firms understand and manage risk, what influences and drives their risk management practices and how regulation impacts on risk management practices); the second area of research is on management accounting change in organizations; and the third area relates to culture and control.

Carolyn Stringer is Lecturer at the University of Otago, and was previously at Monash University. Carolyn's research interests are in the area of performance management and management control research. Her current research involves a longitudinal case study examining performance management practice in a large and complex organization. She has published papers on internal control, outsourcing and accounting education. Carolyn lectures in management accounting and performance management. She is a member of the Institute of Certified Management Accountants Australia.

An Overview of the Theories

The domain of organizational control

Anthony J. Berry, Jane Broadbent and David Otley

Introduction

Organizational control concerns everyone. Whether you are a manager attempting to run a department, a politician trying to frame legislation to control multinational corporations, or just an individual affected by the activities of the many organizations that touch on your life, organizational control is a fundamental concern. In what ways are organizations controlled? By whom and how? And how can we influence what they do? These are some of the questions that this book tries to answer.

We shall approach the topic in a questioning and critical fashion, and primarily from the point of view of a manager working in an organizational hierarchy. What control mechanisms are available to managers, and how can they best operate the levers of power? In trying to answer these questions we need to consider the points of view of other organizational participants and ask how controls affect what they do. Indeed control systems often take on a different complexion when viewed from the perspective of those being controlled rather than those doing the controlling. In addition we shall sometimes step outside the organization and address the issue of corporate governance, or how organizations themselves are controlled by external interest groups. Nonetheless our discussion will centre on the use of controls by managers within organizations, a topic that has become known as management control.

Many people have attempted to define the term management control, and in this and subsequent chapters we shall examine some of the alternative definitions that have been proposed. Let us begin with a simple but widely applied definition: 'Management control is the process of guiding organizations into viable patterns of activity in a changing environment.' Thus managers are concerned to influence the behaviour of other organizational participants so that organizational goals can be achieved. Of course this does not preclude managers from taking actions that will advance only their own interests and may even detract from overall goal achievement. Nor does it imply that organizational goals are fixed or even well-understood by most participants. But without some control mechanisms, organizational behaviour would degenerate into a collection of uncoordinated activities that lacked the cohesion required for continued organizational survival.

As can be seen, discussion of organizational control raises fundamental issues in respect of the nature of organizations and the activities that occur within them. These issues cannot be avoided, although it is all too easy to let them prevent discussion of the more practical issue of the design and implementation of control systems. We shall attempt to steer a middle course by pointing out issues and problems as they arise, while continually keeping in mind the central aim of this book, namely to set down some of the principles governing the design and use of managerial control techniques within managed organizations in both the public and the private sector.

The domain of control

When analyzing a controlled system it is first necessary to define the boundaries of that system. These boundaries are not laid down by some external agency, but are open to definition by the analyst. Thus we may choose to consider the control of individuals, either by themselves or by some external agent, the control of a group of people, the control of an organization or the control of a whole society. Secondly, it is necessary to consider who is exercising control. Again this may be an individual or an organization, or it may even be an organization apparently exercising self-control through a set of designed control mechanisms that relate to no easily defined individual or group. The boundaries of the controlled system and between controller and controlled are thus arbitrary, but they are not unimportant. Some ways of looking at a system may be more helpful than others, so it is up to the analyst to make an appropriate choice.

In general we shall draw our systems boundary around an organization as a legal entity, but there will be occasions when we shall include within the boundary groups such as customers or creditors, who would usually be considered as external to the organization. We shall also assume that the controller is be a manager or a group of managers, such as a board of directors. However we wish to emphasize that these are arbitrary choices that can be varied if a more fruitful analysis can be obtained by so doing.

There is also the question of the system's goals. In what sense do organizations have goals, and how can we establish what they are? This has been an issue of considerable interest to organization theorists, but no conclusive answer has been reached. In a well-known and seminal paper, Cyert and March (1963) assert that 'Individuals have goals; organizations do not', although the remainder of their paper is devoted to discussing how the concept of an organizational objective can be made meaningful. Certainly there is great difficulty in coming to any conclusion on the issue. We can ask a number of questions. Whose goals are we considering, and how stable are they over time? What agreement is necessary between participants before we can accept a goal as belonging to the organization rather than to a group of individuals within it? Indeed who should be regarded as participants, and who are external parties?

One answer to this question has been provided by Barnard (1938), in his construct of the purposive organization. Another is provided by Cyert and March (1963), who speak of the goals of the 'dominant coalition' as essentially being the goals of the organization. While it would be too limiting to believe that any organization had only one purpose, or indeed that the only purposes of members of the organization were those of the dominant coalition, it is a helpful notion to regard organizations as purposive. In that sense control includes both regulating the process of formulating purpose and regulating the processes of purpose achievement. The schools of managerial thought that would claim some of this territory include corporate strategy and policy formulation.

J. D. Thompson (1967) has suggested that these problems can be understood by considering three major themes: the establishment of purpose, the pursuit of effectiveness and the struggle for efficiency. The establishment of purpose refers to the general problem of giving shape and meaning to the patterns of activity and resource allocation within the organization. Purposes are not necessarily stable over time, for they may be formulated in ways that are contingent upon changes, both within and without the organization.

If we define effectiveness as a measure of the achievement of purpose, an effective organization is one that achieves a substantial number of its purposes in any given period. Of course it is possible that an organization's effectiveness will be weaker in the long term than in the short term, or *vice versa*. It appears, then, that the notion of effectiveness can be rather inexact, in that some measure of the achievement of a set of fuzzy purposes may itself be fuzzy. Figure 1.1 illustrates this point.

Given that one might locate a boundary for an organization and test, at that boundary, whether a purpose has been achieved and therefore establish the notion of effectiveness, we might also create a boundary around the notion of effectiveness and within that boundary discuss the question of

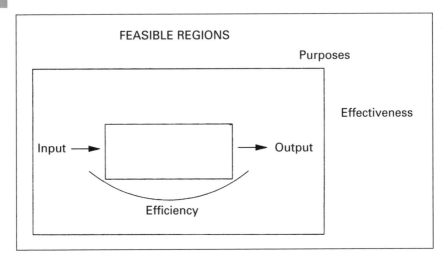

Figure 1.1   Bounding domains for purpose, effectiveness and efficiency

efficiency. Here efficiency is the relationship of outputs to given sets of inputs. These relationships can be expressed in many ways. For example accountants often relate the value of outputs in a market place to the value of inputs in the factor market place, and conclude that efficiency gains will occur either if the value of the outputs rises per unit of input, or if the cost of the inputs falls per unit of output. It is helpful to note that technical efficiency gains measured in this way might be a confusion of relative price changes and gains in technical efficiency in the transformation process. Thompson argues, and we agree, that technical efficiency can only be discussed in a bounded system where the boundaries are closed for analysis, and that effectiveness can only be discussed in a differently bounded system (Figure 1.1). Purpose, however, by its very nature will tend to be unbounded, and the product of social interaction.

These notions of purpose, effectiveness and efficiency lie at the heart of the task of controlling an organization. Regulation of the processes of formulating purposes is an area of considerable interest, as is regulation of the processes of achieving effectiveness. It is a common observation that most accounting control has tended to focus on the processes of achieving efficiency. However recent developments in, for example, strategic accounting have begun to move the focus to the more general problems of organizational management. In this sense the control model offered by Robert Anthony (see for example Anthony & Govindarajan, 2004, that we shall discuss this in Chapter 2 in some depth), talks of strategic control, managerial control and operational control, is clearly a mirror of the layering of purpose, effectiveness and efficiency. These three problems will be with us as we pursue the general puzzles of control, especially goals and their achievement.

For the moment we shall sidestep the complexities arising from the problem of defining goals in a precise manner and substitute 'accepted plan of action' for 'goal' in most control applications. For example many organizations seem to move between periods of relative stability, when agreed plans of action are pursued, and more turbulent periods when various interest groups engage in negotiating and bargaining to establish new agreements. Perhaps the minimum overall goal we need to consider is that of survival. This goal is less problematic in that most organizations seem to have a fundamental commitment to remaining in existence (Lowe and Chua, 1983). Beyond that, the importance assigned to various subsidiary goals appears to be largely a function of the relative power of interest groups espousing particular concerns.

We are thus taking a stakeholder view of an organization, where by various interested parties exert pressure to ensure that the plan of action reflects their individual concerns to the greatest possible extent. The plan finally settled upon will depend on the relative power and influence of the groups involved. Yet it is usually in the interest of most groups that the organization continues to survive. From this perspective it is the feasibility of a plan (that is, its acceptability to disparate groups of interested parties, given their respective bargaining power) that is the fundamental guiding principle upon which subsequent control actions are based. Ideas of optimality are very much the icing on the cake, for identifying and operating within such a feasible region is difficult enough. We are therefore adopting a 'satisficing' (Simon, 1957) approach, where the attainment of satisfactory results is regarded as adequate, rather than pursuing some concept of the best possible result. However this is not to understate the importance of the cultural and symbolic significance of goals. Individuals may be committed to an organization because of its espoused goals, even when these goals do not necessarily guide many of its actions. Indeed it is probably more helpful to think of goals in this symbolic manner, rather than as their being the guiding feature of a control process.

However different organizations exhibit significant differences in the nature and the use made of their goals. Etzioni (1961) has developed a useful typology. He distinguishes between three ideal types of organization; normative, utilitarian and coercive. Normative organizations exist when most participants share the same goals; here the concept of an overall organizational goal is helpful and can be considered as the aggregate of the goals held in common. Utilitarian organizations exist when the goals of participants are irrelevant to the activities of the organization; participants' involvement is on a contractual or instrumental basis. Here some form inducement/contribution analysis (Barnard, 1938) is appropriate, but the derivation of overall organizational goals is not possible or helpful. It can be argued that most business organizations are predominantly of this type. Finally, in coercive organizations the values of the participants are opposed to those of the organization (or perhaps more precisely, to those of the ruling coalition within it). It is the power of this coalition that enables the organization to impose its values on unwilling participants.

Mechanisms of control differ significantly in each of these sets of circumstances. Thus the relationship that exists between individual and organizational goals can be seen as one determinant of the control processes that will be used, rather than the definition of the object of control. One task of the management control system is to assist the organization to identify a feasible set of activities that will provide acceptable inducements to all participants to carry them out. In this way the organization will continue to exist as a viable entity.

However in practice the issue is considerably more complicated than the preceding ideas suggest. Not only do different organizations have different characteristics, but also different parts of the same organization may behave differently. The norms and values prevalent in one part are often quite dissimilar to those found in another. Different forms of involvement also occur at different hierarchical levels, with senior managers exhibiting (or being expected to exhibit) normative involvement, and lower-level workers exhibiting instrumental or coercive involvement.

The study of organizational control therefore involves considerable complexity and has to take account of the vagaries of human behaviour. Nevertheless it is possible to analyze and has been approached in a number of ways. In Chapter 2 we shall take up the approaches of organization theorists. Here we turn to a discussion of the approaches to organization and control in the literature on cybernetics and systems theory.

Cybernetic and systems approaches to control

This section outlines and examines the concept of control from the perspective of cybernetics and general systems theory. The term cybernetics was coined by Norbert Weiner (1948) to denote an area of study that covered 'the entire field of control and communication theory, whether in the machine or the animal'. More recently Pask (1961) has defined it as the study of 'how systems regulate themselves, reproduce themselves, evolve and learn'. Thus cybernetics has merged into the wider field of general systems theory; the aim here is to draw out those concepts which are useful to understanding the process of management control in organizations.

The cybernetic paradigm has underlain much work in management control. For example Hofstede reports that 'a review of nearly 100 books and articles on management control theory issued between 1900 and 1972 reflects entirely the cybernetic paradigm'. From the beginning, cyberneticians have been concerned with the common processes of communication and control among people and machines to attain desirable objectives, and have attempted to map the self-regulating principles found in human biological systems onto machine systems. Others have attempted to extend the self-regulating principles found in the human brain to organizations. Notable works in this area are Stafford Beer's *Decision and Control* (1966) and *Brain of the Firm* (1972). Finally, systems theorists have approached systems as wholes, rather than merely as the sum of their parts. Such approaches have not always been suited to organizational systems, leading to the development of the 'soft systems' approach, which was pioneered by Checkland and expounded in his book *Systems Thinking, Systems Practice* (1981).

We shall begin by outlining the cybernetic approach to the study of controlled systems and then extend it by considering the contribution of general systems theory in general and soft systems theorists in particular. This section will conclude with an evaluation of the contribution that these approaches can make to the study of management control.

The cybernetic concept of control

Cybernetics is intentionally not specific about the nature of the process being controlled; in this way it hopes to derive general principles of control that can be applied to different situations. The basis of controlled activity is seen as reducing deviations between actual process outputs and those which are desired; that is, it focuses on negative feedback. Although this may seem to be a very restricted point of view, part of the usefulness of the cybernetic framework is that the negative feedback mechanism is able to explain much of purposive and adaptive behaviour.

Following the general definition of control put forward by Tocher (1970, 1976) a basic model of a cybernetic control process can be derived. Four necessary conditions must be satisfied before control can be said to exist:

- The existence of an objective.
- A means of measuring process outputs in terms of this objective.
- The ability to predict the effect of proposed control actions.
- The ability to take action to reduce deviations from the objective.

These conditions are schematically represented in Figure 1.2.

The advantage of this particular scheme over similar models – which are often presented in the early pages of management control texts in terms of a

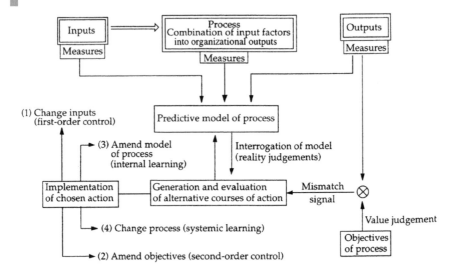

Source: Otley and Berry (1980).

Figure 1.2   Outline scheme of necessary conditions for a controlled process

detector, a comparator and an effector – is that it emphasizes the central role of the predictive model. This is reinforced when anticipatory (or feedforward) control is considered in addition to reactive (or feedback) control. Whereas reactive control waits for the occurrence of an error and then takes action to counteract it, anticipatory control predicts the likely occurrence of an error and takes action to prevent it occurring. Thus control is most effective when the process never deviates from its desired state. In the context of business enterprises, anticipatory controls essentially reflect the operation of planning systems. The more complex the system, the more likely it is that reliance will be placed on anticipatory controls rather than reactive controls. According to Ashby (1956) a lesson that can be drawn from biological systems is that it is advantageous to control not by error but by what gives rise to that error.

Unfortunately these concepts of control cannot be applied in any straightforward manner when analyzing organizational control, an issue explored in some depth by Otley and Berry (1980). Nevertheless the most important contribution by cybernetics may well be the idea that error avoidance can do much to explain apparently goal-seeking behaviour. This point of view is put forward strongly by Morgan (1979): 'Organisms in nature do not orient themselves towards the achievement of given purposes or ends; they do not orient themselves towards the goal of survival. Rather they adopt modes of behaviour and organizational forms which help them avoid certain undesirable states.' Such an approach certainly explains much of organizational and economic behaviour, but it must be recognized that the feedback process is often highly imperfect. As stated by Geoffrey Vickers (1967), one of the most cogent administrative writers informed by a cybernetic perspective, 'In the management of human organizations, feedback is often absent, ambiguous or uninformative and [the cybernetic concept of control] points to the complementary process of mental simulation which enables management to function in such conditions.'

This process of mental simulation is essentially one of attempting to predict the possible outcomes of alternative courses of action. In this context it should be noted that the cybernetic control model presented here allows for the possibility of adaptation and learning. Indeed this is one of the most important features of a viable control system operating in an open system, and will be explored further when general systems theory is considered. It is this cybernetic perspective that informed Lowe (1970) when he defined a management control system as:

> A system of organizational information seeking and gathering, accountability and feedback designed to ensure that the enterprise adapts to changes in its substantive environment and that the work behaviour of its employees is measured by reference to a set of operational sub-goals (which conform to overall objectives) so that the discrepancy between the two can be reconciled and corrected for.

The cybernetic approach is thus a logical and abstract approach to the study of management control systems. It can give some powerful insights into the operation of control systems. However it lacks specificity, and it also tends to assume that control is exercised from outside the system. Therefore self-controlled systems can be better approached by means of the general systems theory framework.

The general systems theory approach

The central concept of the systems approach is that of a system itself. That is, it seeks to explain behaviour by studying the interrelationship of parts rather than the nature of those parts. Therefore it is essentially holistic in nature, in contrast to the reductionist character of much scientific activity. The approach stresses the importance of emergent properties, that is, properties that are characteristic of the level of complexity being studied and may not have meaning at lower levels of analysis. (An example from a physical system is the concept of temperature, which is a property of an assembly of molecules and has no meaning in relation to a single molecule.) Systems can be arranged in a hierarchy of complexity (Boulding, 1956):

1. Static frameworks.
2. Dynamic systems with predetermined motions.
3. Closed loop control or cybernetic systems.
4. Homeostatic systems, such as biological cells.
5. The living plant.
6. Animals.
7. Humans.
8. Organizations.
9. Transcendental systems.

Most control systems theory is derived at a relatively low level of analysis, and an attempt is then made to transfer it to a much higher level of analysis, probably with adverse consequences in terms of applicability.

As noted earlier, a major contributor to the application of cybernetics and general systems theory (GST) to the management of organizations is Stafford Beer. In his book *Brain of the Firm* (1972) he takes the human brain and nervous system as a model for organizational control. He identifies five levels of control, labelled Systems 1 to 5. Systems 1–3 are concerned with the transformation processes required by the whole system and the maintenance of internal stability. System 4 is concerned with the maintenance of dynamic equilibrium with the external world, and system 5 with the self-conscious determination of goals. The interactions between these systems are modelled directly from the neuro-physiological system and are interpreted in terms of managerial situations. Beer's work is intuitive rather than carefully argued, and while it contains much stimulating material it is difficult to assess how much of this derives from the models propounded, and therefore its validity is not demonstrable.

GST is primarily a tool for dealing with very high levels of complexity, particularly in the case of systems that display adaptive and apparently goal-seeking behaviour. That this approach to complexity can be of value to the study of management control is perhaps best illustrated by a definition of accounting put forward by Weick (1979): 'Accounting is the attempt to wrest coherence and meaning out of more reality than we ordinarily deal with.' Although borrowed from a definition of art, this is a good portrayal of the central problem faced in accounting, and in management control more generally. Indeed approaching management control via accounting, as exemplified by Anthony (1965), can be seen as an attempt to deal systematically with the control of a complex, interconnected human activity system. The problems with the approach summarized in Weick's definition can be appreciated by adopting a systemic viewpoint. Thus accounting controls are the result of a great deal of systematic effort being put into the development of organizational controls; the result of putting a similar effort into being systemic remains to be seen.

An important distinction has been made between 'hard' and 'soft' systems approaches. The former tend to relate to physical systems with relatively clear objectives and decision processes, with quantitative measures of performance. The latter tend to relate to systems that include human beings, where objectives are vague and ambiguous, decision processes are ill-defined, possibly irrational and at best only qualitative measures of performance exist. From this distinction it appears that the soft systems approach has most to offer the study of management control.

The leading proponent of this approach, Peter Checkland (1972), claims that systems ideas are used primarily in a process of inquiry, an exploration of the meanings actors attribute to that which they observe. Thus the soft systems methodology deals with the central problem of objectives in a subjective manner. First, an analysis is deliberately conducted in non-systemic terms and the analyst becomes familiar with the rich complexity of the system being studied. Second, a root definition – that is, a fundamental statement of purpose from first principles – of the basic nature of the system that is thought to be relevant to the problem situation is sought. Third, a conceptual model of the system is constructed using the minimum necessary elements to achieve the root definition; this is validated by the data gathered at the analysis stage. The crucial step in this process is obviously the construction of the root definition, and this is also the most subjective part of the process. Smyth and Checkland (1976) have attempted to build some safeguards into the formulation of root definition by using checklists and suggesting that definitions are presented to the participants in the situation for their views. Both safeguards are designed to facilitate what Vickers (1965) would call the process of appreciation, that is, the development of a rich and insightful way of viewing a real-world situation. Such an appreciative judgement requires both factual and value judgements, and therefore any assessment of its validity is itself appreciative.

Despite such safeguards the application of systems methodology to organizations is dependent upon the subjective judgement of the analyst. Whether this is a strength or a weakness depends on your point of view; however it signals a substantial shift away from the methodologies of the physical and biological sciences. The model of scientific activity used in this type of systems approach is quite distinct from that used in the natural sciences.

It may therefore be argued that the systems approach carries with it a conservative ideology (Lilienfeld, 1978) as the analyst works within a framework of cooperative people who agree with the aims of the system. It has been suggested that systems analysis is in the same philosophical tradition as sociological structural functionalism. Although this is clearly true of cybernetics and the hard systems approach, it is less true of the soft systems approach, which is more in the verstehen tradition of thought. This tradition takes its name from the German verb 'to understand' and seeks through detailed knowledge of the system to understand how the participants within the system understand it. As Berry (1983) observes, in this school great stress is laid on the accuracy and honesty of observation, the sensitivity and perception of the observer and the imaginative interpretation of observations.

While there has been much academic criticism of the functionalist approach it is important to recognize that it is less limiting than is often supposed. Burrell and Morgan (1979) point out that organization theorists have often mistakenly equated open systems theory with the use of an organismic analogy. There are also wider perspectives that have been much less fully explored. These involve either taking a more subjective stance (moving to an interpretive position) or being more concerned with radical change than with regulation (regulation refers to the maintenance and continuity of system relationships that have been established or emerged over time). From the perspective of the study of control systems, the subjectivist position poses no particular problems; however regulation is evidently of central importance, although the study of regulatory processes does not necessarily preclude the use of more radical perspectives.

The contribution of systems thinking and cybernetics

GST and cybernetics can contribute to the study of management control systems (MCSs) in various ways. First, a systems point of view can be adopted in MCS analysis. This is the least controversial approach and may constitute little more than analyzing at the organizational level and making a conscious attempt to be holistic rather than reductionist in approach. The most insightful use of this approach has been made by Vickers (1965, 1967), who as a practising administrator has attempted to codify his experience in more general terms by adopting a systems point of view and using cybernetic terminology. In particular he argues for a systemic view point that explains organizational behaviour in terms of ongoing relationships rather than by the imputation of objectives.

Second, there are systems approaches to handling real-world MCS problems, which are perhaps best exemplified by Checkland's (1972) methodology. But although such an approach may provide a means to deal with real-world problems, it does not offer any theoretical basis for the study of management control. Indeed it discounts the possibility of any general theory, arguing that each problem situation is unique and must be dealt with on its own merits.

Third, there are concepts developed in cybernetics and GST that can be used to study MCSs and develop a theory of management control. However there seems to be a gulf between these concepts and their application to the study of management control. For example Schoderbeck *et al.* (1975) lucidly describe the basic concepts of systems theory and their application to management systems, but run into difficulty when applying these concepts to any particular topic. Admittedly this is partly because of their hard systems orientation, but their conclusions are disappointingly diffuse and vague after the initial excitement offered by the concepts. Similarly Amey's (1979) analysis of budgetary planning and control systems ignores the behavioural, organizational, forensic, strategic and political elements of control (McCosh, 1990). Perhaps the most successful text in this area is that by Maciariello (1984), who makes a consistent attempt to apply the cybernetic paradigm to management control systems, but even so achieves only mixed results. Perhaps we shall do no better; the reader is the best judge of that.

Finally, systems ideas have been used in other disciplines related to the study of MCSs, such as the open system and sociotechnical system movements in organization theory. It is notable that all the open system theories considered in this book adopt, explicitly or implicitly, an organismic analogy, drawing on concepts such as survival and functional factors related to that end, such as differentiation, integration and purposive rationality.

In summary, the application of systems thinking and cybernetics to the study of management control raises more questions than it answers. Yet the very fact that these approaches raise questions may be valuable in a field that has been preparadigmatic in its development. In the West the discipline that has probably had the greatest influence on management control to date is accounting, which is a clear application of a systematic approach. The systemic approach of systems theorists may provide a useful countervailing force in the development of more comprehensive theories of management control.

A social system consists of numerous components, each of which is self-controlling and contains models of the behaviour of the whole. In organizational control, the system's environment is also complex, as noted by Buckley (1968): 'The environment of the enterprise is largely composed of other equally groping, loose-limit, more or less flexible, illusion ridden, adaptive organizations.' If management constitutes an attempt to control situations with a greater degree of complexity and uncertainty than the available techniques can cope with, then the systems approach to studying management control at least has the potential to reveal some of the fundamental problems. For example it may indicate areas in which the wrong questions are being asked and inappropriate concepts adopted. It is no sense a complete theory, but it is the most developed one we have and it deserves serious consideration for that reason alone.

Summary

This chapter has introduced the idea of organizational control and some definitions of management control. It has discussed the domain in which control might be exercised, raising interesting questions about purposes and goals and using them, following J. D. Thompson (1967), to connect organizational control to the ideas of purpose, effectiveness and efficiency.

Based on a review of the cybernetic and systems approaches to organizational control, it has been argued that these approaches are not limited to mere description, but offer a systemic frame of thought in which ongoing relationships are the foci of analysis. As Checkland (1981) has demonstrated, there is also value in these approaches for the understanding of real world problems. While the step from the abstract idea to the concrete event is considerable, these approaches do offer possible routes to practical and intelligent theory development and problem solving.

Far from using general systems theory to argue managers are not important we argue that the part played by the manager is still central to organizational control. Also it is possible, as we have seen, to relate theories of learning to the cybernetic concepts of control to show that these approaches are not static. Finally, it should be noted that the classical systems theories discussed in this chapter still have currency. Chapters 13 and 14 will provide overview of contemporary systems issues; that is, control in networks and supply chains. These issues can be usefully explored by retaining an appreciation of the ideas of systems thinking.

Discussion questions

1. What is the difference between systematic and systemic thinking?
2. To what extent can the complexity of organizations be captured by systems thinking (relate your answer to the hierarchy of systems described in this chapter)?
3. Describe a control system in an organization that you know well. To what extent is it able to deal with the complexity it seeks to control?
4. Usng Tocher's (1970, 1976) description of a control system, evaluate the extent to which the following can be controlled: (a) the national economy, (b) a two-year-old child, (c) a team of footballers playing an international match and (d) your bank balance.

Approaches to control in the organizational literature

Anthony J. Berry, Jane Broadbent and David Otley

Introduction

As noted in Chapter 1, not all approaches to control have taken a systems perspective. This chapter provides a broad outline of the work of some of the authors and researchers who have considered the problem of control using various social and organizational frameworks. Social and organizational approaches seek to locate control in their context, and therefore in various ways take into account the organization's environment, structures and the people connected to them. The approaches place differential emphasis on the various elements, including performance management. Subsequent chapters will look in more depth at the impact on control of the structures of organizations and the contexts in which they exist, as well as the roles of the people within them. The intention in this chapter is not to provide prescription for the best way to operate control systems, but to continue the task begun in Chapter 1, of outlining the diverse approaches that have been adopted in seeking to theorize control in organizations. The manner in which control is theorized will of necessity affect the way in which performance is monitored. In approaching this discussion the chapter will review the development of ideas in management control systems by providing a historical overview of the works that have contributed to the current shape of the discipline.

The classical approach is perhaps best represented by the work of Robert Anthony and a series of coauthors. Anthony and Govindarajan's *Management Control Systems* (2004), which is now in its eleventh edition, can be seen as the first contemporary attempt to formalize the subject of management control. They sought to broaden accounting by linking it to other disciplines to provide a framework for management control systems. In so doing they considered the structure and design of relationships in the organizational system as well as its processes – the set of activities the system undertakes.

Anthony *et al.* (1989) constructed a framework of control processes within the organization in order to bound the notion of management control systems. Whilst this framework is now an old one it remains influential so must be considered. The management control processes the authors define are: strategic planning and control, management control, and task control. Strategic planning and control is concerned with longer-term goals and objectives, deciding what these are and evaluating the means by which they can be achieved. It is oriented towards external environmental issues. Task control is the more routine process of ensuring that day-to-day operations in the organization are carried out 'effectively and efficiently (Anthony *et al.*, 1989, p. 11).

Management control links these two elements. It is the process that ensures the strategy of the organization is reflected in the tasks carried out: 'The management control process is the process by which managers of all levels ensure that the people they supervise implement their intended strategies' (Anthony and Govindarajan, 2004, p. 4). This focuses much more on what appear to be their current views of the main aspect of management control. It has some continuity with their early approach but abandons the latter element of the original suggestion that 'Management control is primarily a process for motivating and inspiring people to perform organization activities that will further the organization's goal. It is also a process for detecting and correcting unintentional performance errors and intentional irregularities, such as theft or misuse of resources' (Anthony *et al.*, 1989).

Despite the changes their approach has remained remarkably consistent. They claim that the relationship between strategy, management control and operations (task) control is distinct and hierarchical (with strategy setting the agenda of management control, which in turn sets the agenda for task control), yet the boundaries overlap.

The process of management control described in both works incorporates organizational responsibilities and authority. It is a tool for managers and includes psychological considerations, in that managers must have the ability to communicate and inspire other employees. In both works it is noted that these non-financial elements are important, but little time is given to their consideration. It is taken for granted that the process is goal oriented, and efficient and effective performance is related to the organization's goals. Management control, it is argued, is built on a financially based control system, and as such the budgetary control cycle and performance measurement are central to the authors' thesis that creating responsibility centres provides the answer to management control. In this way performance is built into the core of management control systems.

Thus management control rests very firmly in the domain of accounting, albeit a more managerially based version than the somewhat restricted stewardship function envisaged by Anthony. This observation has been made elsewhere (Lowe and Puxty, 1989), and it is to a critical evaluation of the classical model that we now turn. The enduring influence of Anthony's thinking on the discipline provides the justification for addressing this critique with some rigour.

Lowe and Puxty criticize what they call the 'prevailing orthodoxy in management control' and suggest reasons why the focus should be broadened. Other organizational approaches also address this concern and can be used as a basis upon which to extend the boundaries of the domain – these will be discussed later in the chapter. Lowe and Puxty's seminal critique highlights a number of basic issues that need to be addressed by contemporary designers of management control systems. They argue that the three-tier approach offered by Anthony *et al.* (1989) means that the possibility of offering a holistic view of the organization is lost. Thus interlinkages between the interdependent levels are not considered and the environment in which the organization exists is omitted from consideration. Consequently there is a tendency to see control simply as a feedback process and there is a decoupling of planning and control, such that planning takes place, action follows and finally there is feedback on that action, all rather separately. This can be contrasted with the situation in which there is a dynamic interplay between the planning and control processes, such that feedforward as well as feedback control takes place.

Another crucial issue that Anthony *et al.* do not consider is that of organizational goals. They assume their existence and see the possibility of their existence as completely unproblematic. In so doing they reify the organization, that is, they treat it as an unambiguous, concretely existing object, and neglect the debate on whether it is the organization or the people within the organization that have goals (Cyert and March, 1963; Lowe and Chua, 1983; Pfeffer and Salanick, 1977) A related issue is whether stated goals can be used as an indicator of actual behaviour (Perrow, 1986). This is well debated elsewhere (for example Lowe and Chua, 1983), but it is essential to note that the stated goals of an organization cannot be unproblematically accepted as the goals towards which the organizational members strive.

These weaknesses are evident in some widely used techniques of management control that can be seen as illustrative of the classical approach. Accounting-based controls such as budgeting, standard costing and variance analysis are typical classical controls and are geared to operationalizing the strategy of the organization. They assume a given set of organizational goals, and indeed institutionalize them in the budget. The extent to which the environment of the organization is considered will depend on individual circumstances, but there may well be a tendency for an inward looking attitude (a bias that strategic management accounting – Bromwich, 1990, 2001 – seeks to mitigate, somewhat unsuccessfully given that it has not been as widely adopted as other techniques). In essence the process tends to be one in which the means of control are more important than achieving control (Drucker 1964). Despite the many recent developments in management accounting, these fundamental problems have not been alleviated.

Moving towards different approaches to control

Hopwood (1974) was one of the earliest writers to extend the boundaries of the concept of control. The accounting-type controls of the classical model fit into what Hopwood would see as the administrative category. Hopwood alerts us to the fact that this is not the only element to consider, and that it is also necessary to consider social control and self-control if organizational control is to be achieved. By defining these three elements of control Hopwood provides a bridge between the classical approach and sociological/psychological ideas in the organizational theory literature more generally.

Social controls are reflected in the 'social perspectives and the patterns of social interactions' (ibid., p. 26), or 'the way we do things here'. According to Hopwood, these factors are likely to affect the implementation of administrative controls and therefore organizational control cannot be achieved without reference to the patterns of social interaction and norms.

These themes have been picked up by Merchant (1985, p. 4), who emphasizes the social or behavioural side of control: 'Control is seen as having one basic function: to help ensure the proper behaviours of people in the organisation. . . . Control, as the word applies to the function of management involves influencing human behaviour.' This he calls personnel control, which includes both social control and self-control; it is also linked to what he terms action control and results control.

Results control refers to making individuals responsible for achieving particular results, and then rewarding them for their achievement. This allows the possibility of managers having autonomy of action provided they produce the desired outcomes. These outcomes must be quantifiable, and if this criterion is not met then action control might be used. In this situation the outcome might be difficult to define, but the required actions can be specified, and therefore the control process is geared to ensuring that the correct actions are carried out. Neither of these relate to the social aspects of control with which this section is concerned, but they help to define the domain in which social controls are useful. Thus in areas where it is difficult to define and measure outputs and when it is not entirely clear what actions are required, social controls are important.

For Merchant, social controls include such factors as 'getting the right person for the job', and training and culture. The latter two may well be linked as training can be seen as a socialization process in which a new recruit instilled with the culture of the organization, or 'the way we do things round here'. Merchant offers a 'broad conceptualization of control' ibid., that focuses on the control of behaviour; he also provides some discussion of the implementation of systems. Whilst he sees control of behaviour as important, in his view this comes not just from personnel control but also from action control and results control. However when advocating multiple forms of control he glosses over the drawbacks of this (cost and the possibility of undesirable side effects, ibid., p. 131). Also, whilst some consideration is given to the advantages and disadvantages of the different approaches, the choice between them is left to the individual and therefore is underconceptualized. Moreover possible conflicts between the different elements are not considered. Finally, the 'broad' conceptualization offered by Merchant is very inward looking and tends to neglect the influence of the wider environment on the behaviour of people in organizations.

The social theme is also developed in different ways by Etzioni (1961) and Ouchi (1979, 1980), both of whom provide a three-part analysis of approaches to control, again linking the social and classical aspects but with a rather different emphasis. Etzioni bases his work on the assumption that there are three major sources of control: coercion, economic assets and normative values. All three exist in organizations but some might predominate at different times or in different locations. He is mainly concerned with the notion of power, with power being the means to make subjects comply. If we define control as influencing others to carry out our intentions, then power is a control mechanism. Coercive power relies on the threat of physical pain or restriction of movement, as found in prison situations. Remunerative power is founded on the ability to provide material reward, for example salaries or wages, so this can be seen as the main element of the control an employer has over the employee. Normative power rests on the ability of an organization to provide a symbolic reward to its members, in a 'pure' form this can be found in a religious organization such as a monastery.

When looking at organizational responses, institutional theory, takes up some of these themes but in a different manner. It identifies pillars of isomorphism – coercive, cognitive and normative (Scott, 1995) – that are used in the legitimation of action. There is a growing body of work on the extent to which controls in organizations are the result of institutional currents. According to this approach, organizations legitimate their actions by mimetic practices that develop taken for granted ways of doing things in the context of accepted norms and regulative structures. In this situation management control systems are technologies adopted at the organizational level to support the institutionalization of a particular way of working (ibid.). More recently Soin *et al.* (2002) analyzed the implementation of an activity based costing (ABC) system and found that the system had been affected by other changes to institutional practices. The result was a 'less radicalised version of ABC' (ibid., p. 249) than had been intended by the implementers.

These approaches to control argue that the involvement individuals have with their organization rests on different motivations, and the way in which control is exercised depends on the type of motivation. For example if coercion is the main management control mechanism, this suggests there is no normative involvement and therefore it would be pointless to expect an individual voluntarily to adhere to the norms of the organization. In most organizations there may well be different combinations of the various types of power. For instance, whilst those who work in the caring services might well forego a larger remunerative reward for the normative reward of doing a worthwhile job, they will still require a salary. This highlights the pluralistic nature of control and raises the possibility that different people may respond differently to different approaches.

While attention to the role of power and use of the pluralist frame work are to be applauded, the approach does have its problems in practice. Although the different notions of power are highlighted in the examples discussed so far in this chapter, the implications of its existence are not dealt with rigorously, probably because the original work was not intended as a basis for management action. The practical prescription that we need to recognize power is not a zero-sum issue and therefore conflict is always a possibility and needs to be considered. The extent to which power is seen as either legitimate or illegitimate, or is seeking to institute controls that are either constitutive of behaviour (that is, enforce behaviour) or amenable to substantive justification (legitimating accepted practice) (Broadbent *et al.*, 1991) will determine the probability of conflict. Management control must recognize this and control systems should be designed to reflect the existence of both positive and negative power (the ability to get things done, and *vice versa*). These issues highlight the complexity of designing management control systems.

Contingency approaches

Contingency approaches to control recognize diversity and consider it possible to manage that diversity in a rational way, in that they see controls and the structures of control as related closely to the environment and technologies of organizations and the tasks performed in them. If the latter three elements are recognized then the requisite control system can be adopted. A link can be made between the use of contingency theory in management control and the work in this vein in the organizational literature. In this approach the environment external to the organization is acknowledged. As noted above, contingency theory argues that there is no one best way to approach organizations, but that each organizational design should reflect the environment in which it is found. A seminal study in this vein is that by Burns and Stalker (1961), who differentiate between the mechanistic organization, operating in stable conditions and with a known task technology, and the organismic organization operating in a more uncertain environment with less defined technologies. In the former a bureaucratic structure is appropriate, in the latter the laying down of tight rules is inappropriate or impossible and therefore a more flexible structure is required.

Other writers who acknowledge the importance of the environmental milieu are Hannan and Freeman (1977) and Aldrich (1979), who view the environment as actively shaping the organization. In the population-ecology approach the environment is seen as imposing a 'natural selection' process on firms, and those which survive are those which are suitable for the given environment. Hence it is less a question of adapting to the environment than of survival of the fittest.

Therefore there is some tension between the notion that an organization can survive by adopting the right structure and control system, and the notion that the organization has only a limited space within which to operate in a given environment. Both these approaches recognize that the environment is important, but both see the organization as at the mercy of the environment. Contingency theory perhaps views the environment as somewhat less threatening than does the population-ecology approach. However this is perhaps more a matter of tone than of final outcome. The message for management control is that the environment must be taken into consideration. However there is still doubt about the ability of these approaches to provide a satisfactory basis for action. For example critics of contingency theory approach have pointed to the problem of identifying discriminators that specify the environment or aspects of it sufficiently well to differentiate the situation and provide guidance on to what is appropriate. Perhaps, therefore, an essential task for managers and controllers is to consider variables in the environment of the organization.

Emmanuel and Otley (1985) and Emmanuel et al., (1990) accept that diverse environmental factors might drive the approach to management control, but turn their attention to accounting techniques that could be used to achieve control. They also look at the nature of decisions, and particularly the difference between programmed and non-programmed decisions. In programmed decisions there is a clear and predictable link between action and outcome so the outcome can be planned for; in non-programmed decisions there is a greater degree of uncertainty, making the outcome less predictable and planning more problematic. Clearly there is a strong link between the nature of the environment and the extent to which a decision is programmable. While the authors provide little advice on the design of management control systems, they stress that the multiplicity of variables within and without the organization must be taken into account when designing a system.

Anthropological approaches

In moving away from the classical approach some writers have shifted their focus to the social domain. This type of work has taken many guises, but was popularized by Peters and Waterman (1982), who brought the notion of culture to the forefront of popular management thought. Culture is not easy to define, but it can be broadly described as the norms, values and symbols that enable the members of a society or an organization to make sense of what happens in a similar way. This can be seen in Hofstede's (1980) influential (albeit contested – see McSweeney, 2002) attempt to characterize national cultures. Of course culture is a core factor in anthropology, where it has a much longer pedigree and ranges from communities in exotic locations (Douglas, 1969) to more organizationally based work in Anglophone societies (Douglas, 1986).

Reviews by Allaire and Firsirotu (1984) and Smircich (1983) show that when Peters and Waterman (1982) were introducing the notion of culture into the popular domain there already existed many different ways of approaching the study of culture in organizations. One view held that culture is a variable that can be manipulated to achieve the correct outcome for the organization; another insisted that culture is a dynamic and symbolic element that should be taken account of, but as it cannot be determined externally it cannot be used as a mode of control.

The first of these views was taken up by Peters and Waterman, who suggest that the role of management is to promote an appropriate culture, from which control will naturally flow. The implicit idea is that control will come from internal self-control, rather than being externally imposed by bureaucratic rules and regulations. This assumes that it is possible to impose a culture, which may not necessarily be the case. Socialization through apprenticeship, staff training and selection may well promote cultural control, but it is likely to be tenuous. Whilst helpful in bringing the richer cultural aspects of context to the fore, Peters and Waterman have been criticized for their thesis that certain companies have achieved excellence because of their culture. The authors' categorization of excellence has been questioned, and the companies' position of excellence has not always been sustained, throwing some doubt on the thesis. If a more symbolic view of culture is adopted, then the use of culture as a tool of control must also be questioned. In this view culture is not an independent variable that can be adopted or imposed at will, rather it is constructed by social actors in their daily lives. Peters and Waterman suggest that culture is a thing that is imposed or encouraged by managers, and they do not seem to question the ability of other groups to develop their own culture or to resist cultural imposition.

Bourn and Ezzamel (1986) have studied the NHS and the role of culture in a changing organization with strong professional cultures. They use the framework provided by Ouchi (1980) and the notion of clan control, that is the social control exerted on individuals who are part of a group and identify with the group and its values. They suggest that the moves for change in the NHS (intended to change the control of the service) might not have the intended effect as they would promote a different culture from that which prevailed at the time. This study underlines yet again the importance of considering culture when thinking about organizational control; it also highlights the difficulty of achieving a desired outcome by imposition. Studies of public services, particularly the health services in countries such as the UK and New Zealand, have demonstrated people's resistance to changes that run counter to espoused professional cultures (it should be noted that there is a difference between espoused and taken-for-granted cultures) (Broadbent *et al.*, 2001; Lawrence *et al.*, 1994; Lowe, 2000). Hence it cannot be assumed that culture can be imposed as a means of control.

Brunsson (1985) takes a different approach and considers the role of ideologies. He reflects on what is required to promote action and differentiates between weak and strong ideologies. Action, he argues, is often promoted by the ability to act according to predetermined ideas about what is appropriate – these he sees as ideology. A strong ideology avoids the need for long decision-making processes, with action and reaction being somewhat preprogrammed so there is general agreement on how action should proceed and control is relatively easy. A weak ideology makes action less likely as there is room for dissent. However by its very nature a strong ideology is difficult to change, and should the ideology not be that which is needed (say in a changing environment) then promoting new actions will be very difficult. Whilst this provides an interesting insight into the possibility of change, there is little guidance on how a strong or weak ideology can be recognized. Control in this schema is not so much proactive as reactive, depending on the strength of the ideology of the organization and the extent to which this ideology is aligned to that of the would be controller. Therefore it does not provide insights into operationalizing a control system, although it does give some clue as to the parameters that need to be considered in this respect.

In a processual study Pettigrew (1979) looked at the emergence of organizational culture – the way that reality was constructed in a developing organization. Pettigrew viewed culture as a symbolic artefact and related it to its context and history. In a later study based on the NHS (Pettigrew *et al.*, 1989) the implications of this view of culture were examined. The view put forward is that culture is fundamental to change, but is tentative and sensitive to the possibility of promoting change. The authors point out that a universal recipe for change is not possible, they highlight the influence of local history, politics and people, they are sceptical about rational design and point to the paradox that stability may be necessary to promote change at a later stage. Control in this context is therefore a political balancing act. It involves working within the cultural system and moulding it rather than trying to 'knock it into shape'. Whilst altering us to the part played by cultural factors this study does not provide any overall answer to the issue of control, and neither does it seek to. The discussion is useful in that it highlights the process that should be adopted when developing control systems, but it does not specify the content.

That is not to say that change cannot be achieved, and a number of authors have demonstrated how external forces and internal negotiations can lead to change. Mouritsen (1999) has looked at the extent to which firms might become more flexible in their approach. He demonstrates the negotiated nature of the approach taken by the firms he studied. Dent (1991), in a study of the railway industry, found that a cultured change had taken place. No generalizable conclusions are offered, but this interpretive research sees situations as uniquely contextualized. Laughlin (1991) uses Dent's case study to present a more structured argument about the role of the symbolic elements of an organization in the process of change. Using a 'middle range' theoretical framework (Laughlin, 1995) developed from Jürgen Habermas's critical theory, Laughlin emphasizes interpretive schemes and suggests ways of understanding the processes of change in organizations. The theory provides a framework of possibilities that have to be 'fleshed out' in each individual situation. The main point is the central role of interpretive schemes in determining the path of change. This suggests that interpretive schemes define the level of control that is possible in situations where control is reliant on changing organizational practices and the organizational cultures that have produced them.

While the anthropological approaches to the study of management control are diverse, they all highlight the fact that management control systems are affected by factors that are less tangible than the formal administrative structures that comprise them. Moreover they are all convinced about the central importance of culture in control, albeit in opposite ways: there are those who see it as a tool that can be used by the controller, and those who see it as imposing a constraint, particularly in situations of change. This implies that culture can serve as a useful control tool when there is no change, and if change is needed the desired outcome must be in line with the existing culture as changing culture is difficult. None of the approaches offers guidance on recognizing cultures. This is a considerable disadvantage for those who view culture as a concrete entity and its manipulation as an important control tool. If the more symbolic approach to culture is adopted the possibility of controlling culture disappears and recognition of its impact becomes a matter of the intelligence of the manager (Goleman, 1998) or the ability of the manager to deal with subjectivities. None of the approaches provides direction on the content of control systems. They do however offer good advice on the process that needs to be followed in order to build effective control systems in particular situations. A further drawback is their lack of consideration of power.

Summary

The first two chapters of this volume have provided a broad outline of the various approaches to control in the literature. This chapter has been specifically concerned with the classical or mainstream approach to management control, which is associated with accounting controls and the use of responsibility accounting. In this sense performance is central to management control. Despite Anthony's insistence that psychology is a key part of management control, this has been given little consideration in the classical literature beyond the implicit assumption of economic rationality that linking compensation to performance will motivate employees.

The chapter has also considered various attempts to take the focus away from the narrow accounting base. First, it has discussed the work of Hopwood (1974) and Merchant (1985), who introduced the idea that controls in organizations are multidimensional. Some are administrative and based on organizational structures and procedures; others are based on social relationships and self-control. Second, it has pointed out the need to consider the environment in which organizations operate. Contingency theorists suggest that different environments require different approaches to control and have sought to identify frameworks for matching control to the environmental context. Third, it has considered the less tangible aspects of organizational life and noted the emphasis that anthropological approaches place on the values, ideologies and cultures of those who are subject to control (and those who are controlling).

Finally, the chapter has briefly explained the strengths and weaknesses of the various approaches so that managers will be aware not only of the diverse possibilities, but also of their potential value in different circumstances. The chapter has offered no prescriptions for management control because there are no clear indications of the 'right' or the 'best' way to achieve control and there are no perfect solutions. All the factors discussed above should be considered when developing a management control system. That this is a complex and difficult matter does not mean that we can forget any attempt to control. Rather it means that the developer of a control system must be reflective as well as reflexive. The rest of the book will consider in more depth the various issues relating to control and offer some solutions.

Discussion questions

1. What control systems were or are you subject to as a student at university?
2. What are the advantages of understanding the context in which control systems operate?
3. What are the cases for and against considering management control systems as technical systems?
4. What systems would you use to control a set of computer game developers?
5. What is the difference, if any, between control systems that might be adopted in organizations in the public and private sectors?

Structures of control

Anthony J. Berry, Jane Broadbent and David Otley

Introduction

As Chapters 1 and 2 have shown, there are many approaches to considering control. Different approaches lead to the creation of diverse structures within organisations. When considering the structures of control, then, we can view them through a number of lenses. This chapter will look at the approaches adopted by organizational theorists and by economists. The approaches used by the former are important because they provide ways of structuring organizations and the processes within them. The approaches of economists will be considered because they provide a framework for discussing the question of whether large organizations are the best way of structuring industries and services.

The chapter proceeds as follows. First, consideration given to the structuring of large organizations and the tasks conducted within them. This will be done by reflecting on the influence of classical management theorists and looking at more recent attempts to structure through divisions or matrices. Next the contribution of economists will be addressed, with particular attention to the reasons for forming markets or hierarchies in particular circumstances. Finally the debate on the structural superiority of either markets or hierarchies for organizing the supply of goods and services in contemporary society will be considered.

Organizational theorists and approaches to structures of control

Classical management theory offers a useful starting point for considering control structures. F. W. Taylor (1947) provided an important and still influential account of how tasks could be controlled in organizations. After studying the manual labour involved in a particular task (shovelling pig iron) he identified how the task could be done most efficiently, thus increasing productivity. This identification of the 'one best way' to do a job, coupled with the choice of 'the best man', was called scientific management. Control involved separating the conception and execution of tasks in a workplace. Managers planned and workers carried out the plan at their behest. This may seem an obvious practice to those of us born into today's society, but in the era of craft control this was a revolutionary idea. Under craft control the task was controlled by the craftsman who held the knowledge and expertise needed to carry out the task. Taylor wished to minimize 'soldiering': the hindering of production by natural laziness and adherence to group norms. He also wished to make management more effective. For him an important management task was to identify workers' task skills and then to organize those skills in a scientific fashion to ensure maximum efficiency. Managers had to ensure that the most suitable people for the job were hired and that the necessary tools were available. There was also an element of payment by results, although this was tempered to ensure that workers did not earn enough to engage in drunkenness!

Another influential management theorist was Henri Fayol (1949), who looked at the overall management of the firm. He provided a model that structured the firm as a unified hierarchy, with control and authority coming from the highest level and filtering down the organization. This is illustrated in Figure 3.1.

Fayol, like Taylor, distinguished the role of managers from other functions in the organization. This was in line with his overall idea of the division of labour. Part of managers' duty was to ensure discipline and take responsibility for the actions of their subordinates. For this to happen there had to be unity of command, with a group of workers being responsible to just one

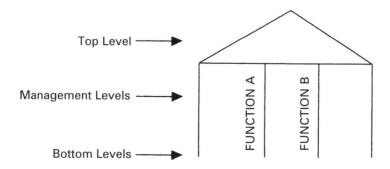

Figure 3.1   The functional hierarchy

superior. Fayol saw the organization as having a unified set of purposes, with individual interests being subordinated to these. Communication, or the passing on of instructions to enable control, mainly followed the top-down hierarchical route, although for efficiency horizontal communication was permitted.

Max Weber formally described the structures of control found in the work of Taylor and Fayol. Weber was not an organizational theorist as such (for an account of his work see Gerth and Mills, 1948). He did not seek to advocate particular ways of organizing, rather he was concerned to understand the society in which he lived and how it was developing. He saw the ways of organizing as typical of the approaches adopted in society in general, in which authority was legitimated by public acceptance of rational-legal principles. This can be contrasted with other societies in which authority was due either to tradition (direct rule by elders or the monarchy by virtue of their position) or to charisma (public acceptance of control by those who were perceived to have special personal qualities, for example a religious leader or a strong political leader). Rational-legal authority came from following a set of rules underpinned by rational calculation. Authority was given to people because they had particular abilities and knowledge, and the whole structure was based on predetermined roles and impersonal relation. The aim was to ensure efficiency.

When providing this description Weber formalized his model of bureaucratic structure. We sometimes use the term bureaucracy in a pejorative fashion to condemn red tape, but it was originally seen as a positive means of improving efficiency. We might also do well to remember that the bureaucratic structures of control contained in the model are still routinely employed in almost all organizations, both large and small. Imagine what an organization without bureaucratic controls would be like.

We cannot consider classical management approaches to the structure of control without some reflection on the Hawthorne experiments (Roethlisberger and Dickson, 1964), which demonstrated the importance of social relations in the work group. These experiments were carried out in the Hawthorne works of the Western Electrical Company, starting in 1924 and continuing for approximately 20 years. Many experiments were conducted, one of which was designed to study the effect of changing physical conditions on output. It was found that changing the physical conditions, irrespective of whether they were made worse or better, resulted in increased output. This, it was argued, was a consequences of the increased interest shown in the work group by managers, which was because of the research. There was some debate about the interpretation of the data collected in this huge project (see for example Rose 1975), but it was agreed that the social composition of the work group might be important as physical aspects of the working environment. Thus the subject of human relations was taken up by organizational theorists. (Later, feminist rereadings of the Hawthorne studies suggested that the work group had been made up of compliant young women with a dominant female leader. The male work group had given up on the experiment much earlier.)

Whilst overall organizational structures were not affected by the Hawthorne findings, the organization of task control did change somewhat. The human relations approach moved away from the basic assumption of the bureaucratic approach that the worker was little more than a cog in a wheel. However it accepted that workers were not just motivated by money. Control of the work process now placed more emphasis on group solidarity and the social needs of workers. One of the areas influenced by this approach to control was budgeting, where employee participation was advocated for the setting of targets.

As we have seen, classical management theorists considered the structures of both organization and task control. The structure of task control was 'nested' in to the organizational structure, which was hierarchical, centralized and final authority lay with top management. However as organizations grew in size, problems with this control structure materialized. Therefore divisional structures were developed to allow specialization alongside task integration.

With divisionalization a large organization was divided into a number of smaller units that organized their own activities to an agreed extent, but remained accountable to the parent organization. The amount of decentralization – that is, the extent to which decisions were made at lower levels of management – differed between organizations and even within divisions of the same organization. The divisionalized structure came into prominence when it was adopted by General Motors. It had various advantages. First, decisions could be made at or near the place of their execution, where there was better knowledge of the environmental conditions. Second, this structure opened the possibility of giving training and responsibility to a wider range of employees, which would not only motivate them but also provide a pool of workers from which to recruit top managers in the future. Third, structure provided a means of filtering information flows to the top managers so that they would not suffer information overload and it would be easier for them to identify strategic issues. The careful allocation of responsibility for decision making would also ensure that decisions could be made faster, as they would not all have to be made at one central point. The main disadvantage was that decisions that were suboptimal for the organization as a whole might be adopted because they were optimal for a particular division.

Divisionalization was organized in a number of ways, but common bases were product or technology differences or geographic location. Whatever the basis, the extent of decentralized decision making varied according to company policy, thus whilst the control structures of divisions may have been similar, the control within them may have differed. (Similarly in centrally managed or unitary organizations there were differences in the levels and extent of decentralization.) In some divisionalized companies control still took a bureaucratic form, so divisionalization may have broken down the unitary bureaucratic structure but it did not replace it completely.

Because decisions had to be taken about the formal structure of the organization (be it unitary or multidivisional) and the extent of centralization or decentralization, organizational theorists considered the extent to which it was possible to provide general rules about the applicability of different structures to different situations. This led to the contingency theories of organizations, which suggested that there were 'best structures' and these were associated with (or were contingent on) other factors in the organization and its environment.

Burns and Stalker (1968) studied the structures of firms and suggested that those which existed in a stable environment and had well recognized technologies (mechanistic systems) should be structured in the way suggested by the classical theorists. In more uncertain environments where there was rapid change and a need to respond to this change, then organismic structures were more appropriate. Organismic structures could adapt much more fluidly and dynamically to the environment in order to survive. Here lateral communication was encouraged, roles could be changed and consultation rather than command was appropriate.

Other contingent variables were suggested. For example Woodward (1965) proposed that the type of technology used in the production process was important, resulting in different spans of control. When the technology was not complex then the span of control could be wider than when the technology was complex. Hence the organizational structure had to reflect the need for diverse spans of control. Company size was also thought to be an important variable. Whatever the contingent variables, once the important ones had been identified then the most appropriate control structure could be used to ensure efficient operation.

Finally, the matrix structure was another approach to structure offered by organizational theorists. Matrix management is to do with providing leadership on both a functional basis and a product basis. For example in the world of education it is common to find a structure with both subject leadership (function) and course leadership (product). Thus a member of staff may be responsible to two different people for different aspects of his or her work. This approach allows for the development and control of expertise within the function, and also allows some integration of different functions in the development of different products. In the latter case faster responses to customers can be made. In this regard matrix management structures come closer to meeting the needs of the organismic organization than do bureaucratic structures. However, having two bosses can be a significant disadvantage, and if the product teams are working on short-term projects then the frequent need to build new teams can cause difficulties.

In summary, organizational theory has suggested a series of structures for use in organizations. These structures provide different solutions to control problems, and in real-life situations have no doubt been adapted to deal with specific problems as they arise. On the whole these solutions are based on an *a priori* view of a legal-rational system and assume the nature of control rests on internal organizational relationships.

In many ways economists have a similar view of the structures available for control. However they have a very different view of why the firm exists, and more consideration is given to the interrelationship of different organizations in the economic environment. It is to this that we now turn.

Markets or hierarchies?

As already noted, economists take a rather different view of organizations from that discussed above. They tend to focus on exchange relationships, which are an essential part of social life. In particular they use the idea of economic rationality to guide decisions on structuring exchange activities. Their basic premise is that division of labour leads to exchanges of goods and services. These transactions must be coordinated, and it is the cost of this, including the cost of information, that determines which method will be used to organize the transactions.

This line of argument can be traced back to Coase (1937) and the notion of ideal markets. It is in the market that transactions are coordinated and buyers and sellers are introduced. Allocation takes place through the price system, which balances supply and demand. The ideal market is one in which allocation is efficiently carried out because of the costless availability of perfect information to all those who wish to engage in the market. Coase pointed out that the allocation process is not cost free, and hence the market is not perfect and exchange relationships can be better organized by means of a contract, especially when the conditions of the exchange are complex. Developing a contract that suits all parties can incur significant costs. When the contractual arrangements are of a longer-term nature, setting up an organization offers an alternative and possibly cheaper way of operating. Thus the cost of information used to coordinate the allocation process is a key variable in the decision about whether transactions can be best organized through the market or in a hierarchical organization.

Williamson (1975) developed these ideas in the context of transaction cost economics. He was specific about both the nature of transaction costs and what gives rise to them. First he raised the issue of bounded rationality, which means that human beings do not necessarily act to maximize the outcome of a set of actions. Because of the complexity of decisions and the limits on people's ability to process information they will seek an outcome that is sufficient to 'satisfy'. March and Simon (1967, p. 141) give the example of the difference between searching a haystack for the sharpest needle (maximizing) and searching for a needle sharp enough to sew with (satisficing). Thus people intend to be rational but can only be rational within the limits of their capacity to process the information available in a complex world. In transaction cost terms the consequences of bounded rationality are increased by complexity.

A second element in transaction costs is opportunism. This occurs when there is information asymmetry between traders. If one trader has better access to information than the other, this allows the first to act in his or her own interest, which can affect allocations in the market and market exchanges will not be fair or effective. This is particular by the case when there are few transactions and few trading partners. With larger numbers, customers who are compromised by a supplier can change to another trading partner. Such switching is not as easy in a limited market.

To bounded rationality and opportunistic behaviour can be added 'atmosphere'. This relates to the preferences individuals have for working in different types of organization, and to groups who hold different sets of values. Thus human factors are considered along with economic transaction costs, resulting in different structures. When there is great uncertainty the desire to minimize the costs arising from bounded rationality will result in transactions being kept within the organization, thus favouring the organizational form of exchange over the market form (Williamson, 1975). Market exchange is favoured when there are many trading partners and the cost of opportunistic behaviour is minimal.

The cost of obtaining information is also a significant consideration. Agency theorists (see Baiman 1982 and 1990 for a thorough overview) focus on the contractual relationship between a superior (manager) and a subordinate and on the cost of the information required by the superior to monitor the contractual performance of the subordinate. Agency theory can be seen as a complement to the markets and hierarchies approach. Spicer and Ballew (1983) argue that agency theory is a special case of organization failure (Williamson 1975), which occurs when organizing in a particular fashion is more expensive than changing to another structure.

Market transactions and hierarchical organization can be seen as the two extremes of a continuum, and adopting some combination of the two may be the best way to achieve efficiency, perhaps in the form of a divisional structure.

Williamson considers several forms of organization operating at different levels of complexity and with different ways of cooperating. Peer group interactions are seen as a simple non-hierarchical way of cooperating to achieve economies of scale in the use of expertise, information and physical assets. As the groups grow larger the need to prevent 'free riding' means that more formal organization is required and a simple hierarchy is preferable. Here there is a recognized superior to coordinate, make decisions and inform.

Coordination problems increase as a firm grows because of the impact of bounded rationality and the impetus to specialize. Williamson posits a structure called the unitary or u-form organization, in which the coordination process is such that several managers are necessary. These managers are in control of functional areas such as production or marketing, and there are at least two management layers. Communicating up and down the hierarchy leads to loss of information and some loss of control. This is exacerbated by the problem of bounded rationality when increasing amounts of information have to be handled. As only a limited amount of information can be considered, some decisions may be neglected. Given the pressing need for attention to day-to-day activities, the danger is that longer-term strategic activities will be ignored.

Williamson suggests that a multidivisional (or M-form) organizational structure is advantageous for large and complex organizations, particularly those which have moved into diverse product markets. With this type of structure there is specialization of managerial decision making and a splitting of responsibility for strategic and day-to-day decisions. Day-to-day decisions are made by quasi-autonomous divisions that concentrate on their own operations. Strategic decisions are made at the centre, which is committed to the future of the organization as a whole and monitors the performance of the divisions. By organizing in this fashion, information loss due to bounded rationality is reduced as the divisions do not have to communicate information about their activities to so many people.

M-form organization may be seen as a blend of market organization and hierarchical organization. At the divisional level there is competition not just between the divisions and their external competitors but also between the divisions for internally allocated resources. The latter may relate to intermediate goods to be transferred between the divisions (producing transfer pricing problems) or basic resources such as capital or workers. The possibility of achieving the advantages of the market alongside strategic direction of the hierarchy can perhaps explain the implementation of internal markets in some bureaucratically and hierarchically organized public services. This phenomenon will be examined in more detail later when we consider more recent developments (see also Chapter 13). First, in order to complete the overview of basic theories we shall look at the work of Ouchi (1979, 1980), who has used the transaction cost approach to examine organizational control.

Ouchi alerts us to the fact that transaction costs are linked to equity or reciprocity in the terms of exchange. When it is difficult to value the goods or services exchanged, then the transaction cost will increase as valuations will need to be made and uncertainty borne. Ouchi is also concerned with measuring output and understanding the way in which inputs are transformed into outputs. When it is easy to measure outputs but the transformation process is not well understood, it makes sense to use a control system that can measure output, which Ouchi considers as most economically dealt with in a market situation. This is because there is little need for internal mediation of the exchange and everything can be measured by the output. Thus the transaction does not need to be organized through extensive contracts.

When outputs are not easily measured but the transaction process is well understood, then the key focus of control is the behaviour of those involved in the transformation process. In this case the most economical control structure is hierarchical organization. This is because the on-going employment relationship does not require constant renegotiation and there is a sense of belonging and commitment to the organization. The costs of monitoring employee behaviour are therefore lower than monitoring them through the market. Figure 3.2 illustrates these relationships.

When it is not easy to measure outputs and the transformation process is not well understood, then neither markets nor hierarchies offer a way of controlling. For this situation Ouchi points to the usefulness of the self- and social controls of the 'clan'. Clan control offers mutual monitoring through the norms and values of the group (an aspect of culture). This type of control is more part of the process of action within the organizations concerned than structure. When evaluating the market-structured approach to control it is important to remember the existence of approaches such as clan control. In the literature markets and hierarchies are often considered but clan control is not discussed.

OUTPUTS	Easily measurable	Not easily measurable
TRANSFORMATION PROCESS		
Well understood	Market/hierarchies	Hierarchies
Not well understood	Markets	Social control of the 'clan'

Figure 3.2 Approach to control of organizations

The use of different structural configurations

The question of which structure is most appropriate is not just an academic one, rather it relates to issues that affect most contemporary organizations. The approach taken by economists to organizational structure has been adopted as a frame of reference, and there is a distinct move towards the adoption of market type answers to the economic problems of countries as different as the UK and the emergent economies in Eastern Europe.

Having reviewed the main background literature in the area, we shall now examine some recent attempts to approach control issues through the market structure. The strength of this approach is illustrated by the fact that it has been used in both the public and the private sector. We shall first consider its use in the public sector.

The belief in the market approach is summed up by Enthoven (1985, p. 42): 'When all alternatives have been considered, it becomes apparent that there is nothing like a competitive market to motivate quality and economy of service.' This belief has formed the basis of much public-sector legislation in the UK and many other countries over the last 20 years. At first the principle was applied to the peripheral activities of organizations such as the National Health Service (NHS). Services such as catering, cleaning and laundry were put out to competitive tender to test the efficiency of the internally organized services. Local governments were also required to open some of their services to competitive tendering. Subsequent legislation made professional services subject to market discipline. For example local authorities legal departments introduced competitive tendering for some of their services and of service-level agreements for others. In the latter case a quasimarket discipline was being attempted, whereby local government departments acted as purchasers and providers of each other's services, rather than as different functional parts of the same organization. This required the formalization of the purchaser's requirements and agreement on service standards. In essence exchange relationships were created within the organization, based on an M-form logic.

Subsequent changes to the organization of UK public services have been in line with what is called new public management (NPM) (Hood, 1991, 1995). A number of changes have been introduced. One is controlling the behaviour of professionals through the use of set targets for their outputs, for example the imposition of a maximum waiting time for treatment in hospitals. Another is the delegation of responsibility to units directly concerned with service provision. In the case of education, for example, the Education Reform Act of 1988 delegated responsibility for service provision to the school level. Now that funding is largely related to pupil numbers and freer choice is possible in respect of school enrolment, competition between schools is being promoted. Thus elements of competition and a market for services are being encouraged (even if entry to the market is strictly controlled). More generally the creation of league tables for schools, hospitals and universities has led to a greater element of competition than previously existed.

Another recent approach is the separation of 'rowing from steering' (Osborne and Gaebler, 1993), with the government becoming more a procurer of services than a direct provider. For example the private finance initiative (PFI) introduced the practice of private sector provision of infra-structure or buildings in which services based. Hence the state purchases, rather than directly provides, some roads, prisons, education and hospital services. In the case of the latter two, the core education and clinical services are still provided by the state, but the buildings and management of the facil-ities are provided by the private sector under contract. The latter arrangement is the outcome of public–private partnership rather than direct competition, but there is an element of competition in the bidding for the initial contract.

Hence the legislative changes implemented over time contain elements of market approach, and since the UK Labour government was elected in 1997 this has been accompanied by attention to aspects of performance manage-ment. For instance there have been moves to measure output (or outcomes), with professionals and organizations being held accountable for achieving them. Performance management is achieved in two ways: by allowing some consumer choice in the take-up of services (that is, a market for consumers) and by requiring some competition to provide the service in the first place (a market for supply). It is questionable whether the imposition of a market-type approach alone would have been effective in achieving control in these situ-ations. This is perhaps the reason that more elements of performance management have been introduced as controls more recently.

One of the problems with developing a market in the public services is providing sufficient information to allow the market to carry out transactions efficiently (Purdy, 1993a; 1993b). Another problem is insufficient use of the information that has been provided (Purdy, 1991, 1993a). It follows that in order to provide such information transaction costs must increase. In the case of PFI there has been concern about the time expended and costs incurred by both public and private sector organizations in the preparation and assess-ment of bids for service provision. This seems to be contrary to the logic of transaction cost economics, which would seek to reduce these costs.

Returning to Ouchi's (1979, 1980) framework, it could be argued that for some activities the process of transforming of inputs to outputs is not well understood. Neither is it always easy to measure output, although some effort has been made to find a suitable measure for doing so. It follows that neither market nor hierarchical control is appropriate for all the activities concerned, but that some degree of clan control is also needed. The legislative changes that have been imposed have tended to reduce the element of professional autonomy that clan control implies, with the government preferring to use performance management. This is perhaps due to its desire to be seen as keeping the promises it has made to the electorate and what it is doing to achieve them (Broadbent and Laughlin, 2003).

In the private sector the market approach is taken for granted and performance management is easier as the single measure of profit is widely accepted. The need for flexibility in response to change is seen as an important strategic issue and theories resting on the centrality of the market structure have been used to explore this (Starkey *et al.*, 1991). The new manufacturing technologies and approaches to management adopted in response to Japanese successes have improved flexibility at many levels. Popular management texts (for example Peters and Waterman, 1982) have stressed the need for flexibility if a firm is to achieve excellence. This assertion is borne our by the economic and political failure of the rigidly organized bureaucratic regimes in Eastern Europe.

In the case of internal reorganization to cope with a rapidly changing environment, perhaps the greatest change has been the redrawing of boundaries of firms so that activities that were once conducted internally are now contracted out. Management buy-outs of sections of firms and the contracting out of peripheral activities are consistent with the advice to go back to basics and to divest other areas. Joint ventures are another means of cooperating in the shorter term. This approach can be seen as a means of controlling a complex environment through the use of contracts. This allows greater flexibility in respect of the activity mix of the firm. The cost of renewing or renegotiating contracts is offset by the benefits of being able to react to change much more quickly. However some of the new approaches to production management, such as the just in time system, rely on very close relationships organized through specific contracts. In this type of relationship the extent of operational flexibility is questionable. Whether this kind of relationship is more aligned to market or hierarchy can also be debated.

The main question at this point is whether the economic approach can help us to define the best structure for control in a given set of circumstances. The superiority of the economic or market model is certainly taken for granted in much current thinking on the provision of public services and universally in the case of the private sector. However some questions need to be asked, based on the insights provided by Ouchi's approach to the matter. He suggests that in some circumstances it is not appropriate to adopt market-type controls, and the key requirement is the ability to measure outputs. There is some evidence that ways are being sought to define and measure outputs in the public sector as this is a fundamental requirement of the

market model. This need to define outputs has grown as the use of performance management approaches has grown. However in some areas there is
grave doubt about the ability of the current output measures to measure the
activity of the organization in a meaningful manner (for the area of education
see Broadbent *et al.*, 1993). This is most pronounced in public sector services
that are geared to individuals (Gorz 1989). If this doubt is grounded in fact
then the market cannot control effectively and performance management
will not be effective. What is more the extra transaction costs incurred when
providing the additional information needed for the market to develop
cannot be set off against any benefit.

The situation in the private sector also needs to be considered. Although
divesting activities and the downsizing operations may be a good way of
achieving short-term flexibility there is still a need for cooperation between
producers. The relationship between suppliers and producers in the just-in-
time system must be close if the system is to work. If contracts are intermit-
tent and the risks interest in a changing environment are passed down to the
suppliers, then the cost of the contract will increase. This will be the result of
producers seeing their risk profile increase because contracts are not guaran-
teed and increasing their prices accordingly. Chapter 13 expands on these
issues.

Choosing an appropriate structure is not merely contingent on the need to
address complexity. Attention must also be paid to long-term stability and
investment in people and capital resources. This requires a consideration of
the patterns of working, the extent to which employees identify with their
firms, the scale of operations and patterns of uncertainty and ambiguity.

Unless these important factors are taken into consideration there is a
danger that the decision to adopt a particular control structure will be an
ideological one, with no concern for efficiency or equity. More research will
enable us to address the intriguing question of whether organizations' choice
of market or hierarchy (or a mixture of the two) is based on objective assessment or ideology. The conjecture that there is not a universal reliance on
markets is evidenced by the growing use of performance management. It is
useful to note that the market approach and performance management
systems both rely on the measurement of outputs – or the designation of
things that can be measured as outputs – if they are to work.

Some final comments

The latter part of this chapter considered whether markets or hierarchies offer
the better way of structuring organizations that provide the goods and services
required in the economy. It has also pointed out the trend for performance

management, which relies on the definition and measurement of outputs in the same way as markets do. The reader might be forgiven for thinking that the suggestions made by organizational theorists have been neglected in the discussion. This is far from the case. Their explication of the idea of a bureaucracy is still extremely influential and indeed is reflected in the whole idea of hierarchy. The two approaches are not mutually exclusive and have many overlaps.

Structure is an important element in the exercise of control in organizations, and whether the structure adopted is considered from the perspective of organizational or economic theory is perhaps less important than recognizing that as yet there are no perfect structures of control. Moreover when questioning whether markets or bureaucracies offer the best organizational structure, the issue of clan control should not be forgotten. Clan control is useful in situations where it is difficult to measure outputs and the process of achieving those outputs is difficult to define.

The issue of clan control can be further explored by reading the work of Merchant (1985), who, as discussed in Chapter 2, outlines three approaches to control: action control, results control and personnel control. Action control involves supervision to ensure that the correct processes are followed and is similar to hierarchical control. Results control requires the outputs to be measurable and monitored to ensure they are as required – this is consistent with performance management and relates to the market approach to control. When neither of the two are possible then personnel control has to be used. This is an extended version of clan control. It involves appointing those who can be trusted to do that which the controller would do in the same situation, and in that sense it tries to avoid the problem of agency by substituting trust for other controls.

Many control systems have adopted action or results control. Personnel controls have not been pre-eminent among the users of models of trust, instead they have adopted aspects of performance management. For example medical practitioners have been encouraged to practice particular approaches to medicine by linking actions such as the adoption of an immunization programme, to their pay. This is based on action control. Schools, hospitals and universities have been subject to a plethora of output measures: exam results, waiting times or the involvement of certain sectors of the community. These are often placed in league tables. In all these examples, assumptions have been made about the relevant processes and outputs. Previously the professionals who undertook these tasks would have been controlled by personnel controls and not performance managed. Professionals would have been trusted and subjected to much less scrutiny in the day-to-day conducting of their tasks. Now the tasks have been redefined in such a way as to minimize the need for personnel control.

Therefore the issue of structure is not the only matter for consideration when control is addressed. It is however, in the context of contemporary debates, a central consideration. The aim of this chapter has not been to present a picture of what control structure should be. Rather it has been to present an overview of some ideas from the organizational and economic fields. It has aimed to show the diversity of approaches available and where these might be of most use. The strengths and weaknesses of the different approaches have also been considered, together with some discussion of current issues and debates. The fact that control structures are a current and controversial topic has been highlighted, and some hesitation about the market solution as a universal panacea has been voiced.

Scott (1995) contrasts institutional theory in economics, sociology and political science. He argues that organizations are the theatres in which institutional values, beliefs and modes of order are visible. Scott explicitly recognizes that modes of order and control are deeply influenced by values and beliefs and are not merely the outcomes of an economic rationale. Rowlinson (1997) concludes that far from fitting into the existing institutional environment, multinational corporations are able to choose an institutional environment that best suits their own choice of control structure and may have the power to persuade national governments to amend their local institutional arrangements to comply with the MNC's desires. However the growing practice of performance management, which is able to emerge once outputs can be quantified, is perhaps the most notable recent development.

Discussion questions

1. Choose an organization with which you are familiar and describe and evaluate the structures of control it has adopted.
2. Evaluate the use of economic models of control and the assumptions behind them.
3. Does the model of control developed by F. W. Taylor have any place in organizations today? Give reasons for and against your conclusion.
4. Evaluate the extent to which an organization can affect its environment.
5. You are the manager of a division of a large multinational company. What benefits might you accrue by controlling the division? Would your argument be the same if you were the managing director of the company as a whole? Give your reasons.
6. Do you think that there are areas of societal activity in which it would not be appropriate to use market-type controls? Argue your case.

4 Procedures for control

Anthony J. Berry, Jane Broadbent
and David Otley

 ## Introduction

The previous chapters addressed the topics of control and control structures. This chapter looks at control procedures, primarily through consideration of planning. It is based on the idea that a plan constitutes a model of the expected or intended future activities of the organization and can serve as a basis for control actions. However it will be argued that the planning procedure is more complex than the situation demands.

Planning may be viewed as consisting of different elements in a simple control cycle. The process starts with defining the pattern of activities to be undertaken in the future; it is the representation of that pattern of activities in physical and/or financial terms that constitutes the plan. The next stage involves undertaking the work contained in the activity programme and measuring what has been done. The third stage consists of drafting reports and statements on the work done, and in the fourth the expected pattern of activities is compared with the actual pattern of activities and a decision is taken about what, if anything, should be done about it. This simple control or planning cycle may be described as a first-order feedback loop.

In the simple feedback control loop the controller or decision maker is required to decide whether to change either the input mix or the transformation process to achieve the desired ends. The desired ends have usually been laid down in the plan. The plan is not the control model; for that the controller needs models of the transformation process in their environmental context to enable her or him to establish another plan or modify the original plan. Hence it is necessary to consider the control models in use; and to consider the kind of planning processes the organization might create. This chapter discusses planning, the management of complexity, the management of uncertainty and whether there is some overall way of fitting these issues together.

Planning

At the heart of a great deal of the literature on planning lie the structural functional ideas put forward by Talcott Parsons (1951). Planning may be viewed as a process of choosing and setting in train activities to achieve certain goals. In any sizeable organization this is a matter of defining activities and differentiating them into subactivities. This differentiation necessarily means that processes for achieving integration are required. As all these activities take place in a changing world it may be necessary to adapt the pattern of activities, and indeed the goals. All this takes place in a social structure where the members of the organization may or may not have the same values, history, traditions, language, skills or knowledge. These four ideas from the structural functional literature – that is, goal attainment, integration, adaptation and social structure – underlie a great deal of what is written about planning and budgeting.

There is a distinction between organizational structure (see Chapter 3) and social structure. The latter comprises the values, beliefs and identities that exist in the organization and identification with it. The former consists of the established roles, authority, responsibilities and accountabilities. Our concern in most parts of this chapter is with in the interplay of social structure and organizational structures and procedures.

BOX 4.1

Accounting costs and social structures

A company owned a fleet of vehicles. The life of each vehicle, with regular maintenance and irregular but well-programmed major overhaul, was about 30 years. The company knew five years ahead which vehicles would be due for overhaul. The company had established a budgeting system, and was attempting to change to a system of flexible budgeting. Clearly the work to be done was very predictable so the company could not understand why it had lost control of the cost of overhaul.

Upon examination it became clear that the standard costs developed for the overhauls were being abused. The company had trouble recruiting skilled workers at the rates of pay it was prepared to offer, so it was decided to introduce a bonus system as a means of increasing the take-home pay of workers

▶

> without changing the daily or hourly rate. The method chosen for this was to place some of the skilled workers' time into a category called idle time. This reduced the amount of time booked for specific pieces of work, which in turn increased the bonus payable for each job. Booked idle time was held to be the responsibility of the management and not of the workers, and it was paid at the rate of the average bonus earned that week in the whole of the overhaul system. So the allocation of time to booked idle time had a ratchet effect in increasing the bonus and therefore take-home pay.

In the above example, drawn from an experience by one of the authors, we can see how the imperatives of the social structure dominated the apparent rationality of an accounting system that reflected the goals/differentiation and integration procedures of this part of the enterprise. In essence the managers were acting intelligently. They were more prepared to set aside an accounting system that did not reflect the full circumstances and they were not prepared to force on their workers unnecessary changes to the patterns of work, effort and use of skill. Here we see that task activities in organizations, be they physical work, accounting or payment, take place within social structures. While these structures may include diverse values and characteristics and may rarely operate with any kind of consensus, or indeed unitary authority, it is clear from this example that the social structure enabled managers to pursue organizational goals when accounting procedures would have caused dysfunctional behaviour.

It is sometimes assumed that organizational plans have an unequivocal, predetermined time span. In the early days of corporate planning, as in national planning, it was common for there to be five-year plans. However the plans executed in the various parts of organizations may have very varied time spans, ranging from a few days or months to many years. So different parts of complex organizations plan over different time spans, with the span of the financial plan being a compromise. For example in the nuclear power industry the time between constructing and decommissioning a power station may be some 45 years, and perhaps much longer. For a fossil fuel power station the duration is 20 to 40 years. Laying a new power supply to your house (which lasts indefinitely) may only take a few weeks. The very long time scales of major projects such as roads, tunnels, very large bridges and so on mean that it is very difficult to predict costs and revenues with any degree of confidence. Even in organizations with much shorter time horizons the time span of thinking and the time span of control vary considerably

Table 4.1 Accuracy of plan forecasts at different managerial levels

	Planning horizon (years)		
	1	2	3
Management level			
Top	0.5	0.11	0.15
Middle	0.11	0.15	–
Lower	0.15	–	–

among the various levels. Table 4.1 illustrates this point showing the probability of achieving accuracy in plans for one, two or three years in the future by different levels of management in a firm producing commodities.

The table suggest that the senior managers were more effective than managers at the lower levels in terms of accurately forecasting revenues and costs in the short-term. However it should be noted that the senior managers' main concern was not short-term control but long-term effectiveness. It can be seen from the table that there was a similarity between some admittedly imprecise notion of time span of control and the error level that was apparently tolerable in the organization (see Berry and Otley, 1986, for a further discussion of this issue). Senior managers, though, were not above using their better short-term performance to claim greater competence than their subordinates. In addition to time there are the problems of complexity and uncertainty. We shall consider these factors in the following sections, but first it should be noted that criticisms of planning are usually based on the dubious argument that as planners cannot estimate accurately they must always be wrong and therefore all estimates are pointless. A second criticism is that if planners are divorced from managerial action they tend to produce idealized plans that managers do not 'own', and therefore interpret rather than follow. In some organizations, because managers have experienced numerous problems with the implementation of plans, the number of planning staff has been reduced and planning has been integrated with managerial work.

Managing complexity

There are many studies and approaches to studying the structures that organizations have developed to manage their inherent complexity. Williamson (1975) discusses the difference between unitary and multidivisional forms of organization, while Harrison (1972) suggests that there are four organizational forms for managing complexity: organizational bureaucracy, the organizational matrix, the person-centred organization and the power-centred

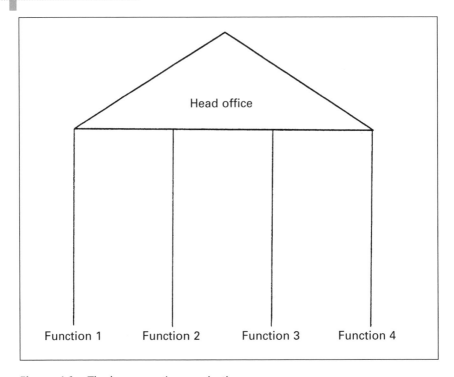

Head office

Function 1   Function 2   Function 3   Function 4

Figure 4.1   The bureaucratic organization

organization. Obviously Williamson, Harrison and other authors (for example Morgan, 1986, who uses metaphors to describe organizations: machines, organisms, psychic prisons and so on) have different pictures in their minds and different ways of thinking about organizations.

Figure 4.1 depicts an organization with a functional bureaucracy. At the top is a head office and each of the four 'arms' represents a major activity, for example purchasing, personnel, manufacturing, marketing, finance and so on, the activities of which are determined and controlled by the head office. Like all bureaucracies, this organization operates with fixed rules, structures and procedures, and certainly its planning and budgeting will be structured by established organizational procedures. The principal criticism of functional bureaucracies is that in a stable situation they are efficient at goal attainment, but in a changing world they tend to be slow to adapt. Clearly the functional model by Parsons is being replayed here: the bureaucratic organization is essentially dedicated to the pursuit of goals through structures of integration to cope with internal differentiation. Control is based on hierarchies and rules, from which are derived plans to ensure compliance and goal attainment.

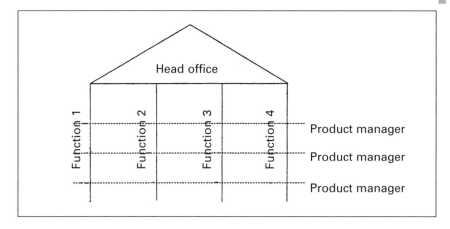

Figure 4.2   The matrix organization

In the matrix organization (Figure 4.2) there are horizontal linkages between the functions because their operations are interdependent. This linking via the planning process and plans enables the interdependent parts to relate to the outside world; that is, it provides the capacity to think about and create adaptive processes. The person-centred organization (the third organizational type suggested by Harrison, 1972) rooted in its social rather than its organizational structure, and goals, differentiation, integration and adaptation flow from the interests of persons as they go about their work. Some professional partnerships are like this.

The Harrison's fourth type of organization the power-centred organization, is akin to a despotism or monarchy and all power flows from one central figure, as in some entrepreneur-created organizations, where the entrepreneur is reluctant to delegate and cannot trust anybody to undertake work on his or her behalf, or indeed on their own behalf. The rest of this chapter will primarily consider functional bureaucracies and matrix organizations, as these are the most common forms of managerial organization.

Processes

Financial planning is part of the control procedure in most organizations. A financial plan is usually based on the four key financial statements; that is, the profit and loss account, which reflects the expected patterns of activity and the consequent revenues and costs; the balance sheet, which represents the asset structure that supports those activities; statements on the sources and application of funds, which show the intermingling of revenues and asset use; and the cash flow, which is a simplified representation of money moving in and out of the organization. Probably the most useful of these four for financial planning and control would be a sophisticated statement of sources and application of funds that encapsulates the changing patterns of financial flows in relation to activity over time. Taken together these four statements provide a picture of resource flows and the consequences of activities.

The financial plan serves as a model for control and fits well with the bureaucratic form of organization, expressing the integration of programmes of activity in financial terms. However as it has been socially constructed and is used in the context of both organizational structure and social structure, it would be unwise to assume that the plan is uncritically accepted as the basis for all future actions (see Chapter 3).

A further criticism arises from consideration of the rationale underlying the plan. Earlier chapters referred to the work of Etzioni (1961) and his typology of normative, instrumental and coercive organizations. If an organization has a normative form the question of goal differences does not arise, although of course there are other problems. If it is a coercive organization, the goals of those being coerced do not matter. If it is an instrumental organization (as are most commercial organizations) there must be some mediation of the different values, goals and so on within the organization. Organizations in pursuit of economic rationality use their need to satisfy capital markets to justify the use of motivation or manipulation to align the organizational members to the institutional goals. Otley (1978) has commented that it might be easier to work in a situation with behavioural congruence; that is, where people can work together despite having disparate views on why it is they are working together. The response of the authoritarian in the face of deviation from institutional norms is to introduce more controls. However the greater the control and number of controls, the greater the deviation that takes place. This endless game has been elegantly charted by Hofstede (1967) and more sharply by Van Gunsteren (1976), who points to the infinite regress of rule-based control: if there is a rule A, then we need a rule B to define when A should be applied. Now that there is a rule B, we need a rule C, and so on. It seems that we cannot solve problems in the social structure by creating additional control procedures in the organizational structure.

Simon (1957) and other researchers note that managers in organizations sometimes behave as though they are not pursuing the same goals; as though the organizational plan and control systems do not wholly provide the criteria for their actions. He offers the following explanation. Given that large organizations deal with complexity via differentiated structures and procedures they tend to create subgoals (and therefore a need for integration). As differentiation is not a simple decomposition of the work of the board but an elaboration of it – in products, technologies, markets and so on – then local rationalities are created, in relation to which local goals emerge. Hence managers working on such local goals are constrained by corporate goals rather than merely subordinated to them.

Complexity

This brings us to what we might term the complexity critique of financial planning and control. Given the nature of complexity and differentiation in organizations, there is clearly a need for integration of both thought and action (a need that is powerfully met by accounting processes). In Anglo-Saxon cultures, great store is generally set on autonomy and autonomous, personally responsible action. In Asian cultures, it is claimed, greater store is generally set dependence and joint action. As in so many things, managing complex organizations lies between these two polar positions of autonomy and dependence. It is a struggle to handle the interdependence between the internal and external worlds of organizations, meeting highly varied environmental demands, opportunities and constraints while trying to maintain the stability of a transformation process and deliver goods and services to the market. Given this, the question arises as to what can be differentiated. It would appear that the notion of the decision maker merely delegating different parts of the task is too simple. As organizations grow in size and complexity it becomes necessary to differentiate both work and decision-making authority about what that work actually is.

In more formal terms, the financial plan – because it is created in a complex organization through highly differentiated procedures – is a somewhat simple descriptive model of the future activities of the organization. Such a plan as model will lack the requisite variety for control that Ashby (1956) demonstrates is required for determining the state of the system and hence controlling it. However the model/plan and the processes that create it will contain substantially more variety and may approach the requisite variety required for control.

Jalland (1989) introduced the elegant notion of parts of organizations forming contracts or compacts that are multidimensioned in nature and rooted in history and understanding. These compacts are spaces or domains within which there is agreement to work and agreement to behave in a certain way. Skills, experience, knowledge and competence are mobilized at, for example, lower levels as part of the bargaining process for resources that enable the organization to function (with variety in the compact and in the process). This way of construing organizations is a late-twentieth century version of Rousseau's social contract, in that the planner's compact creates common frames of understanding that give people the confidence to allocate large amounts of resources and enable managers of differentiated units to handle differentiated tasks, and the differentiated decision-making authority that goes with them. It follows that adaptation should also be handled as a differentiated process, and at two levels: the macro-institutional level, which is about the basic configuration of the enterprise; and at the micro level, which concerns the specific elements of the environment to the organization.

One solution to the problem of complexity is to control by means of vertical coordination. The process of establishing goals, subgoals and so on is characteristic of organizations with a functional bureaucracy. To some extent the technique of management by objectives follows this approach. In a limited number of circumstances this might work, but it is more likely that the debate on goals will be something of a dialectic or a process of negotiation between institutional and internal subsystems. The debate will have to take account of the location of knowledge and the expertise and competence need to undertake work in the complex organization. Depending on the nature of work, there may be considerable complexity when there are 12 or so people, and this is almost certainly the case when there are 20 to 40 people. It is impossible for one person to know everything, ergo the contributions of others are required, and these contributions are unique. So we can again see that the procedures creating a plan or control model are richer and probably more important than the plan itself.

What seems to be arising here is the principle of subsidiarity; that is, in order to cope with complexity, tasks and decision making should take place as close as possible to the point of enactment. This principle, which has become part of the workings of the European Union and the relations between the EU institutions and the regions and local structures of the member states, offers a very interesting model for commercial organizations with differentiated units that could work largely separately from each other. For example in organizations where the interdependence between the units is low the classic multidivisional way of organizing could be introduced. In organizations where interdependence is very high, means have to be found to manage that interdependence and there can be major problems with goals, coordination and control. In an extreme form of subsidiarity, an institution can be seen is an aggregation of parts, and those parts negotiate among themselves about what form the institution should take. In the opposite of the case of an institution dominating its differentiated parts, coordination procedures will emerge to constrain managers' actions. Those of our readers with a knowledge of English history will recall the conflict between King John and the barons, which ended with the barons forcing the king to sign the Magna Carta. This problem was also played out in the evolution of the political structures of the United States. It is also a problem that emerges time and again in debates on the nature of multidivisional organizations.

There can be a rather simple-minded dynamic between integration and adaptation when problems arise in highly complex multidivisional organizations. If problems emerge as a result managing interdependence hierarchically and between the divisions, then the solution proposed is almost inevitably centralization. Conversely if problems arise in centralized or unitary organizations as a result of complexity and ambiguity, then the solution normally proposed is to decentralize or divisionalize. Of course these are polarities, as Peters and Waterman (1982) found, when they observed organizations with what they term tight/loose control structures, meaning that decision-making authority for some matters is held centrally (tight coordination) while for other matters it is delegated (loose coordination to enable adaptation).

More formally, it can be argued that the principle of subsidiarity does not imply either a multidivisional form or a unitary form. What the principle of subsidiarity might do in the designing of organizational control structures is to focus attention on the appropriate location of task and decision-making authority. Note, however, that these approaches all seek to achieve control through vertical coordination, where the purpose is to maintain the integrity of the institution in the interests of the owners or other principal stakeholders, such as managers. The problem that arises here is aggregating differentiated units that work with different technologies and according to different time horizons. In the face of such complexity there is much sense in adopting simplicity in central or institutional control structures. Hence financial models and financial targets, using the conventional balance sheets, profit and loss accounts and cash flow statements, all act to reduce complexity, using common measures and presentations.

Programme planning and budgeting systems, and zero-based budgeting

This section discusses two approaches to managing complexity through financial planning procedures: the integration of programmes with plans and budgets; and the more radical zero-based budgeting, or control by requiring continual rejustification of all actions.

When there is considerable complexity and interdependence in organizations it is essential to find some institutional means of handling it. The story is often told of how Robert McNamara drew on his industrial experience to manage complexities and interdependence in the US Department of Defence (Box 4.2) by introducing programme planning and budgeting systems. The point of such, systems can be seen by referring to models of the organization as a functional bureaucracy or a matrix. In government there may be activities that contribute to some overarching policy, for example the departments in charge of health, education, welfare and housing may all contribute to a policy aimed at improving the economic and social wellbeing of a certain section of the community. If the government were organize its work only on a functional basis there might be discontinuity of policy and a lack of effectiveness. Further more departments might use the policy to secure extra funds but allocate some of these funds to equally worthy but competing projects. In short the efficiency that functional specialization enables may render policies less effective.

BOX 4.2

Organizational cooperation

There are four armed forces in the United States, each of which contributes one member to the Joint Chiefs of Staff Committee, which reports to the secretary of state for defence. These four forces are the US Navy, the US Air Force, the US Army and the US Marines. In any serious fighting these four units have usually had to cooperate in order to provide an effective military force in the theatre of operations. Anomalously the US Air Force has a small army and a small navy, the US Army has some seaborne capability and a great deal of airborne attack capability, and the US Navy has an enormous number of strike aircraft. The US Marines is designed as a flexible force with flexible resources.

When Robert McNamara was secretary of state for defence the Joint Chiefs of Staff presented him with their own solution to whatever problems emerged, and in essence the power of decision making rested not with him but with the Joint Chiefs of Staff. McNamara therefore created civilian directors of theatre operations who reported directly to him. The Joint Chiefs of Staff were told that if they wanted any military resources or funds to purchase those resources they would have to negotiate with the directors of theatre operations, who were the budget holders.

The creation of programme managers across the functions, and hence along the matrix, to coordinate such a policy initiative seems simple enough. However if the programme managers have less authority or political power than the functional managers, then their role will be that of messenger rather than mediator. A solution to this problem would be to give the programme managers authority over budget over allocation and for functional managers to bid for resources. This would enable the programme managers to hold the functional managers to account while themselves being accountable for the policy initiative. Here the matrix managers would have more resources than the functional heads. Hence it is clear that the idea of a programme planning and budgeting system (PPBS) is the creation of a means of integration to ensure the adaptation of programmes needs to become crucial to the behaviour of departments. It is also clear that a form of internal market would exist here, for that is how functions would obtain the resources required to do their work.

In any organization as complex as a government it is unlikely that the exercises of internal market power will be the dominant mode of behaviour. Long-established organizations will have developed all manner of social structures, customs and practices that will mediate against the crude application of internal market arrangements. Furthermore the fact that government policies do not arise in a vacuum but are the outcome of extensive external and internal debate should give the sceptical good cause to doubt that structural changes will give rise to major policy changes. However PPBS can contribute to the pursuit of the rational in the allocation of resources for organizational goals. Its very introduction might cause a political realignment in that cost of programmes will become visible.

Another technique aimed at rational resource allocation is zero-based budgeting (ZBB). This requires all bidders for resources to forget any history or precedent and to justify from a zero base the resources they are requesting from a budget. This somewhat questionable approach, especially in organizations with ongoing commitments, might cause a great deal of irritation and time could be wasted on satisfying the manager that previous behaviour was not perverse. It can be a dangerous weapon in the hands of a new manager for it offers the opportunity to assert authority and perhaps power. ZBB is open to the same criticisms as PPBSs and all other prescriptions for narrowly rational resource controls. A simple representation of a PPBS is provided in Figure 4.3 (note that in this system programme managers allocate resources to functions).

In functional goal disaggregated planning and budgeting the function managers bid for resources in line with a fixed plan, and in turn the programme managers negotiate for resources from the function managers. With a PPBS the situation is reversed the resources are given to the programme managers and the function managers have to bid for resources from them. The programme managers are likely to have a more systemic view of operations to product outputs and to encourage adaptation. Clearly, though, the pathways of differentiation and integration are significantly different.

It is not at all clear that McNamara's ploy (Box 4.2) actually worked well, or that the civilian directors ever managed to gain control of the military. Aaron Wildavsky's (1975) study of the introduction of a PPBS in the US Department of Agriculture suggests that its impact as a means of changing resource allocation was very modest indeed. For while you might choose to

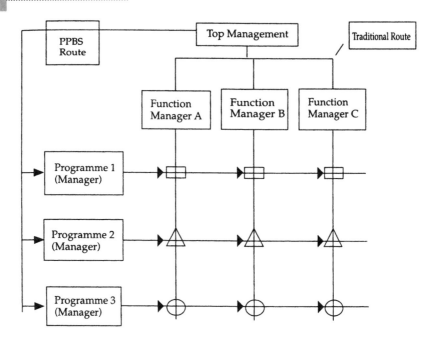

Note that in PPBS the programmes managers are the primary conduct of resources for their functions.

Figure 4.3 Resource flows in a PPBS

organize management structures and systems in a different way by having programme managers, these managers did not effect much change. This could be seen as further support for the idea that social structures both endure and are of great significance. It is easier to change the symbolic representation of what is happening than to change the social structure and how people engage with their work and with each other. Wildavsky's finding that the use of a PPBS prevented some minor control problems but could not stop major ones is memorably expressed in his conclusion that 'some butterflies were caught, but no elephants were stopped'. He found that the government departments were the progenitors of programmes, they possessed the experience to analyze and to create them, and they were a major source of knowledge for the programme managers.

Nonetheless PPBSs are the classic solution to the problems of matrix organizations. They give product managers in matrix organizations the capacity to make crucial decisions about the resource flows required to produce the goods or services for which they are responsible, as well as the data needed to manage the planning and control loops in their particular area of responsibility.

However there are questions about the efficiency of these approaches. There is little governments can do to effect much more than small incremental change in any financial year. As in any large organization, the impetus of past commitments and the limited rationality, together with the political processes of bargaining and negotiating suggest that incrementalism is not merely inevitable but also, according to Braybrooke and Lindblom (1963), desirable for managing major institutions.Because of the plurality of values, the limitation of knowledge, the weight of past decisions, the continuity of programmes, the ambiguity of goals, the shifting relationship between means and ends, the bargaining between one sector of activity and another and so on, incrementalism is essential if the organization is not to fragment (ibid.).

As noted earlier, the rationalist attack on incrementalism led to the notion of zero-based budgeting; that is, managers are supposed to justify anew all the resources required for the following planning period. This is clearly difficult in practice, but it does offer an opportunity for reflection. It is possible to observe the organization in action and then ask how the current configuration of resources came about and whether it is the most effective configuration to achieve what the organization and its units now wish to achieve. So zero-based budgeting has a useful contribution to make, provided it is not treated as merely an analytical exercise but is applied to the day-to-day operational realities of the managers concerned, where future activities are the result of past decisions.

The rediscovery of programme planning and budgeting systems

Johnson and Kaplan (1987), in a critique of management accounting and control, argue that the systematic structures of cost accounting do not connect well with the systemic problems of managing an enterprise. The structures of traditional cost accounting, especially such things as full absorption costing, fit beautifully with the notion of the functional bureaucracy in that they are a classic case of decompositing and disaggregating hierarchical elements to lower-order activities. However if it is important for the bureaucratic functions to work together, then systematic accounting, which takes no cognizance of managing interdependence, is likely to be of limited use.

Johnson and Kaplan's (1987) critique is epitomized by the story in Box 4.3. They argue that it is important to break away from full absorption costing and to create activity pools to which overheads are allocated. These activity pools should be rigorously challenged (following the ideas of zero-based budgeting) to decide upon appropriate cost structures. Then the costs of the activity pools could be allocated to products on a reasoned basis. Clearly this model of activity-based costing is advantageous in that it introduces a critical review.

BOX 4.3

Competing with oneself

The managers of a fish finger factory in Europe found they had some excess production capacity. Their product was selling well and was popular in many markets. They were approached by a major retail operation and asked whether they would manufacture fish fingers to be packaged under the retailer's own brand. The managers believed that this would not threaten their own markets, so they readily agreed and offered a very competitive price to the retailer. In the ensuing years the structure of cost accounting and its full absorption model remained the same, but eventually the company accountant noticed that the retailer's brand now accounted for more than half of total output, and that it was costed with a lower level of cost absorption than their own brand because of their systematic accounting structure. The company found itself in a rather unpleasant predicament as the price of its product was now under pressure in the market. It was difficult for the managers to understand how they had got themselves into this predicament and to think of a way of getting themselves out of it.

In effect the managers had, because of the use of systematic accounting, become rather poorly paid servants of a retail operation. This would not have happened if they had used systemic accounting. They needed such an analysis to see the relationship between the use of resources and the allocation of cost to make sensible decisions. The danger of using a marginal cost analysis was not recognized. However a full absorption cost model can also lead to problems.

As it has application costs, however, it constitutes an alternative method of systematic analysis rather than systemic analysis. This is because it is using observation rather than taking an explanatory approach based in economic or organization theory.

Activity-based costing has become a relatively widespread practice, as has activity-based management. The latter is nothing more than the reconfiguration of programme planning and budgeting systems in a more practical and grounded way. Activity-based management is a horizontal integration process that addresses the systemic issues of the organization, and with the reconfiguration of accounting data flows in support of activity-based management we can begin to see the development of accounting alongside a systemic mode of management control and decision making. It is important to note that the problem of differing of task and decision-making authority, and the question of autonomy and the management of interdependence have not been fully resolved – they have only been reconfigured.

Inevitably, recognition of an activity constitutes recognition of an interdependence that is essentially task-based. There will also be helpful interdependencies between different activity systems. For example the existence of one activity might well make it possible to have a related activity (for example a similar product or service) and the cost of doing them both in the same enterprise will be lower than doing them in separate enterprises. This could be regarded as strategic cost management – achieving cost savings as a result of interdependencies within a very complex system. For instance Boeing and Airbus have both developed families of airliners. In each case the use of common technologies, parts and the operating characteristics of aircraft in use have enabled very considerable cost savings to be made. That is, having developed and built the 757 it was cheaper for Boeing to build the 767 than it would have been for another manufacturer that was starting from scratch. Airbus has followed a similar course with its series of aircraft. Both firms therefore achieved the benefits and also suffered the problems of economics of product range and market scope.

Managing uncertainty

The previous discussion of procedures for dealing with complexity noted that these procedures are about order and ordering. We hope that the reader is not too caught up with the concept of order and stability to forget that in financial plans, especially ones that are projected on a spreadsheet with single-point estimates over ten years, the problem of uncertainty might have been set aside. We live in a state of uncertainty about the future state of the world. We cannot predict anything accurately, the best we can do is to create probability distributions of distant events. Nevertheless nearly all financial plans are couched in single-point estimates (presumably based on probability distributions and therefore the likelihood of their achievement is unknown) and we might ask why this is the case.

The critique of the economic theory of the firm by Cyert and March (1963) includes the observation that managers set out to avoid uncertainty. We probably all tend to avoid uncertainty rather than engage with it, despite the recommendation to the contrary by Donald Michael (1983) and Donald Schön (1983). Schön considers that denial of uncertainty causes one to live in a disconnected way, and that it is imperative to have thought structures and behaviours that connect our experiences and understandings. Schön and Michael are in agreement that managers must learn to live and work with uncertainty. They might find it useful to explore the way in which the anxieties that stem from uncertainty are met by the defences that managers and organizations mobilize within themselves and which inhibit change. Michael argues that only if responsive planning systems are created can organizations come to terms with uncertainty and become intelligent, goal seeking and adaptive. So in terms of our functional quartet of goals, integration, adaptation and social structure, Michael clearly recognizes that the social structure has to bear the costs and difficulties of managing uncertainty through personal and organizational adaptation. He argues that this can only happen if individuals within the social structure give each other support, and that in an uncertain world the most likely outcome of financial planning, or indeed any other human activity, is that we will get it wrong. If an organization refuses to countenance this and either punishes wrongdoers or creates a climate which getting something wrong is unthinkable, then it will condemn itself to being conservative, limited, inward-looking and life-denying (you may well work in such as organization). In order to avoid this the people who make up the social structure have to develop the capacity to learn. It is in the area of awareness of the self and awareness of organizational processes through which defences are mobilized against anxiety that Michael makes his sharpest observation. He argues that managers need considerably more knowledge of themselves, much greater interpersonal sensitivity and a much greater capacity for giving support if organizations are to cope with the ambiguities and uncertainties they face.

You might think that what is being argued for here is something like the management style that prevailed in some Japanese corporations in the 1980s. In these organizations, goals and programmes were formulated after lengthy discussions on a wide range of possibilities, and care was taken to instil a shared understanding of the world of work, how to work together, how to cope with surprises and opportunities, and how to reflect on these and learn anew. In cultures with high dependence and a sense of belonging all this is, possible. But in cultures characterized by egocentric ambition and competition, as in the Anglo-Saxon world, it is much more difficult. What seems to be needed in the Anglo-Saxon world is a process of social adaptation to facilitate the handling of uncertainty about markets and technologies. It is important to note that the technological structure is inanimate, and that the anxieties provoked by uncertainty are provoked in people and do not float in an institutional miasma where they can be located, packaged and locked in a spreadsheet.

The problem of uncertainty can lead organizations to create and mirror the varieties of chaos they face. They do not deal with uncertainty, rather they let it cross their defences and disturb what were believed to be orderly patterns. An example of the latter is a financial plan that results from a multivariate sensitivity analysis and takes no account of the management of consequences.

Another is presenting the future of the enterprise as a probability distribution of the net present value of future expected cash flows, with no consideration of the potential loss to the decision makers. The problem of uncertainty disturbs the apparent stability of budgeting and the meeting of expectations, and it certainly affects the measurement of events. Even more significantly, using observations of the past as the basis for future predictions in an uncertain world is highly problematic. Statisticians ask us to think about variability, measures of variability and the issue of sampling. If observation and measurement are difficult, the elicitation of meaning is even more difficult. The problem of uncertainty requires that interpretative analysis becomes part of the control loop, we cannot merely resort to observation and comparison of what is observed with what was expected. Uncertainty causes us to have unclear expectations and possibly inadequate measures phenomena that occur. Therefore a much richer frame of interpretative analysis is required if controllers are to judge observed activities and decide what can be done to shape future activities.

Thus far we have not addressed the difference between uncertainty and risk. The classic definition is that uncertainty is a state in which all events are equally probable, while risk is a state in which events can be assigned a probability of occurrence. This is a technical distinction, but there are other distinctions too. The topic of risk and control is addressed in detail in Chapter 16.

This takes us back to the discussion of beginning of this chapter, where we touched upon the difference between decision making and control. What seems to emerge here is support for Vickers' (1965) general proposition that when using procedures for control managers do not, and perhaps should not, make decisions, and nor should they believe that they do. Rather, Vickers argues, and we agree, that managers should form an appreciation of that which they are setting out to manage. An appreciation is a multidimensioned, multitheorized understanding of the complexities and uncertainties of the domains in which managers find themselves in relation to the environment. An appreciation, then, creates the context within which action might be considered and resource patterns shifted. It forms the basis of Jalland's (1989) notion of a planning compact, which relates the technological structure of control to the social structure of organizations, with the technological structure containing complexity and the social structure containing uncertainty.

Conclusions

This chapter has considered a range of procedures for control. It raises the question of whether and how we can ensure we have the requisite variety in our planning models and control systems to match the variety in the environment that they seek to control. Given there are differing levels of complexity in the environment along with various degrees of uncertainty this becomes a difficult task. The chapter shows how different organizational form and diverse types of control systems have been used to seek to address the problem of matching the complexity of systems and their environments, ie how the requisite variety (Ashby, 1956) is achieved. Our argument is that the balance sought is rarely achieved and that this remains the biggest challenge for those designing control systems. The paradox remains that in a stable environment it is easier to design controls and it is here that complex controls are least needed. Conversely, in complex situations we as yet have not achieved the requisite complexity in our modelling of controls.

Discussion questions

1. What is the relationship between planning and control?
2. Is it helpful to make plans in areas of high complexity? Give reasons for your conclusion.
3. Evaluate the use of matrix structures in planning and control.
4. How can managers address uncertainty when planning their activities?
5. Evaluate the extent to which techniques such as programme planning and budgeting and zero-based budgeting are helpful to the contemporary manager. Contrast these with activity-based techniques.

The context of control **5**

Anthony J. Berry, Jane Broadbent, David Otley and Dila Agrizzi

Introduction

In order to consider the context of control, this chapter will examine the impact of issues that arise outside the organization, that is, in the environment in which the organization exists. This endeavour should not be seen as imposing a strict delineation of the organization and its environment, nor a one-way relationship between the two. Therefore two points about the nature of control need to be raised: the extent to which the locus of control is within or outside organizations, and the extent to which it is possible to differentiate the organization from its environment. These two issues will be examined in turn.

The locus of control

Whatever their nature, controls are conceived and operated at different levels. For example they may be intra-organizational, internal to the organization and conceived and operated within them. They may be relatively concrete, for example management accounting systems. Alternatively they may be more abstract, for example the values of the organization – the way 'we do things around here, or the organizational culture as it is sometimes called (see Chapter 11). These will not be key themes in this chapter, although it is important to recognize that they are affected by and can in turn affect the context of control in which they are located.

Other control systems are conceived externally – at the societal level, sometimes by governments – but then operated within the organization. Again these systems may be relatively concrete, for example designed to cope with issues such as health and safety or legislative requirements. On a more abstract level are the values and ethics of a society, which influence laws and controls and distinguish deviant from acceptable behaviour. An extreme example is the use of the death penalty as a tool of control. The death penalty is used far more in some societies than in others, and this, it is argued, is related to the values of the societies in question. So the context of control relates not only to concrete external issues but also to the values and ethics of society. As members of organizations are also members of their society, the system of controls in organizations is, according to this logic, related to the abstract and embedded controls that spring from the inner values gained from membership of society.

These extra-organizational factors and their impact are a central topic of this chapter. Their importance lies in the effect they have on the interactions between the values of a given society and the structures produced within it. Values influence the structures that are created, and these structures provide contexts that might be constraining but may not easily be changed. The relationship between societal structures and value systems have been addressed in different ways, and some of the ideas put forward by Anthony Giddens and Jürgen Habermas will be explored later in the chapter.

One final point is that some organizations are created as elements of structures that are devised and implemented at the societal level; these also have the potential to affect each other. Indeed it is the societal role of some organizations to act as devices to control other organizations. Hence there is a possibility of control mechanisms being developed to create systems of interorganizational control, in which one organization's task is to control another (see Chapter 12).

In summary the locus of control is not only an important matter to consider, it is also complex and diverse in that it may be inter-, intra- or extra-organizational, or indeed have aspects of two or all three elements in varying proportions.

Bounding the organization and its environment

If we wish to study the context of control and are focusing control within organizations, then we need to understand the extent to which we can analytically separate the organization from its environment and hence define what the organization is and what is its context. Llewellyn (1998) provides a useful discussion of the role of accounting systems in creating the boundaries of organizations. The fact that something is needed to construct the boundary alerts us to the fact that the relationship between the organization and its environment is likely to be complex. There is a range of theoretical approaches to understanding this relationship. Contingency and functional theorists argue that an organization should adapt to the environment, applying what might be seen as a Darwinian logic. However it is argued that this ignores the fact that actors in the environment can affect and shape an organization. According to the population ecology approach (Hannan and Freeman, 1977) there is a natural selection process in which organizations that are fittest for their environment will survive whilst others will fail. Organizational ecology theory (Trist, 1976), on the other hand, sees the environment and the many organizations within it as comprising a complex ecosystem, evolving together. The environment of any one organization therefore includes many other organizations and each one is part of the environment of the others. Any organization can influence that environment, and the latter is perhaps negotiated and not independently and externally imposed. Llewellyn's (1998) less deterministic analysis shows us that control systems may be active in bounding the organization. Again this demonstrates that control systems may not simply be reactive and static, but also reflexive and mutable.

One example of a set of controls that define the boundary of the organization is the legislative system. In this chapter the organization will be generally assumed to be that defined by legal governance, and the analysis will look closely at controls that are imposed (or are attempted to be imposed) by external bodies of various kinds. External regulation of the legally constituted body will therefore be the main focus of interest. However in the final analysis we shall return to the problem of defining the organization, its environment and their interrelationship, with consideration of the extent to which external controls can be said to be effective.

External regulation and its impact

As noted above, one influential source of control is the machinery of the law, developed through the regulatory and enforcement powers of government. This is not the only source of control; trade and professional groupings may also provide regulation and enforcement. This is most commonly viewed as self-regulation as it avoids government involvement. The extent to which the regulations developed by the government and other associations coincide or accord with the values of society in general will be discussed later. This section is primarily concerned with the formal controls that exist in the organizational environment and are likely to encroach on the control systems within it.

Government legislation

Legislation on structures: extra-organizational controls that may affect interorganizational roles

Government legislation is an important element of control in many organizations and directly controls the actions of organizations in numerous ways. It can create and bound the organization. For example the UK Companies Act of 1985[1] provides the regulative framework for the creation of public and private limited companies. The act allows for limitation of the liability borne by the owners of companies and defines the difference between public and private limited companies. The latter, unlike the former, have shares that cannot be traded in the market. It provides a framework in which companies can, through their articles and memoranda, define their relationships with the outside world as well as internal rules of procedure for relationships with shareholders.

UK legislation allows for the existence of other organizational forms: the Partnership Act of 1890 governs the relationship between partners in a business situation, the Building Societies Act of 1986 regulates building societies, the Charity Commission regulates the operation of charities, local authorities operate within a legal framework, as do health authorities. Without the requisite legislation the organizations in question could not exist in the form they do. The legislation provides broad control over the governance of all the organizations as well as defining the levels of public and private accountability that must be met. The provision of annual accounts to shareholders in a limited company is a good example of how one level of accountability is promoted between the managers and owners of a company. It is interesting to note that much of the accountability imposed on companies is expressed in financial terms and is directed at a specific audience – the board of directors (Laughlin and Gray, 1988, p. 296). Thus external accountability and control has a tendency to be identified with accounting-based information.

Not only does this type of legislation impose organizational boundaries and therefore control the number of organizational types, it also creates opportunities and possibilities for control of and within the organizations. For example a differentiation between markets and hierarchies has been made in earlier chapters as a way of focusing on the controls within organizations. To allow for different approaches to organizational control, the environment in which either markets or hierarchies can exist has to be created. Legislation creates the context that defines the possibilities. This point can be illustrated by the recent history of structural change in the National Health Service (NHS) in the UK.

For many years the NHS was organized as a hierarchy (Mintzbergs, 1993), categorizes it as a professional bureaucracy) controlled by administrators (through resource provision) and professionals (through a system of shared values, or a clan culture). The National Health Service and Community Care Act of 1990 introduced the first of a series of changes when it created structures for the provision and purchase of services, what required a more market-based approach to relationships in the service. This structure would never have been adopted spontaneously in the absence of a legislative framework. Since then various approaches have been taken to the development of structures in the NHS. Under the new legislative framework the overtly market-based purchaser/provider split has given way to a less market-oriented provision of services and the power to define service requirements has passed to primary care groups (PCGs) or trusts (PCTs)[2] (Health Care Act, 1999). Meanwhile the legislation implemented by the NHS Reform and Health Care Professionals Act, 2002 (which included the introduction of PCTs throughout England) has shifted the family health service to PCTs. This has given more control to the primary providers of medical care, thus shifting the balance of control between general practitioners and hospital consultants. The recent changes have elements of both markets and hierarchies, and although the market approach has been attenuated it has not disappeared. The most recent government pronouncements have been about contestability rather than competition (see for example OPSR, 2002).

The nature of legislation can have profound implications for the types control structure that are possible. In the move from hierarchies to the market, privatization has been a popular government policy, and privatization has been used in many countries as a means of changing the organizational structure of public services. It takes a number of forms. In the UK, for example, the privatization of British Telecom left the organization as a whole unit; the initial privatization of British Rail produced Railtrack and a number of competing train operating companies; and the various water authorities were transformed into competing units.

The changes discussed above can be seen as ideological in nature. A number of different positions have been adopted by recent governments, although the overall thrust has been towards market-based approaches. This has been met with some resistance by professionals in the caring services in particular, who have worried about the undermining of their professional autonomy, and by members of the general public, who have been concerned that profit might come before care. Against this is the argument that markets allow efficiency. However Lindblom (1977), in a critique of the competence of markets, shows that governments have provided privileges that enable businesses to function in the market environment. For instance the provision of limited liability confers businesses with a vital privilege. Other examples include tax incentives, influence in policy-making circles and legislation to control the labour force. Without this support business would not be able to function as it does, and this raises the question (which cannot be pursued here in any depth) of the extent to which the market actually functions as an invisible hand.

Imai and Itami (1984) discuss the interpenetration of organization and market in different settings. They examine the US and Japanese economies and demonstrate how market ideas and organizational forms of resource allocation impinge on each other in different ways in the two countries. They emphasize that, whilst analytically separable, in reality the distinction between market and organizational forms of resource allocation is not clear. More recently the notion of partnership between the public and private sectors has been promoted in ideas such as the 'third way' (Giddens, 1998), which seeks to move away from the extreme either/or stand on markets or hierarchies.

Legislation that affects actions: extra-organizational controls that bound organizational actions

Of course not all legislation relates to the structuring of organizations. Some legislation addresses the relationships between the organization and the general community, particularly workers. Health and safety regulations, equal opportunities legislation and pollution controls are examples of this. These define the obligations of the organization very specifically, and by means of inspection and enforcement they control particular activities. They are therefore much more direct than the controls that relate to boundary definitions and the creation of a supportive environment, and they provide a framework for specific actions and obligations. They can also limit the extent to which organizations' own control systems can act autonomously.

Extra-organizational controls: legislation by bodies other than the national government

National governments are not the only legislative source in the increasingly globalized world. For example membership of the European Union has given the regulation of organizations an international dimension. The impact of this can be extensive. For example EU regulations are concerned with many areas of organization and may well come to impinge much more on national practices as the EU's borders expand with the accession of new members countries. The influence of the EU will be felt not only in respect of organizational boundaries and structural regulation, but also in terms of direct intervention to govern the actions of organizations in particular circumstances. The aim is to harmonize practices throughout the EU in the interest of, *inter alia*, maintaining the necessary conditions for the single market to operate. As well as striving to harmonize the more obvious practices, such as accounting, the EU also issues EU-wide directives on broader issues such as the environment. The EU is but one example of an entity that uses transnational regulations to provide the context in which organizations and markets function. Other transnational organizations include Mercosur (or Mercosul in Portuguese: Mercado Comum do Sul), which is the world's fourth largest economic bloc after the EU, the United States and Japan. It was created in 1991 and it comprises Brazil, Argentina, Paraguay and Uruguay. Mercosur's ultimate aim is the integration of South America, and as with the EU its activities extend beyond economic and trade issues to areas such as education, labour, culture, the environment, justice and consumer protection. The World Trade Organization is another body that impacts on trade by creating a set of rules that are internationally applicable.

Formal legislation and delegated powers: the nature of extra-organizational controls

It should be noted that the legislative framework provided by any government (national or supranational) is just a framework. No formal control system can be comprehensive unless the context in which it operates is known and predictable. This is only likely to be the case in very simple situations, and the social world is not simple. Because of this the legislation needs fleshing out. Sometimes this is done through the legal processes in which case law is developed. Case law is an important means of clarifying the law in specific situations, which then can be applied to related areas. Sometimes this fleshing out is achieved through administrative processes, delegating decision-making power to responsible officials. For example in the UK the Education Reform Act (1988) and the National Health Service and Community Care Act (1990) granted the respective secretaries of state the power to rule on particular issues. The granting of power to rule on well-defined matters is an important element of operationalizing laws more generally.

Legislation and the various legal instruments and pronouncements associated with it have to be communicated. In the NHS there are well-used channels through which government policies are communicated to the various health authorities, the bureaucratic structure providing for lines of authority from the secretary of state to the operational units. Direct instruction is therefore possible. Currently included in such instructions to the public sector in general and some privatized organizations are waiting lists targets for the NHS, punctuality targets for train operating companies and performance targets for schools. However doubt has been expressed about the benefits of using externally devised performance targets. Hence the 'star' grading system in the NHS is under question and there is a debate on whether schools should be given the right to set their own performance targets.

External regulations

Economic interest groups

Not all regulations flow from the government; some may even be seen as the means by which government regulation is avoided. This type of control is established by groups working together on a voluntary basis, and adherence to it could be seen as the price of joining a club or exclusive group. For example the UK stock market has some of the most comprehensive controls imposed on companies and these are administered by the body itself, and not through legislation. If a company wishes to be a quoted on the exchange it must comply with the regulations, which are also used to define and maintain boundaries. An example is the 'Chinese wall' in stockbroking firms, created at the inception of the Big Bang in the UK stock exchange. Broking and dealing can be undertaken by the same firm, but confidentiality between and separation of the two areas is required.

Not all associations are so visible. Cartels – groups of firms in the same business acting together to control the market – are illegal in the UK and the United States, but have existed in the past and still operate elsewhere. OPEC is a well-known example of a group of producers working together to control both oil production and oil prices. There is disagreement over how long and how effectively any cartel can exercise control, but some seem to flourish as predatory monopolies.

Some trade associations agree voluntary codes of practice to protect their independence and retain the confidence of the general public. The scheme operated in the UK by the Association of British Travel Agents (ABTA) to protect holidaymakers when travel firms run into financial difficulties can be seen as controlling the trade and maintaining public confidence. Similarly trade unions impose regulations on their members and try to control, through national negotiations on wages and conditions, the employers of their members. In seeking to control employer – employee relations they become part of the environment of employing organizations as well as being organizations in their own right. This type of interrelationship is illustrative of those in Trist's (1976) organizational ecology model.

Normative interest groups

Professional associations are another source of control. These bodies control entry into professions through education and examination programmes and have procedures for expulsion when there is proof of unacceptable behaviour. They have set rules of conduct for their members and many lobby on their members behalf. Accounting professional bodies fulfil all these functions in many countries and some are internationally based. They control the education process by setting minimum standards for registration as students, and they have their own examination systems. Membership of these bodies is usually dependent on passing examinations and having a certain amount of practical experience.

The professional accounting bodies also have some interest in the setting of standards for accounting. They may be closely involved in the consultation processes that generate standard accounting practices. These define the way in which accountants should compile financial data, as this assists the functioning of the capital markets and enables a fairer assessment of the results of companies by the general public. Hence this type of regulation can be seen as a way of achieving the necessary conditions for a market to function. However it should be noted that a number of different accounting associations compile accounting standards, some nationally and some globally based, for example the international accounting standards, and there is a *de facto* market for accounting standards. In this situation there is a possibility that organizations will choose the standards that best suit their circumstances, but the international accounting standards are the a preferred choice of many legislatures. This reflects the preference of the regulatory bodies that are in charge of the organizations. Hence there is a complex web of regulation and choice, which confirms the veracity of the earlier suggestion that organizations can influence their environments and are not simply at their mercy.

Professional associations are interesting in that they illustrate the impact of shared values on controls. They might be viewed as groupings that exist on normative foundations and it could be argued that they exist to protect the values implicit in membership of them.[3] Self-regulation is advocated in the context of a particular view of the expertise of the group. Professional judgement and expertise, it is argued, are intangible and therefore cannot be directly defined or controlled. Professional control must therefore be ensured by instilling in members a set of ethics and codes of conduct. This might also be seen as protecting the culture of the profession. Throughout the world the medical profession adheres to the central value of medical autonomy, and the academic community values its academic freedom. Both communities work hard to maintain their professional autonomy and (as they see it) their integrity.

The central issue to highlight in the context of this chapter is that the values of the professional group impose a strong control on the behaviour of its members. Its formal regulations stem from those values and in some cases are a means of maintaining the right of the profession to regulate itself. It should nevertheless be noted that economic benefits also accrue to such organizations.

Quangos

The purpose of some quasi-autonomous non-governmental organizations, or quangos, is to exercise control over other organizations. Whilst they are set up by the government they are autonomous from it. their task is to control objectively within a policy framework, rather than politically. For example, in many countries regulatory boards have been set up to control the prices charged by privatized utility companies, which because of their near monopoly position could exploit consumers by overcharging. Examples of such quangos in the UK are the Office of Water Regulation (Ofwat), the Office for Electricity Regulation (Ofer), the gas industry regulator (Ofgas) and the telecommunications regulator (Oftel).

The preceding overview of sources of regulation is not exhaustive but it is illustrative. It provides some indication of the nature of regulation and differences in scope. Regulations that provide structures or boundaries for an organization should be differentiated from those which define actions. However control in both cases is extra-organizational and provides interorganizational control structures.

As we have seen, there are numerous sources of regulation. Principal among these is the state, but many other bodies have a strong influence on the control environment and the control regimes of that are imposed or chosen. The question that will be addressed in the next section is how this translates into action (Drucker, 1964). The existence of a regulation does not necessarily mean that it achieves what is intended; nor does it explain why organizations take notice of regulations. Understanding this is essential if we are to understand the context of control.

Regulation: how does it work and why does it work?

Legislation does not always work. People do not always do as they are legally required. For example a drive along any road will reveal the extent to which the speed limit is broken. Police officers have openly admitted that they will not prosecute those exceeding the speed limit on UK motorways by 10 miles per hour or less. This effectively means that one can travel down a motorway at 80 miles per hour with little fear of prosecution. In most countries there are examples of legislation that has failed because of public resistance or lack of support. The 'poll tax' or community charge in the UK was widely resisted because people lost their entitlement to vote in elections if they were not registered for this local tax (the previous tax had been levied on property and did not depend on the number of adult individuals living in a household), and this was argued to be a factor in the discrediting of Prime Minister Thatcher. The community charge was eventually withdrawn and replaced by a tax on property. Its failure illustrates the danger of legislators introducing laws that are likely to be unacceptable to a large proportion of the electorate, and provides a foundation for discussing the relationship between formal regulations and less tangible factors such as social values and culture.

Many social theorists have focused on either the structures in society or the subjective role of the individual. Karl Marx (see for example Marx 1972) concentrated on the structures of society, and particularly the capitalist mode of production. In contrast Goffman (1959) was concerned only with the way in which individuals shape their own social world. For our purposes other theorists are more worthy of consideration because they have attempted to link the two elements together to provide a rather richer picture of society. We shall consider their work because they provide some rationale for recognizing the importance of both tangible and intangible organizational elements in systems of control.

Anthony Giddens has developed a theory of structuration that addresses the relationship between the structures of society and the systems made up by the interdependent actions of the individuals that make up that society. He highlights the relationship between intangible elements such as meanings or values and more tangible structures. A brief introduction to the theory (and an application of it to management control) is provided by Capps *et al.* (1989).

Capps *et al.* use structuration theory to explore the part played by culture in organizational control. Structures provide the rules and resources that people use in their social life, and it is through this use that the structures are maintained and developed. This is what Giddens calls the duality of structure. Three forms of structure are proposed: meaning, morality and domination. Together these provide rules on the communication of meaning, the norms that guide relationships and the power relationships between parties. Capps and her colleagues drew on this theory in a case study of the National Coal Board (NCB) to show the set of practices that create and sustain the structures alongside the production of meaning. They demonstrate how interpretive studies of culture, which look at meanings, can be extended to include considerations of structure and power. More recently Conrad (2004 forthcoming) has used a similar framework in a study of the public utilities in the UK.

Jürgen Habermas (see for example Habermas 1984, 1987) also recognizes the importance of intangible elements in the social world. He differentiates the lifeworld – the stock of taken-for-granted definitions and understanding we have of the world – from the systems of society, which operationalize the values and beliefs of the lifeworld. He also identifies 'steering mechanisms', which steer the systems in a way commensurate with lifeworld values, associating these with money and law. This abstract model of societal development has been adapted for use at the organizational level by Broadbent *et al.* (1991), who argue that the organization can be seen as a microcosm of society, with its own lifeworld, steering mechanisms and systems. The potential effect of these different aspects of organizations on pathways of change have been analyzed by Laughlin (1991). Any process of change that is not led by evolution of the lifeworld, and is therefore at odds with the values of the organization, is likely to be disruptive to the organization and may not achieve what it sets out to do (see Laughlin, 1987, 1991, for a detailed discussion). The value of this type of analysis is that it articulates the argument that the intangible aspects of organizational and social life are at least as important as the tangible ones.

Using ideas developed from the works outlined above, along with those of some lawyers, Laughlin and Broadbent (1997) have examined the implications of legislation that is not in line with the lifeworld of organizations or societies. In particular they have looked at the UK Education Reform Act of 1988 and the UK National Health Service and Community Care Act 1990 to see whether and to what extent these acts have beyond the lifeworld demands of and way organising systems in the organizations with which they are concerned. The implications of this are important to the context of control, especially in respect of the extent to which external legislation *can* control. This brings us back to the question of why people obey laws. How is control achieved through legislation? We argue that the law can only bring about control if it is in harmony with the lifeworld of the society in which it is applied. If it is not, then – as the example of the community charge has illustrated – in the long term either the law will be ignored or it will fail, perhaps causing the downfall of those who seek to impose it. To provide another example, recall the failure of the prohibition of alcohol in the United States in the early twentieth century. Drug legislation may suffer the same fate.

In answer to the questions asked in the heading of this section – how does regulation work and why does it work? – it works when it imposes controls that reflect the values and beliefs of most of a society or organization. This does not mean that everyone will conform as there will always be deviants and different shades of opinion; rather we are referring to its acceptance or implicit acceptance by the majority.

It has to be recognized that control is not simply the result of regulation. If values and beliefs are important components of control they may be so deeply ingrained that they do not require formal regulation. This is apparent in the normative controls (Etzioni, 1961) and clan controls (Ouchi, 1980) mentioned in Chapter 2. Taking a broader perspective, the question of why controls succeed can be related to the notion of legitimacy (Weber, 1948). Authority is gained through the legitimacy accorded to those who seek to control, and legitimacy is achieved in a number of ways. Modern society is seen as being oriented to systems of control that achieve their legitimacy through democratic legal rational structures such as those discussed earlier. On the other hand legitimacy can be achieved through tradition or charisma. These will be considered in turn.

Traditional authority lies with those who have traditionally been accorded that right. In this situation the values of society are such that particular relationships are the norm and to some extent this type of authority is similar to that found in clan control and normative control. For example in some societies the elderly traditionally receive deference. Therefore authority relates to the role of or position held by particular people. Weber cites patriarchy as an important type of domination that rests on tradition. Here control is exercised by a person who holds a given position because he or she is the holder of that position, and for no other reason.

Charismatic authority, on the other hand, is achieved by those who have (or are perceived to have) extraordinary qualities. Religious or national leaders such as Mahatma Gandhi, Mother Theresa and Adolf Hitler can be seen as examples of people who had exercised control through the authority of their persona. This type of control is substantially different from that based on legal-rational or traditional authority as it is personality led and can appear at random. For charismatic authority to be achieved the person in question must have the support of a substantial number of people in an organization or a society. When this is the case the person in question will have a great capacity to control, and this is an important element in the context of control.

Achieving control through external regulation

This section considers how we might conceptualize the context of control and the extent to which external regulation is an important component of that environment. The importance of various regulations in providing a context for the control of individual organizations cannot be denied. The extent to which structures of control are enabled by the external regulatory framework is clear, and both organizations and actors in the environment, depending on their position in the structures, can be powerful in determining the nature of control. Legal regulation has sought to define the boundaries of organizations through the development of governance structures and codes; it has been more successful in some cases than others. The intertwining of the affairs of the companies controlled by Robert Maxwell shows how boundaries can be breached by those who wish to. Also the Enron affair has demonstrated how easy it is to conceal the financial state of a company by developing complex, interlinked entities.

The extent to which the external environment is constitutive of the organization or is constituted by the organization is unclear. In some cases there is little doubt that the organization is constrained by the environmental context in which it operates. On the whole people and organizations do not break laws laid down at the societal level. Equally people do react to cultural values; for example debates on how to address social welfare issues are common but are addressed differently in different countries. Conversely it is possible for organizations to have a strong influence on the outside environment, either directly or indirectly. For example the main employer in a small market town in the south of England was seen by local residents as putting unfair pressure on the local planners by threatening to relocate if the company did not receive planning permission for new offices. It seems likely that in general there is a two-way exchange and that vary in respect of the direction in which power flows.

In summary we can suggest to those who design controls that awareness of environmental influences is essential. Any judgement about a context and its effect cannot be made away from the actual situation and control systems cannot be seen as acontextual technical solutions.

A second important consideration for designers of controls is whether the systems they develop will actually produce the control required. External regulations we imposed in the expectation that the desired effects can be achieved by these means. Members of parliament promote legislation on the assumption that desired consequences will follow; they assume they can change things. The argument presented in this chapter is that controls only work when there is some alignment between the nature of the control and the values of the organization or society in which the control is implemented. One exception to this is when there is direct coercion or physical restraint. for example controls in a situation of slavery or in a prison may work in a rather different fashion (although even in situations like this conflict is possible). Our assumption is that we are dealing with situations in which there is some agreement that authority for decisions should be granted to legitimate authorities, and that on the whole managers and governments are legitimate authorities.

If we restrict the discussion to situations in which direct or physical control is not legitimate, then we have to investigate how we can develop effective external controls. As we have repeatedly argued controls or laws that reflect the values of the organization or society as a whole are essential. It is also possible to use what has been called 'reflexive law' (Teubner, 1983), that is, law that deals with broad frameworks within which practical problems can be resolved. It defines processes enable answers, rather than seeking to provide answers directly. This type of law recognizes that controls developed for one particular situation may not be transferable, either spatially or temporally, but it is useful for developing systems of control at both the micro and the macro level. It allows for the possibility of controls developing and mutating as needs require. With this type of law, regulation would be more easily accepted in that it would be constitutive and amenable to substantive justification rather than constitutive (Broadbent *et al.* 1991). It would therefore be effective and more likely to have the potential for longevity.

There is also a regulatory dimension to control systems. In many cases regulation is needed not only to control but also to sanction those who contravene the law. There are always people who will break the law, and there is often some degree of tolerance of deviation from it. Thus the bounds of acceptable behaviour have to be set and the penalties for breaking them defined. For this reason it is essential for external regulations to work, backed up by a firm value foundation in society. One further question can be raised as a point for future discussion. Is there any law or regulation that is absolute whatever the context? Is there a point about which, morally, there is no debate, and for which external regulation can and should be imposed unilaterally?

Summary

This chapter has discussed the context of control and the effect of external regulation on defining that context. It has examined the part played by external regulation in defining the boundaries of organizations and the relationship between them. Regulation has been described as coming through the rule of law and voluntary adherence to the rules of groups of individuals and organizations. It has been argued that for regulation to be effective it must reflect the values of those it seeks to regulate or it will be ignored, or even undermine the law makers. The use of reflexive law – a law that defines the processes by which agreement on the nature of particular controls is achieved – is recommended as it has the flexibility required to deal with changing values and circumstances.

We cannot pretend that this is the whole story of the context of control; rather we have addressed issues that have the potential to give rise to both passion and conflict and can be illuminated by people from other disciplines, for example political scientists, sociologists and novelists. Deeper insights can be gained by extending the boundary of our considerations and we encourage the interested reader to do this. On a practical level, it is essential to consider the context of control when making any attempt to achieve control.

Discussion questions

1. Do you adhere to all the rules in your organization? Describe the sorts of rule you always keep and explain why.
2. To what extent is government legislation successful in ensuring control?
3. Which quasi-governmental organizations affect your life and how useful are they as control devices.
4. To what extent to extra-organizational controls affect the management control systems in your own organization?
5. To what extent do control systems help to define the boundaries of the organizations in which they are found?

Notes

1. This was updated by the Companies Act of 1989, but the substance was laid down in the earlier legislation.
2. Primary care trusts, like hospital trusts, are quasi-autonomous organizations.
3. Although professional associations might also be seen as 'upmarket' trade unions that protect the monopoly of a set of workers.

Performance management: a framework for analysis

6

David Otley

Introduction

Performance management systems, which tend to be taken for granted by organizations, consist of several interrelated but often loosely coupled parts. The design of these separate parts is often the responsibility of different business functions, such as management information systems, operations management, human resources and finance. When there is a degree of integration, this tends to be focused on budgeting and management accounting-based performance measures. Although management accounting has long been concerned with measuring the performance of business and other organizations, it has often been restricted to financial performance, and has used frameworks and theories drawn primarily from the discipline of economics. More recently some attention has been paid to the development of non-financial performance measures, but this has been done on an *ad hoc* basis using frameworks that have little theoretical underpinning, such as the balanced scorecard. In this chapter we shall broaden this perspective by looking beyond the measurement of performance to the management of performance. Management accounting systems provide information that is intended to be useful to managers, so any assessment of the part played by such information therefore requires us to consider how managers will make use of it. The traditional framework for considering these issues was developed in the 1960s by Robert Anthony of the Harvard Business School, under the title of management control systems.

Anthony classified managerial decision-making and control activities into three major types – strategic planning, management control and operational control – and argued that most managers are usually concerned with only one of these. As the nature of the control process is very different in each case, it is important that a manager's task is correctly identified. Strategic planning is defined as the setting and changing of overall corporate strategies and objectives; management control involves monitoring activities and taking action to ensure that resources are effectively and efficiently used to accomplish organizational objectives; and operational control is concerned with carrying out specific tasks on a day-to-day basis.

Management control is seen as the mediating activity between strategic planning (objectives setting) and task control (the carrying out of specific tasks). It is integrative because it involves the whole organization and is concerned with effective management of the interrelationships between disparate parts. Unlike strategic planning and operational control, Anthony sees management control as routine reporting on the performance of all areas of the organization on a regular basis, so that all areas are systematically reviewed. He also concentrates on techniques that have universal applicability across all types of business and organization. The principal tool for achieving management control is management accounting information. Such information is collected a standard manner from all parts of the organization. Because it is in a quantitative (monetary) form it can easily be aggregated into summaries for higher levels of management, and it is routinely collected and disseminated. Research into the behavioural aspects of management accounting generally, and budgetary control in particular fits neatly into this viewpoint as it emphasizes the social, psychological and motivational aspects of control.

Although this can usefully serve as an initial framework, it would be erroneous to assume that management accounting is the only or even the main means of management control. Anthony's classification assumes away too many problems. Strategic planning cannot be divorced from control, for effective control involves changing plans and objectives. Nor can operational control be kept separate from management control as its technological complexities impinge directly on the control process. The all-important linkages between the three sets of activities are neglected in Anthony's work (see Lowe and Puxty, 1989, for a fuller critique), leading to an overemphasis on accounting controls. As Machin (1983) argues, Anthony himself specified social psychology as the principal source discipline for the study of management control, and it is perhaps surprising that accounting continued to dominate his thinking. In many ways the publication of Anthony's (1965) framework can be seen as the high point of accounting's domination of management control. Machin considers that it was inevitable that mainstream work in management control would swing away from the study of accounting systems alone. Again, it should be emphasized that accounting is just one of the techniques available to assist the control process. The aim of this chapter is to develop a more comprehensive framework for the study of management control systems.

The performance management framework

Four main questions have to be answered when developing a framework for managing organizational performance. The questions remain the same, but organizations need continually to find new answers to them. (We are reminded of the apocryphal economics professor who set the same examination questions every year; there was nothing wrong with this, he claimed, as the answers were different each year!) In an organizational context the answers are different because the context in which the organization is set is constantly changing and new strategies have to be developed to cope with the new operating environment. The questions are as follows:

- What factors does an organization see as crucial to its continued success, and how does it measure and monitor its performance in each of these areas?
- What level of performance does the organization wish to achieve in each of these areas, and how does it go about setting appropriate performance targets?
- What rewards (both monetary and non-monetary) will managers gain by achieving these performance targets (or conversely, what penalties will they suffer by failing to achieve them)?
- What information flows are necessary for the organization to be able to monitor its performance on these dimensions, to learn from its past experiences and to adapt its behaviour in the light of those experiences?

These questions relate very closely to some of the central issues in modern management accounting practice. The first is concerned with performance measurement, not just in financial terms but also in operational terms. It is closely connected to strategy formulation and deployment, and also to the very practical areas of business process management and operations management. The second question is more traditional and has a long pedigree of research on the subject, but it remains important, as reflected in current practices such as benchmarking. The third question has tended to be neglected by those who view performance measurement as being in the purview of human resource management. However the interconnections between the two fields must be recognized to avoid the many counterproductive examples of short-termism driven by financial incentive schemes we see in practice. The final question has been considered by Management Information Systems (MIS) specialists but still needs to be better linked to issues such as the 'learning organization', employee empowerment and emergent strategy.

The following sections will consider each of these questions in turn in order to clarify their meaning. (See Otley, 1999, for a fuller outline of the application of the questions.) The issues raised by the questions will be used in the remainder of the book to provide a framework for analyzing the operation of various aspects of management control systems. However it is first necessary to consider the question of organizational strategy, as this forms the basis of the whole structure of control being developed.

Strategy

Numerous texts have been written on the topic of corporate strategy, and it is not our intention to duplicate those here. The interested reader is referred to such standard texts as Johnson and Scholes (1993) and Morden (1993). Before we can discuss corporate strategy we need to consider the mission, goals and objectives of an organization. Mintzberg (1983) provides some useful definitions, although his terminology is not universally accepted:

1. *Mission*: An organisation's mission is its basic function in society, and is reflected in the products and services that it provides for its customers or clients. The mission of an organisation is essentially a long-term view of its fundamental reasons for existence.
2. *Goals*: An organisation's goals are the intentions behind its decisions or actions. Goals will frequently never be achieved and may be incapable of being measured. Thus, for example, the United Biscuits' goal of giving 'the highest possible standard of living to our employees' is a goal which will be difficult to realise and measure. Therefore, although goals are more specific than a mission statement and tend to have a shorter time-scale, they are not precise measures of performance.
3. *Objectives*: Objectives are goals expressed a form in which they can be measured. Thus, the objective of 'profit before interest and tax to be not less than 20 per cent of capital employed' is an objective capable of precise measurement.

Despite exhortations for organizations to devote more time and effort to the definition of their missions, goals and objectives, such activities are often regarded as little more than public relations exercises. For example how many employees or managers would be able to recite their organization's mission statement, and more importantly, continually use it as a basis for action? What is necessary is more multidimensional view of organizational objectives that gives consideration to the requirements of each stakeholder group.

However a strategy is more than a statement of desired outcomes, whether expressed in terms of mission, goals or objectives. It is essentially a plan of action to achieve those outcomes. Unfortunately, as Coad (1995) succinctly points out, the term strategy is probably one of the most ill-defined in the business vocabulary, having a wide range of connotations. Published definitions vary, with each writer adding his or her own ideas and emphases. For some, strategy refers to a plan as the end product of strategy formulation. Some include objectives as part of the strategy, while others see objectives as what the strategy should achieve. Many mention the allocation of resources as a crucial aspect of strategy. Some prescribe a review of the market and specifically mention competitive position. To complicate matters further, some writers suggest that strategy is a formal logic, explicitly stated, that links together the activities of a business, whilst others suggest that a strategy can emerge from a set of decisions and need not be explicitly stated.

Whilst recognizing the importance of emergent strategy, it is clear that performance cannot be managed unless there is some agreement on the plans the organization is intending to implement and the desired results of those plans. We shall go down an explicitly hierarchical route whereby strategies become codified in performance measures that are used to motivate and monitor performance at lower organizational levels. However when so doing we shall not lose sight of two major issues that stand outside this framework. First, strategies are not solely developed by senior managers; some strategies emerge from what has been found to work at the grass-roots level. The ways in which such emergent strategies can be incorporated into the subsequent strategy re-formulation process is an important aspect of organizational learning. Second, the explicit specification of performance measures is only one means of strategy implementation. Ideas such as 'visioning', whereby employees at all levels are given an insight into the strategic positioning of an organization and have the values of the organization inculcated into their thinking, are also important.

Simons' (1995a) 'levers of control' framework makes an important contribution here. He distinguishes four major 'levers' that can be used to influence the behaviour of organizational participants. The first he calls the belief system, whereby the organization's mission, goals and objectives are conveyed to the staff in a variety of, primarily non-quantitative, ways. By contrast the boundary system conveys information about activities that are not to be undertaken, either because they are not part of the current strategy or because they are viewed as inappropriate for other reasons. Formal performance measurement is the realm of diagnostic and interactive control; these two systems are seen as operating on the same set of formal information, but using it in different ways. Diagnostic control comprises the routine reporting of actual performance against a plan, as in a budgetary control system, while interactive controls are those highlighted by senior managers as being important, and to which they will pay particular attention. Interactive controls are also used to monitor the assumption on which the strategic plan is based and to give early warning of when the strategy may need to be reviewed.

Thus the approach to performance measurement outlined above concentrates on the reporting and use of specific performance measures that are used in a diagnostic or interactive manner. These are clearly only part of the repertoire of control tools available to managers. Nevertheless the formal specification of performance measures and the development of measurement and monitoring systems are major means of performance management in a wide range of organizations, and it is this process that we shall now consider in more detail.

Performance measurement

The starting point when designing a performance measurement system to assist performance management is the business strategy. This specifies the key factors that the organization must attend to in order to be successful. So, the performance measurement system has to be concerned with measures of outcomes or results, and the means by which such results can be achieved. For example a company may wish to achieve a certain return on investment; to realize that aim its strategy is to offer its customers a level of service that is sufficiently high to justify its relatively high prices, and hope that this strategy will enable the business to grow in a profitable manner. Here the overall objective is return on investment, and the means of its achievement is customer service, which may be further refined into more detailed measures of service levels, such speed of response, the value added to services and customer satisfaction ratings. This process is sometimes described as 'strategy mapping' and has recently been promoted as part of the balanced scorecard by Kaplan and Norton (2001b).

The process of setting up the set of performance measures may well stimulate the further development and articulation of strategy. Only when we try to measure performance do we fully understand what achieving it will require. It is tempting to be satisfied with specifying performance indicators, defined here as aspects of performance that are relatively easy to measure but do not capture the underlying dimensions of performance. Many efficiency measures fall into this category, such as measures of idle or non-productive time. Clearly we do not wish our workforce to be unnecessarily idle, but it is also necessary that they work on useful tasks. We are reminded of the story of the accounting professor who paid a student to drive his car around the town during lectures because it reduced the cost per mile!

It is also very easy to set up measures that are inappropriate or easily manipulated. We are suggesting here a top-down approach to the design and specification of performance measures, but it is also important rigorously to test every measure developed to ensure that it is appropriate. Some of our engineering colleagues (Neely, 1998) have referred to this process as 'destructive testing' of performance measures. This involves to examining each performance measure through the eyes of the manager who is accountable for its achievement, and testing whether it might be possible to make the measure look good whilst actually engaging in inappropriate behaviour.

The author vividly recollects looking out of an airport window and watching the baggage being taken off an aircraft. One of the baggage handlers picked up the first small bag to be taken off the aircraft, tucked it under his arm and sprinted several hundred yards across the tarmac to deliver it to a baggage reception point. He then sauntered back to help his colleagues unload the remaining bags onto the baggage train, which eventually made its journey to the reception point about five minutes later. Upon making enquiries it was discovered that the performance measure being used for baggage handling was the time taken for the first bag to hit the conveyor belt. It had not taken long for intelligent employees to work out how to ensure that their performance met the designated target!

One major framework for developing a set of performance measures for an activity or a business unit has been developed by Kaplan and Norton (1992, 1996a, 2001). Their balanced scorecard approach, which is discussed in the following section, provides a structured way of developing an appropriate set of performance measures for the chosen business strategy. It demonstrates that a logical, cohesive system can be devised to integrate both financial and non-financial performance measures. However the choice of which measures to use, avoiding of conflict between them and keeping their number to an adequate minimum are issues for individual companies to address.

The balanced scorecard

The balanced scorecard was the product of a research project conducted by the Harvard Business School and involving 12 leading companies in the United States. It allows managers to look at a business from four important perspectives and provides answers to the following questions:

- How do we look to shareholders? (Financial perspective.)
- How do customers see us? (Customer perspective.)
- What must we excel at? (Internal business perspective.)
- Can we continue to improve and create value? (Innovation and learning perspective.)

As well as defining the four perspectives the balanced scorecard approach suggests that no more than four measures of performance should be defined, although more recently the internal business perspective has been allowed between five to eight measures. This is to focus senior managers' attention on crucial factors rather than being distracted by unnecessary detail. It is said that companies rarely have too few measures. The justification for the four 'boxes' on the scorecard is as follows.

Financial perspective

This is the most traditional perspective and most organizations will already have some measures of financial performance. Most commonly, at the divisional level the overall measure of financial performance is likely to be return on capital employed. However this may be replaced by a less manipulable measure such as residual income, or its more modern counterpart, economic value added. This may be supplemented by measures of sales revenue growth, asset utilization, liquidity and budget achievement. Companies may also wish to include a measure of shareholder value added, as this is ultimately the benefit that shareholders gain from their investment in the company. The measures used here are likely to represent desired results rather than the means by which such results can obtained.

Customer perspective

In order to be successful it is necessary to keep customers happy. Thus measuring how a company is responding to its customers' requirements has become a top priority for most organizations. Customers' concerns tend to fall into one of four categories: time, quality, service and cost. The balanced scorecard requires managers to translate their general customer service goals into specific objectives and measures. For example the cycle time from receiving a customer's order to delivering the completed order is a commonly used measure. But it is vital to ensure that the performance measure targets exactly what the customer requires. One organization put a lot of effort into trying to reduce cycle time, until it became apparent that what most customers actually wanted was not so much a speedy service but a reliable service that was reasonably speedy. Therefore it replaced the cycle time measure with adherence to an agreed delivery date. It may also be important to clarify exactly what the organization's position is in terms of competitive strategy: does it emphasize cost competitiveness or added value products that will be priced at a premium? Developing balanced scorecard measures may require a strategy to be articulated more precisely.

Internal business perspective

Customer-based measures are important but they should be supplemented with measures of exactly what the company must do to deliver the level of service expected by its customers. Thus the internal business perspective box will generally contain measures that relate to the means by which the business objectives will be achieved. To achieve goals on cycle time, quality, productivity and cost, managers must devise measures that are clearly related to employees' actions. This linkage is the most important thread in the process of strategy deployment. That is, a clear link must be maintained between hierarchical levels (and between organizational units) to ensure that the means targeted at one level lead to the results required at the next level. Information systems can play a vital part in helping managers to disaggregate the summary measures. This 'drill-down' capacity is seen as an essential component of an effective information system for use in performance management.

Innovation and learning

All the performance measures in the three areas discussed above are necessarily short term in orientation. They are reported frequently and represent actual achievement over a relatively short period of time (generally weekly and monthly). But in order to remain competitive in a changing environment companies need to adapt and to continue to offer products and services that customers wish to purchase. The measures in the innovation and learning box are intended to promote a longer-term perspective to counteract the short-termism inherent in other measures. Thus new product development and the acquisition of new business and customers may be targeted. Competitive advantage can be gained by having a well-trained and motivated workforce; such measures as employees' skills and attitudes may be included here.

The balanced scorecard therefore provides a structured framework for the development of a simple but comprehensive system of performance measurement. However it is notable that the early publications on the balanced scorecard (Kaplan and Norton, 1992, 1996) contained next to no practical guidance on how to undertake the recommended procedures. Perhaps the considerable popularity of the framework has been due to its lack of specificity, which allows it to be applied in almost any context. Other related frameworks exist, such as the results and determinants framework by Fitzgerald *et al.* (1991), Lynch and Cross's (1995) performance pyramid and Neely *et al.*'s (2003) performance prism. A common thread in all of them is that performance measures should:

- Be linked to corporate strategy.
- Include external as well as internal measures.
- Include non-financial as well as financial measures.
- Make explicit the trade-offs between different dimensions of performance.
- Include all important but difficult to measure factors as well as easily measurable ones.
- Pay attention to how the selected measures will motivate managers and employees.

It could be said that the balanced scorecard essentially adopts a stakeholder perspective on the business. Shareholders and customers are clearly identified, and employees feature sometimes in the internal box and sometimes in the innovation box. Extending the idea of stakeholder analysis might suggest that the balanced scorecard could be extended to include measures that are relevant to each stakeholder group that has to be taken account of. Thus suppliers, local communities, governments and environmental lobbies might all be featured. A common addition in practice is a fifth box entitled 'corporate social responsibility', which covers some of these areas. The framework also focuses attention on internal business processes and on the longer term as well as the short term. Regardless of these extensions, the approach seems to have been found useful in a wide range of organizations – manufacturing and service, public and private – and is relatively easy to adapt to a wide range of situations.

Target setting

Having decided upon the major dimensions of performance that should be measured, the next stage is to set appropriate standards and targets, that is, the level of performance required for each of the measures identified. Clearly, higher levels of performance are more desirable than lower levels, but it may not be feasible to attain these with the current methods of working. The conflict between what is desired and what can reasonably be expected permeates the whole process of target setting. Setting targets for competing performance measures also reveals the trade-offs that may have to be made between different areas. For example high service quality and low prices may not be compatible. Setting targets for the two areas together resolves the conflict and establishes a more explicit strategy. Thus target setting is of major importance to the process of performance management.

It is helpful to distinguish between the process of target setting and the content of the targets set. The way in which target setting is approached is of vital importance to the motivational impact of the eventual targets. A large number of studies suggest that allowing managers to participate in the process of target setting will strengthen their commitment to achieving the targets. That is, being involved in the process is likely to result in greater ownership of and commitment to achieving performance targets. Much of the early research on budgetary control and managerial behaviour studied this in some detail (see for example Hofstede, 1968). It should be borne in mind, however, that managers are likely to view the issue from the standpoint of what is currently feasible and may have to be informed about the need to develop new practices. In addition the way in which the performance targets are expected to be used will influence target-setting behaviour. Managers who believe that a target will be used as a standard against which to judge their managerial performance may be inclined to set 'slack' targets that will be easier to achieve, rather than challenging targets that they may fail to meet but may still motivate them to perform well.

There are several relevant sources of information on the content of the target. What has been achieved in previous periods is always a relevant source of information as it enables judgment of what is actually feasible in given circumstances. But it is necessary to supplement this historical information with information on what is being done elsewhere. External benchmarking has become popular in recent years. This involves finding out the performance levels being achieved by competitors (either by formal collaboration or by gleaning information gleaned from a variety of sources). The requirements of customers and shareholders also provide important information on the performance levels required for future survival. These sources of external information can also provide legitimacy to the target-setting process. A difficult target may be rejected by a manager who feels that it is purely an arbitrary imposition by a demanding superior. However if it is clearly a necessary condition for organizational survival in a competitive market place, then it may be more readily accepted as a challenge.

One of the principal ways in which targets set in different areas are pulled together into a coherent overall statement is the budgeting process. A well-set budget incorporates the standards of performance that are feasible to attain, and represents the financial consequences of the implementation of a plan of action. Ideally the budget is the expected financial outcome of an espoused strategy. Unfortunately this ideal is often not met, with the budget becoming detached from the plans on which it is based. For example repeated budget revisions to meet financial performance targets may cause numbers to be entered into the budget with little or no idea of how these outcomes will be achieved in practice. While the budgetary process has traditionally been of major importance to the overall management of performance, in recent years budgeting has been the subject of increasing criticism (largely due to the difficulty of forecasting), and more radical approaches to performance management and control have been put forward. These have been cogently summarized by Fraser and Hope (2003). The case for improving budgeting rather than abolishing has been put forward by Hansen *et al.* (2003).

Incentives and rewards

The next key issue to address is motivation. It is one thing to set performance targets, but quite another for managers and other employees to be motivated to achieve them. Generally, organizations put into place a number of incentives, both financial and non-financial, to encourage their employees to achieve the performance standards defined in the processes described above. These may include the generation of enthusiasm to achieve a vision that has been communicated throughout the organization and to which, it is hoped, employees will commit themselves, the use of performance appraisal and evaluation methods, and the provision of short-term financial rewards. An appropriate package of incentive and reward arrangements should be central to the design of a performance management system. However in practice such systems are often designed in a very fragmented manner, with different departments being responsible for different aspects of the package.

In an assessment of the reward mechanisms used by organizations to encourage employees to achieve the required levels of performance, Fitzgerald and Moon (1996) suggest that three factors are of particular importance:

- Clarity: do they understand what the company is trying to do?
- Motivation: what benefits, financial or otherwise, will they gain from achieving targets?
- Controllability: are they assessed only on those factors they can control?

A feature of many successful organizations is that they have communicated their vision and mission to employees at all levels. Therefore the employees are clear about the organizational values they should incorporate into their everyday activities. Although it is difficult to codify in quantitative terms, commitment and enthusiasm of this type should not be underrated. The sense of pride that comes from working for a well-known or successful organization can be a vital factor in sustaining competitive advantage. Conversely a downward spiral of poor performance and demotivation, leading to poor employee attitudes, can prove difficult to break out of.

As well as a sense of pride in achievement, more direct incentives come into play. The long-term progression of employees in an organization is usually dependent on their being seen to perform well. The appraisal and evaluation of performance may be the subject of formal procedures and meetings or rely solely on the subjective judgement of a superior, but it is of central importance. The 'things you need to do to get on around here' is an important aspect of organizational culture of which employees rapidly become aware. Also the power politics of an organization have an impact in this area. Even more influential are systems of financial reward tied to performance. Many organizations have introduced performance-related pay, whereby employees earn extra pay for achieving preset performance targets. These have long been the norm in some types of job. For example sales people have traditionally been paid a commission on the sales they make. These mechanisms were used less for middle managers in the UK (although not the United States) until about 1985. However after then there was a great increase in the provision of financial rewards in both the private and the public sectors. A majority of middle managers in both sectors now receive a monetary reward for achieving performance targets.

Such mechanisms can clearly have a major effect on managerial behaviour, making it even more essential for performance measures accurately to reflect what is required of a manager. It is very easy to neglect an important aspect of performance (perhaps because it is difficult to measure) or to give it an inappropriate weighting. Too many organizations have discovered the hard way 'the folly of expecting A whilst rewarding B' (Kerr *et al.*, 1975). The airline baggage handlers mentioned earlier in this chapter were subsequently found to have achieved the speedy delivery of baggage to the passengers at the cost of causing more damage to the bags. However this damage was difficult to measure, in part because it might have been inflicted at departure or transfer airports, and therefore was not the responsibility of the arrival baggage handlers. Great care needs to be taken when designing a performance-related pay system as employees tend to seek to maximize their personal advantage even at the cost of poorer organizational performance.

One major problem area is the use of the budget system as the benchmark for paying performance bonuses. The bonus system is often devised in isolation by a personnel or human resources department. Having decided to introduce a bonus system, they search for suitable measures of performance to base it upon. The budget is often seen as providing such a basis as it already exists in most organizations. However what is often unanticipated is the effect this will have on the operation of the budgetary process. Whereas previously managers may have been willing to set challenging budgetary targets, or at least to submit accurate estimates of future performance, it now becomes advantageous for them to submit 'slack' estimates. As one manager remarked, 'The budget process is like a hurdle race. Before the race starts, we make sure that the hurdles are set at an easily clearable height!'

Finally there is the issue of controllability. It may seem self-evident that managers should be held accountable only for those things they can control, and this is a central tenet of much of the management accountability literature, where considerable effort is made to design performance measures that reflect controllable performance. But there is emerging evidence that this principle is more notable for its breach than its observance. Both Otley (1990) and Merchant (1987) have noted that managers are often held accountable for things outside their control. This may be partly due to the difficulty of splitting the controllable from the non-controllable on a black and white basis. Many things are clearly partly controllable. More fundamentally, managers may have to adapt to uncontrollable environmental changes by revising their operating strategies and plans. Hence they cannot necessarily be held accountable for implementing predetermined plans, only for achieving the desired results. This is essentially what Merchant (1987) describes as results control rather than behaviour control, and it is central to the control of non-programmed activities.

Thus incentives, rewards and the performance appraisal are central to the design of an effective performance management system. However they are often not regarded as part of the performance measurement process and are designed in isolation from it. This is clearly inappropriate. From an economic perspective, the issue is considered at some length in the literature on agency theory, which concentrates on the design of appropriate reward mechanisms under different sets of conditions. However this literature tends to consider the employee as an individual who is motivated solely by financial considerations. The reality is somewhat more complicated than this simple model implies, although it can be used to gain insights into real world behaviour. This topic will be discussed at greater length in a subsequent chapter.

Information flows

The final stage in the performance management process is the provision of information on to the actual results. This is the necessary feedback process that aids adaptation and learning. In practical terms it involves what has become known as an executive information system (EIS). As Crockett (1992) has outlined, to ensure that the right strategic information flows into its EIS a company should:

- Identify the critical success factors and stakeholders' expectations.
- Document the performance measures used to monitor them.
- Determine the EIS reporting formats and frequency.
- Outline the information flows and how the information can be used.

Crockett points out that this process is complicated and time-consuming, and that it involves all levels of management. The EIS should also possess a capacity for 'drill down'; that is, the ability to provide more detailed information on areas that are being investigated in more detail.

The frequency of information provision may differ between hierarchical levels. At low levels very frequent information can be helpful. For example hourly production and quality statistics may be appropriate for use by a production supervisor. At more senior levels, weekly or monthly reports may be more appropriate. However it becomes more difficult to produce meaningful summary information that encompasses many different production processes and customers. Senior managers often find that such aggregate information can only be presented in financial terms. But this does not mean that the focus is only financial. In a sense the financial and accounting information provides a window into the real world of production and marketing. The 'drill down' from aggregate financial information will often need to be non-financial in nature, using such measures as quality, timeliness of delivery and customer satisfaction. This is a real challenge to the designers of EISs, and one that has yet to be fully overcome in practice.

A further issue is the use made of feedback information. At one level a measure of actual performance that shows a target has not been met is a stimulus for corrective action. It indicates that the strategy is not being properly implemented and that corrective action should be taken. However repeated attempts to improve performance may prove fruitless. It may be that the message the data is conveying is that the strategy is now inappropriate. In this case the required action is to review the strategy and to devise other methods of achieving the organization's goals. This is the distinction that Argyris and Schön (1978) make between 'single loop' and 'double loop' learning. Although this may seem a somewhat arcane point, it is also a very important practical issue. In the one case increased pressure is put on operational employees; in the other, the pressure is on senior managers and corporate strategists. It can be quite demotivating and counterproductive to pressure operating staff when they are actually achieving the organization's full potential in the current conditions. Distinguishing ineffective strategy implementation from an inappropriate strategy is a difficult but essential task.

Conclusions

Although the above scheme for the design of a performance management system may appear to be universally applicable, it is clear from practical experience that organizations should tailor each of the steps involved to their own circumstances. There is no single set of performance measures, no single basis for setting standards for those measures, and no universal reward mechanism that constitutes a perfect performance management system in all contexts. Different organizations face different operating environments and must develop strategies that accord with those environments. The so-called contingency theory of management accounting (Otley, 1980) represents one attempt to develop criteria for management accounting systems design that takes account of some of these factors. However the research conducted by Fitzgerald and Moon (1996) in the service sector indicates that effective performance management systems have common characteristics. They conclude that the following are necessary preconditions for the attainment of best practice:

- *Know what you are trying to do.* The design of a performance measurement and management system should be rooted in a clear understanding of exactly what an organization has decided to do in order to exploit its sources of competitive advantage. This understanding should be communicated throughout the organization by meaning of techniques such as visioning and budgeting.
- *Adopt a range of performance measures.* Financial measures alone are insufficient to capture the complexity of modern business operations. Organizations should adopt a range of measures covering the six generic dimensions of performance: financial performance, competitiveness, quality, resource utilization, flexibility and innovation.
- *Extract comparative measures to assess performance.* Both internal and external benchmarking can be used to set standards against which performance is assessed.
- *Report results regularly.* For managers to be able to use performance information proactively it must be relevant and up to date. Appropriate frequency of reporting will differ from task to task, and by hierarchical level.
- *Drive the system from the top down.* Lower-level employees will only take the system seriously if they see it being taken seriously by senior managers.

To these we would add the following:

- *Tie performance measures explicitly to strategy.* It is all too easy to develop a plethora of performance measures; organizations should concentrate on those activities which are vital to their future success. The balanced scorecard offers one framework for doing this.
- *Remember that effectiveness is more fundamental than efficiency.* Ensure that cost reductions are not given greater importance than the achievement of output objectives.

- *Review all performance measures from the bottom up.* Check that the performance measures adopted are not easily manipulated or distorted. Put yourself in the position of employees being measured by the system, and consider how they might respond.
- *Pay attention to incentives and rewards.* It is all too easy to undo the effect of a well-designed measurement and reporting systems by attaching an inappropriate reward system to it.
- *Identify the main risk factors that prevent outcome being achieved.* Consider including measures of key risk factors that need to be monitored; also consider having a measure of organizational flexibility or adaptability (that is, the capability of the organization to deal with the unexpected).

The framework outlined in this chapter may at first sight appear to be normative in nature, and indeed it is partially based on explicitly normative approaches. However it can be used in a non-prescriptive manner to describe how a specific organization has designed and operates its performance management system, within the context of Simons' (1995) wider framework. Whilst we recognize that the framework is incomplete and concentrates on the more formal methods of managing performance in an organization, we believe that it provides a more complete basis for considering the role of accounting and other information system design than has previously existed (see Ferreira and Otley, 2004, for extensions to this framework that make it more comprehensive). Although the framework appears to be universal, more careful consideration indicates that it is in fact contingent. Each organization has its own strategy and exists in its own unique environment; I suggest that its information and performance management systems should be specifically tailored to these circumstances.

Discussion questions

1. In what ways are you subject to performance management? Evaluate the extent to which it controls your behaviour.
2. Discuss the possible elements of a balanced score card for an organization you know well. Evaluate the extent to which it will achieve a balanced performance when the operations environment is (a) favourable and (b) difficult.
3. Evaluate the use of performance management systems in conjunction with remuneration packages for (a) dentists, (b) nuclear scientists and (c) motorway contractors.

Issues and Performance

Accounting systems and control

7

Anthony J. Berry, Jane Broadbent and David Otley

Introduction

This chapter considers the role of accounting systems in organizational control. Every organization, be it small or large, business- or family-run, has some type of accounting system. Accounting systems provide a fundamental way of handling high degrees of complexity by imposing of a set of standard operating procedures; this is a major strength of accounting as a control system. However weaknesses also stem from the imposition of standard systems in complex situations because inventive human minds find ways to report desired results by manipulating the system rather than behaving in expected ways.

Simon *et al.* (1954) suggested that accounting information serves three major functions: attention directing, problem solving and scorecard keeping. Control involves all these functions. Attention must be paid to the process being controlled when the results are not as expected. The idea of management by exception follows directly from this approach. Accounting provides data for problem solving, which may be proactive or reactive; in the latter case this means dealing with issues highlighted by the attention-directing function. Accounting as a means of scorecard keeping results from examination of the extent to which the organization as a whole and the individuals in it meet the set performance targets. When payment for target achievement is used as an incentive, then strong performance management is facilitated by the use of accounting as a control. Thus the performance management of managers and the business units they direct is heavily dependent on accounting-based measures, such as profit, return on investment, residual income or value added.

This chapter will explore the attention-directing and scorecard-keeping functions of accounting based control systems because they are central to the formal and routine control of the organization as well as to performance management. It will also consider the problem-solving function which, whilst a familiar feature of organizational life, tends to be more *ad hoc*, reactive and rarely a simple routine. However routinely collected data often forms the basis of problem recognition and is used extensively in finding solutions, so there are close links between attention-directing routines and decisions taken in respect of unique problems. A note of caution should be sounded before looking at each of these areas in more detail: control is related to many issues other than accounting, that is, accounting is just one element of control systems. Moreover even at the purely technical level, as this chapter will show, the early emphasis on developing accounting controls, particularly budgets, has recently been overshadowed by challenges to their usefulness.

Problem solving: techniques for gathering and organizing data for accounting-based control

The generation of data and information on the internal operations of a firm is the focus of management rather than financial accounting, the latter being geared to providing information for formal and external purposes and legal controls. Management accounting is often defined as providing information for planning and decision making, which might also be considered as a description of problem solving. Collier's (2003, p. 5) definition adds control to the list of elements, reflecting the importance placed in this volume on management control on the issue of accounting. While various elements of accounting systems will be outlined in this chapter, the reader is referred to standard management accounting texts for a more extensive examination of the issues in question for example, Emmanuel *et al.* 1990, provide an overview, while detailed accounts can be found in Collier, 2003; Drury, 2000; Wilson and Chua, 1992). The approaches we shall outline are concerned with providing information for short-term and long-term decisions on activities and with the computation of total product costs, both of which are important to control processes.

Before considering specific techniques, some of the limitations of the models used for management accounting should be noted. First, many management accounting techniques are based on the simple first-order control loop model. This suggests that control requires the formulation of objectives, the development of plans (using predictive models) to achieve these objectives, measurement of the degree of achievement and the monitoring of deviations from the plan so that corrective action can be taken if required (Otley and Berry, 1980; Otley, 1987). Management accounting models tend not to give full consideration to all the stages of this process and mainly focus on the implementation of plans and the monitoring of deviation. The formulation of objectives is often taken as unproblematic; whether we should talk about the goals of the organization or should really refer to the goals of coalitions or individuals is often neglected, and the micro politics of the organization are therefore ignored.

Second, scanning the environment for opportunities has also received scant attention (King, 1975), although some strategic management accounting approaches recognize that an external focus is important (Dixon, 1998; Lord, 1996). Nonetheless much of the management accounting literature is inward looking. For example many works on investment appraisal are based on the assumption that suitable projects will present themselves without any effort on the part of managers.

Third, the use of predictive models has been glossed over, despite the fact that appropriate predictive models facilitate proactive, feedforward control. Feedforward control can be less expensive than reactive feedback control, which can only rectify errors that have already been made. By planning to avoid undesirable consequences considerable savings can be made. Most of the predictive models in management accounting are rooted in economic theories in which profit maximization is the main business objective. Maximization of cash flows has been used as a surrogate for profit maximization. However this is not always the reason why people enter business. For example a comparison scheme for hotel businesses sought to provide hoteliers with an analysis of their financial results. Comparison with the regional average, it was suggested, would enable them to identify areas in which they were weaker than average and hence where the performance might be improved. The scheme was not well supported. Many hoteliers argued that they had set up in the region because they enjoyed the lifestyle. For them, increasing their financial returns was not a primary concern as long as their standard of living was satisfactory. This illustrates that focusing solely on profit maximization ignores why people enter business and what they wish to achieve. Equally we need to be sensitive to the variety of motivations managers have when we consider the use of techniques based on a narrow economic perspective.

We shall now provide a short overview of the main techniques of management accounting.

Information for short-term decisions

An important issue for managers is the effect that short-term changes in activity have on financial results. Techniques have been developed to analyze this and to examine the profitability of operating at different levels of activity.

The interested reader should examine discussions of cost structure, marginal costing and cost–profit–volume analysis in management accounting texts. This approach is based on the fact that in the short term some costs vary in proportion to the volume of output (variable cost) while others (fixed or period costs) do not. The classification of costs into fixed and variable components depends upon the time horizon of the decision being considered. In the very short term most costs are fixed; in the long term all costs become variable. It is therefore vital to consider the time span of the decision being taken before embarking on a cost analysis of this nature.

Of key importance is the contribution made by each unit of production. Contribution is defined as the difference between the variable cost of production and the selling price of each unit. Total contribution can be calculated for any level of activity (within the relevant range) by multiplying the contribution per unit and the activity level. As the contribution accumulates it first covers fixed costs and then provides profits. Therefore profits are not earned incrementally with each unit of production sold. A certain level of activity is required to reach breakeven point – the point at which contribution is sufficient to cover fixed costs. This approach allows the calculation of costs and profits at different levels of production and can be used as a feedforward device to ascertain whether particular activities will be profitable. With regard to limiting resources' or production bottlenecks, the idea of measuring the contribution per unit of limiting resource has been popularized in texts such as that by Goldratt (1984).

The contribution approach can also be used to decide whether components should be made internally or bought from outside suppliers. If spare capacity exists the comparison will be between the internal variable cost and the external purchase price. Any fixed costs that will be incurred by proceeding with production or deciding against it are irrelevant in this situation. Thus the focus is on the marginal cost of the decision, which may be obscured by the use of a full-cost absorption accounting system that allocates fixed costs to units of production.

The contribution technique can also be used to aid some pricing decisions, particularly in secondary pricing situations where there is spare capacity. Here it may be decided that any contribution, however small, is better than no contribution. Thus a lower price than that usually charged may be acceptable, provided the variable costs are covered. It must be remembered however, that short-term decisions, can have long-term consequences.

Information for long-term decisions

The main difference between short-term and long-term decisions is that in long-term decisions the time value of money is of great importance. Here the focus is on the benefits that investment can be expected to produce over a number of years. Estimating of the magnitude of these benefits is a significant difficulty with all investment appraisal techniques, and most tend to assume the existence of good predictive models. In practice models tend to be rather poor and sensitivity analyses are required to ascertain how a decision might be affected by variations in estimates.

There are a number of approaches to the appraisal of long-term investments, three of which will be examined in this section: net present value, payback, and accounting rate of return. The mainstream management accounting texts deal with these techniques under the heading of capital investment appraisal and provide detailed discussions of the benefits of the different approaches. The theoretically favoured techniques focus on the incremental cash flows that are expected to be generated. The reason for this preference lies in the assumption that the objectives of the firm are linked to maximizing shareholders wealth, a surrogate for which is maximization of the net present value of expected future cash flows.

Net present value (NPV) methods take estimated incremental cash flows over the life of a project and discount them to their present value. Discounting is undertaken to account for the fact that cash received in the future has an opportunity cost compared with cash received now. To be acceptable, an investment must have a positive net present value at an appropriate discount rate. A derivative of this approach is the calculation of an internal rate of return (IRR). This rate is simply the discount rate at which the NPV of an investment becomes zero. Here the decision rule is that a project must have a higher IRR than some predetermined hurdle rate. Whilst these approaches are not technically difficult to implement, there are problems with deciding the discount rate to be applied and with forecasting future cash flows.

The problem of estimating an appropriate discount rate to be used in NPV calculations has engaged academics for some time. It may be argued that the discount rate depends on both the cost of capital to the firm and the specific risk associated with the project. In practice the weighted average cost of capital to the firm as a whole can be used to give a discount factor for all capital appraisals. Another refinement is to relate the discount factor to the risk of the particular project, and its interrelationship with other investments. As the discount factor determines whether the NPV is positive or negative it is vital to ensure this is an accurate estimate. It is also important to ensure that inflation is properly dealt with. If cash flows are estimated in real terms, then the real cost of capital must be used; if they are estimated in nominal terms, then a nominal rate is appropriate. Although this seems logical, all too often the discount rate used is inappropriate to the cash flow estimation used.

Forecasting a project's duration and its future cash flows is also problematic, as application of the most sophisticated techniques to the wrong estimates will not produce good results – garbage in, garbage out! Predicting the future is always difficult and cash flow prediction is no different. One solution is to use a Monte Carlo simulation on probabalistic cash flows to produce a probability distribution of NPV estimates. This at least provides the decision maker with an assessment of probable losses or gains should the project be undertaken.

It should be noted that studies to determine whether these sophisticated techniques provide better results as measured by increased earnings per share, have not been able to show a significant relationship (Haka *et al.*, 1985) There are a number of reasons for this and these may be related to the context of their use as well as practical difficulties with their application (for an overview see Northcott, 1991, 1992). Indeed some studies have found an inverse relationship between the use of sophisticated evaluation methods and subsequent performance. However this may well be due to reverse causation, that is, poorly performing firms are more likely to use sophisticated appraisal methods in an attempt to improve their performance.

In the face of the problem of estimating the cost of both capital and cash flows, many firms adopt the less sophisticated technique of payback, that is, the length of time the initial cash investment takes to be recuperated by the cash flows generated by the scheme. This is a much used and well understood technique, and has the advantage of simplicity. If the cost of capital is about 20 per cent then a three year payback will be a fairly robust criterion for project acceptance. Some firms use it only for smaller schemes, some in conjunction with other approaches, and others use it in isolation. A more sophisticated variant is to calculate the discounted payback period, which at least provides an estimate of the time period over which the firm is at risk from its investment.

Debates on the strengths and weaknesses of the above techniques can be found in the literature. Suffice it to say at this stage that the discounting techniques are theoretically superior but are not always used. However their adoption has been growing for some time (Pike, 1983, 1988), perhaps as a result of business education. There is a danger that the techniques will be used to justify decisions that in effect have already been made. If for example an NPV calculation does not achieve satisfactory results, then the cash flows or the discount rate might be changed to produce the required result. The robust debate on the use of the Private Finance Initiative (PFI) to establish new hospitals has raised the question of whether the PFI alternative is in fact 'the only game in town' (Froud, 2003) and therefore has been used to legitimate a decision already made. It seems unlikely that a manager would put forward any plan that did not meet the firm's criterion of positive NPV or required payback as it would be rejected at first sight. However the manager might well be inclined to adjust the estimates in order to promote a project that she or he believes is desirable for her or his own purposes.

The third appraisal technique is different: the accounting rate of return, is the ratio of profit generated by the scheme to the initial (or average) investment. This approach which does not use discounted cash flows is seen as theoretically inferior to NPV because it deals with profit flows rather than cash flows, and these can be manipulated by applying of different accounting policies and techniques. NPV deals with cash flows, which are considered to be more objective and less subject to manipulation than profit flows. (Interestingly this argument ignores the manipulation that can also bias cash flow estimates.) Different accounting rates of return can be obtained from similar schemes that are accounted for using different accounting policies. In particular it raises problems with asset valuation. Despite these problems it is used, probably because it produces similar results to the familiar measurement of return on capital employed, which is used to appraise results *post hoc*.

A fundamental conflict can arise between capital investment appraisal methods based on discounted cash flows, and subsequent managerial performance assessment based on accounting profit and return on investment measures. A good project (on NPV criteria) may have poor accounting returns in its early years; conversely a poor project can initially show good accounting returns. Thus managers may be reluctant to propose a project that is clearly in the firm's best interest because it would adversely affect their performance reports in the short term. This conflict between future-oriented investment appraisal techniques and historically oriented accounting measurement techniques is difficult to resolve. The most straightforward solution is to incorporate the financial impact of a new capital investment into future budgets when it is accepted. The responsible manager's performance should then be monitored in terms of achieving the budgeted figures, rather than any preset return on capital investment target.

As each of the techniques has different aims, and the prescription for action might be different under each, then appropriate action cannot be easily decided. When forecasting cash flows there is always an opportunity for biasing and manipulation in the interests of individuals and against the interest of the organization as a whole. If the appraisal of managers' performance is linked to the results produced, manipulation is likely to happen and can only be minimized (for example by means of post-audit techniques) rather than prevented.

Data for routine control

Information on the costs of existing products or parts of an organization's operation is also needed for decision making and control. In particular the total cost of each product is required for the valuation of inventories in the financial accounts. The technique of absorption costing allocates costs which can be directly identified to the cost object. It then allocates the other indirect costs between the units produced. The total cost of each cost unit is the direct cost of each unit plus the share of indirect costs apportioned to it. Absorption costing is therefore a systematic approach to the construction of total cost information. As well as providing estimates of total cost for the financial accounts, this approach provides information that can be used to make a comparison between different operating units or to price cost objects. Sharing out the indirect costs can be problematic as it is an arbitrary act. This is not necessarily a problem in itself, but when the figures produced are not recognized as arbitrary and are used to form the basis of decisions, problems can arise. Johnson and Kaplan (1991) offer a seminal but contested critique of the relevance of management accounting because of issues such as this. Full cost information can give only a general indication of the long-term viability of a product (if appropriately constructed), whereas variable cost information provides a sound basis for short-term decision making.

Activity-based costing (ABC), developed into activity-based management, has been devised as a more defensible approach to the problem of calculating the cost of a product, department or service. ABC is a systematic approach, but unlike absorption costing it relates costs to the cost object in alignment with the actual processes of transformation it undergoes. This requires an analysis of the 'cost drivers' within a business. For example the cost of filling an order for goods worth £100 is likely to be similar to the cost of filling an order for £10 000. The cost driver in this case is the number of invoices rather than the value of the invoice. Allocating costs by means of cost drivers is argued to produce a more realistic cost, although it still involves arbitrary allocations. Identifying and examining the cost drivers can focus management attention on the activities that incur costs.

The above techniques provide the foundation for many of management accounting's virtues as well as the problems that arise from its inherent shortcomings. Some of these problems relate to the problem of observing and classifying costs in the different ways that are required to use the various techniques, while others relate to the difficulty of using the techniques when predictions are required. Nonetheless the techniques can be used to address the main problems with which management accounting is asked to deal.

Attention directing: budgetary control

Implementing a system of accounting-based control needs more than just techniques for calculating costs. Systems for coordinating the information generated and integrating it with other information in functional areas such as production and marketing are also required. Thus whilst accounting-based control would not be possible without tools to calculate the relevant costs, the process of control is carried out through a different set of activities: those of budgeting. Budgetary control provides the foundation for the other two functions of accounting information systems: attention directing and score-card keeping. It involves the development of plans of action, expressed in financial terms, and the monitoring of subsequent activity to achieve the plans.

Emmanuel *et al.* (1990) alert us to the fact that budgets fulfil many different purposes an organization. Beside being an important element in decision making, budgets serve as:

- A means of authorizing actions.
- A means of forecasting and planning.
- A channel of communication and coordination.
- A means of motivating organizational members.
- A vehicle for performance evaluation and control.

The first four of these are oriented to attention directing, the fifth is more related to scorecard keeping. Different elements of control are to be found in the different functions. In different organizations, each of the above may be given a different emphasis; a budget that is designed to serve one purpose will probably be less effective at serving other purposes. Thus the design of a budgetary control system is essentially a set of compromises, and will result in each purpose being served to a greater or lesser degree.

Budgets as authorization

Formal authorization of spending limits is one way of controlling the actions of subordinates. Thus school governing bodies now have the responsibility, delegated from the local education authority, to spend within a preset budget. They can spend it as they wish (within the requirement to provide education) but they cannot spend more than the set amount. Conversely a budget may be very detailed and authorize spending only on particular items, such as salaries or building maintenance. Whether a budget is presented as an overall figure or item by item reflects the degree of control intended. An item-by-item budget is very much oriented towards behaviour (action) control. However the scope for controlling human beings by simple devices such as budgets can be limited by their resourceful attempts to modify the control that is being sought. Indeed greater control can be achieved by reducing the number of individual controls (Drucker, 1964).

There is a tension between retaining centralized control and delegating decisions to an operational manager. A local manager should have greater knowledge of the local environment so better decisions can be taken more rapidly. However the manager may make decisions that are good for that local operation but do not accord with the overall needs of the organization. This tension between knowledge of what is feasible (generally concentrated at lower levels) and knowledge of what is desirable (generally concentrated at higher levels) is a notable feature of all budgeting systems. Responsibility for either a cost centre (in which the extent of each budget item is centrally determined) or a profit centre (where there is greater delegation of decisions on the budgetary elements) is therefore qualitatively different, as is the control achieved. Any decision about the type of control to be exercised must consider these factors.

Forecasting, planning and communication

The second and third pairs of functions – forecasting and planning, and communicating and coordinating – come into play when developing a budget. The way in which these functions are served can best be illustrated by examining the stages of budget preparation. The nature of the control process can also be illustrated. The interested reader can find more detailed discussions of these issues in mainstream accounting texts (for example Collier, 2003; Drury, 2000; Wilson and Chua, 1992), here there is only space for a brief outline.

The preparation of any budget first requires the forecasting of future activities in all parts of the organization. The activity levels for the various areas must be decided upon and then expressed in monetary terms using forecasts of economic activity, price changes and so on. The individual plans are then amalgamated into an organizational budget (the master budget), which coordinates the different functions, for example, balancing the production and selling plans.

The budget preparation process involves communication between the various functional areas in the organization. The type of communication engaged in is important to the perceptions formed about the budgeting process by the organizational members. As a top-down approach is adopted and plans are imposed from above, organizational members may well view the budget as imposing a severe constraint, perhaps resulting in suspicion and subversion of the budget and the budgeting process. The active participation of budget holders and the possibility of their negotiating the final budget – that is, a bottom-up approach – make it less likely that the budget will be the focus of organizational conflict. However budgeting tends to be both top-down and bottom-up. The budget is passed up and down the organization in several iterations that involve negotiation and bargaining. Top-down and bottom-up refer only to the starting point, and there may be little to choose between them as approaches. Much more important is the way in which changes are negotiated and communicated.

The accounting literature suggests that the generation of budgets should follow the organizational structure of responsibility and accountability. It should also be sufficiently detailed to ensure coordination. Organizational structure does not necessarily determine the type of control system to be operated as it can be altered to achieve a configuration that will enable the desired control, including budgetary control, to be applied. In particular the alignment of cost centre or profit centre responsibilities may be changed in line with changes to the type of control to be exercised.

A budget may be based on standard costs. The forecasting, planning and coordination requirements are particularly stringent in this case. The standard costing approach defines standards for material and labour usage as well as standard costs for each of the quantified elements. According to Miller and O'Leary (1987), standard costing is based on the philosophy of scientific management, which identifies the 'one best way' to achieve a result and then costs it. Subsequently the results are analyzed to determine whether the standard cost per unit has been achieved. Because this technique allows identification of exactly where standards are not being achieved it can be seen as a form of behavioural control. Explanations for non-achievement can be sought and counter measures may be applied. A decision may have to be taken about the degree of deviation from the standards that will be tolerated before an investigation is instigated. Such deviations may not always be the result of poor performance; it may be that inappropriate standards were set. Because it is expensive to develop a standard costing system and investigate deviations standard costing is best applied in organizations where a standard product is produced in large numbers.

Standard costing provides such a tight system of control that products are often deliberately standardized. Whilst common in mass production, this practice is also being taken up by service providers. One example of concerns diagnostic related groups (DRGs) in healthcare. DRGs are groups of medical problems that have similar diagnoses and require similar treatment, generating similar costs. They were originally developed as a basis upon which to reimburse medical insurers in the United States, but are now being used as a way of distributing resources and controlling expenditure in many OECD countries, albeit under a number of different labels.

Thus in different ways the budget preparation process provides a focus for forecasting and planning, and it serves as channel for communication and coordination. However budgetary control requires that a further set of activities.

Motivating and evaluating performance

After the budget is produced and the activity to which it relates is underway, then information on the results must be collected. This is in line with the fifth function of budgeting: feedback control. This involves action to remedy the situation if the required results are not being achieved, and using feedback information to update the planning process. Information on the alignment or otherwise of actual and targeted performance can also be used as the basis for performance evaluation. If performance is evaluated in this way employees will be more motivated to achieve the budgetary targets.

The issue of motivation was an early focus of research, particularly in respect of understanding the effect on managers of using budget targets to evaluate performance. There is evidence that performance is better when clearly defined quantitative targets are set (Tosi, 1975). Whilst a difficult target tends to encourage better performance, if a target is so high as to be perceived as unattainable (and therefore is not accepted by the individual who is responsible for its achievement) the results are likely to be worse than if a lower but acceptable target was set (Locke, 1968). This phenomenon has been demonstrated by Hofstede (1968), who continued the investigation started by Argyris (1952) into the effects of budgets and targets on human behaviour. The conclusions reached by Hofstede reached are as follows.

- Budgets only motivate if the are 'owned' by the manager concerned.
- Provided the budget does not exceed the highest target acceptable to an individual, the results will increase in line with increasing difficulty.
- Participation in budget creation aids acceptance of the budget.
- Cultural and organizational norms plus individual personality influence managers' reactions to particular budget targets.

The title of Hofstede's book – *The Game of Budget Control* – is an apt one as there is considerable gamesmanship in the setting of budgets. Participation in budget setting, for example, can be helpful in ensuring acceptance of the budget, in improving communication and in reducing the likelihood of distortion and manipulation of information. However it can also provide opportunities to bias the budget. For example slack may be built into the targets (Lowe and Shaw, 1968) and managers may affect the budget (Schiff and Lewin, 1970) more than the budget affects them (Argyris, 1952). This is particularly likely when the achievement of targets is linked to remuneration.

Cyert *et al.* (1961) show that the forecast projections of the same figures differ according to the label attached to them. Thus a lower rate of increase is estimated when a figure is labelled sales than when it is labelled costs. It is likely that the forecast is made with an eye to the consequences of error, and a conservative estimate of sales or a generous estimate of costs poses less threat of non-achievement of the target. Both Lowe and Shaw (1968) and Otley (1978) show that biased estimates might not always be in the direction of easier targets. If the current performance is poor, managers might promise improvement and overestimate future performance. This could enable them to continue in their jobs and give them time to solve the problems.

The usefulness of budgetary participation is also contingent on the culture and personality of the manager in question. Those who feel they are in control of their own destiny are more positive about participation than those who see themselves as victims of destiny (Brownell, 1981). The latter group exhibit a poorer performance when participating in budget formation, possibly as a consequence of increased stress from an environment they perceive as uncontrollable and uncertain. Bruns and Waterhouse (1975) suggest that participation is most useful in decentralized organizations that engage in tasks of a well defined and structured nature.

There is likely to be some tension when budgets designed to motivate are also used as vehicles for performance evaluation. This is because a good motivational budget will always be slightly more difficult to attain. Managers who evaluate performance should bear this in mind and not look on small deviations too harshly. Those who use budgets as a basis for planning must also remember that the estimates may contain biases for reasons that are entirely rational from the point of view of the managers who have prepared the budget, but may undermine some of the usefulness of the budget to the organization as a whole.

Whilst there is satisfaction in achieving a set target, a major source of motivation is the reward received for achieving it. However this can encourage bias, which can be difficult to detect in the negotiations that precede the agreement of targets. Therefore budget-based incentive schemes should be designed in such a way as to ensure that individuals' behaviour is in line with the company's objectives (Hopwood, 1973). Good performance is not necessarily the same thing as meeting a budgetary target. Indeed there are organizational structures in which the control of and reward for performance is not best achieved by such detailed control. However accounting measures can still be used in such circumstances, and it is to a consideration of these that we now turn.

Scorecard keeping: performance evaluation and accounting controls

The requirement to adhere to detailed budgets is perhaps most useful as a control when responsibility for costs is delegated to a manager. The reporting of line-by-line results against the budget enables problems to be pinpointed by the delegator. If the responsibility delegated is to achieve a given profit level then the line-by-line detail of the budget is of central interest to the manager to whom responsibility is delegated, but not to the delegator. The profit target is often used as a means of control, with performance being evaluated by achievement of the target. The logic of this type of control is that those who have responsibility are closest to the operations being carried out and know best how to achieve results.

This type of logic achieves its fullest expression in the divisionalized company. Here control is delegated to the operating divisions, whose managers are familiar with the local environment and can therefore make the most suitable decisions. In this situation return on investment (ROI) or residual income (RI) may be used to measure the performance of managers. ROI compares the profit generated with the asset base used to generate that profit, expressed in percentage terms. RI adjusts the profit attained by an imputed interest charge for financing the assets used. Managers are given specific targets, and whilst detailed control of day-to-day operations is not required the targets must be achieved. To this end bonus payments are often used to motivate managers. The well-known technique of economic value added (EVA™, see Stewart, 1994) is a variant of RI.

The development and use of performance measures is not straightforward and problems can arise for many reasons, as noted by Emmanuel *et al.* (1990, p. 176):

- Organizations have many objectives and purposes that cannot be measured easily or effectively by single performance measures.
- Organizations often require cooperative action to be taken. Trying to measure individual performance will not necessarily reflect the cooperative aspects of tasks and may be dysfunctional in that individuals may pursue actions to enhance their individual ratings at the expense of the organization as a whole.
- Specifying tasks and targets in advance may be fruitless because of the ambiguous nature of managerial responsibilities.
- Not all aspects of performance, especially staff quality and morale, which are increasingly important in the modern organization, can be measured in quantitative terms.

- The results may not reflect the effort put into achieving them, especially if the environment proves not to be as was expected when the targets were set.

The main problem is that reward systems reward results and not behaviour. This leads to managerial behaviour being geared to the achievement of results. In a situation where the environment is rapidly changing, the standards against which results are assessed may be inappropriate. Fully depreciated assets may be retained rather than renewed if this helps to achieve ROI targets (Dearden 1962) as the purchase of a new asset will increase the capital base upon which the profits generated are assessed, as well as generating depreciation charges against profit. This retention will be counterproductive if new investment would improve the competitive advantage of the firm's products by improving their quality.

The research findings on participation in budget setting must be borne in mind when performance is being assessed. One finding by Kenis (1979) is particularly worthy of consideration here as it extends the discussion beyond that of budget achievement. Kenis notes that whilst budget achievement is improved by participation, there is no relation between the latter and other measures of overall job performance. Ivanevitch (1976) Milani (1975) and Steers (1975) have found only insignificant connections between budgetary characteristics and job performance, which suggests that quantitative evaluation might have little effect on overall job performance. This may be because managers have no control over some important variables, irrespective of whether or not they are involved in the setting of the budget.

Evaluation styles tend to vary. According to Merchant (1981), large decentralized firms with diverse activities tend to use administrative rather than personal controls. Greater stress is given to formal controls such as budgeting, and lower-level managers participate in the development of budgets. Hopwood (1972) has studied cost centre managers in independent situations and argues that three orientations to evaluation could be identified. In each case there are different approaches to the linking of performance to rewards.

- The budget-constrained approach: rigid insistence on the short-term achievement of the budget.
- The profit-conscious approach: The central focus is the general effectiveness of the unit's operations. This approach is more flexible than the budget-constrained approach, and budgetary information is supplemented by other information. Thus a manager who has a good reason for overspending may still be evaluated favourably.
- The non-accounting approach: budgetary data is viewed as relatively unimportant and other measures of managerial performance are used.

In Hopwood's study, managers who were evaluated according to the non-accounting approach were less cost conscious than those who were evaluated under accounting-based approaches. Those who were subject to the budget-constrained approach reported higher levels of stress, poorer relationships with colleagues and a greater tendency to manipulate financial reports than managers evaluated under the profit-conscious approach.

Otley (1978) repeated some of Hopwood's work in the setting of independent profit centres. He thought that in such a setting, budgetary information would be a more adequate measure of managerial performance than in Hopwood's study. He found that the style of evaluation had little impact on job-related tension or the manipulation of data. Performance evaluation based on budget achievement led to short-termism, but apart from that it was an effective management approach. Otley also found that performance affected the choice of management approach, with better performing managers being more likely to be evaluated according to the more flexible profit conscious approach. Thus the choice of how to use budgetary information in performance evaluation is not straightforward and has the potential to generate unexpected side effects.

Hirst (1981) studied the effect of different environmental conditions. He found that there is a high degree of uncertainty as accounting measures are seen as providing a less complete description of performance than in a more stable environment. Govindarajan (1984) supports this finding, suggesting that in a highly uncertain environment more subjective evaluation procedures are likely to be adopted.

These studies suggest that two central issues need to be resolved in each specific situation. First, the impact of the control system depends on the way in which accounting information is used by managers and the rewards that are contingent upon it. Second, the effect of strong reliance on budgetary measures of performance is contingent upon the strength of the link between managerial behaviour and desired results. This is often quite weak and is more ambiguous in an uncertain environment. Reward systems must be designed with this in mind and must tolerate occasional failure, especially in situations where innovation is needed.

Individual differences between managers must also be borne in mind, and there is some indication that the cognitive style of individuals will affect the structure of the information that will be of most use to them. Highly aggregated data, such as balance sheets and formal accounting reports, are of most use to highly-analytical types (those who use conceptual models to understand situations). Less-analytical types (who see situations more holistically) are better served by disaggregated raw data (Benbasat and Dexter, 1979). Macintosh (1985) suggests that information should be supplied in a manner that is consistent with a manager's cognitive style.

Another important individual difference is the extent to which individuals accept personal responsibility for what happens to them. Those with an external locus of control see events as being outside their control, while those with an internal locus see events as the result of their own behaviour. The latter perform best when involved in budget setting, the former when targets are imposed.

This short overview of the literature on performance evaluation has shown that there are inherent difficulties in finding suitable performance measures, that the approach used by superiors to evaluate individuals will affect performance, and that individual differences and the state of the external environment are important considerations when designing systems. Hence designers of performance evaluation systems must take account of the particular situation and the individuals within it. What works in one situation for a certain set of people may not work in another situation, or even in the same situation when different individuals are involved.

Are budgets necessary?

Despite the almost universal use of budgetary control systems as a major form of integrative control within businesses and other organizations, it has also become increasingly apparent that budgetary control engenders some major problems. These have been well summarized by Neely *et al.* (2001):

- Budgets are time-consuming to put together.
- Their constrain responsiveness and are often a barrier to change.
- They are rarely strategically focused and often contradictory.
- They add little value, especially given the time required to prepare them.
- They concentrate on cost reduction and not value creation.
- They strengthen vertical command and control.
- They do not reflect the emerging network structures that organizations are adopting.
- They encourage 'gaming' and perverse behaviour.
- They are constructed and updated too infrequently, usually annually.
- They are based on unsupported assumptions and guesswork.
- They reinforce departmental barriers rather than encourage knowledge sharing.
- They make people feel undervalued.

Given such a comprehensive list of problems it seems odd that organizations have not revised their budgetary processes. Indeed there has been much call for improvement, and a variety of techniques for better budgeting have been suggested, including:

- Activity-based budgeting.
- Zero-based budgeting.
- Rolling budgets and forecasts.
- Value-based management.
- Profit planning.

However the evidence suggests that although these techniques may have produced some benefits for those who have implemented them, they have not solved the underlying problems with budgeting. Neely *et al.* argue that this is because changing budgetary and planning procedures is a very major and costly activity, and traditional budgetary processes are difficult to discard because 'they remain a centrally coordinated activity (often the only one) within the business. It is usually the only process that covers all areas of organizational activity' (ibid., p. 5–7).

A more radical approach has been put forward under the banner of 'beyond budgeting', which follows the ideas of the executive director of Svenska Handelsbanken, Jan Wallander, who has long rejected the use of budgetary control because of the unpredictability of events. He concludes: 'A budget will . . . either prove roughly right, and then it will be trite, or it will be disastrously wrong, in which case it will be dangerous. My conclusion is thus: Scrap it!' (Wallander, 1999).

The ideas of 'beyond budgeting' are set out by Fraser and Hope (2003), who explore mechanisms that companies can use in stead of traditional budgetary controls. These typically involve the use of a range of non-financial performance measures for line managers. While financial planning is not abandoned, it is kept as a 'back office' function in the finance department rather than being used as the principal means of controlling the activities of line managers.

Other performance management systems may include such mechanisms as balanced scorecards of lagging and leading operational performance measures, activity-based management and other forms of business process management, benchmarking techniques for target setting, and customer relation management models. Managers are thus assessed by a variety of operating performance measures. The assumption is that if managers perform well on these variables the organization's desired financial results will be achieved. The financial results will continue to be monitored by the finance department, but will not generally be used to measure and control the activities of line managers.

In beyond budgeting the principal objective is to avoid what is described as the 'annual performance trap', where the budget is used to set the terms of a fixed performance contract. In other words the line managers' main responsibility is to meet the performance standards laid down in the budget. It is argued that fixed performance contracts usually cause dysfunctional behaviour. Indeed the literature on budgetary control is replete with examples of managers adopting inappropriate methods of conforming to their annual budget. These include manipulating the budget estimates before the budget year has begun (generally to obtain an easier standard), manipulating the figures reported throughout the budget year (so as to adjust the timing of revenue and/or cost recognition) and making inappropriate management decisions (for example postponing maintenance expenditure) in order to produce betters figures than the budget targets. There is often a form of 'big bang' when creative accounting fails to deliver the required results and a major exceptional charge has to be made to the accounts. Abandoning reliance on budgetary control will enable organizations to move from this destructive fixed performance contract towards a more adaptive planning process and the use of a relative performance contract.

The idea is to remove the emphasis on preset budgetary targets and replace them with externally benchmarked performance standards based on the achievements of competitors. A common form of performance target is a league table, referenced either internally (for example different branches of the same company) or externally (for example performance in comparison with leading competitors). Here an arbitrary performance target that is set for a fixed period (typically a year) many months in advance is replaced by a relative performance target that is continually updated in the light of changing market conditions and competitive position. More radically, performance against such targets is evaluated in hindsight; that is, fixed targets are not set at the beginning of the period and targets are adjusted in line with operational experiences and economic circumstances. Rewards may be connected to performance, but typically with an emphasis on work-group rather than individual performance. The objectives to engender a philosophy of doing what is best for the business in the current circumstances, and to encourage team working. Resources are not fully budgeted for in advance but held in a central pool so that they can be distributed at short notice to those areas with the greatest current need for them. The expectation is that these procedures will make forecasting more accurate and more useful. In a fixed target system there is a strong motivation for managers to give biased forecasts, both before and during the budget period.

These measures are believed to be worth implementing in their own right, and some organizations go this far but no further. However the main thrust of the 'beyond budgeting' approach is that their successful implementation provides a starting point for even greater performance improvement, and that a special sort of competitive advantage can be obtained by releasing the energy and initiative of a large number of capable and committed people.

There is little doubt that there is widespread dissatisfaction with budgetary control. It is seen as expensive, time-consuming and having too little added value. Worse, it is viewed as an impediment to proactive and adaptive management. Another factor in the spawning of the radical beyond budgeting approach is the difficulty of forecasting as evidenced by the demise of long-term corporate planning, or at least the reduction of planning horizons in many organizations. If future events are becoming more difficult to predict, then heavy reliance on predictions for planning and control no longer makes sense. The positioning of organizations on the planning-agility spectrum may need to be realigned, and perhaps the beyond budgeting movement is one indication that a realignment is taking place.

One question that should be asked at this point is whether giving up budgeting really is a necessary precondition for performance improvement. Would it not be possible to reduce the importance of budgetary control but maintain it in some form or other? That is, could the message about the usefulness of relative performance targets be acted upon without the total abolition of budgeting? Organizations have attempted to move beyond the fixed annual budgeting model and have used revised budgets and rolling forecasts to try to mitigate the problem of static budgets, but this rarely seems to have been very successful and requires even more effort and expense. An interesting research pursuit would be to analyze the characteristics of companies and their environments that make the abandonment of budgeting desirable.

Perhaps the most fundamental aspect of the beyond budgeting approach is its move away from fixed performance contracts towards 'relative' performance contracts. The problems associated with fixed contracts have been highlighted in the budgeting literature and the 'relative' contract offers an interesting approach to reducing these problems. Unfortunately this idea is not yet well-developed, but it raises the question of whether the problems associated with budgeting might be significantly ameliorated if organizations moved from a fixed to a relative budgetary target. There are parallels here with Hopwood's (1972) distinction between budget-constrained and profit-conscious approaches to evaluation; the latter causes far less dysfunctional behaviour than the former (although there is some evidence that this may be contingent on various environmental and organizational factors). It does appear that being required to meet fixed, rigidly enforced, short-term performance targets – compared with a more flexible approach to evaluation, where some subjective judgment is exercised and long-term effectiveness sought – has substantial behavioural consequences. Some updating of Hopwood's seminal work is long overdue, at both the individual and the organizational level of analysis.

Finally, the validity of the beyond budgeting approach raise, some questions relating to contingency theories of management accounting and control practice. Specifically, is the approach a universal one that can be applied in all organizations, or is it only suitable for organizations facing specific situations? The organizations involved in its initial development are either relatively small or appear to be facing considerable environmental turbulence and uncertainty. Certainly the primary motivation of some of the proponents of beyond budgeting appears to be frustration with their inability effectively to implement business process improvement initiatives. Many have attempted to put business process-oriented improvements into practice, but are critical of how other organizational processes, most notably the budgetary control process, act as a barrier to effective organizational change. Thus perhaps the beyond budgeting approach is most suitable for those organizations in which business process reorganization is most needed.

There is also environmental turbulence to be taken into account. The greater the environmental turbulence, the less that traditional budgetary planning and control processes are used (Samuelson, 2000). Samuelson also quotes Wallander (1999): 'it is better to adapt instead of to plan'. There is clearly a point at which adaptation based on planning ceases to be as effective as adaptation based on environmental scanning and agility. It may be that in selecting an appropriate balance between planning and agility, organizations are deciding how much reliance it is sensible to place on traditional systems of budgetary control.

The beyond budgeting movement is clearly a response to widespread dissatisfaction with traditional budgetary control mechanisms and a desire to implement business processes that map onto the value chain of an organization. Given that a value chain is a horizontal process and most controls have a vertical emphasis, it is perhaps not surprising that budgetary control is seen as a barrier to change. However it is not yet clear whether beyond budgeting offers an effective solution to this problem, even in conditions of high turbulence. It is also unclear what mechanisms should be used instead of budgetary control, or the role that a modified system of budgetary control should play in such circumstances. What does seem important is the way in which the budgetary control system is actually used by senior managers. Rigid reliance on budgeting as the major overall control mechanism in organizations appears to be even more counterproductive than we originally thought. This is an area of both theoretical and practical importance.

Conclusions

The overview in this chapter of the uses of accounting-based controls has illustrated the diversity of the roles played by such controls, as well as the various linkages and tensions that exist between and within these roles. Despite this complexity it is generally agreed that accounting is an important element of control. It is now being introduced in organizations that hitherto have had little financial control at the operational level: schools, probation offices, the arts, hospitals, universities and voluntary organizations. Thus while some scholars and practitioners argue that we should move beyond budgeting, budgeting remains important. The synergies and tensions associated with the use of accounting-based controls need to be clearly understood if we are to exploit the virtues of accounting and not be prey to the weaknesses and dysfunctions that can arise from its misguided use.

If we return to the simple control model upon which management accounting is based (that is, an objective exists for an activity in a quasistable environment that can be described by a predictive model, and it is possible to measure what has been achieved and to allow monitoring to take place), we can see that the type of environment in which accounting-based control is likely to work best is one in which certainty and well-defined relationships exist. The irony is that in this situation any approach to control can be applied. It is when the environment is more uncertain, interdependencies are not easily identified and the future is difficult to predict that we are most in need of some way to help us achieve control. Here an accounting-based approach to control is of little use because it relies on the ability to predict and to translate predictions into financial values. Despite the variability of the circumstances in which accounting information is used there is little variability in its application in Western societies. But accounting still provides an articulation of the one measure that can serve to aggregate or contrast information on all aspects of a diversified business, that is, monetary value. However flawed it may be, it is still a useful means of control, particularly when resources are limited.

However there is some disquiet about the centrality of management accounting information in management control. Johnson and Kaplan (1987) have questioned the relevance of the type of information that management accounting produces. Whilst there has been some contention about the adequacy of the account these authors offer (see for example Ezzamel *et al.*, 1990; Hopper and Armstrong, 1991), they have sparked a debate on the direction that management accounting should take. This has been complemented by the 'beyond budgeting' debate. The outcome of these deliberations will be important for the development of accounting-based control, and for management control in general. There are unlikely to be simple solutions, but the complexity of the task should not discourage us from seeking appropriate solutions.

Discussion questions

1. How do you manage you own financial affairs? Evaluate whether constructing and using a budget would help or hinder the control of your finances.

2. Evaluate the strengths and weaknesses of the claim that budgets are no longer a useful management control system.
3. You are the manager of the local wine bar. Would you manipulate your budget in order to achieve the required result? Explain why and what your employer might do to ensure that you do not do this.
4. Evaluate the extent to which it might be helpful if students played a part in the development of university budgets.
5. Evaluate the extent to which the problems of budgeting identified by Neely *et al.* (2001) can be overcome by adopting different approaches.

8 Performance management practice

Carolyn Stringer

Introduction

This in-depth longitudinal case study examines performance management in a large, complex and diverse organization. The organization was chosen because it was successful, operated in a large range of business areas, and had been using EVA®[1] (economic value added) and the balanced scorecard since the mid 1990s.

This chapter is a response to calls for longitudinal case studies that consider the interrelationships between control system elements (Otley, 1999). Longitudinal case study research on the broad performance management framework in real organizations appears to be rare (Merchant *et al.*, 2003; Otley, 1999, 2001). Otley (2001, p. 246) argues that case studies of real organizations are needed as 'there may be a conflict between the rigour and relevance that is particularly pronounced in this field.' Moreover 'We need to be careful that we do not drive out work that strives to connect with real organizations and their practices' (ibid.)

In a rare example of research an early model of Otley's (1999) performance management framework was used by Moon and Fitzgerald (1996 p. 431) to examine performance measurement at TNT in terms of 'what *dimensions* of performance to measure, how to set *standards* for those measures and what *rewards* are to be associated with the achievement of those standards'.

The research reported in this chapter also draws on Otley's (1999) and a series of questions on the operation of the performance management framework (for example in respect of objectives, strategy, targets, measures, incentives and information flows, and how these elements interrelated). The interviews were generally open-ended and lasted about one hour. Rather than using a structured questionnaire, the interview schedule included a checklist of topics to be covered. The advantage of this approach was that it enabled performance management issues to emerge naturally during the interviews, rather than being raised by the researcher.

Given the sensitive nature of performance management, an exceptional feature of the case study was the degree of access offered by the organization to people and documents. This was achieved by developing trust between the researcher and the organization. The organization's performance management framework was studied between July 2000 and December 2002. This included an initial round of preliminary interviews, a review of the planning and budgeting processes for the financial year to 30 June 2002, an examination of the operations of the organization to 30 June 2002, and a review of the results, including incentive payments to December 2002.

A variety of methods were used to collect data over the two and a half year period, including significant periods of observation (usually around one month), a large number of open-ended interviews with people in the many business areas and at different levels (senior management, operational people), informal conversations (for example at coffee time, during lunch, at the photocopier), telephone conversations with key informants, participant observation at internal meetings (for example strategy sessions, incentives review), and an extensive review of documents. Considerable time was spent on the interviews and observing the operation of performance management, and on the reflexive methodology (see Alvesson and Skoldberg, 2000). The latter involved regular discussions with supervisors about what the researcher had seen and heard during recent visits, and reflecting on the causes of the various behaviours observed. A good description of the approach adopted for data analysis is provided by Atkinson (1992, p. 455): 'That well-established style of work whereby the data are inspected for categories and instances. It is an approach that disaggregates the text (notes or transcripts) into a series of fragments, which are then regrouped under a series of thematic headings.'

The Organization

Sensol was established in the late 1980s.[2] During the early years its organizational strategy was to improve the efficiency and effectiveness of operations in order to make the organization profitable. By the 1990s Sensol's core business was in a declining industry, which prompted it to adopt a diversification strategy.

By the time of the study the organization was operating under a decentralized structure, having changed from autonomous business units to a divisional structure (with business units). The separate divisions operated in diverse business areas. Division A included the core traditional business as well as some new operations. This division had a very high percentage of the market and generated most of the cash for the business. Division B provided a large range of services to most of the other divisions. Division C operated in a highly competitive market and was the market leader in terms of revenue. Revenue growth was achieved by means of acquisitions and price cutting. However Division C remained unprofitable, partly because of the lack of synergy between the business units and the resistance from customers to price increases. Division D also operated in a highly competitive market but had gone from being the star performer to a minor part of the business.

The divisional structure affected the performance management framework because of the highly interrelated nature of the divisions and business units. While the business units were evaluated on their own financial performance, this was complicated by the interrelationships between the businesses. Thirty per cent of total revenues were internally transfer-priced. In one business unit, 70 per cent of the revenues were received from internal business units.

Sensol had a history of restructuring at least once a year, and this had had a significant impact on the entire performance management framework. The restructuring was complex because it required the renegotiation of costs and revenues between the areas being restructured. This had led to a lack of ownership of financial targets, as managers saw the targets as unrealistic because of the changes. It could also have resulted in a lack of accountability as managers and the business units were subject to frequent change, and it might have had a significant affect on the profitability of various parts of the business.

Performance management framework

Sensol's performance management framework was very similar to that introduced by Otley (1999). It included a business planning process whereby the divisional and business unit strategies were developed and the financial targets for the scorecard measures agreed. The business planning targets included operational expenses and revenues, and up to five strategic programmes. The planning targets became inputs into the budgeting process, which in turn became the standards used in variance analysis in the monthly reporting process. The business planning and budgeting targets also became the targets for the annual incentive system.

Balanced scorecard

The uniqueness of Sensol's performance management framework was the combined use of EVA® and the balanced scorecard (Kaplan and Norton,

2001(b)) to measure the achievement of a range of objectives, including sustained profitability, increased shareholder value and meeting the needs of customers and employees. There has been growing recognition of the complementary nature of EVA® and the balanced scorecard (see Otley, 2001).

Sensol's company-wide scorecard was first developed in the mid 1990s to measure the achievement of its financial and social objectives. The scorecard included an 85 per cent weighting on financial measures (EVA®, revenue), and the remaining 15 per cent included measures of service performance, employee satisfaction, and health and safety (Table 8.1). The scorecard reflected the general development of balanced scorecards to include non-financial measures as well as financial ones (Kaplan and Norton, 1992). There has been little further development in linking scorecards to strategy and the development of strategy maps (see Kaplan and Norton, 1996(c), 2001b).

Several problems were clear in respect of the company's use of the scorecard. First, there had been little development of the scorecard measures over time as the company's strategy changed from growth to cost-cutting, and as the business diversified. For example Sensol was having problems with customer satisfaction in all of its businesses. However the customer measure was only used as a service performance measure for the core business and many managers had no influence over the measure. Second, the scorecard measures typically lagged behind rather than led indicators. For example an increase in revenue was not treated as an indicator of future performance. Third, there was evidence of a lack of understanding of and ability to influence EVA® across the business, and EBIT (earnings before tax and interest) was widely used in practice (for example for budgeting and monthly reporting).

Fourth, the use of the scorecard for decision making was slow to evolve. The primary use of the scorecard has been tool as a for reporting-up the organization. There was no mention of a scorecard in the monthly reports in early 2000, the emphasis being on EBIT. By the end of 2000 a few of the business units had begun to develop their own scorecards, and by 2001 some general managers were starting to use scorecards in their business planning presentations. Towards the end of 2002 the scorecard was being used as a communication tool in the organization-wide monthly reports, but its use by the business units varied.

Table 8.1 Sensol's scorecard

Financial component (80%)	Customer component (5%)
Measure: EVA®	Measure: service performance
Internal business component (10%)	Learning and growth component (5%)
Measures: employee satisfaction	Measure: increase in revenue
and health and safety	

Note: The weighting of these measures in the incentive system are shown in brackets.

EVA®

Sensol had used EVA® since the mid 1990s and by the late 1990s had integrated it into the performance management framework (including planning, budgeting, reporting, incentives and capital investment decisions). This was consistent with the recommendations made by Stern Stewart (see Stewart, 1994). Sensol attempted to align EVA® across the performance management framework, and to focus the attention of everyone in the organization on the EVA® drivers they could influence. The underlying assumption appeared to be that as long as everyone was focusing on the strategies that drove EVA® (for example increasing revenues, reducing expenses, reducing capital), this would ultimately result in an increase in EVA®. This approach was consistent with the EVA® literature (see Ittner and Larcker, 2001; Stewart, 1994).

One of the most serious problems Sensol faced with the implementation of EVA® was the lack of understanding of it throughout the business. It was only calculated at the highest levels and was often viewed as a 'black box' adjustment made at the corporate level at the end of the year. Another problem was that many managers had a limited ability to influence EVA®. For example there was limited control over the capital base as many of the businesses had no bank accounts or balance sheets, only some control over their fixed assets, receivables and payables, and the cost of capital was determined at the corporate level.

Despite Sensol's rhetoric of being a value-based organization, EBIT continued to be the primary measure for business planning and EVA® was only calculated at the end of the year. The managers had a good understanding of EBIT and had control over revenues and expenses. Also EBIT was considered to be a good surrogate for EVA® (that is, increasing EBIT would increase EVA®). The case study evidence suggests that managers focused on reducing expenses – rather than increasing revenues or reducing capital – to achieve their financial targets. Focusing on short-term accounting measures such as EBIT can result in managers taking short-term actions (Anthony and Govindarajan, 2004). Stern Stewart has recognized the potential for short-termism with EVA® and recommends that a bonus bank should be used for incentives, which should be paid out over a predetermined period of time (usually three years) (Otley, 1999; Stewart, 1994).

Investigating the performance management framework

The following sections describe the operation of Sensol's performance management framework using the questions asked in Otley (1999).

Objectives

▪ 'What are the key objectives that are central to the organization's overall future success, and how does it go about evaluating its achievement for each of these objectives?' (Otley, 1999, p. 365).

The novelty of Sensol's performance management approach was to combine EVA® with the balanced scorecard approach. Contrary to EVA®'s single objective of creating value for the shareholder, Sensol used the balanced scorecard approach to measure a range of financial and social obligations. However the interrelationship between the performance management elements (for example objectives, strategies, measures, incentives and information flows) signalled to managers that financial measures (EBIT and EVA®) were considerably more important than non-financial ones.

Organizations has to make trade-offs between conflicting objectives (Otley, 1999). This was evident at Sensol in that its recent focus on cost cutting had resulted in one business area reducing overtime, leading to reductions in service performance measures.

Strategies, plans, measures and targets

▪ 'What strategies and plans has the organization adopted and what are the processes and activities that it has decided will be required for it successfully to implement these. How does it assess and measure the performance of these activities?' (Otley, 1999 p. 365).

▪ 'What level of performance does the organization need to achieve in each of the areas defined in the above two questions [here and in preceding subsection], and how does it go about setting appropriate performance targets for them?' (ibid.)

The answers to Otley's first three questions were addressed in the business planning and budgeting processes. During the business planning process the organization's expectations were communicated, the divisions and their business units formulated strategies to meet these expectations, and targets were established. The planning process was coordinated at the Corporate level, which issued business planning guidelines and details of the organization's latest vision, purpose and strategies. The overall company strategy had changed from growth (by increasing revenues and diversifying) to improving profitability and cost cutting.

The key product of the business planning process was an overall business plan for the organization that incorporated the business unit and divisional plans. The process included an initial period of strategy formulation, after which the emphasis shifted to setting financial targets.

Strategy formulation

About six months into the financial year the divisions and their business units began a series of strategy sessions (usually including an off-site retreat) to decide on the future direction of their businesses. Brainstorming sessions were held to identify strategies that would enable them to close the planning 'gap', and internal and external analyses were conducted to identify other strategies and develop strategic programmes. The aim was to identify drivers that would increase economic value added (Stewart, 1994). Next the business units began work on strategies to close the gap between their current performance and their expected performance (for example by improving the profitability of customers and the units' service performance). These strategies were elaborated in detail in their strategic programmes (that is, action plans).

In such a large and diverse organization, overall business planning and budgeting was challenging. Typical problems included the time spent on the process (several months), the tension between standardization and customization of business plans, the lack of time spent on strategic thinking (compared with target setting), and problems associated with the highly interrelated nature of the business (for example agreeing to transfer prices, and the iterative nature of changes) (see Anthony and Govindarajan, 2004, p. 351–3).

Target setting

The longitudinal nature of this study highlights the significant interrelationships between target setting and the other performance elements including setting targets to measure performance against the organizational objectives, setting the minimum and maximum levels for the incentive compensation system, and setting the target level to be used in the monthly reporting process. These targets were measured by EBIT, and then by EVA® once the year-end balances had been calculated. Forecasting was used at the beginning of the process to stretch targets. There was little emphasis on target setting for the non-financial measures in the scorecard, which were negotiated between the senior managers and the corporate managers towards the end of the process.

Sensol described its target setting process as top down and bottom up. This meant that the various businesses were expected to do top-down planning by providing initial EBIT targets early in the process. Forecasting and modelling were sometimes used at this stage. Some managers argued that the initial targets were actually 'best guesses' of what they thought the business areas could achieve, given the proposed strategies. This was followed by bottom-up budgeting to specify how the financial targets would be achieved.

The financial planning template included a base element (last year's operations plus or minus any known changes, such as wage increases or volume changes), plus a strategic element of up to five strategic programmes, which were often broken down into a large number of smaller projects. Separating the financial planning numbers into two components – a strategy budget and an operational budget – was in line with the proposal by Kaplan and Norton (2001a, b).

The final step was to establish the target levels for the annual incentive compensation system, which was 'capped'. The minimum target was that which was required to be achieved and below which no incentive payments would be made, the median target (was that in the business plan, and the maximum target was for outstanding performance. Setting three target levels for such a diverse range of businesses had proved a challenge and a range of approaches had been tired (for example modelling). It appeared that many managers had little understanding of how the target levels were set.

The managers interviewed made a number of comments on the target setting process. First, some claimed that the initial targets amounted to 'plucking numbers out of the air', but these subsequently became real targets to which the managers were held. At the time the initial targets were set, the strategic programmes were only in the early stages of planning and they would not necessarily be implemented. Some managers said they were reluctant to set these targets without conducting bottom-up budgeting at the same time. This meant that the focus tended to be mainly on what had been achieved the previous year. A related point is that if the strategic programmes required substantial resources, they also had to go through the capital investment process.

Second, although the planning process required managers to plan for the following three-year period, the focus was actually on the next year alone as the process started afresh each year. Third, there was a major problem with poor data availability. For example the lack of reliable data on volumes was a considerable problem for at least two of the divisions because volumes were a large factor in their planning forecasts.

Fourth, target setting was a long and iterative process that included extensive periods of negotiation across the organization. It is debatable whether this process could be called planning or budgeting, and approaches varied across the organization. In practice there was extensive information asymmetry at all levels. As Jensen (2001) argues, linking budget targets to incentives can have undesirable consequences. Jensen also highlights problems associated with capping incentive payments. There is some evidence that divisions may try to negotiate lower targets because they know from past experience that their targets can be arbitrarily increased late in the process.

Over the two and a half year study period it became clear that target setting was crucial to the operation of the overall performance management framework (for example strategies, measures, incentives, performance evaluations, information flows). However diversification of the business had increased the complexity of the process and there were mixed results among the divisions. One division reached its maximum target in each of the three years of the study, and the core division in two years. There is some anecdotal evidence that the outstanding financial performance by these two divisions might have been the consequence of achievable targets. Two other divisions failed to reach their targets. Both operated in highly competitive and uncertain markets and were facing serious problems. It is interesting that one of these divisions was able to negotiate a change in the target level for the incentive compensation system.

Transfer pricing

Transfer pricing had a significant impact on the target setting process because the transfer pricing negotiations were conducted at the same time as this process. The decentralized organizational structure and the strong interrelationship between some of the business areas made it difficult to isolate the performance of a single business unit. Some managers expressed concern that some business units were finding it easier to improve performance through the transfer prices charged to internal businesses, rather than by generating more external business. There was also evidence of intense rivalry between some of the business areas.

Another issue was the impact of the transfer pricing negotiations across the business, and there had been a problem with units not reaching agreement on transfer prices before the deadline for the planning and budgeting targets. Once the transfer prices (often based on variable prices) had been agreed, the impact of volume changes could still affect units' performance. There were also problems with the recording and reporting of transfer prices, the lack of information flows between the business areas, mixed approaches to transfer pricing agreements (for example negotiated, imposed, arbitrary, market), the cost of some of the support areas, the lack of freedom to source elsewhere (for example in response to poor service, higher prices compared with the market) and evaluating interrelated business units solely on their own performance. These issues have often been raised in the literature (for example see Anthony and Govindarajan, 2004).

The longitudinal nature of the study facilitated recognition of the impact of transfer pricing on the performance management framework. Initially, discussions with the organization suggested that transfer pricing was not a major issue as transfer pricing agreements were the result of arm's-length negotiation. Moreover transfer pricing did not receive a mention in Sensol's performance management framework. However the significance of transfer pricing became evident when managers in the business units cited it as one of the most significant issues they faced.

Budgeting

The planning process established the overall financial targets and communicated the strategies and programmes across the business. Once these issues had been agreed the budget was prepared (Otley, 1999). As discussed earlier, there was a mixed approach to budgeting, ranging from top down to bottom up. Budgeting was carried out concurrently with the planning and target setting processes because managers wanted to ensure that the targets were achievable.

The final business planning EBIT targets became the budget EBIT targets. Managers could move numbers between line items as long as the end result equalled the business planning EBIT target. In many areas the focus was on what has been achieved the previous year (with account being taken of changes during the year, such as wage increases). At the end of the process considerable effort was put into breaking down the annual targets into monthly targets, although the organization was moving towards quarterly rather than monthly reporting to help reduce the problem of monthly phasing.

The budgets for the EBIT targets were finalized and updated into EVA® targets at the corporate level once the annual reports had been completed. The capital balances were only updated at the end of the year as there was little change in capital balances between the balance dates. Due to delays in the annual reporting process, the final EVA® targets might not be agreed until August or September, even though the financial year began on 1 July. The budget numbers then became inputs into the monthly reporting process.

A key issue for the organization was that while the business planning templates showed the final EBIT target as made up of the base operations plus strategic programmes, this distinction did not exist in the budgeting templates. The result was a lack of visibility of the strategic programmes when the financial numbers were moved into the general ledger account codes. As discussed earlier these strategic programmes were only in the early stage of development, and they might be substantially changed by the time the budgets were finalized. The problem was that whilst managers were focusing on meeting their EBIT targets, delaying or cancelling the programmes could result in a good short-term financial performance through reduced spending, but there were potential long-term consequences, for example future revenues might be affected. To overcome these problems, two of the divisions had developed their own internal strategic programme reporting process, and another was trying to link programme reporting to the scorecard reporting process.

Organizational context

The organizational context had significant implications for the planning and budgeting processes. First, target setting was complicated by the decentralized structure, as the business areas were involved in the complex task of negotiating transfer pricing agreements. Second, Sensol operated in a diverse range of business areas. Some businesses operated in stable environments with little competition, while others operated in highly competitive markets. This diversity necessitated some customization of the business plans, which conflicted with the need for standardization.

Third, the planning and budgeting processes were significantly affected by the organization's frequent restructuring as this involved reallocating revenues and expenses between the restructured areas. Restructuring could delay final target confirmation by months. Finally there were problems with communication across the organization, resulting in a lack of understanding by managers of how the targets were set, the design of the incentive compensation system and how to influence EVA®.

Rewards[3] and sanctions

▮ 'What rewards will managers (and other employees) gain by achieving these performance targets (or, conversely, what penalties will they suffer by failing to achieve them)?' (Otley, 1999, p. 365).

At Sensol the rewards comprised fixed pay (including allowances), the annual incentive compensation system and promotion. While intrinsic rewards (for example the satisfaction of doing interesting work or a good job) were deemed to be important by some managers, most tended to undervalue the motivational impact of intrinsic rewards (for example recognition by seniors). The sanctions managers suffered for failing to achieve their performance targets were mainly related to the incentive compensation system. There was evidence that managers found it hard to deal with poor performers, so the performance evaluation system tended not to differentiate between good and poor performers.

The annual incentive compensation system

Sensol's performance management system was linked to its annual incentive compensation system for senior and middle managers and had been in

Table 8.2 Example of the annual incentive compensation system and the multiplier effect

Base amount ($)		Organizational performance (0–200%)		Individual performance multiplier (0–200%)		Incentive payment ($)
10 000	x	0 (below threshold)	x	50 (acceptable)	=	0
10 000	x	50 (threshold)	x	50 (acceptable)	=	2 500
10 000	x	100 (at target)	x	100 (achieved target)	=	10 000
10 000	x	200 (maximum)	x	100 (achieved target)	=	20 000
10 000	x	200 (maximum)	x	200 (maximum)	=	40 000

operation for several years. The system had evolved from the provision of *ad hoc* bonuses at the end of the financial year, based on what management thought the organization could afford, to a complex, detailed, formula-based system.

The annual payment consisted of a base amount, an amount based on organizational performance and an amount based on the individual's achievement of preset objectives. The three amounts were multiplied together. An example of this is shown in Table 8.2.

The base amount consisted of up to 30 per cent of total salary and the amount of incentive 'at risk' increased by salary grade. If a manager's organizational performance was 'at target' (in which case the multiplier was 100 per cent) and she or he achieved the individual performance target (a multiplier of 100 per cent) then that manager received $10 000. It was generally expected that managers would achieve their targets, and the amount they could earn for exceptional performance was capped at four times the base amount.

The organizational performance multiplier was based on performance measures in the company-wide scorecard. The targets for these measures were set during the business planning process. The weightings were 85 per cent financial measures (80 per cent EVA®, 5 per cent revenue growth) and 15 per cent non-financial measures (see Table 8.1). Incentive payments were based on a weighting of all the measures, although the minimum EVA® target had to be achieved throughout the company (company level and divisional). The higher weighting for company-wide performance was intended to encourage managers to focus on the interests of the company as a whole.

The first part of the performance evaluation process involved top-down objective setting that allowed for some negotiation by managers. The objective-setting process was similar to the process of management by objectives and the development of personal scorecards (see Kaplan and Norton, 2001 (a)(b)). All managers who were eligible for an annual incentive payment were required to set formal objectives, about five of which were linked to the company scorecard and some were personal. In practice the objective-setting process was weak as many individuals either have no objectives or their objectives had been altered by restructuring or other events.

This was followed by the performance evaluation at the end of the year. Managers were rated between 0 per cent (unacceptable performance) and 200 per cent (outstanding). The performance evaluation process included individual meetings to discuss each manager's achievement of the objectives set earlier in the year and to agree on the performance rating. However adherence to this varied widely, with some meetings failing to take place while others amounted to in-depth evaluation.

As already noted, the incentive system was designed to encourage managers across the diverse business areas to work together for the good of the company as a whole. However over time it had become clear that managers focused mainly on the performance of their business unit, as this was something they could influence directly, and they had been able to 'double dip' as short-term financial performance was highly weighted by their superiors in their individual performance rating (worth 50 per cent). This highlights the importance of human resource practices, which tend to be ignored in the control literature (Otley, 1999).

The incentive system was perceived by managers as being 'managed' for two main reasons: the year-end accounting adjustments had an impact on the the size of payments; and it was thought that their superiors had already set the ratings before the individual meetings in order to ensure consistent ratings across the divisions. Moreover the operation of the system was affected by lack of understanding about how the system worked and how to influence the associated measures (for example EVA®), and stories abounded about the impact of the system on the behaviour of managers.

Information flows

■ 'What are the information flows (feedback and feedforward loops) that are necessary to enable the organization to learn from its experience, and to adapt its current behaviour in the light of that experience?' (Otley, 1999, p. 365).

Poor information flows in some parts of the business meant that some people either did not have the information they needed or did not trust the information supplied to them. In this situation managers tended to collect their own information and develop their own databases. This was a significant problem for the organization, and for the performance management framework, so it introduced a new information system.

The monthly reporting process was the main reporting system and comprised a typical feedback loop. The input into the process was from the budgeting templates and variances between actual and budget were shown. The monthly reports also included forecasts of financial performance to the end of the year. For example in December a division would report its actual performance over the previous six months and its forecast performance for the following six months. In practice managers tended to make very conservative forecasts, and one of the reasons for the change to quarterly reporting was to try to improve these forecasts.

It is interesting that there was no reporting on the impact of transfer pricing between the divisions and business units. There was also some concern about the poor recording and reporting of transfer prices (for example it could be difficult to ascertain what a transfer price was for), the difficulty of reconciling transfer pricing across the organization, and the general lack of information flow between the business areas.

Monthly reporting on the scorecard measures developed considerably during the research period. During the early stage of the research the focus was on performance on the EBIT targets, but by the end the scorecard had become prominent and there was considerable discussion of scorecard performance.

Conclusion

While Sensol's organizational objectives included social as well as financial objectives, the primary focus was on financial objectives and this was obvious in the performance management framework. The long and detailed business planning process concentrated primarily on setting the business unit and divisional budget targets, and less time was spent on strategic issues. Despite attempts by head office to use sophisticated tools to create 'stretch' targets, it appeared that managers were motivated to negotiate achievable targets because of the link between these and the incentive compensation system. The 'balanced' scorecard measures were actually unbalanced as 85 per cent of the weightings were based on short-term financial measures (EVA®, revenue growth). Also the principal measure used throughout the organization was EBIT, with EVA® often being seen as a 'black box' adjustment at the end of the year. The short-term financial focus was reinforced by the emphasis on financial factors in the reporting process.

This focus also affected the performance evaluation process. While the organizational rhetoric espoused working together in the interest of the company as a whole, the business units were evaluated on their individual EBIT and EVA® performance. As the senior managers were primarily evaluated on the short-term financial performance of their business units, they evaluated their subordinates the same way. This resulted in managers being able to 'double dip', meaning that financial performance was heavily weighted in both the individual, as well as the organizational performance component of performance targets. Finally, the bonuses were paid annually rather than being banked and paid out over a period of time. This approach is recommended by Stern Stewart to avoid the potential for short-term reactions to EVA® results (Stewart, 1994).

The findings of the study support the observation by others support (for example Malmi, 2001; Malmi and Ikäheimo, 2003) that it is far from clear what organizations mean when they say they have adopted EVA® or the balanced scorecard. Malmi and Ikäheimo (2003) found that organizations that had adopted EVA® used a diverse range of measures (not primarily EVA®), and all used short-term incentives. The description of the performance management framework provided in this chapter makes it seem as though the operation and consequences of the framework were clear, but this was not the case. Over the course of the study it was necessary to piece together the various parts of the 'puzzle' of the framework: business planning and budgeting (for example target setting), information flows, year-end adjustments, performance evaluation and the incentive system. The study involved an examination of the use, rather than simply the existence, of the performance management processes.

Notes

1. EVA® is the registered trademark of Stern Stewart (see http://www.eva.com/).
2. The company's name has been changed to ensure anonymity.
3. Here rewards should be understood in the widest sense and not just as short-term financial rewards, important though these may be.

Divisional control and performance

Mick Broadbent and John Cullen

Introduction

Chapter 3 discussed how an increase in an organisation's size can lead to problems if a centralized and unitary control structure is maintained, and how divisional structures are developed to address the problem of allowing sufficient specialization while integrating the tasks carried out. The chapter also discussed how divisional structures can lead to suboptimal decisions being taken by divisional management. The work of Williamson (1970, 1975) was used to support the notion of multidivisional (M-form) organization being adopted to cope with the growing complexity of larger organizations, and particularly those operating in diverse product markets. M-form organization integrates the concept of markets and hierarchies within one organization: at the divisional level through market-focused day-to-day activities, and at the group or head office level through hierarchies setting strategies for the divisions. Put more simply, strategic decisions are vested in top management while operating decisions are the prerogative of divisional managers (Ezzamel, 1992).

Contingency theory approaches to control (introduced in Chapter 2) argue there is no one optimal way to structure an organization, but that structure should reflect the environment in which it is found. The contingency literature suggests that environmental complexity is significantly correlated with the extent of decentralization and that product diversification has caused many organizations to divisionalize their structures (Chandler, 1962). Lorsch and Allen (1973) link greater market differentiation and independence between products to divisionalization along product lines, while organizations operating in integrated markets tend to remain undivisionalized.

Chapter 4 introduced the notion of subsidiarity as a means of coping with complexity; in this case task and decision-making authority should be delegated as close as possible to the point of enactment. The principle of subsidiary does not imply either a divisional or a unitary form, but consideration of the appropriate location of task and decision-making authority, which as argued above leads to the separation of strategy and operational decision making and control in divisionalized companies.

Having linked the threads developed in earlier chapters of this book, this chapter explores the issues raised in greater detail, initially returning to the arguments put forward by Chandler (1962) and others, and then moving towards a control model for divisionalized companies and consideration of the problems that creates. The traditional approaches to control and performance measurement through the accounting system will be expanded to include the notions of shareholder and stakeholder returns, as will non-accounting controls (see for example Kaplan and Norton, 1992, 1993, 1996b, 2000, 2001a, 2001b). The separation of strategies and operational decision making will be questioned using, *inter alia*, the work of Goold and Campbell (1987a, 1987b, 2002, 2003). The chapter will present empirical evidence on the use of performance measures in divisionalized companies.

The M-model arguments revisited

Dermer (1977) emphasizes that understanding the way an organization structures itself through differentiation and the allocation of responsibilities through decentralization is necessary in order to study control. Organizations differentiate their activities into subunits so that each has a more homogeneous and manageable environment. Differentiation can take many forms, the two major ones being differentiation by function and by product. Decentralization determines the organizational structure, the scope of each unit and its potential range of activities. Differentiation determines what each unit is capable of doing, while decentralization determines what decisions each unit is responsible for and the degree of discretion allowed to each subunit. Ezzamel and Hilton (1980a, 1980b) bring these two concepts together by classifying decentralized structures as 'functional' or 'federal'. Functional decentralization is the delegation of decision-making power to lower levels of management on the basis of functional specification, for example production or marketing, while federal decentralization involves partitioning the firm into two or more quasi-autonomous subunits, divisions or business units whose activities are cocoordinated primarily through price mechanisms such as product lines, customers or geographical location.

Loft (1991), writing about the history of management accounting, notes that at the turn of the nineteenth century the US economy had several huge vertically integrated firms, which had successfully adopted a centralized (or U-form) organizational structure by employing decentralized decision making through differentiation into highly specialized units. Hence top management could coordinate activities, direct strategy and policy. Johnson and Kaplan (1987), using the Williamson's (1975) argument, maintained that such large companies recognized the benefits of a well managed hierarchy over those of market exchange(s). At this stage the firms were not divisionalized, rather they were decentralized and it was not until after the First World War that divisionalized companies started to emerge, well known examples being Du Pont and General Motors.

The links between decentralization and environmental uncertainty are well stated in the contingency theory literature. The work of Burns and Stalker (1961), who identified mechanistic and organic organizational structures, led to research suggesting that environmental complexity is significantly linked to the extent of decentralization within an organization. Chandler (1962) found that product diversification is linked to decentralized structures; this finding was supported by Lorsch and Allen (1973). This led to the conclusion that, as firms differentiate their products, divisionalization will take place as a consequence of the independence of different lines. This argument can be augmented by the analysis of technology as a contingent variable. For example Woodward (1958) and Perrow (1967, 1970) maintain that different organizational structures are a reflection of their technologies. If a large company that operates in several diverse product markets and uses several different production technologies were to decentralize, divisionalization would be the likely result. This conclusion is supported by the general systems theory literature, which argues that organizations, like individuals, seek to cope with their environments. If the environment is uncertain and highly complex, then the creation of subunits or divisions within an organization as a coping mechanism would be appropriate. Thompson (1967) summarizes this approach, stating that organizations cope with uncertainty by 'creating certain parts specifically to deal with it'.

The arguments put forward so far in this chapter follow those of Chandler (1962), supported by Johnson and Kaplan (1987) and summarized by Loft (1991, p. 26) as follows: 'the environment caused large companies to follow certain strategies, which in turn 'caused' the multi divisional company'. However there is uncertainty about this. Loft suggests an opposite cause that may be equally valid: 'large companies' strategy of trying to dominate the market by driving competitors out, or swallowing them up, leads to monopoly and oligopoly and in turn to bureaucracy and wastefulness' (ibid.)

Returning to the mainstream literature, Scott (1971) separates the development of a firm into four stages and links these to organizational structures

Table 9.1   The Scott matrix: four stages of organizational development

	Owner manager	Growth in size	Growth in complexity but central strategy	Highly diverse, no central strategy: set by business units
Stage	1	2	3	4
Product line	Single	Single	Multiple	Multiple
Distribution	Single	Single	Multiple	Multiple
Organizational structure	Little or no formal structure	Functionally based and integrated	Product-market based and quasi-autonomous	Product-market based and largely autonomous

Source: Adapted from Scott (1971).

and their respective attributes (Table 9.1). The Scott matrix views the development of organizational structures through growth in size and complexity. The initial growth in size leads to the development of decentralized, functionally based organizations. With increased complexity the structure becomes product based and quasi-autonomous, with strategy held centrally – the classic multidivisional company. In the final stage, as organizations become even more diverse, the central strategy is replaced by the delegation of individual strategies to divisions or strategic business units. This matrix presents a logical progression of structure, but any large diversified company may adopt different control mechanisms for different divisions at any point in time, so control in a core business division will be different from that in a peripheral business unit. These arguments will be developed later in this chapter).

Multidivisional organizations

The major advantage of decentralized and multidivisional organizations (M-form) is that different layers of management can concentrate on those issues with which they are best placed to deal (Emmanuel *et al.*, 1990). M-form organization, if applied appropriately, enables effective performance and profit maximization (Williamson, 1975) through three attributes. The first is the efficient allocation of resources within the organization. If the organization is compared to a capital market, where lenders with surplus units seek out borrowers who require those units for investment through a risk–return trade-off, then headquarters or central management allocates resources between divisions on an equally competitive basis. Funds raised externally are obtained at a lower cost than any individual division could obtain on its own.

They are then allocated on a competitive basis between divisions and the efficiency of the funds is monitored through the use of performance indicators, thus providing a control loop for the allocation of resources.

Second, by delegating day-to-day and operational decision making to largely autonomous divisions, higher levels of management are not overburdened by detailed information as this is filtered out at lower levels of the communication channel. Such channels can be used for summarized information flows and strategy dissemination. The concentration of divisions into particular areas of activity also reduces lateral information flows, as interdivisional transactions are reduced.

Third, the M-form minimizes suboptimal behaviour. The vesting of strategic decisions in top management and the delegation of day-to-day operating decisions to the divisional level reduces the risk and complexity of decision making as there is specialization at each of the levels. Because the organization is a collection of interdependent units, transactions between these units reduces the potential for the opportunistic behaviour that would be possible in transactions external to the organization. The use of control systems and performance-monitoring devices, linked to a flexible reward system, can ensure optimal behaviour. Headquarters can, if required, mediate disputes between divisions without recourse to legal intermediaries.

According to this theory, hierarchies should only replace markets if it is more economic to organize transactions through such hierarchies, so the managerial costs of divisionalization must be less than those incurred by operating through the markets. The delegation of decision making to divisional managers will automatically increase the managerial costs as increased monitoring will be necessary to ensure that delegated authority is not misused. Scapens and Roberts (1993) argue that decentralization is often ambiguous because of a mismatch between the commercial unity of a division and the arbitrary divisions created by the system of profit centres. This argument is supported by Otley (1990) in a case study of British Coal. As divisional level managers are given greater decision-making responsibility they expect greater rewards because of that responsibility, as well as a share in the success of the divisional activities.

It is possible for the performance of one division to be enhanced at the expense of the organization as a whole, and the competitive nature of divisionalization may breed separatist attitudes and overcompetitive behaviour amongst divisions. Since the loss of central control that comes from decentralization and divisionalization means a higher incidence of non-programmed decisions (Emmanuel *et al.*, 1990) by divisional managers, it is essential that these decisions are based on organizational goals rather than being solely divisionally based.

The use of divisionalized structures may be counterproductive when there is excessive interdependence amongst divisions, for example when the organizational goal is indivisible amongst divisions, or when organizational resources are so complementary that separation of the divisions reduces the scope for scale economies. The interdependence of production functions may result in high management costs in respect of managing divisional relationships and this may negate the benefits obtained from divisionalization. Hopper (1988) argues that such costs arise from the requirement for corporate controls over the managerial labour process, and the growth of management itself means that it has to be managed through the monitoring process.

Williamson (1970, 1975) argues that the divisionalized organizational structure possesses the requisite control apparatus for profit maximization:

- An incentive mechanism, including pecuniary and non-pecuniary rewards, that can be adapted to monitor the effort made by divisional managers attain the goals of central management.
- An internal audit system, to review and evaluate the performance of divisional managers.
- An allocation system to assign resources (cash flows) to the highest yielding projects after the evaluation of divisional investment proposals.

Williamson also suggests procedures for implementing the divisional structures:

- Identify divisional boundaries.
- Assign quasi-autonomous status to each division, thus determining the extent of divisional autonomy.
- Allocate company resources to divisions.
- Use performance measures and reward schemes to monitor and reward divisional activities.
- Engage in strategic planning whenever possible.

Ezzamel and Hart (1987) point out that the management accounting literature has devoted little attention to the identification of divisional boundaries, the assignment of quasi-autonomous status to divisions and the conducting of strategic planning. We hope to redress this by considering these issues in the following section.

Control in divisionalized organizations

The discussion in this section will draw heavily on the work of Ezzamel and Hart (1987), who maintain that divisional control involves both financial and structural control devices, and that these interact with and to some extent constrain one another. According to them the overall control apparatus may encompass a variety of individual controls that relate to:

- Defining the divisional environment.
- Determining divisional size.
- Defining and cocoordinating divisional interdependence.
- Determining the extent of divisional decision-making autonomy.
- Determining the characteristics of information and information flow.
- Designing an internal audit system.
- Designing an appropriate reward system.

The above serve as interacting variables that may constrain managerial action and be subject to other managers' manipulations. Each will be considered in turn.

The divisional environment will be a subset of the environment faced by the organization as a whole. The degree of differentiation required by each division to meet the demands of its environment will create internal diversity. The greater the differentiation, the greater the problem of integrating the various divisions. Divisions operating in relatively certain environments will engage in more formalized organizational practices, whilst those operating in more complex environments will have less formalized systems. The greater the environmental variety the greater the potential for disunity and dysfunctional behaviour amongst divisions, yet each division is unlikely to be fully independent of the others. The organization must achieve integration between units in order to remain a whole. Lorsch and Allen (1973) maintain that the greater the differentiation between divisions the harder the task of integration, with a resulting complexity of integrative devices: task forces, committees, divisional specialists working at head office and so on. In the case of conglomerate companies, which by definition are highly diverse and operate in different product markets, Lorsch and Allen have identified performance evaluation systems that directly link financial performance to monetary rewards, while in vertically integrated firms, with greater interdependence and operating in a similar environment the performance evaluation systems are more formally administered and put less emphasis on financial results than on operating criteria.

Divisional size may reflect a compromise between economic efficiency and administrative efficiency. While classical economics suggests there are optimum sizes for particular units, divisional managers may wish to increase the size of their divisions beyond this norm for personal reward. Conversely head office staff may wish to restrict the size to below this norm in order to limit the power base of individual divisional managers.

Divisional interdependence includes relationships between central management and divisional managers, between divisional managers themselves, between divisional managers and their operating units, and between operating units within a division. Interdependence can take several forms (Ezzamel and Hart, 1987), and is related to demand and transfer pricing issues as well as technological issues and behavioural practices. Each must be coordinated to avoid managers engaging in behaviour that furthers their own interests but is contrary to the interests of the organization as a whole. It is suggested that in order to improve the effectiveness and usefulness of accounting procedures, accountants should team up with designers of organizations and behavioural scientists.

The level of autonomy granted to divisional managers is stated clearly by Williamson (1970, 1975): central managers take strategic decisions, whilst operating decisions are delegated to divisional managers. Williamson argues that this splitting of responsibilities can lead to suboptimal decision making and reduced organizational effectiveness. The evidence cited comes from studies of traditional US divisionalized companies, but more recent work by Goold and Campbell (2002, 2003) and others (to be discussed later in the chapter) confirms the sometimes clouded nature of the two levels of decision making, particularly in the case of strategic business units (see Scott, 1971, fig. 7.1).

Even with strategic business units and more traditional divisions, it is essential for central management to maintain control of the process of allocating resources amongst competing units. This process can regulate the growth of any one division and determine its ultimate size and importance in the organization. Rationing the resources distributed to divisions that do not conform with central strategies can be a powerful incentive to conform. Ezzamel and Hart (1987) maintain a commonsense view about the amount of decision-making discretion granted to divisional managers. They imply that divisional discretion should be limited in decision areas characterized by excessive interdependence, as well as in areas of crucial importance to the organization as a whole. Lorsch and Allen (1973), in the study quoted earlier, found that divisional managers in conglomerates had greater autonomy in decision making than did their counterparts in vertically integrated organizations. Other academic studies are inconclusive and conflicting. Logic suggests that divisional managers facing an environment that is different from that of the organization as a whole, and who are operating with few interdependencies, will have a greater range of decision-making responsibilities than divisional managers working in contrary circumstances. Information flows between the various levels of management can reduce the degree of operational uncertainty. If decentralization and divisionalization through subsidiarity is to work, then the gathering of *ex ante* information for decision making should be done at the appropriate level; equally, reliable *ex post* information should be available for performance evaluation. When output is difficult to observe and verify, then the focus is likely to shift to 'softer' information flows. There has been much criticism of the use of 'hard' accounting information for the evaluation of divisional performance: see for example Ezzamel *et al.* (1990), who argue for the use of soft information for performance evaluation. Other proponents of this approach are Kaplan and Norton (1992, 1993), whose work will be discussed later. According to Ezzamel and Hart (1987) the internal auditing of divisional organizations can take the form of advanced, contemporaneous or *ex post*. An advanced audit involves reviewing a division's proposed course of action; a contemporaneous audit entails continuous monitoring of divisional performance; and *ex post* auditing involves end-of-period performance evaluation. Williamson (1970, 1975) views auditing as a necessary cost of using a hierarchical system, as opposed to a market one. Auditing, he argues, is necessary to ensure the greater efficiencies generated by internal transactions.

Traditional accounting methods of measuring divisional performance

This section provides an overview of the issues involved in using accounting methods to measure divisional performance. The bulk of the related literature consists of management accounting texts, many of which assume that management accounting exists in splendid isolation from rather than being a subset of management control.

Measures of divisional performance are usually financially based. There is substantial evidence (for example Minchington and Francis, 2000; Reece and Cool, 1978; Tomkins, 1973; Vancil, 1979) of the continued use of profit measures and return on investment ratios as the main measures of divisional performance. Solomons (1965) notes three reasons why some sort of index of divisional profitability is useful.

- It can serve as a guide for central management to assess the efficiency of each division as an economic entity.
- It can help central managers to assess the efficiency with which divisional managers are discharging their duties.
- It can guide divisional managers when making decisions about the daily activities of their divisions.

While these three reasons provide a basic rationale for the use of divisional performance indexes in a single organization, Skinner (1990) suggests that performance indexes be used to make interfirm comparisons and set up benchmarks whereby the results of a division can be compared with the results of a whole company in a similar industry. Recent developments in segmental company reporting also emphasize this external focus. Solomons (1965) concentrates on central managers and divisional managers, thus excluding operating managers whose efficiency has a direct effect on profitability. The three reasons stated by Solomons agree with Williamson's (1970, 1975) argument that through effective resource allocation and performance evaluation by central management, divisionalized organizations can pursue profit maximization.

A major challenge with this approach is to devise performance measures that do not encourage divisional managers to pursue policies that benefit their own division but are detrimental to the organization as a whole. Shillinglaw (1982) suggests three rules to which divisional profit measures must comply before they can be regarded as acceptable (see also Drury, 1985):

- Divisional profits should not be raised by any actions that reduce total organizational profit.
- Each division's profit should be as independent as possible of performance efficiency and managerial decisions elsewhere in the company.
- Each division's profit should reflect items that are subject to a substantial degree of control by the divisional manager or his or her subordinates.

Traditional measures of divisional performance include profit, return on investment (ROI), residual income (RI) and discounted cash flow (DCF); a more recent measure is economic value added (EVA®). Each will be considered in turn. It should be borne in mind that the nature of interdependence in divisionalized companies and the manner in which strategy is devolved may not produce clear divisional boundaries, thus the responsibility of the managers and hence the performance measures may also be unclear.

Profit

Profit is an appropriate measure of performance if the divisional manager is responsible for all the variables used in its calculation. There are, however, problems with profit measurement, definition and calculation, and with common costs, common revenues and transfer prices. Absolute profit can be defined in many ways using different accounting bases. Deciding which level of profit to apply may also present problems – that is, contribution margin, direct divisional profit, controllable divisional profit, income before taxation or net income.

Return on investment and residual income

Return on investment (ROI) or return on capital employed (ROCE) are very commonly used indexes of managerial and divisional performance. According to Skinner (1990), surveys from a number of countries have shown that about 70 per cent of divisionalized companies use profit – most often in the form of ROI ratios – as their main measure of divisional financial performance. Francis and Minchington (2000) support this view.

The return on investment measure has many advantages: it is a true efficiency ratio that focuses attention on both assets and profits; it is widely used (but also abused) by managers; and it provides a basis for comparing performance between divisions, between divisions and outside companies and between divisions and alternative schemes for investment of funds. ROI is a ratio that divisional managers will be required to maintain or improve over time. A divisional manager may be able to maintain the ratio by replacing assets as necessary and making progressive improvements in profits, but there is no strong encouragement to make the division grow in size, hence the use of absolute profit in parallel with ROI. Horngren (1962) suggests that the change in ROI is often more significant than its absolute level, whilst Amey (1969) argues that profit maximization must be the true objective.

The use of ROI can lead to the suboptimization of resources. A divisional manager may reject a new capital investment project that is in the company's best long-term interests as it has a positive net present value, because of the effect that such a project would have on the division's short-term ROI (see the example in Box 9.1). Because new projects usually originate at the operational level (Bower, 1986; King, 1975) it is possible for divisional managers to filter out such projects before central management knows of their existence. While

---

BOX 9.1

Rejecting an acceptable investment

A division of a large conglomerate has achieved a fairly consistent ROI of about 20 per cent for over last five years. This is above the return for the company as a whole, which has ranged from 11 per cent to 15 per cent over the same period with a cost of capital of about 10 per cent. The divisional management team has been considering a new investment in advanced manufacturing technology. The estimated return on the new investment is 18 per cent, with a positive net present value of £68,500 and an internal rate of return of 14 per cent. The divisional management team decides not to submit the proposed investment to headquarters for approval as it would reduce the ROI of the division in the short term.

the bulk of academic literature supports this view, Lillis (1992) repudiates this generalist conclusion in her study of three large divisionalized firms.

Solomons (1965) argues that the use of residual income overcomes these difficulties. Residual income imputes a cost of capital on the investment base, which when deducted from profits (or net earnings) gives an absolute figure rather than a percentage. The charge for capital is useful for evaluating performance and guiding investment decisions. Divisional managers, Solomons argues, will have an incentive to pursue all projects whose estimated internal rates of return is greater than the cost of capital as this can increase absolute residual income. Solomons also argues that residual income is the long-term counterpart of discounted cash flow, thus making it consistent with wealth maximization in the classical economics model. This assertion has been criticized by Amey (1969), who argues that, amongst other things, the cost of capital might be inappropriate. ROI, regardless of the definitional problems with its two components – profit and investment – does provide a measure of efficiency. Such a measure, however, may encourage managers to pursue short-term goals and have a very narrow view of the organization's objectives. Swieringa and Weick (1987) maintain that a measure such as ROI at least promotes action within the organization, whilst Covaleski *et al.* (1987) link this internal measure to external pressure from financial markets. Financial measures of performance tend to concentrate on the short term; that is, on the effect that actions have on the figures for the current financial year. In fact the time scale may be even shorter: Tomkins (1973) found that a very large proportion of divisionalized companies in the UK (46 out of 53) appraised their divisions against detailed financial budgets on a time scale of a month or less. So projects that reduce short-term financial performance figures are likely to be held back by divisional managers unless specific provision is made for them in the capital budgeting process. More recent empirical work will be presented towards the end of this chapter.

The use of financial performance targets encourages divisional managers to make decisions that are consistent with the achievement of a corporate finance objective, but this ignores the fact that organizations have multiple objectives, many of which cannot be easily measured. This narrowness of objectives will be considered in some detail after the next section.

Discounted cash flow

The discounted cash flow approach to divisional performance compares the expected net present value of the division at the beginning and end of a given period. It has clear links to the economic value concepts of financial performance measurement, which have not been adopted for corporate financial reporting. While future cash flow may be difficult to estimate, the academic and practical problem is to establish a discount rate or cost of capital for application to the estimated cash flow.

Less formal approaches to establishing a discount rate include the use of past divisional returns, the returns achieved by a company that is comparable to the division, the budget returns of the division, the average return of the industry in which the division operates, and management judgement. More formal approaches include the weighted average cost of capital adjusted for risk levels, and the use of the capital asset pricing model (CAPM) to derive covariances for divisional returns. Establishing a weighted average cost of capital for a division can be computationally difficult – there are problems with gearing levels for divisions, and with the issue of the holding company not holding securities issued by divisions and traded in capital markets, although Williamson (1970, 1975) likens the relationship to a capital market in a very positive manner.

Although theoretically superior, the CAPM approach has several computation problems, including the following:

- Thode (1986) argues that four conditions must be met before the CAPM can be adopted: selection of a company of equal business risk to the division; quantification of the proxy company's business risk; no scale economies or other synergies must exist; and the growth opportunities of the division must exactly match those of the proxy company. According to Thode it is highly unlikely that these conditions will occur simultaneously.
- A potential problem may arise because of the changing expectations of managers who in the past have applied a single corporate rate to appraisals and who are now asked to use different rates for each division (Welch and Kainen, 1983). Some divisions may have projects rejected that might otherwise have been accepted, with implications for divisional growth, profitability and management rewards. This change of approach to the application of discount rates may be culturally unacceptable to divisional managers.
- The use of divisional costs of capital to evaluate all projects in a division is likely to bias divisional managers in favour of riskier projects. There is normally a portfolio of projects with high, medium or low returns, and using one cost of capital to evaluate all projects may lead to rejection of low-return but low-risk projects.

Grinyer (1986) argues that the CAPM approach, which emphasizes systematic risk, will not be adopted by managers who are subject to total risk not just the systematic element.

The discounted cash flow model is academically more robust, but profitability indexes such as ROI remain the dominant divisional measure of performance. This emphasis on accounting measurement and asset valuation has resulted in broad criticisms of such performance appraisal techniques, however the accounting-based measures have recently been augmented by value-based measures, which will be considered next.

Value-based measures

Recent additions to the more general performance measurement portfolio can be applied to divisional performance measurement. These measures reflect the view that financial metrics can be employed in a modified form to evaluate the performance of a company, and hence a division, by taking a shareholder wealth perspective. The measures include economic value added (EVA) and cash flow return on investment (CFROI) and form part of the value-based management agenda summarized by Cooper *et al.* (2001).

Both EVA and CFROI are sponsored by different consultancy companies. Both provide a shareholder perspective of divisional performance that is more objective than profit and more akin to wealth measurement. Because of space limitations only EVA will be considered here. EVA takes into account the opportunity cost of funds in a similar manner to residual income (RI), and thus addresses the problems alluded to above.

Put simply, EVA takes a company's net operating profit after taxes and deducts a charge for the capital used to generate those profits, in a similar manner to RI. However EVA differs from RI as the profit flows are adjusted to provide a more cash-flow-based measure. These adjustments follow three principles (SMAC, 1997): any non-cash-flow related charges affecting both income statement and balance sheet are reversed; any expense that is considered to be an investment for the future is capitalized and added to the asset base; and the asset base must reflect its replacement value.

The capital charge is the weighted average cost of capital multiplied by the replacement cost of the asset base. The former is difficult to establish at the company level and will require a specific cost of capital for each division. This necessitates the apportionment of both debt and equity finance to each division and the use of discount rates that reflect the different risk situation in each division. As we have already demonstrated, this is fraught with problems. Minchington and Francis (2000, p. 99) argue that EVA 'takes the key business factors that create cash flow for the organization and presents them in a single measure'. Assuming that EVA is a useful measure of performance, Ehrbar (1998) suggests four ways in which wealth could be created within the model: cutting costs, investing in value-adding projects, reducing the cost of capital, and releasing the capital associated with underperforming assets. There are no creative ideas on how value adding-projects are nurtured, developed and operationalized. Hence they provide solutions similar to those that could be derived by the use of much simpler accounting matrices for performance measurement.

A more balanced view of divisional performance

Traditionally there has been a tendency for management accounting control to concentrate solely on internal issues. There has also been a tendency to focus solely on financial measures of performance, which mainly attend to the effect that actions have on one year's profits, return on investment or residual income. As mentioned earlier, projects that could lower the short-term financial performance figures are likely to be held back by a divisional management team unless specific provision is made for them in the capital budgeting process. As also argued earlier, placing too much stress on corporate financial objectives may mean ignoring the fact that organizations have multiple objectives, many of which are not easily measured in financial terms. Using one key measure of financial performance is almost certain to produce dysfunctional management behaviour in respect of one or more other objectives, such as sales growth, market share, employee relations, quality or social responsibility. It is to the need to link financial measures of performance to non-financial measures of performance that we now turn.

The reader may be familiar with the work of Bromwich and Bhimani (1989), who pointed out that there was mounting empirical evidence of the need for management accounting to become more externally focused so as to enable the organization to look outwards to the final goods market. This followed a call for strategic management accounting by Simmonds (1981), which was further developed by Bromwich (1990). While discussing the joint use of financial and non-financial measures of performance, we must also discuss the link between performance measures and the strategy being followed by the organization.

As early as 1979 Parker argued for a balanced assessment of divisional performance, to be measured by a composite mix of quantitative and qualitative indices. Parker considered that much of the traditional divisional performance literature was based on a simplistic and unrealistic view of corporate and divisional goals: 'Given the existing range of changing corporate and divisional goals, the divisional profit test taken by itself is inadequate as a measure of any division's progress towards the attainment of the corporate goal set' (Parker, 1979, p. 316). He went on to suggest an alternative approach to divisional performance measurement that accountants could adopt for the benefit of the decentralized company as a whole. According to Parker (ibid., p. 317) accountants should:

- Discard the belief that accounting measures could be used to promote goal congruence among divisional managers.
- Recognize the need to preserve some degree of autonomy in divisional operations.
- Review the possible methods of assessing divisional performance with a view to accounting for the needs and objectives of all levels of management, above and within the division.
- Move beyond the single profit-based index to provide extra measures of divisional performance to account for a broader range of success criteria.

He suggested the following as possible additions to the traditional profit/ROI (and now EVA) measures of performance:

- Financial management ability: stock and asset turnover, gearing ratio, sources and application of funds, fixed asset statistics (for example age), maintenance expenditure, depreciation policies.
- Productivity: profit before interest and tax.
- Marketing: sales volume, market share, sales effort indicators (for example, number of visits per customer).
- Research and development: research and development costs to sales, research and development cost per employee, project performance indicators.
- Social responsibility: social budget, narrative report.
- Employee relations: time lost because of accidents, hours lost as a percentage of hours worked.

Other writers (Dearden, 1968; Johnson and Kaplan, 1987; Kaplan, 1984) have suggested before and since that profit/ROI is too narrow a view. However Parker's main argument was that there is a plurality of objectives in a company and its divisions so there must be a more balanced view of performance and the indicators used to appraise it.

The idea of a balanced view was further developed by Kaplan and Norton (1992, 1993), who introduced the idea of a balanced scorecard (Figure 9.1) to give managers a quick but comprehensive overview of the business:

The balanced scorecard includes financial measures that tell the results of actions already taken. And it complements the financial measures with operational measures on customer satisfaction, internal processes, and the organisation's innovation and improvement activities – operational measures that are the drivers of future financial performance (Kaplan and Norton, 1992, p. 71).

Financial perspective		Customer perspective	
Goals	*Measures*	*Goals*	*Measures*
Survive	Cash flow	New products	Percentage of sales from new products, percentage of sales from proprietary products
Succeed	Quarterly sales growth and operating income by division		
Prosper	Increased market share and ROI	Responsive supply	On-time delivery (defined by customer)
		Preferred supplier	Share of key accounts' purchases, ranking by key accounts
		Customer partnership	Number of cooperative engineering efforts

Internal business perspective		Innovation and learning perspective	
Goals	*Measures*	*Goals*	*Measures*
Technology capability	Manufacturing geometry *vs* competition	Technology leadership	Time to develop next generation
Manufacturing excellence	Cycle time, unit cost yield	Manufacturing learning	Process time to maturity
Design productivity	Silicon efficiency, engineering efficiency	Product focus	Percentage of products that equal 80% of sales
New product introduction	Actual introduction schedule *vs* plan	Time to market	New product introduction *vs* competition

Source: Kaplan and Norton (1993), p. 76.

Figure 9.1   The balanced scorecard

An important feature of this approach is that it looks at both internal and external matters of concern to the organization. The balanced scorecard introduces the idea of competitor benchmarking in relation to new product introductions and technology capability. Another important feature is that it considers the key elements of a company's strategy. Different divisions may be following different strategies and the items in the scorecard will need to reflect this. A final important feature is that financial and non-financial measures are linked. There is no suggestion that financial performance measures should be discarded altogether – periodic financial statements remind managers that improved quality, response time, productivity or new products only benefit the company when they are translated into improved sales and market share, reduced expenses or higher asset turnover. An example of the development of a balanced scorecard by Kaplan and Norton for a divisionalized organization is provided in Box 9.2.

BOX 9.2

'FMC Corporation is one of the most diversified companies in the United States, producing more than 300 product lines in 21 divisions organised into five business segments: industrial chemicals, performance chemicals, precious metals, defence systems, and machinery and equipment. Based in Chicago, FMC has worldwide revenues in excess of $4 billion.

'If we were going to create value by managing a group of diversified companies, we had to understand and provide strategic focus to their operations. We had to be sure that each division had a strategy that would give it sustainable competitive advantage. In addition, through measurement of their operations, whether or not the divisions were meeting their strategic objectives.

'If you are going to ask a division or the corporation to change its strategy, you had better change the system of measurement to be consistent with the new strategy. We acknowledged that the company may have become too short-term and too internally focused in its business measures. Defining what should replace the financial focus was more difficult. We wanted managers to sustain their search for continuous improvement, but we also wanted them to identify the opportunities for breakthrough performance.

'A new measurement system was needed to lead operating managers beyond achieving internal goals to searching for competitive breakthroughs in the global market-place. The system would have to focus on measures of customer service, market position and new products that could generate long-term value for the business. We used the scorecard as the focal point for the discussion. It forced division managers to answer these questions: How do we become our customers' most valued supplier? How do we become more externally focused? What is my division's competitive advantage? What is my competitive vulnerability?

'We decided to try a pilot programme. We selected six division managers to develop prototype scorecards for their operations. Each division had to perform a strategic analysis to identify its sources of competitive advantage. The 15 to

▶

20 measures in the balanced scorecard had to be organisation-specific and had to communicate clearly what short-term measures of operating performance were consistent with a long term trajectory of strategic success.

'We definitely wanted the division managers to perform their own strategic analysis and to develop their own measures. That was an essential part of creating a consensus between senior and divisional management on operating objectives. Senior management did, however, place some conditions on the output.'

Source: Kaplan and Norton (1993)

Kaplan and Norton (1996) stress the importance of the link between an organization's strategy and its management control system, and describe the way in which companies use the balanced scorecard as the foundation of an integrated and iterative strategic management system. This strategic management focus is taken further with their introduction of a strategy map:

> A strategy map enables an organization to describe and illustrate, in clear and general language, its objectives, initiatives, and targets; the measures used to assess its performance (such as market share and customer surveys); and the linkages that are the foundation for strategic direction (Kaplan and Norton, 2000, p. 170).

The strategy map embeds the different items on an organization's balanced scorecard into a cause and effect chain, which connects desired outcomes with the drivers of results. (Examples of strategy maps can be found in Kaplan and Norton, 2000, and Cullen *et al.*, 2003.)

When applying the balanced scorecard to a divisional organization it is important to remember that the nature of the linkage between the four perspectives has been the topic of some debate in the academic literature. Otley (1999) reflects on the general assumption that the financial and customer perspectives can be viewed as results measures, whereas the internal business and innovation and learning perspectives can be viewed as a means by which results are obtained. Norreklit (2000) criticizes the view that there is a linear causal link between the different perspectives and offers an alternative view: that the four perspectives are in fact interdependent. Norreklit also suggests that to be successful the balanced scorecard needs to be rooted in employee commitment. This requires the use of a more interactive style (Simons, 1995a), with an ongoing debate on performance measures serving as an important driver of strategy formation and implementation. Therefore careful attention has to be paid to the process of implementation and to understanding the relationship between the different perspectives.

Brief mention should be made of other models of performance measurement that take a much broader and longer-term perspective. These include the European Foundation for Quality Management excellence model (EFQM, 1999) and the service profit chain (Heskett *et al.*, 1997). Both of these share characteristics with the balanced scorecard approach and may in fact be used in combination with that approach. The stated aim of the EFQM model is to help organizations to be successful by measuring whether they are on the path to excellence, helping them to understand the gaps in their performance, and stimulating solutions. The model is based on the premise that excellent results in respect of performance, customers, people and society are achieved by leader driving policy and strategy, people, partnership and resources, and processes.

The service profit chain model identifies a series of causal relationships that result in profits and growth; that is, there is a direct and strong relationship between profit, growth, customer loyalty, customer satisfaction, the value of goods and services delivered to customers, service quality and productivity, and employee capability, satisfaction and loyalty. Silvestro and Cross (2000) have explored the use of the service profit chain at stores in a UK supermarket chain. Whilst their empirical evidence supports the general notion of the service profit chain, they suggest that the basic model is too simplistic and further work is required to increase its sophistication.

Finally, there is widespread use of similar models of performance measurement in the public sector. The UK government seems to view performance measurement as a key tool in its effort to modernize the National Health Service and has linked performance and incentives. For example funds provided through the Modernisation Agency and the awarding foundation status are both linked to performance. In local government, the concept of best value has been developed by the introduction of comprehensive performance assessment and associated balanced scorecard approaches to incorporate various stakeholders' views. Performance measurement tools are being used at different levels of the public sector in a way that mimics their use in divisionalized commercial organizations. Needless to say there has been a heated debate on the suitability of such measures in the public sector. However we shall not consider this here. Rather we shall look further at the link between performance measures and the strategy being followed by organizations.

Strategic analysis

As mentioned earlier in this chapter, the work of Williamson (1970, 1975) is based on the premise that central managers take strategic decisions, whilst divisional managers attend to operational decisions. We shall now look at a range of studies that challenge this assumption. The main thrust of these studies is the need for the divisional performance measurement system to accommodate the fact that many divisional managers are responsible for the development of their own business strategy. Business strategy refers to the way in which a company competes in a given business and positions itself among its competitors (Simons, 1990). This contrasts with corporate strategy, which is concerned with determining which business(es) to compete in and the most effective way of allocating scarce resources among business units (ibid.).

Kaplan and Norton (1992, 1993, 1996b, 2000) highlight the need to link the performance measurement system to the key elements of the organizational strategy. They point out that different divisions in organizations may follow different strategies, and therefore the items in the balanced scorecard must reflect these differences. Hall (1978) has described how General Electric, recognizing the need to differentiate between divisions, introduced the concept of strategic business units (SBUs). SBU planning is based on the following principles (ibid., p. 394):

- The diversified firm should be managed as a portfolio of businesses, with each business unit serving a clearly defined product market and having a clearly defined strategy.
- Each business unit should develop a strategy that is tailored to its capabilities and competitive needs, but consistent with the organization's overall capabilities and needs.

Four steps are taken when operationalizing SBUs (ibid., p. 396):

- Identification of strategic business elements, or units.
- Strategic analysis of these units to ascertain their competitive position and long-term product market attractiveness.
- Strategic management of these units, given their overall positioning.
- Strategic follow-up and reappraisal of SBU and corporate performance.

Using the concept of strategy as a position, Hall emphasizes the need for different performance measurement and appraisal systems for business units holding positions in the different strategic classifications of dogs, question marks, stars and cash cows. He suggests that organizations have generally failed to develop the managerial control aspects of the process. According to him it is illogical to go through the process of SBU analysis and then continue to measure and reward SBU management against a profit target:

> Most firms have gone only half way with the SBU concept – they position the product market segments and then go right on rewarding and promoting managers on traditional criteria. In the end the companies which make the SBU concept work will be those which change all management systems; developing and rewarding SBU managers differentially depending on their SBU position and the strategic handling which is appropriate for their element of the portfolio (ibid., p. 402).

This link between strategy and control systems formed the basis of further work by Govindarajan and Gupta (1985) and Simons (1987b). Govindarajan and Gupta (1985) examined the link between strategy, incentive bonus systems and effectiveness at the SBU level in diversified firms. The results of the study can be summarized as follows: (1) greater attention should be paid to long-term gains (for example in respect of product development, market development, personnel development, political/public affairs) and the use of subjective (non-formulaic) approaches when determining an SBU general manager's contribution to effectiveness; and (2) the relationship between the extent of the bonus system's reliance on short-term criteria and SBU effectiveness is effectively independent of SBU strategy. Govindarajan and Gupta provide empirical support for the idea that, in terms of SBU effectiveness, the utility of any incentive bonus scheme to influence an SBU general manager's behaviour is contingent on the strategy of the focal SBU.

Simons (1987b) carried out an empirical study of the relationship between business strategy and accounting-based control systems. Building on Miles and Snow's (1978) typology for identifying generic strategies (prospector, defender, analyzer), Simons studied firms classified as either prospectors or defenders to determine whether management control systems differed between the two groups. He found that successful prospector firms seemed to attach a great deal of importance to the use of forecast data, set tight budget goals and monitored outputs carefully. In prospector firms cost control was reduced. Large prospector firms emphasized frequent reporting and the use of uniform control systems, which were modified when necessary. Defenders, particularly large firms, appeared to use their management control systems less intensively. In fact negative correlations were noted between profit performance and factors such as tight budget goals and performance monitoring. Defenders emphasized bonuses for the achievement of budget targets and tended to make few changes to their control systems.

Goold and Campbell (1987a, 1987b) took this a stage further by carrying out a major empirical study of the management of diversification in 16 large UK companies:

> For senior managers at the corporate headquarters of most large companies, diversity is a fact of life. The portfolio of these companies frequently includes businesses from several industries, at different stages of maturity, with different growth option and different financial performance. Understanding and controlling each of the businesses in a portfolio of this sort is a severe test of corporate management (Goold and Campbell, 1987a, p. 42).

Goold and Campbell identify three main central management styles (strategic planning, strategic control and financial control) and three main philosophies for constructing and managing a diverse portfolio (core business, diverse business and manageable business). A brief description of the different philosophies and management styles is provided in Box 9.3.

BOX 9.3

PHILOSOPHIES

Core business

Company commits itself to a few industries and sets out to win big in those industries.

Manageable business

The emphasis is on selecting businesses for the portfolio which can be effectively managed using short-term financial controls. There may be extensive diversity in terms of industries, but there is homogeneity in the nature of the businesses.

Diverse business

The emphasis is on diversity rather than focus. The centre seeks to build a portfolio that spreads risk across industries and geographic areas, as well as ensuring that the portfolio is balanced in terms of growth, profitability and cash flow.

CENTRAL MANAGEMENT STYLE

Strategic planning

Corporate management in Strategic Planning companies believe that the centre should participate in and influence the development of business unit strategies. Their influence takes two forms: establishing a planning process,

▶

and contributing to strategic thinking. In general they place less emphasis on financial controls.

Financial control

Financial Control companies focus on annual profit targets. There are no long-term planning systems and no strategy documents. The centre limits its role to approving investments and budgets, and monitoring performance. Targets are expected to be stretching, and once they are agreed they become part of a contract between the business unit and the centre. Failure to deliver the promised figures can result in management changes.

Strategic control

The centre of Strategic Control companies is concerned with the plans of its business units but it believes in autonomy for business unit managers. Plans are reviewed in a formal planning process with the objective being to upgrade the quality of the thinking. However the centre does not want to advocate strategies or interfere with the major decisions. Control is maintained by the use of financial targets and strategic objectives.

Source: Goold and Campbell (1987b), p. 27

An important finding by Goold and Campbell is that companies tend to employ a uniform style across most of their businesses, and that changes in style rarely occur. Companies with a core business philosophy tend to adopt a strategic planning style, those with a manageable business philosophy adopt a financial control style, and those with a diverse business philosophy use a strategic control style. This relationship is shown in Table 9.2. Comparing this with the Scott (1971) matrix (see Table 9.1), Goold and Campbell discuss specific control issues in stages 3 and 4 in more depth by considering the different management philosophies and styles associated with these stages.

Of particular interest to us is the degree of responsibility given to business unit managers. This can be linked to the concept of strategic business units discussed above (Hall, 1978). Primary responsibility for proposing strategy and achieving results lies with the business unit manager and not with central management. Companies in this situation delegate strategic responsibility to ensure that strategies are based on detailed knowledge of specific product markets, to increase the units' 'ownership' of strategy, and to reduce the over-load on the chief executive and senior management. Goold (1991) agrees

Table 9.2   Management of a diverse portfolio

	Philosophies		
	Core business	Manageable businesses	Diverse businesses
Diversity across industries	Low	Very high	High
Diversity across types of business	Fairly low	Low	High
Style at centre	Strategic planning	Financial control	Strategic control
How mismatches are avoided	Core business mainly responsive to strategic planning	Portfolio selection and retention of 'manageable' businesses	Structure into homogeneous groups
Growth	Mainly organic	Mainly acquisition	Organic and acquisition
Drawbacks	Limited industry diversity, maturation of core businesses, non-core businesses	Limits to acquisition-based growth, vulnerable to aggressive competition, does not build	Low key centre, limited central added value, cultural complexity

Source: Goold and Campbell (1987a), p. 50.

with these objectives but emphasizes that such delegation can only work if two basic conditions are met:

■ The centre must monitor whether the business unit is on track with its strategy. Unless the centre knows when to intervene, delegation amounts to abdication of responsibility.

■ The managers of business units must know what is counted as good performance by the centre. Without clear goals, the whole concept of decentralized responsibility suffers, since the conditions under which managers can operate free from central intervention are ill defined (ibid., p. 69).

In companies with a strategic control style the formal strategic control process typically consists of the following stages (ibid.):

■ Periodic strategy reviews of each business: the businesses propose a number of strategic objectives or milestones and negotiate with the centre until agreement is reached. These objectives are non-financial indicators of underlying competitive position, and provide a longer-term, more strategic focus to financial objectives.

- Annual operating plans: explicit non-financial objectives derived from the strategic plan are often included with the financial objectives in annual operating plans.
- Formal monitoring of strategic results: some companies combine this with monitoring of the budget or operating plan, in others it is a separate process.
- Personal rewards and central intervention: explicit strategic objectives are built into personal reward schemes and complement financial performance in guiding central intervention. Most companies avoid a formula-based link between the achievement of strategic objectives and personal rewards, and prefer a more direct and flexible link.

The last two of these points can be related to the work of Simons (1990, p. 136), who introduces the idea of interactive management control as opposed to programmed control:

> Management controls become interactive when business managers use planning and control procedures to actively monitor and intervene in on-going decision activities of subordinates. Since this intervention provides an opportunity for top management to debate and challenge underlying data, assumptions and action plans, interactive management controls demand regular attention from operating subordinates at all levels of the company. Programmed controls, by contrast, rely heavily on staff specialists in preparing and interpreting information. Data are transmitted through formal reporting procedures and operating managers are involved infrequently and on an exception basis.

Simons focuses on business strategy and the way in which top managers use interactive control systems, including performance measures, to monitor the progress of a business unit towards its business goals. He argues that top managers make selected control systems interactive in order personally to monitor the strategic uncertainties that they believe are crucial to achieving the organization's goals. He also suggests, in a similar way to Goold (1991), that the use of interactive control systems can be linked to the use of subjective reward systems that are not formula based. For instance, one company in Simons' study had a reward system based on effort. As a result of the debate on the interactive management control process, new strategies and tactics have emerged over time. Simons shows how management control systems are important not only for strategy implementation but also for strategy formulation, while Mintzberg, (1978) discusses how interactive control systems can be used to manage emergent strategy. Similar points are considered by Dent (1990), who demonstrates how embryonic management notions can become manifest through new systems of planning, accountability and performance measurement. These can in turn provide the necessary conditions for organizational reform and the emergence of new strategies.

In a further development of his ideas, Simons (1995a) talks about levers of control. In this regard he refers to interactive control systems and diagnostic control systems. The latter are in fact just another name for programmed control systems. What is interesting is the way in which he introduces the idea of belief systems (organizational culture) into his levers of control. The levers of control are as follows:

- Belief systems: used to inspire and direct the search for new opportunities.
- Boundary systems: used to set limits on opportunity-seeking behaviour.
- Diagnostic control systems: used to motivate, monitor and reward achievement of specified goals.
- Interactive control systems: used to stimulate organizational learning and the emergence of new ideas and strategies.

Simons suggests that the levers work in opposite ways to ensure effective strategy implementation and development. Two of the levers (belief systems and interactive control systems) create positive and inspirational forces. The other two (boundary systems and diagnostic control systems) create constraints and ensure compliance with orders. According to Simons, effective top managers use the levers to inspire commitment to the organizations purposes, stake out the territory for experimentation and competition, coordinate and monitor the execution of current strategies, and stimulate and guide the search for future strategies. An interesting question is the extent to which these levers permeate through the organization to management at the divisional level.

Finally, we shall look at more recent developments. In their ongoing work on corporate parenting styles, Goold and Campbell (1998) suggest that business unit boundaries and corporate reporting structures can have a major impact on both value creation and value destruction. They argue that any decisions on business unit definitions and corporate structures should rest on potential value creation and not be determined by history, ambition or politics. Nilsson (2000) explored the issue of parenting style, value creation and management control in a study of four corporate groups based in Sweden. Nilsson found strong evidence that the groups in the study were attempting 'to develop philosophies of control which allow simultaneous co-ordination and situational adaptation of the management control systems at both corporate and business-unit levels' (ibid., p. 110). Interestingly, Nilsson suggests that this may be due to a particular leadership culture in Swedish firms that encourages far-reaching decentralization in which management by objectives plays a central role.

In an extension of their work on corporate parenting, Goold and Campbell (2003) consider the development of new organizational forms such as structured networks. They view structured networks as embracing both the benefits of focus and autonomy associated with SBU-based structures, and the benefits of interdependence traditionally associated with matrix-based organizations, the inference being that the potential 'silo' effect of traditional SBUs is replaced by influences from other parts of the organization. Different types of parenting (minimum corporate parenting; value-added parenting, shared services – Goold and Campbell, 2002) require different approaches to management control.

Divisional performance measurement in practice

Any empirical consideration of the use of different performance measures for divisions in an organization must take account of performance measures operating at the organizational (company) level. Cooper *et al.* (2001) have studied the use of value-based management (VBM) and stakeholder value management approaches against a backdrop of traditional measures of company performance. The study was of 74 large, UK-based companies in a broad range of industries.

The researchers attempted to classify the companies into three categories: (1) those following traditional accounting approaches to performance management, (2) those following the techniques of VBM, and (3) those following stakeholder management approaches. However this proved problematic 'as the majority did not fit neatly into any [of the] three classifications' (ibid., p. 10), with none of the firms exclusively adopting the VBM or stakeholder approach and all retaining traditional measures of performance. The authors see this as an 'evolutionary' aspect of performance management. Regardless of their emphasis, all the organizations recognized the importance of shareholders, employees and customers as stakeholders and thus may have implicitly been using a balanced scorecard approach. However traditional accounting-based measures remained dominant in performance management and measurement.

Corporate performance measures are not the only relevant ones to consider. It is essential for any divisional performance measurement systems to be seen in the context of these corporate performance measures. In addition all performance measures must reflect the objectives of the division and its degree of autonomy or interdependence.

Malmi and Ikäheimo (2003) studied the application of VBM in six Finnish companies. All the organizations were fairly large and divisionalized. In some VBM was applied at the group level, while in others it was applied to one of the divisions. In three of the companies EVA® was calculated at the group and divisional levels, but not at the business unit level. One of the companies combined EVA® with the balanced scorecard and planned to use both financial and non-financial indicators to back this strategy. Interestingly the chief financial officer of this company thought that VBM was of little value unless it was linked to operations through a balanced scorecard. The two other companies also calculated EVA® for their business units. Malmi and Ikäheimo (2003) conclude that in some of the companies the use of VBM had an impact on measurement at almost all levels, whereas in others only the highest level had been affected by the VBM measures.

Finally, Minchington and Francis (2000) looked at divisional performance measures in a questionnaire-based study of 258 companies in a cross-section of UK industries. They found that for the majority of divisions profit was the principal objective and traditional accounting performance measures were still dominant (Table 9.3). Seventy-two per cent of the companies had introduced performance-related pay linked to financial measures. Interestingly they found a low awareness of the EVA® and balanced scorecard approaches. Major criticisms of the newer measurement concepts, including EVA®, shareholder value analysis and the balanced scorecard, were the complications caused by their adoption and the fact that non-financial managers found it difficult to understand them. EVA® was considered to be an effective measure for top management but of limited use at the divisional level.

Only 15 per cent of the respondents calculated divisional costs of capital and very few calculated division-specific costs. The application of a company-wide cost of capital to all divisions limited the application of measures such

Table 9.3 Divisional objectives and performance measures (per cent)

	Correctly used	Being considered	Not being considered	Not aware of
Ability to stay within budget	99	1	0	0
Balanced scorecard approach	24	21	29	26
Economic value added (EVA®)	10	18	46	26
Residual income	6	2	56	36
Return on capital employed	71	6	18	5
Shareholder value analysis	15	13	53	19
Target cash flow	70	7	17	6
Target profit	94	3	2	1
Value drivers	28	18	35	19

Source: Minchington and Francis (2000), p. 104.

as residual income and EVA®. The current and replacement cost of asset values was only calculated by 4 per cent of the respondents, again limiting the use of more recent performance measurement techniques. However, the balanced scorecard was growing in popularity as a divisional performance measurement tool, as were value-based measurement systems. It may be that the 'evolutionary' aspect of company performance noted by Cooper *et al.* (2001) is also present at the divisional level.

Conclusion

This chapter has pointed out that management control and performance measurement systems, particularly in respect of combining financial and non-financial measures in the strategic control process, need to be understood in their organizational context. Control and performance measurement in divisionalized companies is highly complex, and the linkages between strategy, structure and organizational content are nowhere near as clear as Williamson's (1970, 1975) model suggests.

Our review of the literature has revealed only limited use of the recent value-based measures of performance. Whilst the more balanced approaches are growing in popularity, the emphasis remains on the more traditional accounting measures of performance, despite studies stretching back over half a century highlighting the problems with such measures.

Discussion questions

1. Critically discuss the use of financial measures of performance to measure divisional performance.
2. Discuss the view (Simons, 1995) that performance measures are an important part of strategy formation as well as strategy implementation.

Strategy and control   **10**

Alan F. Coad

Introduction

During the last 40 years the study of management has been dominated by two concepts: strategy and control. Much of the resulting literature has been tele-ological. Strategy is often described as top management's definition of what an organization should be doing. Control is then achieved by means of cyber-netics, through goal-related feedback and adjustment. However there is another body of literature, more recent and rooted in a more empirical research tradition, that regards strategy and control as something other than the creation of top management. According to this perspective, organizations and their environments are made up of a variety of stakeholders attempting to satisfy their wants amidst a host of conflicts and constraints. Strategy in this light is not the sole prerogative of top management, but rather the outcome of complex social, political and learning processes.

This chapter explores how the relationship between strategy and control has evolved in management literature since the 1960s. Initially it examines the question 'What is strategy?', suggesting it is a multifaceted concept with subtle layers of meaning. The remainder of the chapter is organized by divid-ing the literature into three distinct periods of time. The period from the 1960s to the mid 1970s is described as the era of grand design and systematic planning, the years from the mid 1970s to the end of the 1980s are depicted as the era of strategic positioning, and the period from the 1990s onwards is termed the era of complexity. Such a division is a contrivance to lend struc-ture to a relatively short chapter. Inevitably there are no clear divisions between these periods; the research traditions overlap and have many complementary features. We have also had to be selective in our exploration. So no claim is made of comprehensive coverage of all perspectives.

Nevertheless it is hoped that the chapter provides an effective introduction to how our understanding of the relationship between strategy and control has evolved in recent decades.

What is strategy?

Today it seems unremarkable when groups as diverse as business leaders, trade unionists, public sector workers and elected politicians litter their speech with the words 'strategy' or 'strategic'. Their intention is usually to convey the importance of their ideas and to suggest a sense of elevated aims, coherent thinking and careful planning. But such everyday use of these terms is a relatively recent phenomenon, stemming largely from the acutely competitive *zeitgeist* of the 1980s. Those who espoused the political spirit of neoliberal economics were more than happy to borrow concepts and vocabulary from the then emerging discipline of strategic management, and the now commonplace use of the words strategy and strategic masks their sometimes subtle layers of meaning.

The word strategy is derived from the Greek *strategia*, meaning the art of the general. The translation of the term in the business vocabulary drew heavily on the military and competitive sources of the word, such that strategy came to be seen as 'something an organization needs or uses in order to win, or establish its legitimacy in a world of competitive rivalry . . . strategy is what makes a firm unique, a winner, or a survivor' (Thomas, 1993, p. 3). But published definitions of the term vary, with each writer adding his or her own ideas and emphasis. For some, strategy refers to a plan, the end product of strategy formulation (Newman and Logan, 1971). Some include objectives as part of the strategy (Andrews, 1971; Quinn, 1980) whilst others see objectives as what the strategy is to achieve (Ackoff, 1974). Many mention the allocation of resources as a critical aspect of strategy (Hofer and Schendel, 1978). Some prescribe a review of the market and specifically mention competitive position (Porter, 1985). To complicate matters further, some writers suggest that strategy is derived from a formal logic, explicitly stated, that links together the activities of business (Ansoff, 1979), while others indicate that a strategy can emerge from a set of decisions and need not be explicitly stated (Mintzberg and Waters, 1985). More recently the development of core competences (Pralahad and Hamel, 1990) and the importance of learning in organizations (Senge, 1990) have been stressed as key components of strategy. Still others have applied linguistic theory to suggest strategy is essentially a discourse enabling those in organizations who accept its key constructs to enjoy the benefits of power arising from hierarchical status and perceived expertise (Knights and Morgan, 1991).

Clearly the word strategy is used in many different ways. However within this diversity there are two major themes that help us get to grips with this slippery concept. First, there is the idea of strategy as a position. This notion involves identifying where an organization locates itself in its environment. By this definition, strategy is the mediating force, or 'match' (Hofer and Schendel, 1978), between the internal and external context. In ecological terms, strategy is an environmental niche; in economic terms, a place that generates rent; in management terms, a product-market domain, the place in the environment where resources are concentrated. Strategy by this definition is a version of positional analysis, concerned with the status of an organization relative to competition and other aspects of its environment, such as customers, suppliers, investors, and the governments of the countries within which it operates. A feature of this concept of strategy is that all organizations can be said to have a strategy. Thus while the match between an organization's resources and its environment may or may not be explicitly developed, and while it may or may not be a good match, the characteristics of this match can be described for all organizations (ibid.).

The second major theme is the idea of strategy as a process. Chandler (1962), Ansoff (1965) and Andrews (1971) were among the first to propose a distinction between the process of strategy and its content. This distinction has tended to divide researchers ever since. Strategy process research has been concerned with how strategy is formed and implemented, while what is being decided has been claimed as the province of position-oriented research. The questions of who is involved in strategy and why strategy arises have been addressed by both groups, but in different ways. The business unit, the company and populations of organizations have been the focus of position research, whereas process research is largely preoccupied with individuals and groups within organizations. The question 'why' has been seen primarily as one of economic performance by position researchers, whereas process researchers have looked to logical, political, cognitive and institutional rationales.

However this distinction between process and position research has left both streams theoretically weakened. Most scholars would agree that the content of a strategy is likely to be affected by the processes whereby a strategy is developed and implemented. Also, it is possible that these processes are affected by the content and outcomes of previous strategic decisions. For example close examination of positioning strategies (for example Miles and Snow's (1978) prospectors, analyzers, defenders and reactors) infers a variety of organizational processes. Moreover many of the prescriptions for the processes of strategy (for example Andrews' (1971) search of the environment to identify opportunities that could be exploited by company strengths) imply a search for environmental niches, that is, positions.

This overlapping of two key themes in the strategy literature is accommodated by Stacey's (1996) model of the strategy concept. He emphasizes the importance of thinking of strategy as a game people play. This overcomes a tendency to depersonalize strategy. Much of the strategy literature infers an objective reality in which the organization moves in response to changes in the environment (Glaister and Thwaites, 1993). Unconsciously we begin to see strategy in mechanical terms where one thing moves in predetermined ways in relation to another thing. This oversimplifies strategic management because organizations and their environments are not things but groupings of people interacting with one another. By focusing on strategy as a game, we remind ourselves to examine the moves, countermoves and further responses by inter- and intraorganizational players that are the dynamics governing success or failure.

Stacey's model of the gaming process is shown in Figure 10.1. Starting at the left-hand side, people in the environment of organization A do something that is discovered by people within that organization. The latter choose how to respond and then act upon that choice. Their actions then have consequences for people in the environment, for example competitors, customers, suppliers, distributors and legislators, who choose how to respond to the actions of the people in organization A. And so the game goes on. People both within and outside the organization interact through a series of feedback loops, resulting in discovery, decisions and action that control and develop their organization.

Figure 10.1 shows that we can look back in time from the present (*to*), and if we are able to perceive a pattern in past actions we call this pattern the past strategy of the organization. Similarly if we are able to look forward (to *tf*) we may discern a pattern, or strategy, in our expectations of future actions. For Stacey, then, strategy is a perceived pattern in actions past or yet to come. The emphasis on perceptions is important because strategy does not have an objective reality independent of the observer: we cannot touch or feel a strategy. Strategy is a label that people apply to patterns in action. Moreover different people might apply different labels, focusing on different attributes of the unfolding action. This leads us to the concept of multiple realities, whereby different organizational actors perceive the patterns of the strategy game in different ways, which may lead to different prescriptions of how to act in the future. The remainder of this chapter focuses on the ways in which organizational actors make sense of their environment, and how this contributes to the development of strategy and control in organizations. As indicated earlier, different researchers have deployed very different methodologies when exploring these phenomena, and in the sections that follow, developments in the strategy literature are divided into three main periods of time.

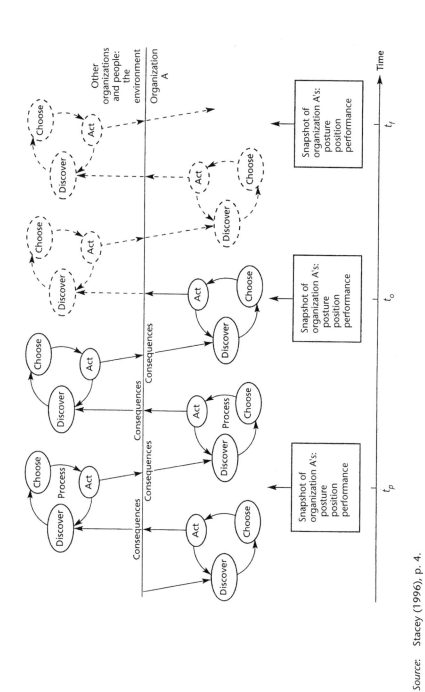

Source: Stacey (1996), p. 4.

Figure 10.1 The strategy concept

The 1960s to the mid 1970s: the era of grand design and systematic planning

Much of the early literature on strategic management conceived the strategy process as a grand design by top management and systematic planning and control throughout an organization. Early influences can be found in the work of Selznick (1957), who introduced the notion of distinctive competence, argued the need to match an organization's internal state with its environmental expectations and discussed the role of building policy into an organization's social structure as a basis for change and the implementation of strategy. But the real impetus for these perspectives came from the works by Ansoff (1965) and Learned et al. (1965). In respect of Stacey's (1996) three elements of the strategy process – discovery, choice and action – grand design and systematic planning perspectives prescribe a discovery phase comprising a comprehensive appraisal of an organization's strengths and weaknesses, its environmental threats and opportunities, together with a recognition of the values and expectations of influential stakeholders (usually assumed to be top management).

This knowledge is usually summarized in the form of a position statement (such as a SWOT analysis), which gives an indication of where current strategies are likely to lead the organization in the future. If a gap exists between predicted performance and managerial expectations, the gap should be closed by selecting appropriate strategies. The 'choice' phase, then, comprises the identification of possible strategies and their evaluation according to a favoured set of criteria. The criteria prescribed for assessing strategies are often summarized under classifications such as tests of 'fit' with environmental opportunities and threats, feasibility in respect of the resource capability of the focal organization, and acceptability to influential stakeholders. Together these stages of discovery and choice are referred to as strategy formulation. Lastly, the action phase involves formal implementation of chosen strategies by designing an appropriate organizational structure, adopting a management style that will influence the organizational culture in a way regarded as instrumental by top management, and establishing appropriate control systems to check that actions align with managerial expectations.

It must be acknowledged that this description is a simplification of early thinking in this tradition. However it presents a picture that has tended to dominate the subject of strategic management, and will be familiar to readers of popular textbooks on the subject (see Dess and Miller, 1997; Johnson and Scholes, 2003). Furthermore it should be emphasized that the grand design and systematic planning perspectives do not comprise a monolithic, uniform body of explanation and prescription. On the contrary, they comprise a number of approaches that appear to be very different. For example some writers (such as Andrews, 1971) regard strategy formation as a creative, conscious intellectual process of organizational design, whereas others (such as Ansoff, 1979) regard strategy as the outcome of systematic, formal planning and control. Nevertheless these perspectives have all adopted a teleological view, where organizational order is assumed to have been created by grand design. They also assume that organizations follow particular strategies because that is what the senior managers have decided. Consistent with this belief in the designing influence of top management is the belief that the circular process of discovery, choice and action that is strategic management is a deliberate and intentional one. The validity of these beliefs will be examined in subsequent sections. For now we shall concentrate on what came to be understood as the relationship between strategy and control that emerged alongside the work of these early influences on strategic thinking.

Grand design, systematic planning and control

From the mid 1960s to the mid 1980s the dominant view of the connection between strategy and control was based on the work of R. N. Anthony, who defined management control as 'the process by which managers assure that resources are obtained and used effectively in the accomplishment of the organisation's objectives' (Anthony, 1970, p. 5). This definition distinguished management control from both strategic planning and operational control and led to the development of formal, systematic, organization-wide data-handling systems to facilitate management control (Machin, 1983). This perspective was reinforced by the tendency in the strategy literature conceptually to separate strategy formulation from strategy implementation. Hence strategic planning sets the strategies and management controls check they are being pursued appropriately. Control is effected through negative feedback. The management control system measures the performance of a process and compares it with a standard. If the performance fails to meet the standard, subsequent performance is adjusted to ensure compliance. Therefore, the model is, essentially cybernetic, although only a very simple kind of cybernetics is involved (Lowe and Puxty, 1989).

It was noted in Chapter 2 that Anthony's perspective brought into close alignment the concepts of management control systems and management accounting systems. For him, management control is built around financial information on revenues, costs and resources. The information covers both planned and actual levels, such as are found in a budget. In addition to financial information, the system may include data on the volume of resources and number of personnel, as well as the quantity and quality of output. Plans are presented and approved on certain dates each year. Reports on actual outcomes are submitted, reviewed and evaluated in a prearranged sequence. Overall the management control process is depicted as an integrated one, encompassing programming, budgeting, reporting, analysis and corrective action.

Disquiet with the Anthony model

Despite its plausibility and widespread acceptance, Anthony's model of management control has a number of serious limitations. Some of these have been referred to in Chapter 2. Here, it is worth emphasizing that a number of limitations came to be recognized in the strategy literature during the 1980s and led to a variety of prescriptions in the rational-comprehensive tradition that came to be labelled 'strategic control'. In particular, Anthony's model stresses financial objectives and, via the budgetary control system, usually concentrates only on the coming 12 months. It pays little explicit attention to longer-term goals and objectives. Moreover by virtually ignoring issues such as organizations' environments and their positioning relative to other entities, it fails to accommodate constructs that are fundamental to the concepts of strategy and control. Furthermore it plays down the potential of management control systems to influence strategy formation and draws unnecessarily restrictive boundaries around concepts such as management control and strategic planning.

Prescriptions for strategic control

The prescriptions for strategic control systems that emerged in the strategy literature during the 1980s broadly fall into two categories. First, there are those elements of the system which are concerned with ensuring that the firm's strategy is on track. These may be referred to as implementation controls. Second, there are recommendations for systematic approaches to checking that the present strategy remains relevant in changing circumstances. This is the role of strategic control systems, which enable top management to respond to unforeseen external and internal developments with changes in strategy. These may be referred to as relevance controls.

Strategy implementation control is concerned with whether or not a firm's strategy is being implemented as planned. By analogy with budgetary control systems, this requires that objectives be established and performance measured against the objectives to assess whether strategy is going according to plan. However there is a fundamental problem here, in that strategic objectives tend to be relatively long term. Hrebiniak and Joyce (1986) point to a tendency for managers to focus more on short-term than on long-term objectives. Controls set against objectives that are several years ahead will not be as influential as controls set against this year's targets. Therefore they suggest that strategic control systems should specify short-term goals (milestones) that need to be achieved in order for the strategy to be implemented in the long term. The strategic milestones are not targets in themselves, but rather are things that are realized on the way (for example the completion of a new call centre overseas).

Relevance controls are concerned with a much broader question: should the firm's overall strategy be changed in the light of unfolding events and trends? Hurst (1982) reasons that there are differences between strategic control systems and budgetary control. Strategic control requires more data from more sources, particularly external sources, and may be concerned with competitive benchmarks and non-financial measures, as well as with long-term outcomes. Strategic control may therefore be less precise and less formal than budgetary control, and is concerned more with the accuracy of the premises on which a managerial strategy has been based than with quantitative deviations from a standard. Relevance control requires systematic and continuous strategic surveillance of internal and environmental factors to determine if the assumptions on which a managerial strategy has been based remain valid. It has been argued that control processes such as these provide top management with the information they need to decide when to intervene to adjust strategy (Schreyogg and Steinmann, 1987).

Disquiet with grand design and systematic planning

At the same time as these recommendations for the development of strategic control systems were being made, considerable disquiet was being expressed about the efficacy of formal, systematic corporate planning and control systems. *Business Week* documented the troubles in a cover story: 'After more than a decade of near-dictatorial sway over the future of U.S. corporations, the reign of the strategic planner may be at an end . . . few of the supposedly brilliant strategies concocted by planners were successfully implemented' (*Business Week*, 17 September 1984, p. 62). Indeed Goold and Quinn (1990b) found that very few companies were using formal strategic control measures to monitor strategic progress and ensure the implementation of strategic plans. But at the same time as this disquiet was being expressed, a fresh wind from economics was blowing new life into the subject of strategic management. Dominated by the work of Porter (1980, 1985), it drew on the branch of economics called industrial organization to emphasize a 'positioning' view of strategy.

The mid 1970s to the end of the 1980s: the era of strategic positioning

Advocates of strategic positioning retained the fundamental premises of grand design and planning based on systematic analysis by top management and comprehensive implementation by the organization as a whole. But their views differed in one fundamental respect. Whilst supporters of grand design and systematic planning placed no limits on the number of strategies that were possible in any given situation, supporters of strategic positioning argued that there were few fundamental strategies – key positions in the economic marketplace – that could be so defended against current and future competition as to yield superior profits compared with other companies in a particular industry. So an important object of strategic positioning was to identify the limited number of strategies, referred to as 'generic', that could be used as a basis for analyzing the current strategies of organizations and selecting of appropriate future strategies.

Some of the earliest examples of strategic positioning came from firms of consultants. For example the Boston Consulting Group developed a growth-share matrix, which was used to analyze products or business units according to their market share and the potential for growth in the market, and to recommend generic strategies depending on their position in the matrix (Henderson, 1979). Another approach was to study the profit impact of market strategies (PIMS), developed in 1972 by General Electric in the United States. PIMS studies identified a number of variables – such as market position, perceptions of product quality, and investment intensity – and used them to predict returns on investment, market share and profits (Schoeffler *et al.*, 1974). But the greatest impetus for strategic positioning was provided by Porter (1980, 1985), who introduced a number of concepts that offered a relatively systematic and rigorous foundation for competitor analysis. In summary, Porter argued that strategy formulation should comprise an analysis of the competitive structure of an industry to determine the industry's long-term prospects for profitability, a value chain analysis of a firm to identify its strengths and weaknesses relative to those of others, and the specification of a plan of action to build a sustainable competitive advantage by configuring the value chain in such a way as to position the firm using one of three generic strategies. Porter's three key concepts – five forces analysis of industry struc-ture, the value chain, and generic strategies – are examined below.

Five forces analysis

Porter (1980) reminds us that competition does not arise solely from intense rivalry amongst companies that produce more or less the same product or

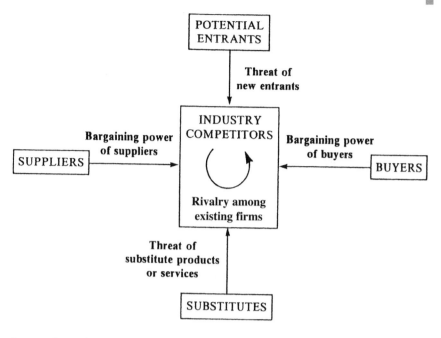

Source: Porter (1980), p. 4.

Figure 10.2   Forces driving industry competition

provide a similar service. Competition also comes from the threat of new entrants into an industry, the threats posed by substitute products, the bargaining power of customers and the bargaining power of suppliers. These five forces are summarized in Figure 10.2.

Five forces analysis is an industry-level analysis to assess the attractiveness of an entire industry relative to that of other industries. Here the term industry refers to a group of companies that produce more or less the same products. New entrants pose a threat because they have the potential to bring extra capacity to the industry, thereby increasing supply and reducing prices. Established firms lose market share and economies of scale, and the resulting impact on volume, costs and prices significantly reduces profits. The threat posed by substitute products is that they limit a firm's ability to charge high prices. When substitutes exist the firm is likely to find that demand is price elastic: if it raises its selling price its customers are likely to switch to the substitute products. In circumstances where customers' bargaining power is strong, industry profitability may be forced down by customers demanding price discounts and high quality. Conversely when suppliers' bargaining power is strong, industry profitability may be reduced by suppliers raising their prices (and therefore industry costs) or reducing the quality of their supplies (and therefore the industry's ability to charge premium prices). The impact of intense rivalry amongst industry competitors is sometimes difficult to predict. Rivalry can be beneficial if promotional activity stimulates demand and the push for efficiency reduces costs. But if demand is stagnant or declining, intense rivalry often reduces profitability because of the increased costs of promotional activity and price competition.

Value chain analysis

Porter (1985) introduced a framework for analyzing a company's activities, with the latter being divided into primary and support activities (Figure 10.3). Primary activities are to do with the flow of the product to the customer, and include inbound logistics (for example receiving, storing and distributing materials), operations (for example the transformation of inputs to the final product), outbound logistics (collecting, storing and distributing the product to the final customer), marketing and sales, and service (post-sale activities that enhance or maintain the value of a product/service, such as installation, repair, warranty, training). Support activities aid the primary activities through procurement (the purchase of inputs used throughout the firm's value chain), technology development (know-how, procedures and scientific development embodied in other activities), human resource management, and firm infrastructure (general management systems for planning, finance and quality control, and links with regulatory bodies).

Value chain analysis is a systematic way of examining the activities of a company and how they interact with each other. The concept of value relates to how consumers view the company's product/service in relation to competitive offerings. The term 'margin' at the right-hand side of Figure 10.3 indicates that profit margins are determined by the difference between what customers are willing to pay for the company's products and the costs incurred as a result of the way in which the value chain is managed. Consistent with his notion of generic strategies, Porter (1985) suggests that a successful organization will have a theme throughout the value chain (for example cost leadership), and that this will be evident in many of its activities. However it is the totality of the value chain that needs to be considered, so Porter emphasizes that the linkages and relationships between the various value activities often determine whether competitive advantage will be achieved. The linkages between value activities and with the value chains of suppliers, distributors and customers often provide distinct cost advantages or become the basis on which an organization's products or services are differentiated from competitive offerings. Moreover these sources of competitive advantage may be sustainable, because although competitors may find it relatively easy to copy individual products

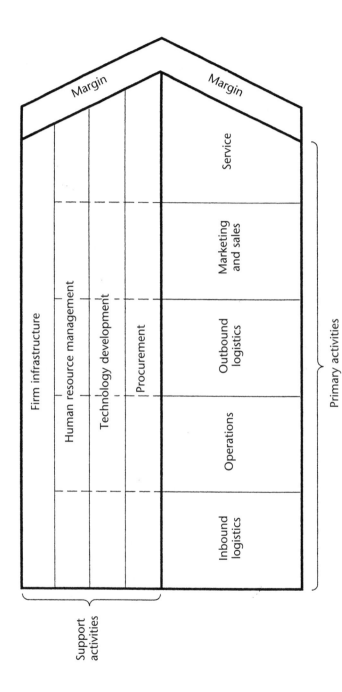

Source: Porter (1985), p. 3.

Figure 10.3 Porter's generic value chain

or activities, it is far more difficult for them to identify, let alone copy, the linkages in a firm's value chain.

Porter's generic strategies

Porter (1985) argues that there are only two ways a firm can achieve competitive advantage, namely low cost or differentiation. These combine with the scope of a particular business (the range of market segments targeted by the company) to produce three generic strategies to achieve above average profits in a particular industry: overall cost leadership, differentiation, and focus. A company with overall cost leadership holds the position of lowest-cost producer in an industry. It obtains competitive advantage and high profits through its ability to sell at lower prices than its competitors. Differentiation strategists make products or services that are unique in terms of attributes that are desirable to customers. The differentiation strategy can be based on variables such as product/service quality, access to distribution channels, financing facilities and after-sales service. Its success depends on attracting sufficient customers who are willing to pay a premium price for the differential characteristics offered. Finally, focus strategists segment the total market and focus on a sector that they can perhaps serve more effectively than their competitors (by means of low cost or differentiation).

Controversially, Porter (1985) argues that firms must have a clear strategy and should avoid the temptation to be all things to all people. For him, firms that attempt all the generic strategies become 'stuck in the middle' and are destined for below average performance.

Strategic positioning and control

The main implications of strategic positioning for control appear to be the regular (re-)analysis of industry structure, value chains and competitive position, and the modification, if necessary, of future plans. But the strategic positioning perspective has also generated some very specific proposals, especially in the accounting literature. For example Simmonds (1981) introduced the idea of strategic management accounting, defined as, 'the provision and analysis of management accounting data about a business and its competitors for use in developing and monitoring the business strategy, particularly relative levels and trends in real costs and prices, volume, market share, cash flow and the proportion demanded of a firm's total resources' (ibid., p. 26). The logic of strategic management accounting is founded on the requirements of business strategists, who need ongoing measurements of changes in strategic position if they are to adjust their actions effectively. Simmonds argues that such strategic indicators are rarely disclosed by conventional accounting, with its emphasis on profit. In fact, when a firm's competitive position has been improved it is often at the cost of current profit because of the costs of competing with other firms. Conversely increased profit may reflect a decline in competitive position as a result of reduced spending on maintaining market share (for example on marketing or R&D). So strategic management accounting views profit not as being largely determined by a firm's internal efficiency, but rather as stemming from the firm's position relative to current and potential competitors. This leads to Simmonds' specification of management accounting systems that emphasize the importance of relative costs, prices, volume of demand and financial standing.

Subsequent publications in the positioning tradition drew directly on the work of Porter (1980, 1985). In particular Shank and Govindarajan (1992, 1993) promoted the use of accounting inputs to value chain analysis under the title 'strategic cost management'. Their prescriptions require identification of a firm's value chain, the assignment of operating costs and asset values to activities, and examination of cost drivers as a basis for developing sustainable competitive advantage. In this analysis, cost leadership is attained by controlling costs (for example by controlling scale, learning and capacity utilization), and reconfiguring the value chain (by developing more efficient ways to design, produce, distribute or market products). Differentiation, on the other hand, calls for a set of supporting tactics that are clearly distinct from those for a cost leadership strategy. Whilst with cost leadership the key to achieving target margins is likely to be effective cost control, the focus of differentiation is more likely to be the firm's ability to command a premium price. So in the pursuit of differentiation, absolute cost minimization may not be an objective. Rather decision makers will be concerned with examining the overall impact on sales of increasing costs such as marketing expenditure, the production of high-quality products or services, and engaging in research and development.

The concept of strategic cost management was further developed by Shank (1989) and Shank and Govindarajan (1992, 1993), who extended the value chain analysis to take account of interdependence between the activities of buyers and suppliers. They argue that if value chain analysis focuses merely on an individual firm, cost analysis begins with the purchase of raw materials and ends with the sale of the finished goods. Hence it ignores the possibility of exploiting linkages with suppliers and customers by overlooking the determinants of purchasing price, the logistics of distribution and the benchmarking of activities and costs throughout the supply chain. In their methodology Shank and Govindarajan assume that the analysis is performed by a firm that looks beyond its boundaries to its buyers and suppliers in the supply chain. However more recent literature has indicated that buyers and suppliers can also perform value chain analysis cooperatively. This requires them to share information on costs, activities and performance in order to find ways of reducing costs or increasing margins for the benefit of the entire supply chain. Inevitably this can cause concern about the exchange of sensitive information, the fair division of costs and benefits, and the appropriation of investments in specific assets (Dekker, 2003).

Continuing disquiet

The influence of strategic positioning on the development of strategic management should not be underestimated. The 1980s witnessed a proliferation of courses, conferences, university faculties, academic journals and consulting firms. After years of general pronouncements about the processes of grand design and systematic planning, strategic positioning added substance to the field by focusing on the content of strategies and opening up its prescriptions to substantial investigation. But alongside the apparent success of strategic management, disquiet about the subject was being expressed in literature rooted in a more empirical research tradition. This literature regarded strategy and control as something other than the creation of top management. It viewed organizations as made up of a variety of stakeholders attempting to satisfy their wants amidst a host of conflicts and constraints. Strategy in this light was not the prerogative of top management, but rather the outcome of organizational struggles. It was what the organization actually did rather than what top management intended it to do. The resulting order was not the creation of an overall designer, rather it emerged from the interactions among organizational actors (Dermer, 1988, 1990; Johnson, 1987; Mintzberg and Waters, 1985). The argument of these authors was that the prescriptions of grand design, systematic planning and strategic positioning were not so much wrong as excessively narrow. Their focus on the economic and quantifiable aspects of strategy making had resulted in exclusion of the cognitive, social and political factors that make up the reality of much of organizational life. The influence of this more empirical research tradition caused strategy researchers to accommodate the earlier prescriptions of design, planning and positioning, alongside other perspectives that addressed some of the complexities of the strategic management process. Some of these issues will be addressed in the next section.

The 1990s onwards: the era of complexity

Learning and strategy

A major strand of the empirical literature depicts strategy making as a process of learning in organizations. In the late 1950s Lindblom (1959) applied the terms 'muddling through' and 'disjointed incrementalism' to the making of decisions in public administration (see also Braybrooke and Lindblom, 1963). He suggested that policy making was a serial, remedial and fragmented process whose purpose was to solve problems rather than address overall objectives or make connections between different decisions. But Lindblom fell short of producing an overall theory of strategy formation. This was left to Quinn (1980), who agreed with Lindlom on the incremental nature of the process but not on its disjointedness. Quinn's work stands in contrast to the rational-analytical approaches favoured by Ansoff (1965), Learned *et al.* (1965) and Porter (1980, 1985). He argued that managers in major enterprises consciously move forward incrementally. For Quinn (1980), business enterprises comprise a number of subsystems with different people and different information needs. Each subsystem observes company-wide issues in a disciplined way, but does so incrementally and opportunistically. As each subsystem has limited knowledge and resources it tends to act incrementally; the organization as a whole also tends to behave in this way. Skilful managers who use this step-by-step approach are not 'muddling through'. Rather they are deliberately using it as an approach to improve the quality of strategic decision making and purposive action.

Whilst we may question the applicability of Quinn's notion of logical incrementalism to all organizations in all circumstances, it did introduce the importance of learning to the strategy literature. The later work of Prahalad and Hamel (1990) continued the theme of 'learning' and became particularly influential during the 1990s. They believe that a company's competitive advantage is derived from deeply rooted abilities, termed 'core competencies'. These allow the firm to diversify into new markets by reapplying and reconfiguring what it does best. Moreover, because these competences are hidden they cannot easily be imitated. Hence the secret of success lies not with great products but with the unique set of abilities that allow a firm to create great products. According to Prahalad and Hamel (1990) core competences are the outcome of the collective learning of an organization, especially in terms of how to coordinate diverse production skills and integrate multiple technologies. Thus managers are encouraged to view their organization not as a collection of products or business divisions, but rather as a portfolio of resources and capabilities that can be combined in various ways. But even this notion of a learning organization came to be criticized for its emphasis on what is constant and persistent, rather than what is creative and revolutionary.

While the study of strategic management has tended to emphasize control, order and predictability, Stacey (1996) argues that disorder and chaos are intrinsic properties of organizations, and the constant disturbances faced by managers often contain creative opportunities that can be harnessed to produce learning that transcends established strategic thinking. Stacey draws on chaos theory to assert that organizations should be seen as dynamic systems in a permanent state of disequilibrium, and that managers should deliberately inject disturbances as a basis for permanent revolution in their strategic thinking. This view is complemented by that of Hamel (1996, 1997), who argues for a revolutionary approach to strategy in which companies no longer play by established rules of competition but instead seek to change radically the basis of competition in their industry.

Overall, significant variations in the processes of learning are evident in the strategy literature: ranging from incrementalism to chaos and revolution. The emphasis on learning has brought a reality to the study of strategy formation that was missing in the prescriptions for grand design, systematic planning and positioning. Based largely on empirical research, studies in the learning tradition have told us not so much what organizations are supposed to do as what they actually do when faced with complex and dynamic situations. But learning is only one aspect of the complex process of strategy formation. Another is the politics of strategy making, to which we now turn.

Politics and strategy

When considering the politics of strategy formation it is useful to distinguish micro politics from macro politics. The former regards the strategy process as the outcome of bargaining and compromise among conflicting individuals and groups within an organization, while the latter examines how the organization as a whole can promote its own welfare by controlling or cooperating with other organizations.

Studies of micro politics view organizations as coalitions of individuals or interest groups with different values, beliefs, information, interests and perceptions of reality. Since most important decisions involve the allocation of scarce resources, these differences give rise to conflict, and make power the most important resource. In this situation strategies and goals emerge from bargaining, negotiation and jockeying for position among the stakeholders, rather than solely being the outcome of analysis and planning by top management (Bolman and Deal, 1997). Of course conflict has negative aspects. Too much of it can immobilize an organization by diverting the efforts of its members into unproductive activities. Nonetheless if an organization comprises diverse socioeconomic groups the inevitable conflict may bring positive benefits. For example it could energize the organization by countering any tendency for lethargy, staleness and apathetic compliance. It could encourage self-evaluation to challenge established strategic thinking. Consequently it could help stimulate organizational learning by keeping the organization in touch with what is happening in its environment and by being an important source of innovation.

The basic unit of analysis in micro politics is the interest group. Each group is presumed to have its own perspective and rationality, and to operate consistently within that rationality (Dermer and Lucas, 1986).The multirational nature of organizations generates conflict in that the stakeholders compete to control strategy. But there is no presumption of managerial prerogative. Managerial plans do not necessarily determine the contents of the strategic agenda (Dermer, 1990). Strategic concerns can originate anywhere in the organization, and the role of 'change entrepreneur' can be assumed by anyone with the necessary motivation and power; and sources of power are the media through which conflicts of interest are resolved.

While micro politics is concerned with individuals and groups within an organization, macro politics focuses on the interdependence between an organization and its environment. Organizations have to deal with many stakeholder groups, including competitors, buyers, suppliers, unions, investors, regulators and pressure groups. Stakeholder analysis attempts to cope with the messiness of macro politics by means of a rational approach. Freeman (1984) argues that the construction of strategic programmes for stakeholder groups should be based on an analysis of stakeholder behaviour to predict the potential of the group in response to strategic manoeuvring. He suggests four generic strategies: offensive, such as trying to change the stakeholder's objectives; defensive, such as linking the issue to others that the stakeholder views more favourably; maintaining the current position; and changing the rules. In this sense Freeman's approach to macro politics can be interpreted as a rational approach to strategic positioning. But the importance of relations with stakeholder groups may be more fundamental to strategic success than is suggested by Freeman.

In an influential text Kay (1993) combines the stakeholder perspective with that of core competences, to set out the advantages of viewing companies as a type of community. In this perspective resources can be bought as commodities, and therefore cannot be a source of competitive advantage. For Kay the strength of successful companies lies in the network of relationships they have built up with their employees, suppliers and customers. This network delivers distinctive capabilities through the unique organizational knowledge that arises from collaboration and interaction, by establishing a cooperative ethic among the participants, and by establishing those organizational routines which are the repositories of organizational knowledge. The validity of this perspective has been borne out by the rapid rise of cooperative arrangements between organizations during the last two decades.

The term collective strategy is used by Astley and Fombrun (1983) to describe the situation in which strategy formation is the result of a process of collaboration and negotiation between separate organizations acting in partnership. Collective strategies have become increasingly popular because individual organizations do not always have the resources and competences needed to cope with increasingly complex environments. It may be more economically viable to obtain specific materials, skills, technologies, finance or access to markets by cooperating with other organizations than through individual acquisition. A number of collective strategies can be combined to form hybrid arrangements that bridge the extremes between pure forms of market transaction and pure forms of hierarchy (Williamson, 1975, 1985). These range from loose market-like relationships such as networks, to tight contractual relationships such as joint ventures. The appropriateness of each method will depend on such things as the scale of the venture, the risk of assets being appropriated by one or more of the partners, and the degree of trust between the partners (Dekker, 2003).

Institutions and strategy

While the learning and political perspectives tend to emphasise differences and change within and around organizations, another body of theory encourages us to consider the similarities among organizations. Modern institutional theory dates from the work of Meyer and Rowan (1977), who argued that organizations tend to adopt the strategies, structures and practices that are socially expected of them. Such behaviour brings social approval and increases the likelihood that external actors will assist the organization, for example by providing finance, becoming loyal customers or speaking favourably of the organization in public. According to Meyer and Rowan, social pressures that occur at the industry level tend to apply roughly equally to all organizations in the industry. These pressures cause organizations to converge on similar strategies and structures. So instead of the rational actor model of the strategist as a manager who dispassionately analyzes the external world and makes competitive choices, institutional theorists depict actors as collectively acquiescing to the expectations of the institutional setting. This process is known as institutional isomorphism, whereby organizations with similar pressures come to resemble one another in the pursuit of social legitimacy. As Johnson and Greenwood (2002, p. 46) explain:

> Organizations behave in accordance with . . . socially constructed reality because to do so reduces ambiguity and uncertainty. Shared understandings of appropriate practice permit ordered exchanges. Over time, however, these shared understandings, or collective beliefs, become reinforced by regulatory processes involving state agencies and professional bodies, which normatively and/or coercively press conformity upon constituent communities.

Following this logic, institutional theorists argue that the rules of competition within a particular industry are similar for all the constituent organizations. For example firms of solicitors may prefer not to see themselves as a business in a competitive sense, but as offering services of a high professional standard. Similarity is more marked than difference: firms of solicitors offer similar services and build relationships with clients in similar ways. Competitive behaviour is constrained by conventions of acceptable conduct. Not conforming to these expectations is likely to be frowned upon even if competitive advantage could be achieved (ibid.).

Institutional theories also provide explanations for the apparently faddish nature of strategic management. As we have seen, in the 1980s there was a preoccupation with finding suitable positions to compete in the market place in which. This was heavily influenced by the work of Porter (1980, 1985), which emphasized the competitive forces within an industry and adapting a firm's value chain to locate the firm favourably in relation to those forces. In the 1990s, in contrast, the emphasis shifted to the development of core competences upon which competitive advantage could be built.

A further feature of institutional theories is the possible contradiction between social expectations and organizational efficiency. This sometimes causes organizations to decouple the formal structure from actual work practices. That is, they adopt structures and practices that are in keeping with institutionalized expectations but have little effect on the real work of the organization. For example apparently rational accounting control systems may have little impact on the day-to-day operations of an organization, or senior managers may enthusiastically advocate particular strategies without translating their rhetoric into action. Thus organizations may appear to conform to social expectations, but the conformity is ceremonial rather than substantive.

Complexity and control

The inclusion of the learning, political and institutional perspectives in the literature on strategic management allows a more realistic portrayal of the context in which strategic management takes place. It is a complex context in which organizations simultaneously require both stability to implement current strategies via using approaches to control that use planning and monitoring and the institutionalization of effective practices, and instability to encourage innovation via group learning and political modes of decision making. In this context an important role for managements is to use their positions of power to influence the structural arrangements and dynamics of organizations so as to provide an appropriate balance between stable institutionalized practices and the discontinuities of learning and political behaviour.

Scholars are a long way from providing prescriptions for the management of inevitable tensions. The legacy of Burns and Stalker (1961) is an 'either/or' way of thinking about the design of organizations. There is a widely held belief that formal bureaucratic controls are inappropriate for organizations facing a high degree of uncertainty. Changing contexts apparently require more organic practices: coordination is achieved through the use of informal, personal communications rather than rules and standard operating procedures. The implication is that organizations have to choose between designs for order or disorder, for consistency or disturbance, and for continuity or change.

I argue that this dichotomy has been overstated. Katz and Khan (1978) observe that organizations possess both 'maintaining systems', which insulate them from change and uncertainty and perpetuate the *status quo*, and 'adaptive systems', which stimulate innovation and experimentation. An issue that remains largely unaddressed in the literature is whether a balance between these types of system should be achieved by the conscious intervention of senior management, or left to some form of self-organization by the organizational participants.

In this regard we can compare and contrast the approaches to control taken in the 1980s by two large successful organizations, as described in case studies in Bruns and Kaplan (1987). Dent (1987) studied the structure and processes of control systems at Eurocorp, a company that developed, manufactured and distributed a wide range of computing products, while Simons (1987a; see also Simons 1990, 2000) investigated the control processes at Johnson & Johnson, which produced pharmaceutical, cosmetic and health care products. Both of these companies were large, and contingency studies suggest that increased size leads to task specialization, especially when scale economies can be obtained. This in turn creates task interdependence and pressure for the development of bureaucratic planning and control procedures (Mintzberg, 1979). In addition both companies faced considerable environmental uncertainty, which in general tends to produce pressure for decentralized decision making – giving discretion to those with specialized market knowledge – and management through organic arrangements (ibid.).

Superficially, Eurocorp's control system was designed according to traditional principles. Formal planning procedures existed, but they were not continuous activities. With the rapid pace of change in the company's product markets, plans quickly became obsolete. Planning provided corporate direction, but in practice operational coordination was achieved through a complex pattern of spontaneous interactions. Dent (1987) argues that the structure of the control system was significant in supporting this interaction. Responsibility exceeded authority: managers depended on others to achieve their own unit's performance targets. This created tensions in the organization, in that managers had to think beyond their functional tasks and to negotiate with the managers of other units to act on their behalf.

Meanwhile Johnson & Johnson coped with its uncertain environment by formalizing frequent superior–subordinate interaction. Simons (1990) distinguished two types of control process. He uses the term 'interactive control' to describe the situation in which business managers used planning and control procedures to monitor and intervene in decision-making activities. Long-range and financial planning systems were used interactively: superiors were formally involved in ongoing negotiations with subordinates regarding revisions to plans in the light of actual outcomes. This interaction took place in tandem with the second type of control process, which Simons (2000) calls 'diagnostic control'. This was used in areas of the business that were less exposed to uncertainty. Here managers directed their attention primarily to ensuring that predetermined control procedures were established and maintained by designated subordinates, and intervened only if outcomes were not in accordance with predetermined standards.

Obviously the richness of the case studies by Dent and Simons cannot be conveyed in two short paragraphs and the reader is encouraged to refer to their works. Nevertheless we can observe two significantly different ways of coming to terms with some of the issues discussed in this chapter. Both cases demonstrate the paradox of 'fit' and 'split' (Pascale, 1990). At Eurocorp stability, central control and synergies (fit) were encouraged by the annual planning cycle, in which broad competitive issues were examined, resources were allocated and profit consciousness was established through the specification of units' financial objectives. However new perspectives and innovative actions (split) were encouraged by decentralized decision making and overlapping responsibilities, which resulted in informal negotiations between the managers of different units. Hence learning needs were primarily accommodated by horizontal interaction and self-organized political negotiation. In contrast at Johnson & Johnson stable activities were subject to diagnostic controls. But continual re-examination of current strategies was formally designed into the routine and there was frequent interaction between superiors and subordinates, who used the long-term and financial planning systems in a highly interactive manner.

Both approaches encouraged organizational learning and the identification of strategic issues by stakeholders throughout the organization. It may be that to some extent the approaches were substitutable and involved certain trade-offs. Dent (1987) observes that the processes at Eurocorp were inefficient. Lacking formal authority over other units, managers expended a lot of time and effort on persuading others. Sometimes there was suspicion that agreed actions would not be taken. Stress levels were high and frictions emerged. Nevertheless it is far from clear that alternative approaches would have been less costly. For example at Johnson & Johnson interactive controls necessitated continual replanning and frequent communication between superiors and subordinates, which was also very costly.

If such approaches are substitutable, they call into question simple contingency models that infer that mutually exclusive modes of control are appropriate in different circumstances. The case studies describe significantly different ways of dealing with the complexities of strategy formation. On the one hand most large organizations require routines, planning and control systems to be institutionalized in order to provide stability and direction for the organization. On the other hand they require the differences of opinion that create constructive tension and form the basis of dialogue, learning and innovation.

Conclusion

For the past 40 years the management literature has been dominated by the concepts of strategy and control. For much of this time the prevailing view of the relationship between the two was that of Anthony (1965), for whom strategy was the domain of top management and control systems were needed to ensure effective implementation. However in more recent years this view has been criticized as being too optimistic about the possibility of synoptic, rational analysis by top management and the cooperative execution of strategies. A more empirical research tradition has encouraged the inclusion of learning, political and institutional perspectives on the context in which strategic management takes place. In this more realistic approach the role of senior managers moves away from dictating strategic direction towards using their power to establish appropriate structures that institutionalize both stability – in the form of planning and control systems to bring order to the operationalization of current strategies – and instability, to encourage innovation via group learning and political modes of decision making. We are far from being able to prescribe measures to reconcile this tension, so it is in dealing with these contradictory forces that practitioners and academics will face some of their greatest challenges in respect of the relationship between strategy and control.

Discussion questions

1. Management control has been defined as the 'process by which managers assure that resources are obtained and used effectively in the accomplishment of the organisation's objectives' (Anthony, 1965). Discuss.

2. Compare and contrast Anthony's (1965) view of strategy and control with Simons' (1995) 'levers of control'.

3. Discuss how the concept of risk is related to the concepts of strategy and control.

4. Discuss the implications of stakeholder theories for performance measurement in organizations.

5. What is the role of strategic management in the establishment of organizational culture? What insights into this role might we gain from political theories?

6. Neoclassical economics suggests that organizations tend towards an equilibrium size. Discuss the implications of learning in organizations for equilibrium theories.

7. Prevailing theories of corporate governance suggest that the overall objective of economic organizations is the maximization of shareholder wealth. Discuss the implications of stakeholder theories for corporate governance.

11 Culture and control

Tobias Scheytt and Kim Soin

Introduction

Culture is a complex phenomenon. The term has been used in many contexts to describe the essence that binds together diverse groups, including the members of nations, regions, ethnicities, organizations and professions, and even families. However culture is difficult to define. It is 'a tricky concept as it is easily used to cover everything and consequently nothing' (Alvesson, 2002, p. 3). When travelling abroad we can see the differences between a foreign culture and our own, but usually we cannot explain where the differences stem from.

In order to interpret and understand cultures we have to consider the contexts in which they are shaped. To do this we have to 'unlearn' the everyday understanding that culture is defined by the 'pleasures in life', such as books, movies, music, art or 'ways of expressing oneself', for example through fashion, modes of communication or the type of car one drives. Similarly, organizational culture is not defined by artefacts such as logos, website designs, clothing conventions, company anthems or mission statements. Instead these artefacts can be viewed as outcomes or reifications of a specific culture, with its shared traditions, norms, beliefs, values, rules and convictions. Hence artefacts that are often held up as being *the* culture, merely reflect or symbolize a specific (organizational) culture (Smircich, 1983).

Accordingly, systems and practices of control are man-made artefacts that to a certain extent are an expression of a specific organizational culture. Control is a social and organizational practice that takes place in an environment that is culturally predefined. Thus it is important to recognize that control is never culturally neutral, but is influenced by and influences the cultural context in which it is executed. That is why the (often underestimated) cultural specificity of control must be included in theories of management control (Ahrens and Dent, 1998).

This chapter examines the complex interrelationship between culture and control, starting with an account of the conceptualization of culture. This is followed by a discussion of a model of the relationship between control and culture, namely Simons' (1995a, 1995b) 'levers of control' model, with a particular focus on the 'belief systems' lever. The penultimate section develops our understanding of the multifaceted nature of organizational culture, drawing on models by Alvesson and Berg (1992) and Macintosh (1994). That section highlights the existence of subcultures and demonstrates that the general orientation of organizations can result in differing control cultures. The final section offers some conclusions about the relationship between culture and control.

The concept of organizational culture

Culture is not a new phenomenon in the field of organizational research. Indeed in the late 1930s Arnold (1937) emphasized the importance of cultural artefacts for organizations by defining four elements that are common to all organizations: (1) a common creed or set of rituals that integrate the members of the group, (2) a set of attitudes by which the creed becomes effective, (3) a set of individual habits that lead to natural cooperation, and (4) mythological or historical traditions that suggest the creed is transcendental. However the notion of organizational culture was not properly addressed until the late 1970s and 1980s, when the strengthening Japanese economy was perceived as a threat to Western economies, and particularly that of the United States. Practitioner-oriented books such as that by Ouchi (1981) revealed the secrets of the success of Japanese companies: a strong, clan-like and commitment-oriented organizational culture, shaped by the basic rules of Japanese society. Another influential text was that by Peters and Waterman (1982), which drew on empirical studies of high-performing Fortune-500 companies. Based on the finding that successful companies paid considerable attention to the development of their culture, Peters and Waterman identified cultural factors that were crucial to business excellence, thereby fostering a lively debate among researchers on the relationship between culture and performance. However the attempts to link culture directly to performance were shattered by the decline of both the Japanese economy and the companies that had been held up as examples of excellence in the 1990s. Indeed in the ten years that followed more than 50 per cent of the companies highlighted by Peters and Waterman vanished from the Fortune 500 list following mergers, takeovers or economic decline.

Since then discussions on organizational culture have broadened in focus. Culture is no longer seen as the key factor in success, but as a perspective to explain processes in organizations and help members of organizations (for example managers, see Schein, 1985) and researchers (for example Allaire and Firsirotu, 1984; Alvesson, 1994; Smircich, 1983) to understand the multifaceted nature of organizational life. In anthropology (for example Geertz, 1973) and in organization theory (for example Alvesson and Berg 1992; Czarniawska, 1992; Frost *et al.*, 1985; Parker, 2000) culture is often understood as the system of common symbols and meanings collectively ascribed to circumstances. Organizational culture therefore determines the 'process of reality construction that allows people to see and understand particular events, actions, objects, utterances, or situations in distinctive ways' (Morgan, 1988, p. 128). In turn the common history of these processes of reality construction in diverse situations leads to the condensation and validation of ascribed meanings, values and beliefs. Organizational culture therefore provides patterns of interpretation that help the members of a group or association to understand the experienced reality, to explain the common history and to comprehend incidents that happen in the community.

There are two broad ways of conceptualizing organizational culture. First, the organization *has* a culture. Here the 'made' or designed artefacts that symbolize the organization are identified as the organizational culture. They are seen as related to basic assumptions, ideologies and styles of thinking. Nevertheless the artefacts, and therefore the organizational culture, can be formed or changed by deliberate action (for the broader topic of management and organization see Deal and Kennedy, 1982; Peters and Waterman, 1982; for the design of management control systems see Langfield-Smith, 1995; Simons, 1995a, 1995b). Those with the greatest potential to form or shape an organizational culture are the managers or leaders of the organization (Schein, 1985). Contingency approaches to the analysis and design of cultural artefacts are employed to guide the formation of (organizational or control) culture.

Second, the organization *is* a culture. From this perspective, organizations are cultural systems with idiosyncratic rules and processes that are difficult to observe, understand and enact – particularly for someone who is not part of the culture (Czarniawska, 1992). The culture of the organization consists of basic assumptions, ideologies, traditions, styles of thinking and acting that cannot be decontextualized, and therefore cannot be deliberately changed. To understand an organizational culture one has to interpret it within its context, since the functional mechanisms of the culture cannot be understood from outside. Therefore ethnographical and interpretive methods are applied, through which observed phenomena are taken as symbols and representations of the basic cultural roots of the organization (for the broader topic

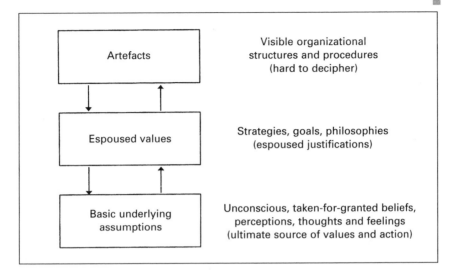

Figure 11.1 Levels of culture

of management and organization see Alvesson and Berg 1992; Parker, 2000; Smircich, 1983; Trice and Beyer, 1993; for management accounting see Ahrens, 1996, 1997; Ahrens and Dent, 1998).

These two conceptualizations may be viewed as different (or opposing) perspectives that in combination allow us comprehensively to interpret organizational and/or control cultures. This relates to the model by Schein (1985), which contrasts the idea that an organization *has* a culture in its man-made, crafted cultural artefacts with the idea that an organization *is* a complex cultural entity (Figure 11.1).

The cultural levers of control

The observation and design of control systems has to take account of the interrelationship between the three levels of culture shown in Figure 11.1. We may conclude that control is – like all types of organizational practice – culturally influenced and one of the observable artefacts in the organization. However what Schein calls the 'basic underlying assumptions' are the main driving forces behind culture, as well as important for the design and employment of control systems.

Simons' (1995a) 'levers of control' comprehensively addresses the various levels of culture in relation to control. It identifies the belief system as one lever of control that is predominantly related to organizational culture. The belief system links core values to business strategy and inspires participants to commit themselves to the organization's purpose. It helps to foster the creative and innovative potential of the organization, empower individuals and encourage them to search for new opportunities. Furthermore it helps to bind this potential to the organization's visions, missions and strategic directions, and motivates individuals to search for new ways of creating value and achieving desired levels of performance.

The belief system is used by managers to 'inspire and direct the search for new opportunities' (Simons, 1995a, p. 7). In general it nurtures the search for new ideas and business opportunities. In relation to strategy formation, these practices are aimed at fostering the development of what Mintzberg (1991) calls 'emergent strategy', that is, the day-to-day creation or identification of opportunities for new businesses, which in turn add to the organization's intended strategy. Managers are able to change or direct the belief system by defining mission statements, visions, credos and so on. Hence the belief system of the organization influences both the intended and the emergent strategy development process and may be summarized as follows:

- The belief system comprises an explicit set of beliefs that define basic values, purposes and direction, including how value is to be created, the desired level of performance and human relationships.
- Its values lies in providing momentum to and guidance on the seeking of opportunities.
- It does so by means of mission statements, vision statements, credos and statements of purpose.
- It is of greatest utility when opportunities expand dramatically, and when top managers are wise enough to change the strategic direction of the organization or energize the workforce.
- It is senior managers who write the substantive drafts and staff groups who facilitate communication, feedback and awareness.

Clearly the belief system is related to and interacts with the culture of the organization and its employment is aimed at espoused values and basic assumptions (Schein, 1985). It can therefore be viewed as a powerful measure to control the behaviour of the members of the organization, rather than just as a simple technical mechanism for management control. Hence, following Simons (1995a), it is clear that managers use the belief system in their efforts to control the business and it is therefore a lever of control in the same way as the diagnostic control system, the boundary systems and the interactive control system.

Although Simons' model suggests that certain aspects of culture exist at the surface and can be influenced by means of rule setting, policy making, governance processes, mission statements and performance measurement systems, it does not discuss three factors that should be considered against the background of an interpretative understanding of organizational culture. First, while the model offers a general conceptualization of how belief systems can be changed, it does not explicitly consider variations in the cultures of different organizations. For instance organizations come in diverse forms (for example small versus large, privately versus publicly owned, profit-oriented versus not-for-profit) and have different belief systems. Second, as organizational culture is, according to Schein's (1985) model, related to basic underlying assumptions, measures to control the belief system tend to scratch the surface of rather than fundamentally change a culture. Third, the practices that Simons (1995a) suggests for using this lever might indirectly influence the basic assumptions underlying the cultural artefacts. For example we know from a substantial body of critical and Foucauldian literature that guidelines, sanctions and punishment for misbehaviour should be viewed as disciplinary measures (see for example Hopwood, 1987; Hoskin and Macve, 1986; Miller 1994; Miller and O'Leary, 1987; Puxty, 1993). The management control system can therefore be used as a subtle means to exert power in an organization. In particular the implementation of the control system, even when overtly directed at improving the information base or the quality of decision making, is influenced by the – mostly concealed – interest of powerful individuals or groups in the organization (Berry *et al.*, 1985; Hopper *et al.*, 1987, Laughlin, 1987; Power and Laughlin, 1992). This can result in changes in the style of communication, forms of cooperation and the identity of organizational members (Alvesson and Willmott, 2002; Munro, 1999; Willmott, 1993).

We argue that these shortcomings of Simons' model are a consequence of his conceptualization of culture. In particular the notion that a lever of control can be used to change an organization does not fully take account of the multifaceted nature of organizational culture. The hypothesis that belief systems are levers implies that the culture of an organization is well known and that there is a fixed set of explicitly defined values and beliefs that can be deliberately changed – thus following the notion that an organization has a culture, rather than being a cultural entity in itself. As the interpretive strand of organization studies tells us, organizational culture is a more intricate phenomenon. It permeates organizational practices and procedures, but is based on concealed factors. What can be directly changed, however, and this is addressed in Simons' model, are the organization's artefacts, procedures and processes, which constitute the explicit part of a specific culture. The implicit aspects of culture that Schein (1985) calls the 'ultimate source of values and action' – for example the world views, patterns of sense making and interpretation embedded in the organization – are not addressed by Simons. Hence the suggestion that the belief system is a lever that can be employed to control an organization by defining (new) shared values and beliefs does not reflect the full complexity of organizational culture.

The multifaceted nature of organizational culture

The interrelationship between organizations, their specific cultures and control practices has been addressed in the literature on management control. For example the contingency view of management control (Otley, 1980) explains how environmental factors cause control systems to vary across organizations, as well as affecting their market position, overall strategy, profit orientation and stage of development. This has spawned a large body of literature on the relationship between organizational culture and the design and use of control systems.

In line with this, we argue that there are a number of internal and external factors that affect the basic levels of control and lead to a context-specific view of the relationship between control and culture. In this sense we can speak of a control culture that is determined by the specific situation and characteristics of an organization, and these factors are important when considering how to design and use a control system.

One important aspect of organizational culture is that it has various components. Figure 11.2 shows cultural influences that can affect in the way

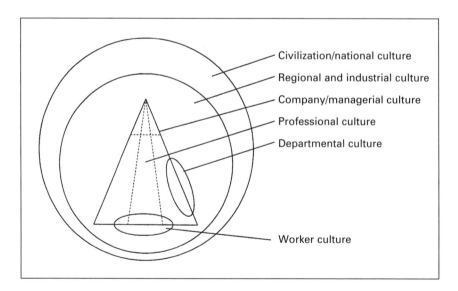

Source: Alvesson and Berg (1992).

Figure 11.2 Layers of culture within and surrounding organizations

in which management control is practised in an organization. Some of these influences are external (such as national or regional cultures) and others are internal (for example departmental culture, professional culture).

A number of studies have considered the impact of national or regional culture on the design and implementation of control systems (for example Bhimani, 1996; Groot and Lukka, 2000; Harrison and McKinnon, 1999; Lebas and Weigenstein, 1986; Scheytt *et al.*, 2003). The members of an organization are also members of families and other organizations and bodies, such as unions, sports clubs or church congregations, all of which have their own culture. Broadly speaking, all the processes of education, socialization and coercion experienced by the members of an organization influence the culture of the organization, as does their explicit and implicit or 'tacit' knowledge (Nonaka, 1994). Hence the influence of external cultures on the organization's reality can be seen as an ongoing and elemental process, and it is important to take account of, interpret and understand the broad cultural background in which control takes place and management control systems are applied.

Ahrens (1996) describes the impact of specific national cultures on the practices of management accounting and control. The research was undertaken in a German and a UK brewery and focused, among other things, on the difference between the styles of accountability in the two countries. At the UK company Ahrens noted there was a severe shortage of funds for maintenance. This had resulted, for example, in a leaking roof in a warehouse where cans and kegs of beer were stored. Although the maintenance manager had expressed concern about the state of the building, money for repairs had not been granted. The reason for this was the company's preference to direct resources to activities that would produce short-term profits; repairing the roof would be a long-term investment. As the accountability of managers was clearly related to profit, costs and market measures – as opposed to maintenance, even though matters of hygiene, health and safety were involved – the roof was not repaired during the two-year observation period. Ahrens then transferred this story to another national culture by telling the managers of the German brewery about the situation and asking for their views. The managers' response was that they would ensure the roof was repaired because as well as the need to adhere to legal and company regulations it would be good practice in terms of operational procedures. Thus the British style of accountability and control culture was characterized by financial objectives (minimizing costs and maximizing profits), while in the German company the integrity of operational processes had precedence over bottom-line profits. So despite their similarities in respect of professional expertise, products and organizational structure, there were clear cultural differences between them in the case of management control.

However there are two reasons why organizational culture is not just an imprint of the national and social culture in which it is set. First, organizations have a unique culture that is partly shaped by their organizational history. Second, one may not speak of *the* organizational culture. Rather, following Alvesson and Berg's (1992) model, there are organizational subcultures that must be considered when looking at the interplay between control and culture.

Ezzamel *et al.* (2001, 2004) studied the impact of workers' culture on the accounting and control systems at an engineering plant. The workers at the plant were highly autonomous and had specialist skills in relation to the production process and its planning and design. The organization of work practices was left up to them as long as production levels were maintained. In exchange for this autonomy they offered flexibility and cooperation in ensuring that the production targets were met. Standard costing systems were the primary management accounting tools and were largely geared to reassuring the parent company about efficiency rather than serving any internal purpose. However changes in the external environment – namely increased competition and the resulting loss of market share – prompted an attempt to change the work practices via a range of management accounting and control mechanisms (for example activity-based costing/management and through-put accounting). These were resisted by the workers and most had to be abandoned. So despite the relentless effort by management to impose stricter controls the workers' culture of autonomy and freedom prevailed and the management was defeated.

We argue that it is the self-understanding of the organization that constitutes the culture of the focal organization, which itself, consists of the diverse self-understandings of groups within and outside the organization. However the concept of self-understanding is blurred, and it is also difficult to identify organizational cultures and subcultures. This is even more the case in 'control cultures' as here the 'hidden practices' of organizing dominate. In particular, control that binds actions and behaviour is carried out in implicit processes of observing, monitoring and surveillance.

A typology of management control regimes can be mapped in relation to the goal and task orientation of the organization. Macintosh (1994) identifies five basic types of control. These are listed below and depicted in Figure 11.3.

- *Bureaucratic controls* have existed in churches and the military for centuries but today are widespread in both public and private sector organizations, for example the civil service. Control is impersonal and the major mechanisms of control are hierarchies, rules, records and formalized procedures. The management accounting and control system is a central part of this.

■ *Charismatic controls* tend to be found in situations where the leader is visionary and perceived as heroic. Control stems from the subordinate/disciple's enthusiasm for the cause, hero worship and personal loyalty.

■ With *market controls* the price mechanism and competition regulate behaviour and promote efficiency in the organization.

■ *Traditional controls* stem from collective wisdom that has amassed over a very long time and can be found in families, schools, professional associations and many public and private organizations. The predominant control mechanism is clan control via rituals, ceremonies and slogans.

■ *Collegial control* is the dominant control mechanism in organizations such as universities, churches, NATO and the United Nations. Control is in the hands of an elite group, such as the professors at universities.

Ezzamel (1994) describes an interesting case of a university where the strong collegial control culture was targeted for change. Faced with a financial crisis the university's central administration sought more rational resource allocation by changing from an incremental to a comprehensive planning, programming and budgeting system. Resources would be channelled into 'acknowledged centres of excellence'. This would require differential budget

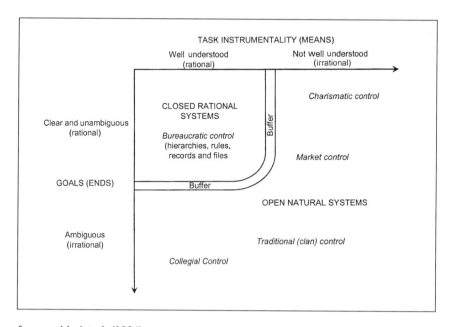

Source: Macintosh (1994).

Figure 11.3 Types of control

reductions among the various academic disciplines and the cutting of 50–80 academic and 100–175 non-teaching posts. In addition to averting the financial crisis, the overall aim was to change the academic culture (which was characterized by job security, academic freedom and liberal work practices) in order to bring about tighter control and accountability. Budgeting mechanisms were to be used to create a more business-like and efficiency-orientated culture. Ironically it was the technical accounting knowledge of some of the academics that enabled successful resistance to the proposed changes and ultimately determined the nature of the budgeting system. This case demonstrates the tensions that can exist between conflicting control regimes in organizations, and particularly in public sector organizations such as universities and the NHS. What can be identified here is a clear conflict between two regimes defined by different cultures. In Macintosh's (1994) terms, the centre was seeking to replace the prevailing collegial control culture with a more bureaucratic one.

Dent's (1991) study of a state railway company demonstrates how the introduction of accounting and control systems can have fundamental effects on organizational culture. Under the existing culture the emphasis was on operational factors such as engineering and logistics – accounting and economic concerns were incidental. Cultural change was brought about by the appointment of business managers to make the railway profitable – the government of the time was opposed to state support of the public sector. The new accounting culture shaped the dominant meanings given to organizational life and hinged on notions of profitability, accountability, (cost) visibility, performance and the customer service. The old culture had not been powerful enough to prevent the changes imposed by a neoliberalist government that inflicted harsh economic criteria on all branches of the public sector.

What can be clearly seen from the above examples is that tensions can arise between control practices and organizational culture, particularly when organizations are in the process of change. Culture determines whether control in an organization is perceived as legitimate or illegitimate by the members of the organization. On the other hand the introduction of a new control regime can change the culture of an organization. However, as the examples demonstrate, the interrelationship between culture and control cannot be depicted as a simple matter of cause and effect and cannot be managed in a technical or mechanistic manner.

Conclusion

The introduction and use of management control systems always takes place at the level of the organization. So when we look at an organization we can usually identify the system of cost accounting, incentive systems, governance structures, explicit strategies, systems of accountability and so on. We can read the mission statements, evaluate the strategies, look at organizational charts and understand them as part of the formal organization. However we must always to take into account the fact that all these systems are bound to the 'ultimate source of values and action' (Schein, 1985): the deeper self-understandings and self-constructions that are found in the organization. That is, the way in which the members of an organization make sense of its systems is fundamentally determined by the culture of the organization.

In order to obtain a clear picture of what transpires in organizations control systems theory has to employ alternative methods of understanding the role and functioning of management control systems. For example an interpretive approach employed to understand the intricate relationship between culture and control. Since patterns of interpretation are defined by the organizational culture and since culture is based on shared values, beliefs and norms, they also provide organizational members with the means to make judgements. They help to distinguish between good and bad, between success and failure and between insiders and outsiders, and therefore support the exclusive characteristics of the organization. Culture is therefore also related to the 'rules governing cognitive and affective aspects of membership in an organization and the means whereby they are shaped and expressed' (Kunda, 1992, p. 8). The ability to judge, however, is closely related to the systems and practices of control in the organization. This is what we identify as the recursive relationship between culture and control.

Knowledge of the nature of this recursive relationship is of particular importance if managers want to implement new systems of control. With regard to the implementation of an ABC system, for example, it makes a difference whether the organization surrounded by the national culture of, say, the UK or that of Germany. It also makes a difference whether a performance management system (in combination with performance-related pay) is implemented in the organizational culture of a low-tech product manufacturing company or that of a software engineering company.

Furthermore as each organization is unique in terms of shared values and beliefs, all control systems have to be adapted to the specificities of the organization. Any attempt to change a culture, for example by implementing a control system, can only be targeted at the artefacts or explicit practices in the organization. Basic assumptions and beliefs cannot be addressed by the control system, even if it may indirectly change the culture. For example the design of a reporting system can be changed, but the way in which the members of the organization use the information provided is difficult to change. Similarly a performance management system can be implemented, but how this might change the patterns of action in the organization cannot be easily or precisely predicted.

Simons' (1995a, 1995b) 'levers of control' model highlights the importance of organizational culture in the context of control practices. However the notion of culture underlying his conceptualization points to a strong understanding of the complex interplay between control practices and the context in which they are embedded. From this perspective, organizational culture can be deliberately changed similar to the way that mission statements, basic values or beliefs, can be directly and explicitly addressed, and hence can be employed to exert a specific type of control over the organization. However Schein's (1985) conceptualization of organizational culture and the examples discussed above suggest that explicit attempts to change a culture can be of limited success or can result in unexpected or unintended consequences. Hence irrespective of which perspective is taken, managers and researchers have to be aware of the contextual and implicit characteristics of every organizational culture. Systems of control in organizations should be interpreted as culturally specific in that cultural factors at different levels influence them. However this does not mean that we cannot say anything about the design of management accounting and control. Rather an enhanced understanding of the diverse aspects of organizational culture might energize, enhance and intensify our discussions on the importance of management control systems in today's organizations.

Discussion questions

1. Describe the culture in your organization and evaluate the extent to which it affects the organization's approach to control.
2. Provide an example of an organization in which the control system has been in conflict with the organizational culture, and discuss the extent to which the desired control has been achieved.
3. In a university setting, what levers of control are used to control students' behaviour? How effective are they?
4. Discuss the strengths and weaknesses of seeking to use culture as a tool to control an organisation.
5. Is it possible to identify organizational culture or national culture? Provide reasons for your conclusion.

Intellectual capital and the management control of knowledge resources

12

Jan Mouritsen

Introduction

During the 1990s the notion of intellectual capital/intangibles was proposed as a new type of resource to be managed in a knowledge and service society. Intellectual capital is concerned with the firm's knowledge – the development, sharing and application of insight, information and reflexivity – and it helps to create knowledge about the firm's activities, for example by using an intellectual capital statement as a management tool to build a portfolio of knowledge resources, to upgrade them and to monitor their effects. Intellectual capital therefore has a management control agenda, and through intellectual capital statements, knowledge resources are made visible, can be tracked over time and can be evaluated. In this respect an intellectual capital statement is of use to firms that wish to systematize their management of knowledge resources.

This chapter firstly defines intellectual capital and then discusses how the management of knowledge resources can be accomplished, using two examples from a research project in this area. It ends by considering what type of knowledge is available in an intellectual capital statement.

A general model of intellectual capital

Intellectual capital is concerned with intangible assets, which are becoming more and more important in the knowledge economy (Austin and Larkey, 2002; Roos *et al.*, 1997; Sveiby, 1997). Distinct from financial capital and tangible assets, intellectual capital generally consists of human capital and structural capital (organizational and customer capital) and the relationships

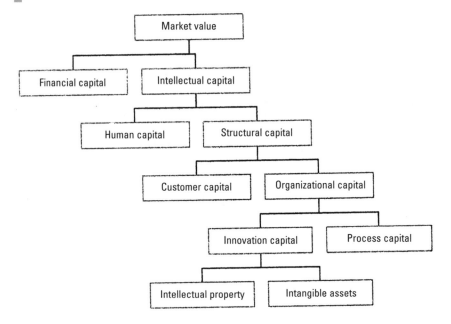

Figure 12.1 The breakdown of market value into financial and intellectual capital

between them. Intellectual capital has often been deemed as important because it can help explain the difference between the market value and the book value of a company. This assertion should not be taken too seriously, but it does justify Figure 12.1, which depicts the breakdown of market value into financial and intellectual capital, and more importantly the breakdown of intellectual capital into human and structural (organizational and customer) capital.

The definitions in Table 12.1 show that the elements of intellectual capital are important assets for firms, but they are not usually reported in accounting systems. Human capital includes people's capacity and motivation to act, their innovative capabilities, skills and competences. Information technology systems, concepts, patents, organizational procedures and knowledge that is retained in the firm are examples of organizational capital. Customer capital consists of relationships with customers, brands and image. Intellectual capital is the product of these factors.

These definitions appeal because they can be neatly expressed in a diagram, as in Figure 12.1, but it is obvious from Table 12.1 that there is no simple mathematical way in which the components can be added together to obtain a value. However the breakdown of the components can be used as a reporting model, and this has been done by Skandia, the Swedish insurance

Table 12.1 Key definitions of the components of intellectual capital

	Human capital	Organizational capital	Customer capital
Karl Erik Sveiby (1997)	'involves capacity to act in a wide variety of situations to create both tangible and intangible assets'	'Internal structure includes patents, concepts, models, and computer and administrative systems'	'The external structure includes relationships with customers and suppliers. It also encompasses brand names, trademarks, and the company's reputation or image'
Thomas Stewart (1997)	'money talks, but it does not think; machines perform, often better than any human being can, but do not invent . . . [the] primary purpose of human capital is innovation – whether of new products and services, or of improving in business processes'	'knowledge that doesn't go home at night . . . it belongs to the organization as a whole. It can be reproduced and shared. [It includes] technologies, inventions, data, publications, . . . strategy and culture, structures and systems, organizational routines and procedures'	It is 'the value of its franchise, its ongoing relationships with the people or organizations to which it sells . . . [such as] market share, customer retention and defection rates, and per customer profitability'
Leif Edvinsson and Michael Malone (1997)	'combined knowledge, skill, innovativeness and ability of the company's individual employees . . . it also includes the company's values, culture, and philosophy. The company cannot own human capital'	'hardware, software, databases, organizational structure, patents trademarks, and everything else of organizational capability that supports those employees' productivity. . . . [It is] everything left at the office when the employees go home. . . . Unlike human capital, structural capital can be owned and thereby traded'	

company that was the first to report externally on its intellectual capital. This will form the basis of the discussion in this chapter. The initial sets of indicators adopted are shown in Table 12.2.

Table 12.2 lists indicators that represent intellectual capital but it is clear that they do not aggregate neatly into a quantification of its value (for a review of measurement approaches see Petty and Guthrie, 2000). In use the indicators are loosely coupled and express very different things. They are there to account for renewal (with a view to tomorrow), customers and processes (with a view to today) and financial results (with a view to yesterday). All these are connected by a human focus. Hence this reporting format presents indicators in a general story line about the relationship between the past, the present and the future. But the story is not complete because we need to understand how knowledge, as a resource, creates value. The template of intellectual capital in Figure 12.1 is a starting point to investigate the firm's intellectual capital rather than assess the worth of that capital.

Knowledge and value creation

Knowledge is a strange resource that philosophers have struggled to understand for centuries, even millennia. Consider Plato's account of a dialogue between Socrates and Theaetetus (Plato, 1996):

Socrates: When you speak of cobbling, you mean by that word precisely a knowledge of shoemaking?

Theaetetus: Precisely.

Socrates: And when you speak of carpentry, you mean just a knowledge of how to make wooden furniture?

Theaetetus: Yes.

Socrates: In both cases, then, you are defining what the craft is a knowledge of?

Theaetetus: Yes.

Socrates: But the question you were asked . . . was not, what are the objects of knowledge, nor yet how many sorts of knowledge there are. We did not want to count them, but to find out what the thing itself – knowledge – is

Prior to this exchange, Socrates had asked Theaetetus to define knowledge. The quotation reflects their conclusion that knowledge cannot be defined in abstract terms, but only in relation to a practical application. Knowledge is useful when it makes a difference to something or somebody. Therefore knowledge is not just a thing in itself but has to be related to certain practices. Hence knowledge can only be understood in relation to a purpose and this

Table 12.2 Skandia's indicators

	American Skandia	Skandia Real Estate	Skandiabanken	Skandia Life UK Group	Dial	Skandialink
Financial focus	• Return on capital employed • Operating result • Value added per employee	• Direct yield • Net operating income • Market value • Total yield	• Operating income • Income/expense ratio • Capital ratio	• Return on capital employed • Operating result • Assets under management	• Gross premiums written • Gross premiums written per employee	• Gross premiums written • Operating result • Assets under management
Customer focus	• Number of contracts • Savings per contract • Surrender ratio • Points of sale	• Customer satisfaction index • Average lease • Average rent • Telephone accessibility	• Number of customers	• Number of contracts • Savings per contract • Service awards	• Telephone accessibility • Number of individual policies • Customer satisfaction index	• Number of contracts • Surrender rate
Human focus	• Number of employees • Number of managers • Of whom, women • Training cost per employee	• Human capital index • Employee turnover • Average years of service with company • College graduates as a proportion of total staff	• Average number of employees • Of whom, women	• Number of employees	• Average age • Number of employees • Time in training	• Number of employees • Human capital index • Share of employees with secondary education or higher • Share of employees with 3 or more years of service
Process focus	• Number of contracts per employee • Adm. expense per gross premium written • IT expense/admin. expense	• Occupancy rate • Financial occupancy rate • Net operating income per sq. m. • Cost per square metre	• Payroll costs/administrative expenses	• Number of contracts per employee	• IT-employees as a proportion of total employees	• Administrative expenses/gross premiums written • IT expenses/administrative expense
Renewal and development focus	• Share of gross premiums written from new launches • Increase in net premiums written • Development expense/adm. expense • Share of staff under 40 years	• Property turnover: purchases • Property turnover: sales • Change and development of existing holdings • Training expenses/administrative expenses	• Total assets • Share of new customers • Deposits and borrowing, general public • Lending and leasing • Net asset value of funds	• Increase in net premiums, new sales • Pension products, share of new sales • Increase in assets under management	• Increase in gross premiums written • Share of direct payments in claims assessment systems • Number of ideas filed with idea group	• Number of contracts per employee • Fund switches via Telelink • Fund switches via Internet

purpose contains one version of its value, namely as something that is useful to something or somebody. This value is only loosely coupled to financial value because organizations do not always do things that are valued financially in the market place. A university may be good at teaching, but given the manner of funding it may not be rich. Even if being good at certain things may be related to financial success over time, this does not always hold. There is therefore a distinction between a firm's competence and its financial success at a particular time. So if market value is composed of financial capital and intellectual capital (Figure 12.1), we should be concerned – the relationship may not hold at this particular time because there is a journey between renewal for the future, relations in the present and the financial results of the past. This is recognized in certain types of strategy. Building on competency theory, Grant (1998) states that:

> The starting point for the formulation of strategy must be some statement of the firm's identity and purpose – conventionally this takes the form of a mission statement which answers the question: 'What is our business?' But in a world where customer preferences are volatile, the identity of customers is changing, and the technologies for serving customer requirements are continually evolving, an externally focused orientation does not provide a secure foundation for formulating long-term strategy. When the external is in a state of flux, the firm's own resources and capabilities may be a much more stable basis on which to define its identity. Hence, a definition of a business in terms of what it is capable of doing may offer a more durable basis for strategy than a definition based upon the needs which the business seeks to satisfy.

According to Grant the market (where financial valuation takes place) may not be a strong asset because it is fragile. Hence it is more appropriate to concentrate on the firm's own resources and competences when the external world is in a state of flux. Here the firm's capabilities and competences, or what Socrates would call knowledge, are the important things to be managed.

The main point is that value can be attached to what the firm can do, rather than how it can serve the market (in the short term). There is a relationship between a firm's ability to do things and its expected financial value in a market economy, but this is open and problematical rather than a simple solution. There are at least ways of addressing this problem. One is to be more specific about the relationship between indicators and effects. Another is to develop a causal model of how intellectual capital is valuable. For example Lev's (2001) value chain scorecard links discovery and learning, and implementation and commercialization (Table 12.3).

Table 12.3 Value chain scorecard

Discovery and learning	Implementation	Commercialization
Internal renewal • Research and development • Workforce training and development • Organizational capital processes	Intellectual property • Patents, trademarks and copyrights • Licensing agreements • Coded know-how	Customers • Marketing alliances • Brand values • Customer churn and value • Online sales
Acquired capabilities • Technology purchase • Spillover utilization • Capital expenditures	Technological feasibility • Clinical tests, food and drug administration approval • Beta tests, working pilots • First mover	Performance • Revenues, earnings and market share • Innovation revenues • Patent and knowhow royalties • Knowledge earnings and assets
Networking • R&D alliances and joint ventures • Supplier and customer integration • Communities of practice	Internet • Threshold traffic • Online purchases • Major internet alliances	Growth prospects • Product pipeline and launch dates • Expected efficiencies and savings • Planned initiatives • Expected break-even and cash burn rate

Source: Lev (2001).

This scorecard indicates that discovery and learning come before implementation, which also precedes commercialization. The scorecard subordinates the intellectual capital components in Skandia's reporting model to knowledge development and application in the firm. Despite the fact that the firm in question is one of high R&D intensity and has a place in the new economy, there is little attention to human capital. Instead there is much more focus on the formal processes of knowledge generation. All the elements of the value chain scorecard are related but it is not an additive model. Rather it is a structural model that (potentially) can be estimated by statistical means.

Another approach that can be followed also attempts to link measurements, but through a strategic approach rather than a statistical model (Roos *et al.*, 1997). Here the indicators are made relevant by means of narratives. While the indicators can be grouped into accounting categories such as employees, customers, processes and technology, if this is what the observable transactions are about, these categories have to be connected and this can only be done by means of a narrative (Mouritsen *et al.*, 2003). The narrative represents the firm's interpretation of how the network of knowledge resources contributes to the user. Like the value chain scorecard, the narrative relates the sequence of activities that make knowledge resources productive, but it also specifies how the firm assembles, upgrades and manages knowledge resources in accordance with the purpose they are to serve. Typically this purpose is related to a user. The narrative approach requires the intellectual capital statement to be concerned with:

- A plot: the intellectual capital has to be able to solve a certain problem, and the narrative explains how the firm can do this.
- Actors: the intellectual capital statement has to explain how actors intervene to mobilize (develop, apply and share) knowledge to achieve the desired end.
- The actors are selected according to their role in the narrative rather than on the basis of whether they are internal or external to the firm. The user is typically a valuable actor in that the user is a medium through which the firm can reflect on its knowledge resources in order to identify which ones it must draw on to provide a particular service.

The narrative is therefore a mechanism to help the firm reflect on and communicate its ambitions and the connections between those ambitions and its efforts to develop, share and apply knowledge. It concerns the logic of the knowledge economy, as reflected in the firm's business model.

The intellectual capital statement

The intellectual capital statement is a reporting and management tool that makes knowledge and intangibles manageable. However as we learned from Socrates' dialogue with Theaetetus, knowledge is not a thing but more an ambition to thrive on abilities, insights, information, intelligence and reflexivity. To become manageable, knowledge has to be translated into knowledge resources or containers in which knowledge can be situated and about which decisions can be made. In the literature a number of types of container of knowledge have been proposed: the person, the network, the IT system, the customer, procedures and processes, culture, incentive systems and so on. From a management control perspective, knowledge is useful if it can be rendered manageable, that is, orchestrated to meet corporate ends. Even if much is made of the person in knowledge management, the person is really only useful as a knowledge container in the meeting of corporate objectives.

Writing the intellectual capital statement

The intellectual capital statement consists of four elements that together express the company's knowledge management. These elements link users of the company's goods or services with its need for knowledge resources, a set of initiatives to improve knowledge management and a set of indicators to define, measure and follow up initiatives (Figure 12.2).

The first element is the narrative, which expresses the company's ambition to increase value for users. This helps it to define what it needs to know and how knowledge can be best directed to produce a service or a product that will have value to a user. This value can be called the use value, and a set of knowledge resources are needed to create it. The knowledge narrative shows which types of knowledge resource are required to create the use value. To identify the elements of a knowledge narrative it is useful to answer the following questions:

- What product or service does the company provide?
- How does it make a difference for the user?
- What knowledge resources are necessary to supply the product or service?
- How does the constellation of knowledge resources produce the service/product?

The second element consists of knowledge management challenges, or knowledge resources that need to be strengthened through in-house development or external acquisition. These are long-term challenges that define

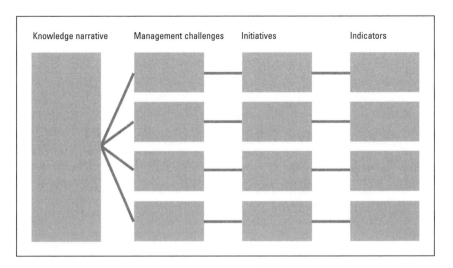

Figure 12.2 The elements of an intellectual capital statement

the business model of knowledge. They can take the form of close cooperation with innovative customers, expertise in specific fields or insight into the
company's control processes. The starting point for addressing these challenges might be to do something about the existing knowledge resources, or
to introduce new types of knowledge resource not found within the
company. To obtain an idea of the firm's management challenges the following questions could be addressed:

- How are the knowledge resources related?
- Which existing knowledge resources should be strengthened?
- What new knowledge resources are needed?

The third element comprises initiatives to address the management challenges in terms of compiling, developing and procuring knowledge resources
and monitoring their size and effect. This could mean investing in IT, hiring
more R&D consultants or software engineers, or conducting training
programmes in company processes and procedures. Vocational and social
activities could also be introduced to increase employee satisfaction.

Initiatives must be able to work in the long term, and specific ones may be
repeated over several years. They may involve specific players, for example
one to hire personnel, another to launch training initiatives and one to
develop the required procedures and routines. Develop a set of initiatives
requires the following questions to be answered:

- What initiatives – actual and potential – can be identified?
- What initiatives should be given priority?

The fourth element consists of a set of indicators that monitor whether the
initiatives have been launched or whether the management challenges are
being met. Indicators make initiatives visible through measurement, and they
make evaluation possible. Some are directly related to specific initiatives such
as training days or investment in IT. Others are related only indirectly to
initiatives, such as the number of R&D consultants employed or the number
of newly appointed software engineers. Indicators can measure:

- Effects: how do activities work?
- Activities: what does the firm do to upgrade knowledge resources?
- Resource mix: what is the composition of knowledge resources?

These elements together represent the analysis of the company's intellectual
capital. The elements are interrelated, and their relevance becomes clear when
seen in context. The indicators show how initiatives are launched and put

into effect. The initiatives formalize the problems identified as management challenges. The challenges single out what has to be done if knowledge resources are to be developed. The knowledge narrative sums up, communicates and reorientates what the company's skills and capacity do or must do for users, and what knowledge resources are needed within the company.

The process of identifying a suitable intellectual capital statement

The design of the intellectual capital statement is of particular concern because typically firms face difficulties if they start by defining their knowledge narrative and then logically deduce the management challenges, efforts and indicators. This is not too surprising because firms' competences may offer a more stable basis for sustained value creation than their markets, and typically strategy starts from markets (Grant, 1988). For a competence-based strategy it might be more useful to start with the firm's own resources and competences when designing the intellectual capital statement. The design is important for knowledge development and learning because it determines how relevant learning can be promoted. In contrast to many other organizational resources, learning and knowledge do not have their own object and therefore have to be oriented towards a purpose. One has to know something about a particular something, and to learn something about a particular something. Therefore organizations have to develop an appreciation of the object of knowledge and learning along the development of the strategies that develop them. This puts pressure on the intellectual capital statement because its four elements (narrative, challenges, efforts and indicators) are not always developed sequentially. Often their development is a puzzle-solving activity in which they are gradually forged by playing with all the relevant knowledge resources in an interactive manner. It is easier to start with the practices of knowledge and learning than with their abstract strategies and ambitions.

Table 12.4 illustrates how it is possible to create a varied set of information to develop an appreciation of how it is that knowledge and learning exist and are relevant to the organization. Working to fill in the boxes of this model, a pattern gradually emerges about how different types of knowledge resources contribute to knowledge and learning, and how it is that the development of these knowledge resources may be helpful in advancing the particular kinds of knowledge and learning of relevance to the ambitions of knowledge.

The purpose of Table 12.4 is to help map and evaluate initiatives related to knowledge management and learning. It has two columns on current status and two on assessment. Some organizations are able to answer the questions in all the sections, while others are only able to answer some of them. This could reflect insufficient knowledge management or that not all the initiatives

Table 12.4 Template for the development of knowledge and learning

Knowledge resources	Existing actions and initiatives	Existing objectives and strategies	Assessment of initiative effect	Assessment of objective ambition level
Customers/ users	What actions and initiatives have been taken to: • ensure the right customer portfolio? • upgrade customer relations and customer competences? • promote customer satisfaction?	What objectives exist for: • customer mix? • upgrading customer relations and customer competences? • customer satisfaction?	How do the company's initiatives contribute to creating something of value to its users?	• Are the existing objectives sufficiently ambitious? • Are some initiatives more crucial to success than others? • Do we need to develop new types of actions?
Employees	What actions and initiatives have been taken to: • ensure the right employee portfolio? • train and upgrade employees? • promote employee satisfaction?	What objectives exist for: • employee mix? • training and upgrading employees? • employee satisfaction?	How do initiatives affect employees' contribution to creating a better company?	• Are the existing objectives sufficiently ambitious? • Are some initiatives more crucial to success than others? • Do we need to develop new types of action?
Business processes	What actions and initiatives have been taken to document and rationalize business processes?	What objectives exist for documentation and rationalization of business processes?	How does the company create initiatives to increase the value of its business processes?	• Are the existing objectives sufficiently ambitious? • Are some initiatives more crucial to success than others? • Do we need to develop new types of initiative?

Knowledge processes	What actions and initiatives have been taken to document and rationalize knowledge processes?	What objectives exist for ensuring the documentation and rationalization of knowledge processes?	How does the company create initiatives to increase the value of its knowledge processes?	• Are the existing objectives sufficiently ambitious? • Are some initiatives more crucial to success than others? • Do we need to develop new types of initiative?
Production technology	What actions and initiatives have been taken to: • ensure the right production technology portfolio? • upgrade existing production technologies?	What objectives exist for: • ensuring the right portfolio of production technologies? • upgrading the existing production technologies?	How do initiatives to develop the company's production technologies make the company stronger?	• Are the existing objectives sufficiently ambitious? • Are some initiatives more crucial to success than others? • Do we need to develop new types of initiative?
Knowledge/ infrastructure	What actions and initiatives have been taken to: • ensure the right knowledge infrastructure? • upgrade the existing knowledge infrastructure?	What objectives exist for: • ensuring the right knowledge infrastructure? • upgrading the existing knowledge infrastructure?	How do initiatives to develop the company's knowledge infrastructure enable the company to share knowledge better?	• Are the existing objectives sufficiently ambitious? • Are some initiatives more crucial to success than others? • Do we need to develop new types of initiative?

are relevant. The two assessment columns allow reflection on the relevance of the initiatives, and initially relevance is judged against concrete local problems, but the answers to the issues raised in these columns also draw on an – often implicit – understanding of the knowledge management challenges of the organization.

The table facilitates the collection of information to form the basis of the four elements of the intellectual capital statement and formulate a proposition about how and when organizational learning is relevant, and when individuals' creativity is be relevant and when it is not. The point of the intellectual capital statement is that it shows a network of knowledge resources that have to be aligned. Sometimes it is more useful to stabilize certain forms of knowledge and make them an organization-wide resource, and in other situations certain types of knowledge may have to be transformed through creative measures. Thus knowledge can both function in relation to coordinating organization-wide activities, which requires stability of knowledge, or it can be used to transform the setting, which requires knowledge to be transformed though learning.

This suggests that knowledge and learning are managerial issues. There are decisions to be made in respect of economizing, organizing and modularizing. Economizing requires decisions about putting limits on learning (through education, development activities and so on). Organizing requires decisions about where to accumulate knowledge (in people, processes, technologies), and modularization requires decisions about the variation of knowledge (as in best practices). Even if learning is generally important, it is not a general good. It is also a factor for which management decisions about composition, investment and size have to be made.

Answering the questions in Table 12.4 allows existing and potential initiatives to be pulled together in a series of management challenges that function as an 'umbrella' or 'common denominator' for initiatives of certain durability. Examples of such challenges are:

- The recruitment, retention and development of employees and competences.
- Development of the company's processes.
- Mixing knowledge and competences across the company.
- Establishing visibility in the market.
- Building partnerships with customers.
- Accumulating insight into users' needs.

The table also facilitates formulation of the knowledge narrative (the knowledge management strategy), organized around the possible use-value that is created through recognizing the full extent of the knowledge resources of the organization. The knowledge narrative creates a meaningful interrelationship between knowledge resources, products, services and user value. It links a number of single elements by way of, among others, the words 'because' and 'therefore'. Hence, the narrative is an explanation – in this case an explanation or account of the knowledge management strategy of the organization.

Reading the intellectual capital statement

There are numerous indicators in intellectual capital statements, but it is often difficult to read them. They have somehow to be divorced from the text and images. Somehow therefore a reader has to find how the firm's intellectual resources are marshalled – just as the conventional financial statement presents information on financial resources. The objectives in reading the financial statements will also be relevant for reading the intellectual capital statement. The first task is to present the indicators in such a way that they say something about general management problems. In the case of the financial statement this concerns the firm's solidity, the composition of its assets and liabilities, its investments for growth and improvement, and its profitability. Similarly, intellectual capital information includes the composition of knowledge assets, the firm's efforts to upgrade resources, and the effect of knowledge and intellectual resources. This is illustrated in Table 12.5.

The form presented in Figure 12.3 facilitates analysis of each of the firm's knowledge resources – employees, customer relations, processes and technologies – such questions can be asked. The knowledge resources column enables a portfolio assessment of the company. The reader will determine whether the company's knowledge resource portfolio is competitive and can meet future needs. The activities column facilitates evaluation of the management's ability to develop employee competences, the organization as a whole and customer relations. The effects column provides the information needed to assess whether the company's knowledge management set-up and activities work,

Table 12.5 Parallels between the financial and intellectual capital statements

Financial statement	*Intellectual capital statement*
What are the company's assets and liabilities?	What do the company's knowledge resources comprise?
What has the company invested?	What has the company done to strengthen its knowledge resources?
What is the company's return on investment?	What are the effects of the company's knowledge work?

Knowledge resources \ Evaluation criteria	Effects – what happens	Activities – what is done	Resources – what is created
Employees	• • •	• • •	• • •
Customers	• • •	• • •	• • •
Processes	• • •	• • •	• • •
Technologies	• • •	• • •	• • •

Figure 12.3 Form for analyzing intellectual capital indicators

enabling an assessment of company stability. The columns can be read randomly as they are not closely interlinked. However, they become interlinked when the statements are set side by side and the reader uses them to develop his or her version of what is going on in the company. Analysts are likely to concentrate on an overall assessment of the company and its management, and the extent to which it will be able to meet future challenges by developing suitable knowledge resources and using them wisely. Analysts would also be interested to know why a company would wish to operate with a short supply of knowledge resources. The knowledge resources column can indicate what the company should offer employees in terms of educational opportunities, challenging technologies or innovative projects. The activities column can form the basis for evaluating employee development opportunities. The effects column facilitates measurement of employees' satisfaction with the company as a workplace and the effectiveness of the company's knowledge management. Experience with intellectual capital statements has shown that they can be powerful tools to communicate a company's identity and position to current and prospective employees.

Analysts are also likely to evaluate the company from the perspective of current and potential customers. The knowledge resource column can reveal how many and what types of customer relations the company has and how this changes over time, enabling analysis of the company's ability to supply suitable services to its customers. The activities column provides the basis for assessing customer and user relationship development initiatives, and the knowledge resource portfolio shows whether there are any risks in the customer base. Finally, the effects column facilitates assessment of whether customers are satisfied with the company's goods or services and how stable the company is.

The case of COWI consulting

COWI is a Danish consulting company that caters to international industrial, construction, transport and environmental organizations. The company was established in 1930 and today has over 2800 employees, around 2000 of whom work in Denmark. Most of the employees have received further education. The group's turnover for 2000/1 was DKK 1720 million. COWI's intellectual capital statement only includes the parent company: COWI A/S.

According to the head of knowledge management, 'having prepared intellectual capital statements for some years, I wonder about two things in particular: how could I ever have imagined it would be easy, and how were we able to do without it?' COWI's first intellectual capital statement was primarily aimed at providing information to the public. While this is still considered important, the statement has gradually become an internal management tool. In addition to the annual statement, reviews are conducted every one to four months. This is possible because nearly all the data required for the statement are recorded, thus allowing automatic processing. Knowledge/intellectual capital reporting has become an everyday activity. The project group that produced the first intellectual capital statement has now been disbanded and the statement is no longer published as a separate document but as a vital part of the annual report.

> For a company such as ours, customer relations are quite crucial. What do we know about our customers, and what do they know about us? The intellectual capital statement makes any gaps in this knowledge conspicuous to everybody . . . [B]ut also inside the organization we obtain important new information . . . we obtain a much better insight into each other's work, strengths and weaknesses: 'Oh, is this how my department looks in comparison with others?' 'So that's why they do it like this or that' (head of knowledge management).

According to the head of knowledge management the intellectual capital statement has revitalized COWI's external communications. The text of the annual report was previously flooded with facts that are now systematically presented in tables and figures, leaving space in the text for more entertaining and illustrative stories about the company.

We shall now look at COWI's intellectual capital statement. The analysis will be conducted in two steps. First, the numbers in the intellectual capital statement will be separated from the text and made readable according to a general analytical model. Second, the numbers will be reintegrated with the text on strategies and activities in the statement.

Step 1: Reading the intellectual capital indicators

The indicators in COWI's intellectual capital statement (Figure 12.4) are distributed broadly across the whole area covered by the analytical model. The spread of types of indicator is therefore considerable. A direct interpretation of the indicators is as follows.

Resources

- The company's employee base is very stable in terms of age and education, but there is a consistently high level of employee loss. The number of professional networks is increasing, which indicates that the company is strengthening its professional development.
- The customer base shows a slow but steady increase, and COWI is gradually augmenting the activity in this area.
- The proportion of customers from the private sector is relatively low, meaning that a large part of the company's turnover is dependent on state budgets. This may constitute a risk.

Activities

- COWI have focussed slightly more on their customers, and the proportion of resources used on development activities is fixed. This indicates that the company has systematically organized its development activities.

Effects

- COWI has a stable workforce. The number of remarks in the company's Quality Assurance audit is also stable.
- The number of customers has increased significantly, but there are no time series available to determine whether the customer base is stable.
- Even though the market in some areas is turbulent the company has continued to grow. All the indicators for organizational development are stable: stable development activities, stable upgrading investment and (in general) stable development effects. This stability should not be mistaken for stagnation as it reflects change at a constant rate. Whether this rate is rapid enough is another matter.

This reading is general, but it does highlight business concerns, and it facilitates hypotheses on the particular workings of the firm. These hypotheses have to be tested, and for this purpose the intellectual capital statement has to be viewed in terms of relevance and perspective, which is the purpose of the second step in the reading of the statement.

Step 2: Understanding the numbers

The generalized reading of the intellectual capital statement produces a story line on how these indicators work and a business model of how knowledge is to work. This is a strategic ambition, obviously, and the numbers alone cannot judge it. So, the reader has to be concerned with the relationships between the knowledge strategy, the durable management challenges that make up the business model, the efforts to develop the business model, and the indicators suggest monitoring the implementation of efforts. The four elements are translation mechanisms where all the elements help redefine what the others are about. Figure 12.5 shows COWI's presentation of its intellectual capital story line (see also Figure 12.2).

Figure 12.5 illustrates the translations of the text of the intellectual capital statement and creates a representation which speaks to a reader's logic – is this really a good firm? And how may the analysis of the indicators presented in Figure 12.4 help assess this question? Here COWI presents the purpose of intellectual capital, which is to develop an appreciation of the user's value of the service through a particular offering that requires certain knowledge resources. The figure then explains how the translation between this ambition and certain activities take place: The ambition to create interdisciplinary solutions translates into cooperation with customer, project management and knowledge sharing. These again translate into various actions, ranging from develop markets and increase cooperation between groups to control quality. This is then visualized by a series of indicators to support this, including customer profile, level of interdisciplinary cooperation and quality audits. They are not all available in indicators, which can be seen by comparing Figures 12.4 and 12.5. Some are only for internal use. But the translations show how this idea of interdisciplinary solutions get actualized and the various elements help refine and redefine each other. Now we know how interdisciplinary solutions relate to quality audits. We may not agree, but the proposition has been made. And this is what makes it possible to resist and say this is not a good business model; or say that the business model is not actually followed, or to say that there is a lacuna in the business model of management challenges. It provides reflexivity.

This story is a proposition. Readers then evaluate it. They question and

	Effects	1997	1998	1999	2000	Activities
Employees	Job satisfaction index		65		68	Number of professional networks
	Sickness absence	2.1	2.5	2.2	2.6	Degree of organization
	Loss of employees (%)		13	13	11	Proportion of working hours
	Proportion of employees					spent on further training
	with COWI shares (%)			79	70	
	Image among engineering students			No. 2	No. 2	
Customers	Media exposure			238	131	Number of presentations
	Percentage of new customers				24	per 100 employees
	Percentage loss of customers				8	Number of publications
						per 100 employees
Processes	Remarks per QA audit			5.1	5.7	Proportion of time spent on
						development
						• of which internally financed
						• of which externally financed
						QA audits carried out
Technologies						

Figure 12.4 Indicators in COWI's intellectual capital statement

inquire and probe into both the logic of the story – the explanation – and they ask themselves whether the numbers presented will persuade them about the story. The numbers (Table 12.2) are evaluated against two sets of questions: (1) are they concerned with the types of insight that a person would require, and (2) do they develop in a way that convinces about a desirable path of development. These are conclusion to be arrived at by the reader and the numbers cannot do this by themselves. Part of the reader's reservoir of resources to do this is the story presented in Figure 12.2 that provides a logic that again can be evaluated against two questions. (1) Is this a logical story, and (2) is it a viable business model?

1997	1998	1999	2000	Resources	1997	1998	1999	2000
	29	33	32	Number of employees	1563	1544	1571	2000
	7.4	8	13	Average age	42	42	42	42.1
				Average years of education	5.8	5.9	6.7	6.7
0.6	0.5	1.1	1.1	Written-off value of years				
				of education	4.3	4.2	4.6	4.6
				Proportion of employees				
				with top education			4.4	4.7
				Work experience			16.2	16.2
				Number of years service			10.2	9.8
				Number of employees with project				
				management experience		56	58	57
				Proportion of time spent on travel	4.1	4.1	5.2	6.4
				Proportion of employees posted				
				abroad long term		1.8	3.8	2.8
				Cross-disciplinary cooperation				
				(% working hours)	29	30	30	30
				Customers' distribution, proportion				
7.5	3.5	19	13	of private sector customers		33	26	24
				Number of individual customers			1274	1484
8.8	6.2	17	6	Number of on-going projects			5152	5102
				Average turnover per project				
				(thousand DKK)			915	1010
				International customers			15	17
				International projects				
				(% working hours)			29	30
				Number of best practices				
	7.3	5.7	5.9	on the intranet	612	699	773	
5.2	5.8	4.1	4.2	Number of projects per employee			17	18
	1.4	1.6	1.7	Trade within the COWI group			2.3	2.7
		49	83	Exchange of employees with				
				the COWI group			1.1	1.1

The intellectual capital statement as a management tool

The arguments and example presented thus far illustrates how practically it is possible to establish and read an intellectual capital statement, but one question still lingers: Why is it necessary to go to all this trouble? It is not just clear that a firm has to develop its knowledge (resources)?

Intellectual capital is concerned to make a network of knowledge resources and explain how they cohere which is in contrast to most formulations of knowledge management more generally where knowledge is seen

Knowledge narrative elements	Management challenges	Actions	Indicators
Use value COWI offers well-defined and formulated interdisciplinary descriptions of requirements in engineering, finance and the environment. This is achieved by combining front-line competences within these fields	• Supply complete solutions in close cooperation with the customer	• Develop international or private markets	• Customer profile • Proportion of international customers • Proportion of international projects
		• Enhance our image with customers	• Number of speeches, articles and publications • Customer satisfaction
Product or service COWI supplies interdisciplinary development-oriented consulting services. These are total solutions (analyses, planning and design) in engineering, finance and the environment	• Well-organized project processes	• Increase cooperation among group companies	• interdisciplinary cooperation • Cross-organizational cooperation • Intragroup trading (expatriation, trade)
		• Improve project processes	
		• Improve development processes	
Knowledge resource In order to supply these services we need high-level interdisciplinary competences and the ability to combine them		• Control quality at all organizational levels	• Internal and external quality audits: number and reprimands • Number of errors and expenses
		• Optimize management systems	
	• Right mix of competences and skills	• Visualize internal and external knowledge	• Number of internal and external professional networks • Number of best practice cases • Number with educational profile and length of education • Number with length of long service

Figure 12.5 COWI's intellectual capital story line

From \ To	Tacit knowledge	Explicit knowledge
Tacit knowledge	Apprenticeship On-the-job-training Coffee breaks Group work	Dialogue Use of metaphors and analogies
Explicit knowledge	Experience Learning by doing	Documentation Coordination

Figure 12.6 Knowledge management techniques

to be situated in the heads of people (Nonaka and Takeuchi, 1991, 1995; Nonaka, 1994). The management problem is here to make people share their insights and experiences so that individual and tacit knowledge is transformed into collective and codified knowledge. The means to do this are illustrated in Figure 12.6.

The key challenge is to transform individual knowledge into collective knowledge. The intellectual capital approach offers an alternative. It is less concerned with the individual creative person and more concerns with the linkages between a constellation of knowledge resources to produce a use value of the company's services. If working, the intellectual capital statement has an effect because it creates a new version of the firm that was not seen previously. It surveys the management aspects of knowledge when it shows the composition of resources, the investments in upgrades and effects related to knowledge. Knowledge resources can be tracked over time, and it is possible to engage in evaluative activities – it is possible for managers and others to say whether they like what they see. Suddenly knowledge is not tacit any more and it is not outside the domain of direct management attention. Knowledge gets translated into resources and suddenly it is possible to perform management – to trace, to evaluate, to change and to monitor consequences and effects. Knowledge has been made ordinary, and the prospect of a knowledge society is not as daunting. The intellectual capital statement says that it is a network of knowledge resources organized around a purpose related to users, and it says that to understand all this it has to be made amenable to comparison and evaluation. Numbers are needed here, because otherwise this tracking would be impossible.

When companies embark on intellectual capital management, their ability to act is metaphorically brought from the individual's 'darkness' within into the 'light' of the numbers where it is subjected to a wide set of management activities. Refocusing knowledge management by means of intellectual capital statements allows management to develop it into a project that exceeds the individual's sphere. Intellectual capital is constituted by a of phenomena, relations and incidents normally separated from each other in time and place as well as in logic and ontology are subjected to coordinated management measures with the proposition to produce a certain value for users of the company's service.

In the same way as financial and management accounting pull financial decisions out of the daily chaotic detail, intellectual capital statements pull knowledge management out of dispersed, chaotic day-to-day situations, compare activities in new ways and identify new or hidden relations. Subsequently, the new knowledge is put back into the day-to-day decision situations. The result is some form of coherence across the organization's different knowledge resources, more opportunities for coordination and attention to the effects of knowledge management activities.

In the case of COWI, the intellectual capital statement makes a claim about the firm's management of intellectual resources: it claims that intellectual resources are organized around the ambition to create interdisciplinary solutions via cooperation with customer, project management and knowledge sharing which again are materialized by such activities as develop markets, increase cooperation between groups and control quality that are made visible and understandable by a series of indicators to support this, including customer profile, level of interdisciplinary cooperation and quality audits. The relevance and trustworthiness of the intellectual capital statement is obviously a matter for the readership to determine. And this readership determines how it wants to intervene either as managers to decide whether, for example, to increase number of patents or not. Or as suppliers of resources to decide whether this is a risky firm (financial resources), a capable firm (a user/customer) or whether it will develop competences (prospective employees). They are all interested in understanding the firm's knowledge resources; and they act on this understanding by changing the firm or adding to it.

This is where the managerial concerns for economizing, organizing and modularizing knowledge come in. Economizing asks questions about how much should be invested? In the case of COWI, investments are routinely allocated to upgrade people. But is it really necessary to make education a routine? Or will this stiffen the company? Can training be too institutionalized and is it thus worth the investment? And is the workforce too stable – is it a problem that people do not leave and thus that turn around is too small?

Organizing asks questions about location of knowledge. Is it in people, or in quality management systems? In COWI, it could be in people; but there is obviously the possibility that knowledge resources are made productive through the project management system where various resources are oriented towards a purpose – a customer. Is the project management system able to offset the risk of people leaving the firm? How does this influence the evaluation of risk?

And the concerns about modularization concerns the ambition to predictably link various kinds of knowledge, and in the case of COWI the normative and directing role of project management systems may make organizational knowledge sharing more obvious than organizational knowledge development.

The central proposition of intellectual capital statements is to detect knowledge that functions and communicate such knowledge within the organization to affect company activities. This is not an issue that can be solved by a division into tacit knowledge – which seems to be outside management's 'control' – and explicit knowledge. Managers will then look for control – also in the knowledge management field – At least, this is the promise made by intellectual capital statements.

Discussion questions

1. What are the elements of intellectual capital, and how can they be explained?
2. How are intangibles/intellectual capital related to knowledge?
3. Explain the distinction between writing an intellectual capital statement and reading an intellectual capital statement.
4. What is a knowledge narrative?
5. Explain the difference between the value chain scoreboard and the intellectual capital statement.

13 Control in networks

Anthony J. Berry

Introduction

This chapter explores control in networks, which are a subject of interest in a wide range of academic disciplines. A network may be described as a set of nodal points (for example firms in an economy) interconnected by a series of linkages, whereby single firms are linked to every other firm. The study of such networks can concentrate on the nodes (for example a single firm's strategy for working), the linkages (for example communications) or the larger system that encompasses both of them. Depending on the theoretical assumptions and perspectives adopted, the study of networks can take differing forms.

According to Adam Smith (1937) the relationship among firms in markets may involve some conspiring together, but he also thought that the competition in markets could serve as an invisible hand in controlling firms. Alternatively Alfred Chandler (1977) saw the firm as a powerful actor with a visible hand. With networks of embedded firms (Grabner, 1993) there may be collaborative working. This represents a modification of the concepts visible and invisible hands to include the notion of firms operating hand in hand.

Much of the study of management control has been undertaken within organizations, which explains to the rather managerial, legal and ownership imperatives that underpin traditional control approaches. This is not unexpected since the discipline developed to address control problems within firms. In this tradition the issue of legitimacy is resolved by (silent) appeal to the legitimacy given to ownership, with property rights sustained by statutory law. Here the environment in which the firm operates is of great significance, and ownership and control are intertwined. However when we consider the issue of control in networks we must deal with the fact that ownership and control may be separated and factor and product markets may be closely related.

The debate on the organization of economic activity was stimulated by transaction cost analysis (Williamson, 1970), which developed into new institutional economics. This led to the polarization of control into either hierarchical or market control, with hierarchies being viewed as a nexus of treaties and/or contracts (Aoki, 1990a). Ouchi (1980) draws attention to the significance of social factors with his discussion of clans and cultures. He sees these as either alternative organizational forms of control or as determining the choice of hierarchical or market-based control. As both are ideal types, the space between them can be seen as a domain of hybrid forms of relationship and control, including networks, alliances and (tightly) specified supply chains.

Network organization has been the focus of much practical and academic interest (Nohria and Eccles, 1992), with some scholars viewing networks from an essentially economic stance and others taking an organizational and interpersonal perspective. Harrison (1972) includes networks as one of four organizational cultural forms (functional, task network, power and personal). The most common description of the matrix organization is that of a network with both lateral and hierarchical links. Others depict the network as a set of actors, either individuals or persons in organizational roles (Nohria and Eccles, 1992). Examples here are professional or trade associations and kiretsus (sets of firms working together to produce one product, such as a motor car).

Oliver and Ebers (1998) have used network analysis techniques to analyze the theoretical and empirical nature of 158 research papers published in three US journals and one European journal. They note that there are four theoretical approaches to studying networks: contingent decision-making and strategy (study of the nodes in a network), (social) network relations[1] (study of social linking), interorganizational power and control (study of nodes and links) and interorganizational governance structures (study of nodes and links). Most of the papers address theory formation and explore the formation of networks, rather than explain network performance or outcomes. Oliver and Ebers claim that there is a central paradigm, which has a positive quantitative method and a focus on the forces that drive networking. They suggest that there are four substantive configurations of variables, with social networks at one end of the spectrum and governance (mostly approached via institutional economics or institutional economics plus strategy) at the other, with power/control lying inbetween.

Much of the literature concentrates on the strategic interests of dominant firms in creating networks (for example Moller and Svahn, 2003); the interested reader might also wish to examine the place of the network in entrepreneurship, (see O'Donnell et al., 2001). There is also a new network science (Herman, 2003).

This chapter is concerned with control and therefore will not consider firms' strategies, social networks or network governance – except when these touch on considerations of control – as to do so would require several more chapters.

Taking an approach that differentiates by level of complexity, networks exist at three levels: intrafirm (for example production with activities in different divisions), interfirm (for example a supply chain or distribution cascade) and extrafirm (for example trade associations, the European Union and the World Trade Organization). This chapter explores control in intra- and interfirm networks, with some attention to issues arising at the extrafirm level.

Exploring the network concept

Following Yeung (1994) a business network is defined here as 'an integrated and coordinated set of economic and non-economic relations embedded within, among and outside business firms'. While this definition, from an economic perspective, slightly conflates the inter- and extrafirm levels, as will become clear below it allows attention both to the structure and the processes of control.

The characteristics of a business network have been summarized by Christensen *et al.* (1990) as follows:

1. Two or more firms have some sort of commercial relationship.
2. Each of these firms is dependent upon the assets controlled by the other partners in the network.
3. The partners in the network have some form of independence as well.
4. A network relationship has transaction specific investments from both sides which are a semi specific character. It takes time to develop such a relationship.
5. A firm can take part in more than one network.
6. Different power relationships can result (one model identifies an asymmetric power structure where one firm dominates the network; another is based upon a symmetrical balance of power among the partners).
7. Inside the network there must be some incentives available to govern the exchanges. Agreements rely on negotiations and consensus.
8. Management of networks is contingent upon the strategic interest of partners and the power structure involved. It can take a range of forms from an economic approach based upon self interest to forms based upon trust and behavioural adaptation.

This typology is heavily influenced by economic rationality and is to some extent based on a resource-dependent analysis (Yeung, 1994). The consequence of creating networks and the social relations that precede them or emerge from them is not explored. There is an assumption that even in joint programmes a conflict of interests may arise at any time. The form of business networks ranges from market to hierarchy via licensing/franchising, alliances, cooperative agreements, joint ventures and conglomerates (ibid.). These appear to depend on the degree and nature of the interdependence among the partners as they develop the network.

The issue of interdependence in the social as well as the technical aspects of networks has been taken up by Swedberg and Granovetter (1992). They define business networks as 'a regular set of contacts or similar connections among individuals and groups' (ibid.). Thus the survival and flourishing of firms involves not only a set of market relationships but also a set of social relations.

Taking account of the social context of market relations (the extrafirm issues) alerts us to the notion that trust is an important lubricant of the social system with the idea that the existence of trust is pivotal to the economy and not only to social relations (Etzioni, 1988). It may be argued that network relations are based on solidarity, trust, confidence and appropriate behaviour. These 'elements of trust, cooperation and social order and cohesion are the basic agreements forming Durkheim's non contractual basis of contracts' (Yeung, 1994). Of course trust is not an absolute concept as there can be low-trust and high-trust relationships. To some extent these ideas are a recapitulation of the 1960s behavioural critique of the economic theory of the firm. Indeed the work of Yeung may be seen as a critique of the technical or economic theory of networks.

In management control texts the control of operations is typically addressed through a consideration of budgets and processes such as cost management and activity-based management. Here a broader view of operations is taken, with attention being paid to modes of network control, financial control and clan control issues in embedded operations. Embeddedness means that a firm is linked by medium- or long-term contracts to suppliers and purchasers in a complex chain (Christensen *et al.*, 1990).

The remainder of this chapter explores some of the characteristics of the embedded firm, discusses the control problems in such networks and considers financial management and social and organizational processes within and between partner firms.

Operations and organizations

Here we shall consider operations in two forms: operations that take place wholly within a given organization (intrafirm) and operations that take place among a number of participating firms (interfirm processes). Intrafirm operations in a complex organization often require the contribution of many subunits or divisions. Figure 13.1 provides a simplified example of an operation to produce a product or service, with a series of steps from inputs to outputs in a convergent procedure. The transfers into and out of the organization involve

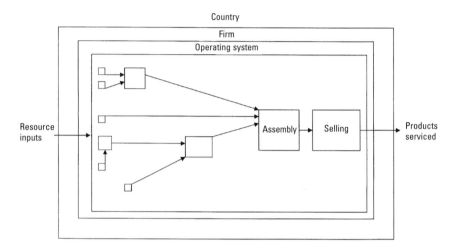

Figure 13.1(a) A firm and its boundaries within a country

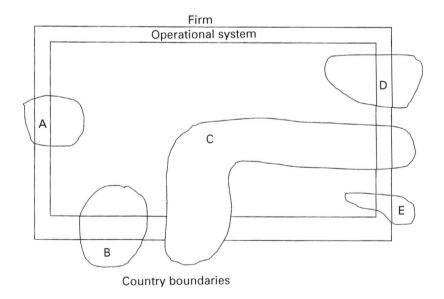

Figure 13.1(b) A firm and its boundaries across countries (each 'blob' is a country)

transactions at the boundary. Here the term of boundary is used in two different ways: to indicate the legal and institutional boundary of the organization,
which is marked by the usual (market) transactions of purchase and sales; and
to refer to the social and cultural boundaries of the organization, which may
be considerably fuzzier than the legal or transactional boundary.

In Figure 13.1(a) the operating system lies wholly within the legal boundary of the organization and that boundary lies within a country boundary.
This represents a firm operating as an independent trader. In Figure 13.1(b)
the example is made more complicated by relaxing the country constraint.
The steps of the operation remain the same and still lie within the organizational boundary, but they now take place in a number of countries, as in the
case of multinational firms such as Ford, Shell, Unilever and so on. For example in a car assembly plant in the UK the materials and parts may be provided
from Spain, Italy and Germany, the engines made in Germany and Spain, and
the product marketed in several other European countries. Indeed the
concept of country can be more a matter of design and marketing than of
operations. The automotive industry is said to represent the first truly global
network of provisioning, manufacturing and marketing and sales. Here there
are legal control issues that cross social, cultural and national boundaries, and
intrafirm and interfirm issues in respect of controlling the network system.

In Figure 13.2 the steps of the operation take place in legally separate organizations. Here the firms are, to a greater or lesser extent, dependent upon
each other for the functioning of the operating system. Following Grabner
(1993), we can refer to these firms as embedded in networks. These simple

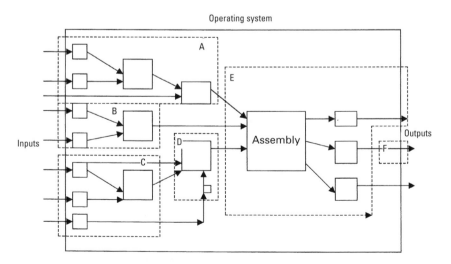

Figure 13.2 The embedded firms (dotted lines) in a production system

examples lead us to a consideration of the problems of control within independent firms and within firms embedded in networks. Note that the positioning of boundaries to denote what is inside the system, network or chain is arbitrary, but is based on the relative significance of the contribution of the actors to the operation in question.

In the case of an embedded network, operations take place both within and outside the boundaries of specific enterprises. For example supplying ladies' lingerie to a retail shop involves textile technology firms, dye manufacturers, fashion designers, textile manufacturers, suppliers of trimmings, suppliers of cutting machines, garment makers or assemblers, merchants, and retail houses working together to design, manufacture, merchandise, market and sell the garments. These relationships may stretch over two to three years for one season's offerings. Technology is significant here as it adds a further boundary to the system and can prevent other firms from joining the system as a single technological approach is required in interfirm networks if problems are to be avoided. This involves the standardization of materials, production equipment and procedures for control, including electronic data exchange. Thus in any complex operational network or chain that produces goods or provides services, most operating systems involve transactions across many boundaries.

The evolution from hierarchy to network

With the Fordist production system all stages of design and production took place within large, vertically integrated companies, with outside suppliers only being used for non-significant inputs. The move away from this in search of economic efficiency through specialization and flexibility has been called post-Fordism. An extreme example of the latter is a footloose low-technology assembler that operates in one place for a short period of time and then moves on to a cheaper location.

In this section we shall explore the process of evolution from integrated operations to decentralization (alternative hierarchical control) and finally network membership, contracting out or franchising. The complexity and wide range of activities in some organizations make it difficult to implement decisions and report actions. There are time lags between recognizing problems, making decisions about them and taking action because the various aspects of problem solving are passed up the hierarchy in complex organizations. Decentralization and divisionalization are the first step towards remedying this, with responsibility and accountability being delegated within the organization and hence reducing the burden on senior managers. Alfred Chandler (1977) and others have demonstrated that divisionalized firms grow faster and are more profitable (efficient) than unitary firms.

Decentralization is a form of differentiation to cope with internal and external complexity and uncertainty. It requires new modes of integrating the decentralized units, including new rules for the transfer of products and services. When this becomes too difficult, quasi market controls may be introduced. One UK food producer followed this path and made each division an investment centre, with performance-related rewards for the managers (a form of market control). However when faced with the need to reconsider the cost base of its procurement, production and distribution chains it found it could not make the necessary changes without dismantling the divisional structure and quasi market controls. It then had the difficult task of unravelling its market-based controls and reintroducing more hierarchical ones, even though these had to support a lateral (cross-divisional) flow of work. Alternative approaches to such problems are to contract out troublesome activities (for example the manufacture of some products or parts and the provision of some services), arrange a management buyout of the operations in question and thereby set up a subcontracting arrangement, or establish franchises. The competitive behaviour adopted by these new and legally separate units is perceived to drive down costs and improve returns on capital.

Thus the complexity and uncertainty of intrafirm operations can lead to variations in control structures and procedures through changes in hierarchy, rules and forms of market. These are not only economic and technical matters, as questions of identity, motivation, belonging and loyalty are involved too. In the case of franchising there is usually a strong attempt to align the interests of the franchiser and franchisee, usually through tight contractual conditions. Complexity and uncertainty can also lead independent firms to embed themselves in a chain of operating systems. Of course the independent firm and the embedded firm mark either end of a continuum, and many firms operate in a more hybrid mode, with some operations remaining largely within their own control and some taking place in the network or chain.

These ideas have been taken up by the UK and other governments. There has been a move away from the public provision of services by large, unitary, state organizations and towards privatization or restructuring. The UK government has restructured its service ministries into a central policy unit that contracts out the delivery of services. The agencies that provide these services are subject to strict control through contracts, service agreements, cash limits and so on, and the now well-rewarded managers are expected to meet the government's targets. This could be viewed as a form of internal franchising.

The system dynamics work by Forester (1961) demonstrates that if actors in a network operate independently then instabilities can arise. This point can be illustrated by Senge's (1990) example of a brewery whose retailers responded at various times to an expected growth in demand and a consequent shortage of supply by overordering, which led to substantial overproduction. One solution to such predicaments is to create significant capacity to prevent instabilities (for example buffer stocks or excess production capacity). While the cost of holding stocks of goods at intermediate stages in a chain may be lower than the cost incurred by, say, a shortage during a peak demand period, it is more expensive than if the firms in a network act in concert to minimize stock holding at all stages of the operation. The latter practice was developed by Japanese firms to reduce their fixed and working capital and increase their returns on capital. It has since been widely copied and lies at the heart of the economics of supply chain management.

Modes of control in networks

We have seen how the need for flexible specialization and efficiency in the face of market uncertainty and volatility can lead to the establishment of chains or networks. However it is important that stability and predictability prevail within the network to ensure the intrafirm delivery of goods or services. This can be characterized as the need for control over economic returns or appropriations (Dekker, 2004) as well as over the task systems of production.

There are two standard modes of control. First, direct control is personal supervision of those doing the work, perhaps through rules administered by tiers of staff. However even in quite simple organizations direct control is difficult, and in complex organizations it can be impossible. Second, control may be indirect, but this too is difficult to establish and maintain in organizations with a high degree of variability, in terms of technology and staff knowledge. Geographic dispersion of the operating units adds to the problem.

Three considerations arise when setting up a system of independent firms (either inter-firm networks or chains). First, a decision has to be made about which firms should join the system. How and by whom should the partners be chosen (ibid.). Second, there is the matter of establishing (or modifying) the operating system. This includes the drawing up of plans and production and delivery schedules. Third, there is the question of managing the operating system once it is established. Control might be through dominance, collaboration or competition.[2]

Dominance means that a powerful firm in the network is able to ensure compliance to its requirements. This is characteristic of many advanced networks with numerous embedded firms. For example in the past 20 years food retailing has been dominated in the UK by a small number of firms that channel goods from manufacturers and suppliers to customers via super- and hypermarkets. These firms enjoy considerable economies of scale. They have lower operating costs (fewer sales employees), provide a wide range of goods and services in one place (customer convenience), and achieve cost efficiencies in purchasing and distribution. Dominance can be exercised to align incentives and working practices by means of five processes (Gulati and Singh, 1998): command structures and authority systems, incentive systems, standard operating systems, dispute resolution procedures and non-market pricing mechanisms. These can be supplemented by performance measurement and outcome evaluation (Dekker, 2004), or by tight franchising agreements. Some counter strategies have emerged with some suppliers responding to requests for 'open books' by creating production facilities dedicated to a given customer only. This means that information provided is limited and thus renders some accounts visible whilst keeping others invisible.

Collaboration involves joint control of an interfirm network. An example here is the development of an advanced military or commercial aircraft, where close collaboration between the manufacturer of the aircraft, the suppliers of components and engines and the air force or airline in question is essential not only in respect of design and construction but also in the interests of operational efficiency and safety. It also characterized to some extent by the lingerie example provided earlier.

Competition is control via the day-to-day interplay of firms in markets. This does not imply perfect competition – for example, there might be an oligopoly.

In order to explore these three modes of control we shall draw on the ideas of Williamson (1973) and Ouchi (1980) (see also Chapter 3 of this volume). In Figure 13.3 we have related the ideas of control by dominance, collaboration or competition to the idea of cultural control. It is argued persuasively by Scott (1995) that beliefs and values permeate social structures and shape the modes of order and control that are observed in organizations and in hence in networks. In this figure we observe that the control in a network may be a mixture of the ideal types.[3]

At this point we need to consider the nature of the interdependence between firms in a network and the time scales of its establishment and operations.[4] It seems reasonable to argue that the time scale for the operations of an embedded network will depend on the type of system in question and its cycle of production. This could be just days or weeks, while the time taken to negotiate and establish the network could be relatively long, perhaps years because decisions have to be taken about materials, design, technology, lead times, quality specifications and the requirements of the dominant player.

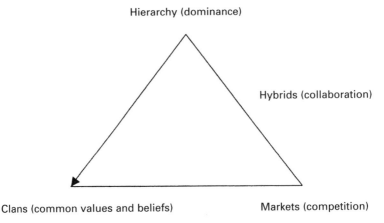

Figure 13.3   Modes of control

Miller (1976) offers a taxonomy of network interdependence:[5]

- Serial: activity A precedes B, which in turn precedes C.
- Reciprocal: A and B are interactively related.
- Mutual: A and B take place jointly.

When the network is fully operational, interdependence may be serial or mutual; during the process of negotiating and establishing the network, interdependence is likely to be reciprocal or mutual.

If we combine the various ideas discussed above, in an established network the time scale will be short, dependence will be serial or mutual and the form of control will be either dominance or collaboration. Control by competition is unlikely as this would mean that the rationale for setting up the network was incorrect and that the short-term switching of suppliers (not just choosing among several suppliers already involved) was possible. For this mode of control to be feasible the operating system would have to be very simple and parts readily available.

During the process of negotiating membership of the network the time scale will be long, interdependence will be created and the mode of control will be competition; that is, organizations will bid to take part in the network. (The most powerful actor in the proposed chain or network might exercise a decisive influence by setting criteria for entry, for example in terms of finance or technological capability.) After the participating firms have been decided upon, the time scale will still be long, control will be by collaboration and interdependence in the design and creation of the network will be reciprocal or mutual. Here joint working groups may be set up to ensure that the best compromises are reached. It is unlikely that such groups will set up a competitive mode of control for this part of the proceedings.

Once the network is established then it is possible that the three activities of negotiating and renegotiating, re-establishing and operating will be taking place at the same time but in different places. Hence the three modes of control – dominance, competition and collaboration – will be present. To some degree the contrasting nature of these control modes will mean that actors will be constrained by the need to continue to collaborate. This apparent paradox of different control modes may produce a loosely coupled network in order to give flexibility. This loose coupling enables alternative logics within the network while at the same time ensuring overall system has the required degree of stability. This might perhaps explain why some authors write about control as being tight-loose as they note the apparently conflicting control modes in an operating network.

Sako (1992) points out that trust and goodwill are essential in interfirm relationships, and both are clearly important in partner selection and network formation. Rousseau *et al.* (1998) consider three types of trust. Calculus-based trust uses information to consider whether the trust in the relationship is sound or sensible. Relational trust is built up via repeated contact and can be nurtured by, *inter alia*, joint participation in development activities (see also Dekker, 2004). Institution-based trust is created when parties are confident that the beliefs, values and legal forms used provide a reliable context for the network. This has particular relevance for networks that cross national boundaries.

Trust between partners is sometimes described as an alternative to a formal control system, or as reinforcing such a system (Adler, 2001; Dekker, 2004; Ring and Van de Ven, 1992). Dekker (2004) argues that up to a certain threshold, trust and control procedures can be complementary, but as trust is virtually cost free there is a danger of it becoming a substitute for formal control. It is conceivable that the trust and control relationship in a network may change with experience. However Tomkins (2001) argues that trust may have a moderating effect on the relationship between control problems and control procedures, that is, in a high trust setting problems will be handled with minimal extra control procedures; in low trust settings greater levels of control are required.

Financial management

The financial management and control of interfirm networks involves many of the problems found in divisionalized organizations particularly when they have adopted investment centre control and varieties of market related transfer pricing policies as a means to facilitate the work of the operation of the intrafirm networks across the boundaries of countries or markets. Managers have to construct increasingly elaborate rules and procedures to ensure that the network does not come to resemble a series of independent firms. Given national accounting practices, it is likely but not necessarily the case, that the recognition of costs and revenues will be consistent. In the interfirm network all the familiar problems of optimization and suboptimization appear, with the added complexity of legal independence and perhaps a struggle to ensure that the economic returns to the participating firms are appropriate, however that is determined. Firms involved in collaborations can negotiate about the specificity of assets for particular purposes, products or services and also perhaps about knowledge and skill specificity. They can also negotiate cost measurement rules. Emerging evidence of such network behaviour is considered below. Accounting problems can be multiplied if participants are members of more than one network. For example in one UK automotive company the managers measured production costs in several ways to cope with different customers' requirements for cost reduction; they found it simpler to vary the allocation rules rather than change any aspect of production, hence they reported different costs for identical production processes.

Some dominant actors require access to cost information and the adoption of costing systems to enable assessment of the cost structure of the network over time. For example some Japanese firms require this of their first-level suppliers. This sounds simpler than it is in practice. Supply chain research (Berry *et al.*, 2000; Tomkins, 2001) has found that supply chains are sometimes managed link by link with little or no systemic analysis, even though the managers understand the entire chain. Nonetheless it is desirable to have statistics on fixed and marginal costs over time, and on cost in relation to volume so that the impact of cost-reduction programmes can be assessed and any problems addressed.

In collaborative networks we can expect to find some sharing of information costs and other financial matters. In some construction projects the dominant actor has created gain-sharing processes (Seal *et al.*, 1999) where there is one account for the project and all the participating firms are required to reveal their costs (and production problems). All extra profits on the contract are then shared between the participants. Given the one-off nature of construction projects, each firm can limit its commitment. A successful collaboration can enable the network to be the basis of successful future contract bidding.

In an extensive case study of interfirm accounting and coordination, Hakansson and Lind (2004) found that established accounting practices played a key role in the dyad they observed, that there was a systematic combining of accounting with overlapping accountability, and that accounting was a basic facilitating process. The information that flowed between the companies was not restricted to routine matters, and that information sharing was part of the problem solving process. Interestingly, all three forms of control (hierarchical, market and cooperation/collaboration) were present.

Most of the research in this area has looked at the limitations of accounting between dyads, and it seems that the use of an activity-based cost system throughout an interfirm network is not yet feasible. However a radical shift is promised by powerful computing technology. Berry *et al.* (2000) report that one UK-based multinational has developed a computerized information system that enables it to 'look globally along the 39 product chains in real time', as well as to examine accounts at the nodes (local and global manufacturing, distribution and sales) of the intrafirm network. This allows the company to manage each chain from the centre, and to examine capacity and capacity constraints in the 15 manufacturing countries, the supply systems in over 40 countries and sales in over 100 countries. Thus technology has reinforced the dominance of the centre over all operations. It would be very interesting to see whether an interfirm network could utilize similar information technology to the same effect.

In a study of three Japanese supply systems (all managed by dominant actors) Cooper and Slagmulder (2004) found that interorganizational cost management (IOCM) was characterized by three elements:

- Functionality-price-quality.
- Interorganizational cost investigations.
- Concurrent cost management. This was used only for high-value items and was either parallel or simultaneous.

They note that these practices were observed in several clusters, increasing in complexity. These could all involve interorganizational work groups. The clusters of practices were perceived to be associated with each of five relational contexts. The contexts were based upon either interaction characteristics (design dependence, resource sharing, supplier participation, bilateral commitment) or governance structure (incentives and protection).

Table 13.1 sets out Cooper and Slagmulder's findings (the definition of dependence is ours, following Miller, 1976). As can be seen, their findings do not contradict the thrust of the arguments in this chapter.

The cost management clusters were developed contemporaneously with the relational context. The driving logic for this was superior joint performance. This was difficult to establish *a priori* so the collaboration was a calculated gamble. The primary justification for these actions was based upon a discounted cash flow analysis of future savings. The value for the enhanced

Table 13.1 Relational contexts and IOCM clusters

Relational context	Cluster 1 only	Clusters 1 and 2	All 3	Dependence	Trust
Pure market (common suppliers)				Autonomy	Price
Pure hierarchy					
Subcontractor	X			Serial	Contract
Major supplier		X		Reciprocal	Competence
Family member			X	Mutual	Goodwill

capability of the partners was unknown, but the companies acknowledged the enhanced design capability emerging from the collaboration. These authors' observations about trust reflect the ideas of Sako (1992).

Networks and social relations: extrafirm issues

So far in this chapter collaboration has been addressed in a rather technical manner and little has been said about the issue of social control as a mode of extrafirm control. Social relations (which result from institutional context and actor behaviour (Scott, 1995), infuse the whole network and can never be separated from it. In a study of business systems in Asia, Whitley (1992) demonstrates that business systems are a product of their social context. This suggests that extrafirm considerations may have a greater influence on network formation and control than products, services and markets. The Anglo Saxon suspicion of, for example, trade associations and lobbying may be related to social individualism, unlike the social and cultural preferences that shape business networks in Germany, Italy and France. For example there is a great difference between the roles of the chambers of commerce in French cities (membership is mandatory and they have powers of taxation) and those in the UK (voluntary membership and no taxation). One consequence of this is that French chambers of commerce have created significant educational institutes (for example INSEAD, HEC), thus demonstrating the possibilities for those who work collaboratively.

To illustrate the significance of these observations, consider the findings of a study of the American automotive component supply industry, where alliances had been established between US and Japanese companies. The researchers reported that the Americans considered they had learned nothing from the collaboration, while the Japanese were puzzled about the attitudes and behaviour of the US participants. It seems that the clan-based control with which the Japanese were familiar, based on open discussions and the sharing of problems, knowledge and data, were not understood by the Americans, who were accustomed to control based on rules or market competition. Hence the dynamics of collaboration can be different for firms from different cultures. Nevertheless it is important for non-Japanese actors in a Japanese network to have the ability to engage in the required reciprocal or mutual dependence. If they cannot do that they might be treated as incidental contractors and subjected to market-based control, as can be seen in some Japanese manufacturing chains with sweatshop contractors on the margins.

Some theorists (for example Trist, 1976) view networks as ecosystems, that is, systems of systems (each firm being a complex system in itself), where the need for coordination can be met by creating informal, *ad hoc* reference or steering groups. These groups would consist of staff from some or all of the firms and would be set up to handle particular problems, as Cooper and Slagmulder (2004) have observed in the case of cost management. Change in networks can be difficult if a number of organizations have come together very successfully for a specific purpose. It may not be assumed that the network will be able to take on a further and different collaborative task (Huxham and Vangen, 1996). Ongoing collaboration will require ongoing negotiation. This is not so much a matter of building trust as building a new coalition of willing participants.

To assume that all that is needed for success is to design an operating system that can be run satisfactorily to achieve the expected benefits is to ignore potential social problems. The matrix form of organization has been adopted by divisionalized organizations in order to bring about coherence and reduce conflict among divisions, yet it is clear that multinational firms still find that cultural issues can pose major problems, as the extensive literature on this topic demonstrates. The cultural problems that arose in the US/Japanese venture mentioned above have been repeated many times in other alliances or joint ventures. But it is arguable that people of different cultures, are equally able to understand the benefits of an embedded system or network to work towards it. Nevertheless people from cultures with a greater disposition towards collective working will be better at engaging in micro social processes to realize long-term benefits.

▍ Other issues

A number of issues have yet to be examined. These include a consideration of networks from the perspectives of decision making and strategy, and social relations and governance. It was argued earlier that three ideal types of control – dominance, competition and collaboration – can exist simultaneously in an interfirm network. Recent researchers have used very similar models, not surprisingly as many of their studies have been based on the work of Williamson (1973) and Ouchi (1980). However there are a number of difficult questions to be answered.

If control in an interfirm network is expressed both through managerial systems and as the product of its institutional context, the question remains as to how these extrafirm contexts shape interfirm networks? Which of the elements of the social and economic context have the most enduring effect on network creation and network functioning? To answer the question there is a need for further observation of the behaviour and outcomes of networks, with attention to the issues of uncertainty and risk management. These should be considered in the context of the determining forces of the social and political processes in the environment.

It is argued that there are two principal motives for creating networks: dominant actors seek to gain market control by creating networks while avoiding ownership and limiting capital expenditure and other commitments; or partners create a network of more or less symmetrical power relations as a means to enhance or protect their market position. We need to undertake studies to understand the implications of the different motivations.

The managers of networks must be able to handle the complexity, ambiguity and conflict that will arise through different conceptions of structure and design. They must be adept at switching modes of behaviour from negotiating, establishing, modifying and operating in networks of firms. How can these capabilities be developed?

Given that control can encourage defensiveness, how can control procedures be designed to prevent the network resisting change? Can the partners remove or limit the defensive routines that exist in their firms (secretiveness, personal fiefdoms, lust for power, conflict of ambitions, narcissistic leadership) and will therefore exist in the network in the form of fear of being exploited, lack of generosity, readiness to blame others, political bargaining, and failure to understanding the partners' needs. If such routines are not addressed they may prevent changes, and the inevitable lack of trust might shatter the network. The fate of many joint ventures suggests that this is a real problem. So how can a control system be created that helps the partners need to learn both about the inside of the network and the environment? Cooper and Slagmulder's (2004) work suggests that this may be best done by means of interorganizational work groups with open boundaries.

Finally there has been little critical analysis of networks across developed, developing and underdeveloped countries. Addressing this will require attention to cultural and religious differences, and how these can be mediated and managed. The insights provided by Huxham and Vangen (1996) into cross-sectoral networks indicate the scale of this problem.

Discussion questions

1. Consider a network system with which you are familiar. If you agree that interfirm networks are central to economic development, how can control be exercised within them?
2. To what extent do social networks dominate the control processes in interfirm networks?
3. What limitations does financial management have in the assessment of network performance?

Notes

1. Most of the work on social networks stems from the work of Mitchell (1969).
2. Richardson (1972) identifies three similar control relationships: hierarchical, market (following Williamson, 1973) and cooperation.
3. There are network organizations (religious bodies, political movements) whose *raison d'être* is to promote values and beliefs but these appear to choose a mode of control that can be hierarchical or a mixture of the types.
4. Some scholars assert that firms can choose their culture, but here we follow the view that firms are the visible expression of their institutional context (Scott, 1995).
5. Thompson (1967) proposes a similar taxonomy: pooled, sequential and reciprocal interdependence.

14 Control of supply chains

Anthony J. Berry, John Cullen and Willie Seal

Introduction

It has been argued that traditional management accounting control systems do not readily support supply chain management initiatives. This chapter explores the development of supply chain concepts and the growing interest in supply chain accounting. Supply chain management is:

> The strategic management process [that unifies] the systematic planning and control of technologies, materials and services, from identification of need by the ultimate customer. It encompasses planning, designing, purchasing, production, logistics and quality. The objectives are to optimise performance in meeting agreed customer service requirements, minimising cost, whilst optimising the use of all resources throughout the entire supply chain (DTI, 1997).

Interfirm supply chains involve the organization working beyond its legal and organizational boundaries and building relationships with suppliers and customers along the value chain. However the traditional management control systems are internally focused and do not consider the potential for exploiting linkages with the firm's suppliers and customers. Therefore they must be adapted to handle the management of new organizational forms (such as strategic alliances, partnerships, networks and virtual organizations), the growth of which has been a significant factor in securing competitive advantage in a dynamic market. In essence, management control systems must be capable of identifying costs and value-adding processes across traditional organizational boundaries and focus on supporting cooperative ventures between organizations.

Evaluation of supply chains

Changes in the technology and organization of production, lean production (Womack *et al.*, 1990), closer supplier relationships (Lamming, 1993), world-class manufacturing and flexible specialization have transformed manufacturing and the provision of services. In the case of Japan, (Akoi, 1988; Okimoto, 1986; Sako, 1992) this has involved the establishment of long-term relationships with customers and suppliers. The term supply chain management originated in the 1980s, when it referred to internal business functions of purchasing, manufacturing, sales and distribution (Harland, 1996). Since then it has been extended beyond the firm to incorporate management operations across organizational boundaries (ibid.) Sako (1992) identifies four main theoretical approaches to the study of supply chains:

- Transaction cost economics, following Coase (1937) and Williamson (1979).
- Relational contract theory, influenced by Macaulay (1963) and Macneil (1974).
- The sociological approach to networks adopted by Granovetter (1985) and Frances and Garnsey (1996).
- Networks as management strategies, for example Miles and Snow (1986) and Nohria and Eccles (1992).

The adoption of cooperative strategies requires re-examination of accounting governance and control systems that assume arm's-length transactions (Gietzmann, 1996) as this assumption presents a major obstacle to the formation of alliances or partnerships (Stuart and McCutcheon, 1996). Success in partnerships requires commitment, coordination, trust, the sharing of risks and information and participation and joint problem solving (Mohr and Speckman, 1994) to reduce transaction and production costs (Dyer and Ouchi, 1993; Williamson, 1975). The need for trust is pointed out by many authors (for example Pruitt, 1981; Stuart and McCutcheon, 1996) but it takes time to build (Turnbull *et al.*, 1992). Sako (1992) identifies three types of trust:

- Contractual trust, which relates to the keeping of promises.
- Competence trust: the trust that partners have the ability to carry out the work.
- Goodwill trust: this allows more discretion and implies the possibility of greater commitment.

In these cases, trust appears to be about accepting that the other party will behave well and not exploit other parties.

Supply chain partnerships constitute a considerable organizational innovation (Teece, 1996) and can be a viable and advantageous way to achieve the benefits of vertical integration (Johnston and Lawrence, 1988). Much of the literature seeks to achieve success for both customers and suppliers in partnerships, resulting in a win–win situation (Kanter, 1994; Macbeth and Ferguson, 1994; Helper and Sako, 1995).

The supply chain literature has its origins in studies of Japanese companies, especially car manufacturers. Whether the social structure found in Japanese companies is crucial to the operation of supply chains is unclear, but it is argued that the societal values and beliefs shape the economic arrangements of corporations and markets (Scott, 1995; Whitley, 1994). Japan and other Asian countries are viewed as having a more dependent culture than that in the UK, and this is held to explain some aspects of interorganizational behaviour where trust is implied but may actually be more a matter of social obligation. The issues of dependence, power and dominance in network formation and functioning have been addressed by Zheng *et al.*, 1997), who states that in the pharmaceutical and automotive industries the final manufacturer is dominant, in the retail consumer goods sector the final retailer exercises considerable power, and in the electronic components industry there is no one dominant actor.

Castells (1996, p. 194) argues that the trend in the UK towards supply chain integration and networking does not mean that the UK is shifting to the Asian model:

> Countries and institutions continue to shape the organisational requirements of the new economy, in an interaction between the logic of production, the changing technological base, and the institutional features of the social environment. The architecture and composition of business networks being formed around the world are influenced by the national characteristics of societies where such networks are embedded.

Moreover, as noted by Turnbull *et al.* (1992, pp. 167–8), there is a lack of trust (or in our terms, social obligation) in the UK, and this extends to Japanese-style techniques: 'After more than ten years of price freezes, volume cuts, multiple sourcing and the like, many suppliers view the latest moves to JIT as another means by which the vehicle assemblers intend to put the squeeze on.' This assertion is backed by Frances and Garnsey (1996), who have found that large UK food stores use accounting techniques as control mechanisms that extend beyond their own boundaries to control suppliers.

Table 14.1 Control at the various stages of the supply chain development

Stages of transition	Interfirm control	Intrafirm control
The *autonomous firm* in an arm's-length relationship with free buyers and sellers. Firm A is independent from firm B	None	
Serial dependence: the output of firm A goes directly into the production system of firm B	Management control is handled by the dominant actor	Management control is handled via common transfer pricing policies
Reciprocal dependence: firm A and firm B are dependent upon each other to the extent that firm A and firm B affect each other's behaviour	Management control has developed to include some attention to each other's costs	Management control procedures reflect interaction between units
Mutual dependence: the behaviours of firm A and firm B are interlinked	Management control represented in a jointly constructed financial representation of the supply chain	Management control is set within the context of broad business considerations

This has given rise to barriers to entry and increased the stores' market power and concentration.

Earlier chapters considered the issue of control in relation to the hierarchical and market forms of organization (see also Williamson, 1979). Between these two lie a number of alliances or what are sometimes called hybrid forms, which can exist in supply chains within firms (intrafirm) and between firms (interfirm). Four of these are shown in Table 14.1.

These four types can also be seen as steps in the creation of a managed supply chain, with three stages of transition: from autonomy to serial dependence, where the two firms are loosely tied together; from serial dependence to reciprocal dependence, where the interplay of the two firms is recognized and managed; and from reciprocal dependence to mutual dependence, where full partnership behaviour is evident. This suggests that the development of management control and accounting will closely follow the position of the firms in respect of the degree of autonomy or dependence. In autonomous firms there will be no attention to interfirm supply chain accounting.

Management control and accounting

The establishment of a supply chain requires changes to be made to the organization of production and the control of costs by the customer and the supplier. The success of Japanese suppliers and assemblers in respect of the return on assets (RoA) achieved by each company in the partnership and the poor results achieved in the UK has been noted by Lamming (1993). In his view '... lean accounting would provide the means for such information, upon which lean production might be based in the search for reducing costs, improving value and gaining a better understanding of the behaviour of both' (ibid., p. 200).

As supply chains develop, via outsourcing and/or partnerships, lean supply arrangements (Saunders, 1994) are required as a large part of the cost of production is accounted for by supplied goods. Saunders notes that 'costs are an important dimension of performance in supply chains and it is a factor that needs to be managed on an integrated basis' (ibid., p. 213). He argues for a more proactive role for purchasing and supply managers and for a more holistic and systematic approach, leading to a 'total cost of supply' or 'total cost of ownership'. He proposes the use of activity-based costing, target costing and an open book policy to improve supply chain effectiveness. The conflict between partnership and the asset management basis of accounting has been pointed out by Gietzmann (1996), who argues that some modification of accounting governance is necessary, based upon trust and commitment. The use of Japanese supply chain and accounting practices has proved difficult for UK firms that have introduced them without sufficient attention to governance issues (ibid.)

Supply chains are essentially horizontal and require integration along the chain. The search for more effective operational cost models was given impetus by the recognition of cost drivers (Porter, 1985). These facilitate the analysis of costs in the value chain in the pursuit of competitive advantage. This new focus on a wider array of sources of costs improves on the situation where 'accounting systems do contain useful data, but they often get in the way of strategic cost analysis' (ibid., p. 63). However the inward vertical integration models of accounting still ignore value created outside the firm's boundaries (Partridge and Perren, 1994).

Subsequent research has emphasized that the identification of cost drivers and analysis of the costs in the value chain are essential to the attainment of competitive advantage (Bromwich, 1991; Hergert and Morris, 1989; Partridge and Perren, 1994; Shank and Govindarajan, 1992). Quillian (1991, p. 9) notes that activity-based costing (ABC), process value analysis and performance measurement 'can act as a catalyst for integrating isolated logistics functions, leading to substantial improvements in costs, cycle times, inventories and levels of customer service'. Complementing Quillian's study of suppliers, Lee and Seraph (1995) have examined supply issues from the purchaser's perspective. They note that ABC can be used as a basis for price negotiation and as a means of exploring how suppliers have arrived at a price. Taken together, these two studies suggest that suppliers and buyers can usefully join forces to achieve common efficiencies, but they do not indicate how any consequent savings could be shared.

For assemblers who purchase a large proportion of their parts, supply chain efficiency is crucial for competitiveness. In the case of Nissan, 'achieving total cost control throughout the whole supply chain has [been] a critical challenge' (Carr and Ng, 1995, p. 348). These authors report that Nissan used a multidisciplinary team approach to supply cost management and noted that the openness of the suppliers' books – or transparency – was limited (see also Lamming, 1993). Two major suppliers showed 'concern as to whether Nissan would exploit its position of power, particularly in the light of its tougher circumstances' (ibid., p. 361).

Supply chain advocates speak mostly about cost control but they also emphasize partnership which is intended to bring benefits to all participants in a shared destiny. It is necessary at least to align performance with the shared destiny principle (Harland, 1996), and with some agreement on the measures to be used (Hope and Hope, 1995). This might be achieved by applying the balanced scorecard method to the problem, combining its four elements (customer, internal business, innovation and learning) with a financial perspective.

Interest in the part played by management control systems in the development of interorganizational relationships has grown rapidly in recent years. Berry *et al.* (2000) examine techniques such as open book accounting, target costing, total cost approaches and performance measurement systems to measure improvements in the supply chain. Mouritsen *et al.* (2001a) discuss the ways in which interorganizational management controls, such as target cost management/functional analysis and open book accounting, create new possibilities for management intervention in processes both internal and external to the organization. Seal *et al.* (1999) researched the role of accounting in the establishment of a strategic supply partnership. They found that accounting played a constitutional role in the development of the partnerships in question and there was a willingness to look at processes that would cross the organizational boundaries. However there were problems with the common systems and boundaries created around the open book relationship. Finally, Cooper and Slagmulder (2004) have explored interorganizational cost management during product design and the characteristics of the relationships associated with them. They were both traditional relationships based on markets and hierarchies and additional hybrid relationships. The authors suggest that the firms in the study had developed interorganizational cost management techniques to overcome an information asymmetry between buyers and suppliers.

A number of papers have focused on trust in interorganizational relationships (for example Dekker, 2004; Seal *et al.*, 2004; Tomkins, 2001; Van der Meer-Kooistra and Vosselmann, 2000) and the role of accounting. Dekker (2004), in a study of a strategic alliance in the railway industry, found that the chosen management control systems – through the support they offered to the realisation of the alliance's goals and the creation of mutual transparency – enhanced the relationship of trust between the partners. The control mechanisms largely consisted of management accounting practices (for example budgeting, open book accounting) and the findings suggest that management accounting can be an essential part of governance in interorganizational relationships. Interestingly, Tomkins (2001) raises issues about trust and questions information characteristics at different stages of business development and the information needs of types of alliances at different stages of development. He suggests that accounting systems must be 'lean' and that leanness can be obtained by carefully balancing trust and information sharing.

Some logistical research has provided empirical evidence of the use of management accounting techniques to facilitate re-engineering. For example Goldsby and Closs (2000) report on the use of activity-based costing to re-engineer the reverse logistics channel in the Michigan beverage industry. Farris and Hutchinson (2002) discuss the concept of cash-to-cash (C2C), which they see as the new supply chain management metric. C2C is the length of time between cash payment for supplies and the collection of accounts receivable generated by the sale of the goods. Managing the C2C cycle involves both a cross-functional approach within the firm and a collaborative approach throughout the supply chain. Farris and Hutchinson discuss the significant benefits gained by Dell Computer Corporation and Cisco Systems from the use of this approach. In broader terms, they report that companies with best-in-class supply chain management practices outperform their average-performing competitors by 10–30 per cent on delivery time, 40–60 per cent on C2C cycle time and 50–80 per cent on inventory reduction. Finally, Bernon and Cullen (2004), in a study of retail reverse logistics processes, argue that if a holistic supply chain approach is taken when managing of the reverse logistics process, then benefits can be gained in both economic and environmental terms. Included in their analysis is the potential for using quality-costing and opportunity-costing techniques to reduce costs throughout the supply chain, including the management of returned products.

Having considered some of the literature on management control and accounting, we shall now look at some empirical work conducted by the authors.

Control in supply chains

Berry *et al.* (2000) investigated management control accounting practices in the UK in relation to the development of supply chain management. The data is from case studies of three interfirm supply chains, one at each of the following stages of development: serial dependence, reciprocal dependence and mutual dependence. Representatives of 13 other companies were interviewed using a semistructured schedule. Their stages of supply chain development are shown in Table 14.2.

Strategic decision making

The benefit of vertical integration (coordination) via hierarchy was that many stages of the complex supply chain could be managed in-house. However because the larger multinational companies operated in many regions, countries

Table 14.2 Stages of supply chain development

	Interfirm	*Intrafirm*
Management of suppliers (serial dependence; Lamming:* stress)	6 firms	No evidence gathered in this study
Collaboration with suppliers (reciprocal dependence; Lamming:* resolved)	2 firms	3 firms
Systemic management of a chain (mutual dependence; Lamming:* partnerships)	3 firms	2 firms
Average turnover	£700 million	£2540 million

* Lamming (1993) constructed a four-phase model of customer–supplier relationships that recognized different phases of development. The four phases were the traditional approach, stress, resolved and partnership. In the traditional model, the supplier with the lowest bid would be awarded a contract. In the stress phases, favoured suppliers were encouraged to invest and gain benefits from competitive advantage available in new practices and plants. Although, the involvement of suppliers was driven by attempts to reduce costs. In the resolved phase, there was increased recognition of the importance of relationships and this resulted in more collaboration. In the partnership phases, it was recognized that the resolved model was not sufficiently progressive for best-practice relationships. Best practice was identified as being a partnership between two firms, showing respect and valuing each other's contribution, engaged in the relationship.

and markets, managing in-house presented considerable difficulties. The use of supply chain management as a tool for strategic integration was evident in the intrafirm cases, but it had not been possible to develop the same degree of strategic integration in the interfirm cases, which perhaps served to reduce supply chain effectiveness. The introduction of supply chain management had led to a significant increase in functional integration and the use of multifunctional teams was very common. This was taking place in the context of 'delayering', so that the complexity of the teams' work was also increasing. Hence it appeared that the development of the intrafirm supply chains had produced very radical changes in the firms in question. Changes in the interfirm companies were more limited, but radical solutions to the problem of integrating the companies in the chain were being sought. The solution adopted by a textile firm that was not included in the study was physically to separate its manufacturing plants in order to dedicate one plant to one customer and integrate their production and distribution systems.

Relational contracting and shared destiny

One of the firms in the study was a (serial dependent) supplier to a number of multinational companies in the automotive business and therefore had experience of several approaches to managing a supply chain. The firm's relationships with these customers varied markedly. In the case of those which had proved to be hard bargainers it was likely to take many more years before for the relations to become fully cooperative. The firm assumed that the customers were attempting to secure compliance and cost reduction, or were trying to extract more of the profits from the system. In contrast customers with some understanding of collaboration were given more attention and there was a greater readiness to share productivity and product technology improvements with these customers and parallel suppliers. However the firm was unwilling to open its accounting books to detailed scrutiny, and was certainly unwilling to enter into detailed discussions of its cost structures with any of its customers.

Decision-making and control cycle: planning, budgeting and reporting

In virtually all the companies the routine management control and accounting cycles remained in place despite the introduction of accounting innovations. In most there had been little impact on the financial planning, budgeting and reporting regimes. Despite identifying the need to understand processes, and introducing *ad hoc* systems to provide the necessary information, there was still a tendency to provide routine monthly reports under traditional functional responsibility headings. However there was also evidence, in line with the stages of development model, of horizontal integration practices being created alongside the typical vertical integration procedures of management accounting.

One major issue in this new environment was that the order-fulfilling cycles were becoming much shorter and out of harmony with the common monthly and annual cycles of management accounting. There was evidence that the attention directing elements of the formal management systems were being by-passed by physical, real time observations and action taken without formal cost analysis.

Supply chain thinking was based partly on the concept of extending cost management to include upstream processes and inputs to the firm. Hence cost management had extended from production to embrace accounting and procurement. There was also evidence of horizontal information systems, kaizen costing, benchmarking, open book accounting, value engineering and target costing. The changes in management control accounting practice broadly fitted the stages of development model. Cost management for efficiency and effectiveness was largely changing in line with the stages of the development model, with more impact as interdependence grew.

Costing practices: how costs were measured

Supply chain management had stimulated cost management procedures to control internal costs, especially the cost of resources and their procurement. Common to most firms the use of standard costs was to measure product profitability; the advent of supply chain management had had no effect on this. However the speed of change and the shortening of cycles had led to standards not being used for detailed variance analysis. While there were cost management procedures in many of the companies, these were part of general management and were not directly related to supply chain management. There was little evidence of the use of marginal and variable costs, except when the cost of a principal material input so dwarfed other costs that the material cost was an estimate of variable costs. There was little evidence of life-cycle costing in any of the firms in the study. The expectation that ABM/C, would find a ready application in the interfirm supply chain was not observed. ABM/C had been applied in major companies with an intrafirm supply chain. The interfirm supply systems in this research were not analysed using cost models that followed the structures of the chains.

Cost of suppliers

There was little or no evidence that the benefits and costs of changing the process of managing suppliers had been analysed. Decisions had been taken on the basis that reducing the number of suppliers and making staff reductions would have positive outcomes. Few of the companies had appropriate accounting procedures for recording and tracking the costs of purchasing.

In the case of interfirm chains it was observed that a change to relationships of serial dependence produced dominance in the chain. Reduction in the number of suppliers meant that the reciprocal dependence had to be managed. So reduction of the number of suppliers (dominance to ensure efficiency) was followed by efforts to build collaborative advantage. The intrafirm companies were following the same processes, but in a more sophisticated way. These processes took place with very little formal cost–benefit analysis and little impact on management accounting.

All the companies calculated the cost of holding stock and the use of lean production to reduce cycle times was common. The expectation that supply chain management would lead to target costing, becoming a central theme was not borne out, except in the case of one Japanese-owned company. There was no evidence of throughput costing in any of the companies.

Cost minimization requires knowledge of the marginal costs of the production processes along a chain. Two of the intrafirm companies had knowledge of marginal cost and the models of the processes and hence were able to consider this issue. Few if any of the firms' supply chains suffered capacity constraints. If capacity was problematic it was because different supply chains were using the same production and distribution facilities.

These findings fitted with the earlier evidence on ABM/C. The further along the supply chain stages the greater the likelihood that ABC techniques were applied to the chain. The existence of 'open books' reflected development through the supply chain stages. In cases of market or serial dependence the books were closed. As reciprocal dependence developed the books were opened to improve the chain relationship. However the degree of openness should not be overstated as there were no a general invitations to peruse companies' accounts. In one case of interfirm reciprocal dependence it was accepted that the customers should provide the supplier with information (including cost and value added calculations) on procedures between the delivery of components and their subsequent use in the assembly process.

Performance management

As firms moved along the supply chain stages the degree of attention given to performance measurement and management increased. The decision-making challenge in the later stages was whether to continue to 'bolt on' additional supply chain performance measurements or to switch to a supply chain management approach that integrated a process-driven structure with an integrated information system. The main focus of reporting in the firms had not changed, but the impact of supply chain development at each stage had led to consideration of the need for reporting along and about the chain.

There was evidence of integration of planning processes and additional reporting for supply chain issues. The common monthly and annual cycles of management accounting were challenged by the shortening cycle of order fulfilment (ordering, procurement, manufacture and delivery). The accounting cycles were too slow to be of use in monitoring and managing the order fulfilment process so physical measures were being used instead.

Supply chain thinking complicated the locus of responsibility and accountability in a manner very similar to programme planning and budgeting structures. In one intrafirm company, new demands relating to the supply chain forced operational integration. The structures of responsibility and accountability and the financial transfer rules had been redefined, which had affected the performance measures. This had had a direct impact on managers who had become accustomed to divisional performance-related pay. Consequently there were significant problems with integrating the intraorganizational supply chain.

In general this problem was due to management accounting and control procedures being used for short, medium and long-term integration. In the newer world of supply chain thinking, vertical integration of the management accounting and control cycle still exists to provide a longer term view (as does financial reporting). However there was evidence in two of the companies of the use of information and control systems for intrafunctional integration in the short or medium term. One of the companies, whose entire strategic focus was on creating partnerships, used a version of the balanced scorecard (Kaplan and Norton, 1992) to measure performance in partnership situations. There was also evidence that progress through the supply chain stages had had a parallel impact on reporting procedures.

The study was not primarily about Electronic Data Interchange (EDI). However the early stages of supply development using simple linking exchanges, such as ordering and scheduling. At the most developed companies the use of EDI was via complex logistics systems, to which could be added systems for accounting.

Efficiency

For the companies in our study, cost management was central to supply chain management. This was in line with the observation by Saunders (1994) and by Lee and Seraph (1995) that as companies move to lean manufacturing there is a tendency to purchase subassembled input materials. The overall relationship between labour and material costs does not change, but it changes for the final assembler. As the proportion of input costs in input and transformation costs increase the focus of management moves from production to procurement. There was evidence in some of the companies that the penetration of management control and accounting into the small details of organizational work was being pushed up the hierarchy, although this was levelling out. This occurred because the companies used physical measures as the basis of decisions, with an eye to the consequences of costs. In the intrafirm supply chains, and to a lesser extent in the interfirm ones too, the point at which physical and accounting measures were integrated was shifting.

Effectiveness (optimization)

We expected that management accounting procedures based on a more systemic approach to cost management would be applied in the inter- and intrafirm supply chains because they offered a means of moving away from single, overhead rate calculations. In fact there was little evidence of the application of Business Process Engineering, ABM or ABC. The interfirm chains were managed link by link, with little or no consideration of the sequence of the links. In one interfirm chain the firms did examine interorganizational processes and accounting information, but this involved only a single link.[1] The intrafirm chains should have been more amenable to these approaches but those classified as reciprocally dependent were not changing rapidly, while those in mutual dependence had changed to more sophisticated modelling.

Strategic cost management

There was little or no evidence in the companies with interfirm chains of the use of management accounting for strategic management. There was no evidence of strategic management control,[2] although management accountants were involved in strategic management, which included getting a grip on input costs. In intrafirm cases of mutual dependence the firms were close to having an integrated logistics, procurement, production and market model. This included accounting data, thus creating an on-line strategic management tool.

Horizontal information systems

In two of the companies in interfirm chains (one of which was serial dependent and the other reciprocally dependent), horizontal information systems were very much project based, but these were additions to extant practices. Horizontal information systems were most developed in the companies in mutually dependent intrafirm chains, which had developed very sophisticated logistical models of procurement, production and distribution that extended to the flows in their suppliers' factories. However marketing and accounting data had not been integrated into supply chain management. This was to be the next major step.

Two cutting edge intrafirm examples

In general the greatest impact of supply chains on management accounting was found in intrafirm chains in multinational companies. This was the product of converging a number of practices and technologies, including computing power. The building of very complex logistics models, the use of satellite communications technology (fast and always available), local access to global systems, the application of systemic thinking as a mode of integration, moves towards lean manufacturing and world class manufacturing, the need for rich information for decision-making, control and analysis and the capacity to manage beyond the legal boundaries by modes of dominance (serial dependence, reciprocal dependence and mutual dependence) were being brought together to establish process-driven integrated information systems (PDIIS). However these new (if embryonic) systems were being introduced alongside the extant systems and had not displaced them as the new had to be embedded before the old were abandoned. They had not removed the need for local operating information systems, but when integrated with accounting they potentially provided a tool for strategic analysis and management control. Two of the companies were close to achieving this, and several more were moving in that direction – that is, from reciprocal to mutual dependence.

Evidence from other case studies

Strategic Alliance (Seal *et al.*, 1999)

Seal *et al.* (1999) studied two British-owned manufacturing companies in the automotive industry that were thinking of establishing strategic supply partnership. In the assembler company, materials accounted for 80 per cent of manufacturing costs, so managing supply chain costs was a crucial element of overall cost control. The company was seeking closer ties (involving information sharing and R & D collaboration) with a supplier of strategic components. For its part the supplier wished to establish the degree of cooperation and trust that the two companies had realized in their US operations. In the UK the two companies had been doing business for approximately 25 years but until recently their relationship had been at arm's length. For the proposed strategic alliance, the initial supply agreement was based on a document drawn up by the assembler that stressed an open and trusting relationship that 'delivers tangible and measurable benefits to both sides over a long period, and allows the sharing of ideas and information'. It had a cost reduction target of 6 per cent per annum for controllable costs but would accommodate changes in the price of raw materials and exchange rate movements by reference to agreed public data. The agreement specified areas that should be subject to continuous improvement, a management review process and a governance procedure. The proposed alliance would involve cross-company teams seeking out and designing mutually beneficial technical projects. These would be jointly funded, but the assembler would have first use of the developments a predetermined period.

Subsequent development of the alliance agreement changed the 6 per cent cost reduction to a reduction in 'all-in cost'. Although this potentially made agreement with the supplier easier, it raised technical challenges in respect of measuring the reduction and distributing the benefits between parties. There was common ground with regard to moving some of the value-added work to the supplier, as had happened in the United States. However there was a problem with timing as it would not be 'politically acceptable' to move work from the assembler before the core business had grown sufficiently to take up any slack created by outsourcing. For an open book agreement on operational matters, negotiations were needed on the boundaries of activities and in respect of demonstrating benefits that were quantitative but not necessarily financial. Differences and weaknesses in both firms' cost systems also presented technical difficulties for the open book agreement.

The case of Dextron (Seal *et al.*, 2004)

Dextron designed, assembled and built computers in a plant with 300 employees. It had two main products: a personal computer and a computer aimed at the business market. For both products, chips were the most expensive bought-in items, accounting for approximately 50 per cent of the total production cost. The company operated in a very competitive market and its purchasing style had had to be adapted to cope with growing competitive pressure. Until 1995 purchasing had been rather traditional with strongish bonds between the suppliers and Dextron. As competitive pressure became severe, during the period 1995–98 the company sought to improve the efficiency of its production by introducing supply logistics integrated management. This involved the creation of cross-functional teams to increase the company's customer focus and break away from the rather compartmentalized 'silo' model that had hitherto characterized the company's production process. A key aspect of this was the setting up of a cost management group (CMG) in early 1996. Initially the group consisted of a project accountant and a project engineer, but later more members were added. By the end of 1997 the CMG was involved in reducing supply chain costs through the benchmarking of suppliers, value engineering, identifying the total cost of ownership, setting up hubs in appropriate geographical locations, quality costing and developing a sophisticated supplier management programme.

As Dextron's supply chain initiative progressed, from 1998 some effort was made to move away from adversarial forms of relationship and to engage in collaboration for mutual advantage. During this phase the CMG identified opportunities for marketing, benchmarking and tear-down analysis, Enterprise Resource Planning (ERP) systems and the reduction of inventories. The part played by accountants in the CMG was broadened and they took on extra production, commercial, organizational and change management roles in addition to the substantial accounting contribution that they were already making. Over time the CMG had evolved from initiating *ad hoc* studies on cost reduction to become the focus of continuous change in supply chain practices. Although the team was multifunctional it was dominated by accountants, who did their best to promote best practice in Dextron's supply chain.

School Trends (Cullen and Mather, 2003)

School Trends employed 120 people and had a turnover of around £8 million. Its core business was customized primary and secondary school wear. The study explored, through action research, the entire supply chain, from the suppliers of garments to all internal processes in School Trends, inventory management, decorating subcontractors, logistics operations and customers in the primary school and secondary school sectors. The activities in School Trends (including boundary-spanning activities) were mapped and a form was devised to identify weaknesses in the process and possible solutions. Also examined were external relationships, costs and benefits, lessons learned and discrepancies between planned completion date and actual completion date. A key purpose of this exploration was to investigate the cost of waste (process and product).

Members of the supply chain were then interviewed to enable process mapping across the organizational boundaries. 'Weakness forms' were completed and action points identified. The discussions involved challenging existing practices, for example norms of delivery and style of packaging, and action was taken to share benefits throughout the supply chain. For example packaging and the positioning of logos was causing problems for the logistics provider. Through joint action the problem areas were identified and changes were made. This improved both the performance of the logistics operator and the handling of packaging at School Trends. The sharing of information was facilitated by the introduction of a new software system.

The whole approach was focused on opening up discussions with different partners in the supply chain about sharing information. As a result significant changes were made to internal and external processes. However it should be noted that agreement on information sharing was only achieved because good relationships already existed among the supply chain.

Conclusions

Most supply chains are managed as a set of discrete links, with little or no attention to managing the chain as a whole. This reflects the construct of supply chains as observed sets of connections and not as manageable sets of interfirm behaviours, which in turn reflects the question of ownership and asset protection. Many companies in supply chains do not see themselves as surrendering to the needs of the integrated chain, but as managing their destiny by engaging in a series of relationships that bring mutual advantages. This fits with argument by Scott (1995) that economic arrangements reflect the (changing) social structure.

Reference has been made in this chapter to integrated information systems (PDIIS), including electronic data interchange and enterprise resource planning systems. Whilst Berry *et al.* (2000) found that a few years ago most of these focused on intrafirm activities, further developments in information technology have enabled strategic information sharing across organizational boundaries. It is important to recognize, however, that information technology mainly acts as an enabler (Cullen *et al.*, 2001) and that a taking advantage of the available opportunities depends on understanding of relational aspects of supply chain management.

Recent studies, many of which are empirical in nature, have considered the use of management control systems in the management of new forms of organization, such as strategic alliances, joint ventures and virtual organizations. For example, there is concern about the way in which management accounting practices are being configured in the context of the relationship between trust and information. Equally there is debate about their appropriateness at different stages of business relationship development. Finally, much of the debate in this area is relevant to accounting in networks, as discussed in Chapter 13.

Discussion questions

1. Critically evaluate whether management accounting control systems help or hinder the development of supply chain relationships.

2. Discuss the notion that management accounting control systems differ at different stages of business relationships (Tomkins, 2001).

Notes

1. Lamming (1993) has made a similar observation.
2. In the sense that strategic management accounting refers to strategic decisions about cost structures in relation to competitors' cost structures.

15 Management controls in the public services: the example of schools

Gloria Agyemang and Jane Broadbent

Overview

During the last 25 years the nature of management control in the public services has changed considerably all over the world. Both governments and public service managers have sought to address the problems that result from changing ideological positions and environmental pressures. The former include differing positions on the role of government in planning and delivering services. Related pressures include the impact of globalization, the impact of external regulators (as noted in Chapter 5) and changing technologies, among many others. The varying combinations have led to diverse systems and structures of management control, and to the imposition of controls that have affected interorganizational relationships and control systems. To explore these various approaches we shall look at the example of UK schools. Particular attention will be paid to the partnership policy adopted by the New Labour government as it is indicative of the thinking that is currently influencing the approaches of government in many nation states. Before this a more general discussion of the trajectory of change will be provided.

It would be impossible and indeed foolish to try to define a starting point for the changes that have taken place in the public services. There has been continual pressure for efficiency and economies in the sector in order to make best use of the limited resources available.[1] However a starting date for this analysis must be chosen so we shall settle for 1979, the year of the election of the Thatcher government in the UK. This Conservative administration started to introduce changes that reflected an approach adopted by economies all over the world, but perhaps most quickly and aggressively in New Zealand. This approach was called new public management (Hood, 1991, 1995) and espoused the view that private sector practices should be adopted, including the delegation of financial control, performance measurement and rewards for achieving them. However there was distrust of professional power so tight control of outcomes was used as a means of control.

In the context of schools in the UK (similar things happened elsewhere – see Broadbent *et al.*, 1999, for a comparison with New Zealand) the Education Reform Act of 1988 took financial and management control away from local education authorities and delegated it to schools under the Local Management of Schools scheme. The Act also established a national curriculum and a regime of testing to ensure that the curriculum was followed and the desired standards achieved. Thus financial freedom came at some cost to professional autonomy. A market-based ideology was also implicit in the change. Market forces and the accompanying competition were seen as means of encouraging efficiency whilst minimizing the costs of direct control. In essence there was an attempt to introduce the idea of 'the survival of the fittest'. In some areas of economic activity, markets were produced by selling off parts of the infrastructure, thus privatizing them and removing their monopoly – as in the case of the utilities. In other areas competition was introduced in different ways. In education the idea of having catchment areas that defined the populations schools would serve was abandoned. Instead schools were financed on an age-weighted pupil basis, with funding following the pupils. Thus schools had to compete to attract sufficient pupils to secure the funds to pay for the number of teachers required to provide a full national curriculum. Whilst the nature of this competition varied in practice – some schools were in a position to select pupils rather than pupils choosing them – the idea of competition came to be embedded.

New public management (NPM) has had many different incarnations (Olsen *et al.*, 1998) and is no longer new. However the drift from the public administration of services to the management of their provision has never ceased. It is reflected in fragmentation of the education provided to our future policy makers and managers into political science, MBA and now MPA (master of public administration) courses. Thus we are now less likely to speak about the public sector than about the public services. As citizens we have become accustomed to the notion of competition between service providers and to the rhetoric of performance measurement and outcome indicators. At the same time those who run the services tend to complain about the strictness of the regulatory bodies that are responsible for what they do and how they do it. Thus NPM has produced a contradiction in the provision of public services. On the one hand is the seeming freedom brought by the market mechanism, on the other is tight central control of what professionals practice.

With the election of the New Labour government in 1997 another element was introduced to the complex set of assumptions and relationships. New Labour championed the use of partnership as a means of exploiting the best of public and private sector thinking for the benefit of society as a whole. This notion of partnership can be found in the concept of the 'third way' (Giddens, 1998). The third way specified a move away from both hierarchies and the markets as means of organizing, and proposed a different way of shaping relationships between the economy, the state and the public and private sectors. It envisaged a new mixed economy with 'a synergy between public and private sectors, utilizing the dynamics of the market but with public interest in mind' (ibid., p. 100). There should be a balance between regulation and deregulation, with the government decentralizing various activities but continuing to be involved in target setting and directing. The neoliberalist philosophy of the previous Conservative government, which had espoused the power of the market, was rejected. There would also be a move away from the 'nanny state', 'command control' and hierarchies traditionally associated with the Labour Party. The third way offered 'progress, moderateness, modernization, pragmatism and the language of partnerships' (Newman, 2001, p. 44).

The introduction of public private partnerships brought other changes to the provision of public services. These partnerships may be viewed as an extension of the idea of contracting out services, which had been prevalent since the early privatization of certain public services. Refuse collection and catering and cleaning services were early candidates for this type of short-term contract. This was followed by partnership in the provision of infrastructure (Broadbent and Laughlin, 2004) through the use of private sector financing (the Private Finance Initiative, PFI). Here long-term contracts of 30–60 years are the norm, and because of the length of the relationship there is a need for closer partnership. In the area of education, PFI contracts have been signed for the refurbishment of schools. Other areas in which this mode of procurement has been adopted are hospitals, prisons and transport infrastructure, including roads and bridges.

Whether the dynamic that the third way envisaged will be achieved will take some time to determine, given the length of the partnership relationships. However, the introduction of changes over time indicates that the development of management controls in relation to public services is unlikely to come to a halt. A concrete example of the impact of the new measures can be provided by considering the control of UK schools, and it is to this that we now turn. The emphasis will be on the extent to which legislation informed by the ethos of the third way has affected the modes of management control in the sector, although it should be remembered that the process started with the changes that emerged from the Education Reform Act of 1988.[2]

Control in schools: core aspects

New Labour came to government in May 1997 with an educational mission. Prime Minister Tony Blair described his three priorities in government as 'education, education and education', and it was through education that New Labour's economic and social agendas would be achieved. The discourse of the third way defined the manner in which the government would govern and achieve these agendas. This new way of thinking was to shape the policies for education.

Within a short time the government's education policy started to emerge, initially in a 1997 white paper on 'Excellence in Schools' and then in The School Standards and Framework Act of 1998 (SSFA). These two documents communicated the changes that the government sought for the management and control of schools in order to promote excellence and raise educational standards. The self-management of schools, performance measurement and target setting would be retained, and partnership working would be added.

School selfmanagement

As noted earlier, the principle of school self-management was enshrined in law by the Conservative government through the Education Reform Act. At that point the local education authorities (LEAs), which had previously held control over all but a small part of overall school budgets were somewhat sidelined. School autonomy was granted in the belief that empowering the service providers would give them a sense of ownership and motivate them to improve their schools' performance. Moreover they knew best what would work in their own area. School governing bodies were made responsible for the conduct of schools and for formulating development strategies. Head teachers became the equivalent of chief executive officers and operated under the strategic framework set by the governing bodies. The head teachers were responsible for the leadership, direction and management of their schools.

School self-management was extended by the Labour government, but with greater emphasis on accountability and a strong focus on performance and raising standards.

The Local Management of Schools funding scheme was reformulated into a scheme called Fair Funding by the SSFA and schools were given funds for activities that had not previously been in their remit. These included budgets for school meals, curriculum, advisory and training services, personnel and financial and legal services. The schools could choose to purchase these services from the market or enter into purchasing arrangements with their LEA. The governing bodies were made responsible for the budgets.

Working with the LEAs

With increased empowerment and autonomy came greater accountability, and the government put in place checks and balances to ensure that all schools worked to raise the standard of education. While the schools were autonomous, partners were needed to contribute to their work. One such partner was the LEA (or its equivalent as in some areas the LEA's tasks had been contracted out to private sector providers). Under the SSFA 1998, 'The Code of Practice: LEA – School Relations' set out the way in which schools and LEAs should interact. It offered practical guidelines to ensure an 'effective relationship' between schools and the LEAs, and listed seven principles that should underpin the relationship. Both schools and LEAs had the overriding duty of raising educational standards, although school self-management meant that the schools were primarily responsible for this; the LEAs should not intervene unnecessarily but must monitor the school's performance. Intervention by the LEA, should be 'in inverse proportion to success', with weaker schools receiving more LEA intervention and support. There was to be 'zero tolerance' of underperformance. LEAs and schools should work in partnership to achieve value for money and avoid bureaucracy. A complicated system of joint accountability between the two was created, with the long term aim of 'bolstering schools' internal capacity to generate their own improvement' (DfEE, 1999, p. 14).[3]

The SSFA 1998 required the LEAs to promote high standards in education, and to this end they were provided with funds from the Fair Funding scheme to support school improvement, access, special educational provision and strategic management. As part of school improvement, they should set performance targets and suggest ways of achieving those targets. They also had to find ways of supporting failing schools. In their access role the LEAs would manage the distribution of school places, manage capital programmes, administer school admission and provide home-to-school transport, school meals and advice and support to pupils excluded from schools. With regard to special educational provision, they should assess the need for special education, make statements,[4] secure provision in the light of individual statements, monitor that provision and provide guidance and information to parents. Strategic management included strategic planning for the education service, and administering the service in terms of personnel, monitoring, expenditure auditing and other provisions. None of these roles were school-specific and had to be carried out for all schools.

Although the schools were responsible for day-to-day management and decision making, the government wanted to place checks and balances on them and 'The role assigned to LEAs is central to achieving this. LEAs are the main means through which external support and intervention can be applied in a way which is sensitive to each school's performance and circumstances' (Code of Practice, DfEE, 1999, para. 6 p. 2). The LEAs should provide 'leadership, facilitate partnerships and networks, promote co-operation and co-ordination between education and other service providers; carrying out research, disseminating best practice and providing information and advice' (ibid., 1999, para. 28, p. 8). This was a significant departure from the policies of the previous government, which had encouraged schools to opt out of the local education ambit. Thus the LEAs were given a new sense of purpose (Hannon, 1999) and a new interorganizational control relationship was formed.

This control/accountability relationship between the LEAs and schools was different from the previous relationship in that it did not involve direct control but the use of influence and persuasion. Moreover it was not voluntary but created by legislation, and arguably both schools and LEAs came to be tightly regulated by the government as its demands on them increased. In short, while schools were ostensibly autonomous and LEAs played a number of management roles, the DfEE had the ultimate power to direct the two organizations.

Partnership and consultation in the control of schools

The principle underlying the new partnership between the schools and LEAs was explained in the code of practice on LEA–school relations: 'LEAs, governing bodies and head teachers working in partnership can have a powerful impact in raising standards' (DfEE, 1999, para. 39d, p. 11). Schools were encouraged not to 'deny the proper involvement of the LEA'. However, as noted earlier, the LEAs should only intervene 'in inverse proportion to success'. This meant that stronger schools whose performance had improved should be left to get on with their work while weaker schools with underperforming pupils should receive more support from the LEAs.

The partnership involved consultation and communication, with the LEAs consulting the schools on every aspect of LEA work that pertained to schools. In theory the LEAs retained some vestigial control over the schools in that they still allocated the overall budget, and although this was done according to a formula they could influence the formula. However in the age of partnership, consultation was required. Schools had to be consulted about the introduction and removal of formula items, as well as about changes to the age weighting in the pupil-led part of the formula and changes in other areas. Another matter that required consultation was the preparation of the education development plan – the SSFA required the LEAs to consult head teachers, governing bodies and other partners to agree its contents. Schools, although autonomous, were expected to interact with other schools in order to share best practices. The LEAs were expected to facilitate this. Thus school performance was made the responsibility of several stakeholders.

In a subsequent green paper (DfES, 2001, para. 6.66, p. 92) the importance of partnership was reiterated and the concept was extended. World class education, it was argued, 'depends on creating between educators, parents, communities, business and Government, a powerful partnership committed to the achievement of the highest standards for every child and young person'.

Private companies were invited to take part in cross-sectoral partnerships in education action zones (EAZs),[5] which were created to help raise standards in areas where performance was poor. The LEAs were expected to act as brokers for private sector companies that wished to deliver services to schools. This was designed to encourage schools to look beyond the services provided by the LEAs in order to obtain better value for money. This requirement was also included in the Fair Funding regulations. However the EAZs were disbanded in 2003 due to lack of private sector interest, demonstrating the difficulty of achieving cross-sectoral partnerships.

Using performance indicators and targets to manage performance

Target setting for examination performance was introduced by the 1997 Education Act. These targets were applied to pupils' performance in the National Curriculum Standard Attainment Tests (SATs) and public examinations, and it was the responsibility of the governing body to set and publish the annual targets. The level at which the targets were set for each school, and for all schools in aggregate, had to contribute to the attainment of overall national targets (made explicit in DfEE, 1999, para. 64, p. 22). Schools had to agree their targets with the LEAs and the latter had to ensure that the targets were challenging. The LEAs were also expected to set their own area performance targets, and these could not be a simple aggregate of the schools' targets. In addition to examination targets, schools and LEAs had to set targets for school attendance in order to reduce truancy and other unauthorized absences. The targets were made known to parents and other partners, and at the end of the year they were informed of the results vis-à-vis the targets.

The government's expectation was that the output standards would be used to manage activities in schools and ensure the attainment of performance standards set at the national level. In 1998 it had introduced new public service agreements on output targets and service standards. The PSAs were intended to foster a culture of good performance throughout the public sector, demonstrating the importance of performance management as a tool for control. 'Clarity and ambition about what we want to achieve and how it will be judged are a crucial start. That's what PSAs have achieved at a strategic level. But this needs to be understood, communicated and shared by everyone involved: *an important first task for managers. . . . We want to see a new performance culture inside our public services'* (Milburn, 1999, emphasis added).

The DfEE set 11 performance targets, eight of which related to schools. Performance was measured in terms of educational achievements of school children's results in public examinations. For example two of the targets were aimed at increasing the percentage of children achieving five or more GCSEs at grades A*–C and an increase in the percentage of children reaching level four in literacy and numeracy in the Standard Assessment Tests (SATs). Other targets were related to class size, the number of nursery places and the reduction of truancy. These targets were replicated in schools and at the LEA level. Arguably the DfEE presumed arguably that its plans at the national level would cascade down into local level plans. Carter (1989) argues that performance indicators were used either as 'tin-openers' to help diagnose problems or as 'dials' for measuring performance. In this instance it seems they were used as dials. But the PSAs and performance targets were also aimed at increasing the accountability of schools and LEAs in respect of achieving the targets. Performance indicators were therefore a means of effecting managerial control within the organizations responsible for delivering the services. The role central government set itself was to identify clear goals and standards and to provide performance indicators to be used as a means of political control (Newman, 2001). The ethos of the third way might have been framed to give service providers some freedom in the delivery of services, but like all NPM measures it also paradoxically sought to regulate in order to achieve the aims of the state.

Development planning as a management tool

In addition to the requirement to report on progress towards meeting the performance targets, schools and LEAs had to prepare school development plans, detailing activities and priorities for school improvement. The LEAs were also required to prepare an education development plan (EDP), identifying actions that would be taken to raise the educational standards in their localities, the time span of these actions, the individuals who would be responsible for them and success criteria for the elements of the plan. The EDPs were prepared in consultation with schools and other partners, such as the diocesan boards of Church schools, other religious bodies' education services, local health authorities, colleges and various public and private voluntary organizations. They also included the achievement targets agreed with the DfES for the key stages, and represented the LEAs' overall strategy for school improvement.

The EDPs had to be approved by the secretary of state for education, so this was another way of exerting central control over LEAs and schools. It also ensured that the national targets would be considered (Derrington, 2000). 'In deciding whether or not to approve a plan, he [the secretary of state] will have taken account of the extent to which the EDP has been consulted on and agreed at local level. The Secretary of State may withhold or withdraw approval from the EDP if it does not meet the statutory requirements which are set out in regulations' (DfEE, 1999, para. 37, p. 9). The extent of this prescription meant that the EDPs had a standard set of priorities (Arnold, 1999) and were 'in effect the LEA's licence to operate' (Hannon, 1999, p. 211) – it seemed that without central government approval of their plans and actions the LEAs would not be allowed a role. The fact that improving standards was central to the government's strategy warranted this degree of control (DfEE, 2000).

Capacity building: funding

The government was determined to increase investment in education and considered that 'investment in human capital will be the foundation of success in the knowledge-based global economy' (DfEE, 1999). It pledged to make an average increase in funding of at least 6 per cent in real terms each year during the period 1999–2003. It also increased the devolution of funds to schools so that they would have greater financial responsibility for their activities. The idea was that if more resources were held by schools, the head teachers and governors would have an incentive to scrutinize the use to which the money was put and judge its effectiveness in improving educational performance (DfEE, 1999, p. 6).

There was also an increase in targeted funding to support government initiatives and areas of economic deprivation. This was part of the drive for inclusion and equality, in line with the principles of the third way. One related project was the Excellence in Cities scheme, which provided extra resources to secondary schools in cities. Funds were allocated to provide gifted and talented pupils with focused programmes of study, employ successful individuals to act as learning mentors, provide learning support units for excluded and disruptive pupils, and finance beacon schools and specialist schools in the cities. The government also committed itself to providing funds to develop facilities, improve buildings and enhance IT provision in schools. It was suggested that better facilities and buildings would improve the educational achievement of children. In addition public–private partnerships and PFI initiatives such as the New Deal for Schools were announced. The New Deal for Schools involved the provision of £1.083 billion for capital programmes during the 1997–2002 parliament. Finally, there were schemes that enabled LEAs to develop school buildings under the private finance initiative, in which private sector organizations delivered services in buildings they had built and financed. The LEAs headed these schemes on behalf of the schools, and some tension arose in places where school governors felt this diluted their control over their own activities.

Inspections and the consequences of failure for schools and LEAs

Having set up a control framework in terms of policy, funding, processes, targets and outputs for the school sector, the final control tool is inspection and audit. The government operates on the premise that good performance means less intervention, but where there are problems there will be sanctions. Schools can be closed and new schools opened under the Fresh Start Initiative.

The inspections follow a national standard framework developed and operated by the Office for Standards in Education (OFSTED). Introduced by the Education Reform Act of 1988, the inspections have been the cause of much stress to schools. Nowadays LEAs are also inspected. Schools are inspected at least once every six years, and much of the focus is on classroom observation. The inspection team subsequently issues a report on educational standards, the quality of education provision, leadership and management (including financial management) and the spiritual, moral, social and cultural development of pupils. On receipt of the Inspection report the governing body is required to prepare an action plan for addressing key findings. In effect the action plan is another development plan in that it specifies targets, priorities and staff development. Both the inspection report and the action plan must be sent to appropriate stakeholders: parents, the LEA and the diocesan authorities (for Church schools). They are also made available on the OFSTED website.

When schools are considered to have problems or causes for concern there are additional consequences. There are four categories of such schools: schools that require special measures because they are failing or are likely to fail to provide their pupils with an acceptable standard of education; schools with serious weaknesses, where the inspectors have identified significant weaknesses in one or more areas; underachieving schools, where the pupils and the school, are achieving less than schools in comparable circumstances; and schools with failing sixth forms. Each school so designated is required to prepare an action plan for tackling its problems. In addition schools that are put under 'special measures' are officially inspected or monitored each term. If a school remains under special measures for more than two years and shows no sign of improving it may be closed and a new school reopened with a new governing body and new management as a 'fresh start school'.

If a school shows signs of failing the LEA has specific powers of intervention under the SSFA. It may issue a formal warning notice that requires the school to take specific action, appoint additional governors, suspend the delegated budget, and issue directions if discipline has broken down. Intervention only takes place after the 'monitoring has identified weaknesses or underperformance and should be in proportion to the scale of the problem' (DfEE, 1999, para. 39c, p. 10). The implication is that because of its regular monitoring activities the LEA should have been aware of the problems, or early warning signs of them, and taken action to handle the situation sensitively.

The different types of LEA intervention are subject to rules laid down in the SSFA 1998. For example formal warning to the governing body should be issued if pupils' standards of performance are low, if there has been a serious breakdown in the way a school is managed, and if the safety of pupils or staff is threatened by a breakdown of discipline (DfEE, 1999, para. 114). The appointment of additional governors takes place if a school has been found to require special measures or the governors have failed to respond to a formal warning notice. The most drastic action is the suspension of delegated powers.

The LEAs can exert direct control over schools only when there has been a deterioration of educational performance, management or finance. The arrangement is curious in that being in partnership and being a critical friend are expected to be enough. This may be the case but is untenable if problems start and have to be managed more forcefully. LEAs are expected to provide a minimum level of advice and support during normal times, although additional support and guidance can be purchased by schools for a fee. Should a school break down the LEA may be endowed with draconian powers but it also stands to be sanctioned by the secretary of state for not intervening earlier. This can place some stress on the relationship between the LEA and its schools.

LEAs may also be held responsible for schools failing, despite their inability to exert direct control in the run-up to this. The last Education Act passed by the Tory government (in 1997), introduced the joint inspection of LEAs by OFSTED and the Audit Commission. Should an inspection reveal failings or failures the secretary of state has the power to intervene and remove services from the LEA.

Discussion: the mesh of controls

Under the aegis of the third way the control of schools has been a complicated mixture of delegation and centralized control over standards and output. This is achieved through the involvement of LEAs, which monitor what is happening in their area, define the processes of managing and teaching, and measure output although they have little power to exert direct control.

Output controls are strongly evident in the use of performance indicators, which lie at the heart of the control system. The educational achievement targets apply not just to schools and LEAs but also to the government, and their achievement is too important for the state to adopt a hands-off approach. The failure of one is failure for all.

Alongside output control there is a strong element of process control. This has undermined professional control and determined the content of education and the means by which it is planned and delivered. This chapter has touched on process control by means of a short discussion of the inspection regime and planning measures such as school development plans and EDPs. Other measures such as the government's instruction to introduce a 'literacy hour', have also impinged on professional practice. Failure to deliver any one of these measures, as judged by the regulators, can mean that the school will be judged as failing.

Clearly the performance management regime, through the control of processes and outputs, provides a carrot for schools and LEAs in that good results can mean less inspection. However with the carrot comes a stick, and just as success is defined, so is failure. As one colleague has put it, 'they can just as easily hit you with the carrot'. Whilst the targets and rewards are clear, the implementation of controls has changed the responsibilities of the principal parties to education: LEAs, parents and teachers. These parties are expected to work in partnership with each other and with other parties, for example private sector providers. This has created a complex situation: the targets must be achieved, but if they are not, then who is responsible? The schools cannot escape responsibility, as demonstrated by those which have been put under 'special measures' or closed, nor can the LEAs. But if too many targets remain unmet, then the state must also be blamed. The strong central control element accompanied by the complex system of delegation is perhaps designed to minimize the risk that blame will adhere to the government. However there are also risks on opting either for delegation or for centralization, which large companies also have to address.

Conclusion

This chapter has demonstrated how, alongside output and process control, there is room for more subtle influencing strategies that operate through partnerships and are relational rather than simply contractual. The example of schools demonstrates the more general fact that control of public services is more focused on performance management and the achievement of targets than it was in the past. Of course the benefits of knowing what is expected to be achieved and ensuring that it is achieved are immense, providing the targets do not distort other elements of organizational activity. There is a danger that in measuring some elements of performance other less tangible elements will be ignored (Broadbent, 1995). For example there is concern that measuring waiting list times is adversely affecting the treatment of NHS patients (Aggrizzi, 2003). It follows that a performance management regime in an activity as complex as education – and many other parts of the public service – is problematic. Nevertheless it remains a principal item in the government's control tool box.

Discussion questions

1. To what extent is it appropriate to control public sector organizations in the same way as private sector ones?
2. Is it appropriate to make LEAs responsible for the achievements of the schools in their areas without giving them direct powers of control?
3. Evaluate the effectiveness of performance indicators such as league tables as a tool of control.
4. Is the concept of a 'failing' organization useful in controlling public sector organizations? If so, why?
5. Is resource allocation by LEAs a useful management control tool in schools?

Notes

1. It should be recognized that the allocation of resources is subject to political priorities, so there is relativity in the scarcity of resources in different sectors as well as an absolute scarcity.
2. The first edition of this book provides a more detailed discussion of the earlier changes.
3. The title of the central government department responsible for education was changed by the Labour government from the Department for Education and Employment (DfEE) to the Department for Education and Skills (DfES).
4. Statements define the extra help that pupils with special needs should receive.
5. The Education Action Zones in 2003.

Risk and control: the control of risk and the risk of control

Anthony J. Berry, Paul Collier
and Christine Helliar

Introduction

As the chapters in this volume have suggested, organizations' control systems take many forms and are based on a variety of economic, social and cultural factors. By providing a sense of stability and predictability, control systems limit the risks faced by senior management and, to a lesser extent, all members of the organization. This chapter first explores the manner in which control systems can help with the management of risk and then turns the situation around and examines the risks associated with control.

In the early 1990s researchers had very little knowledge of how managers and organizations perceived risk and how risk entered into management practice (Bettis and Thomas, 1990). That situation has now changed. In the last decade or so policy makers, managers and academics have paid growing attention to risk and risk management. There have been a string of reports and recommendations from governmental and professional bodies on how corporations should manage risk. In the UK the Cadbury code (Cadbury, 1992) was concerned to improve the internal control processes of organizations. In the same year the Treadway report in the United States (COSO, 1992) addressed the part played by internal controls in improving corporate governance. The array of corporate problems that arose in the 1990s added to this concern. Marshall *et al.* (1996) suggest that the risk management failure at Barings, Kidder Peabody and Metallgesellschaft were due to dysfunctional culture, unmanaged organizational knowledge and ineffective controls.

Further developments include the amalgamation of the Cadbury, Greenbury and Hempel recommendations into the Combined Code of the Committee on Corporate Governance, which was updated in 2003. Guidance for directors on control was provided by the Turnbull Committee in 1999, including the recommendation that directors should review the effectiveness of their organization's internal control and report to shareholders that they have done so. Such a review should cover all controls, including financial, operational and compliance controls and risk management.

The rest of the chapter consists of four sections. The first looks at current ideas on corporate risk management, especially those based on internal controls. Next the organizational and psychological aspects of risk are considered. This is extended in the third section by a discussion drawn from the social science literature on risk. The final section discusses the risks of control. Examples are provided from previous and current research.

The control of risk by organizations

Enterprise risk management processes

Almost all the recent literature on risk management is based on the managerialist, functionalist or positivist-realist conception of risk. Jopeck (2000) notes five steps to risk reduction in an ongoing cycle of planning and directing: risk analysis, elevation and presentation, decision making, implementation, and evaluation. He suggests that risk analysis should comprise asset assessment, threat assessment, vulnerability assessment, qualifying and quantifying risk, countermeasure identification, and analysis. He also considers three views of risk: risk averse, risk tolerant and risk accepting. In a similar vein, Muir (2000) reports on a joint project by the Australian Treasury, the Australian Financial Markets Association and Arthur Andersen to investigate how companies identified operational risk. Subsequently a blueprint was proposed for managing that risk. This is known as the Standards for the Control of Operational Risk (SCOR) and recognizes more than 100 risk management standards. These include reputation damage and financial loss resulting from a breakdown in human resources, processes or technology.

Meagher and O'Neill (2000) introduced the idea of enterprise-wide risk management (EWRM) as a structured and disciplined approach to aligning strategy, processes, people, technology and knowledge – for the purpose of evaluating and managing the uncertainties that an enterprise faces – into a logical, complete and integrated structure. The authors suggest a seven-step process:

- Establish the business risk management process.
- Assess business risks.
- Develop business risk management strategies.

- Design and implement risk management capabilities.
- Monitor the risk management process.
- Continuously improve the risk management process.
- Ensure the availability of information for decision-making.

EWRM uses a first-order control loop and depends on a rational understanding of information recognition, assessment, decision making and monitoring for its logic. Meagher and O'Neill note that a risk management system should have a good supply of modelling tools and allow for the incorporation of new tools. Merkley (2001) queries whether EWRM matters and answers in the affirmative because consistency of behaviour ensures reliability.

Brooke (2000) considers how managers accept some risks, asks how much risk is too much, and counterposes the risk of inaction with the cost of risk reduction, noting that not all risk can be eliminated. McNamee (2000) offers a rational framework for addressing business risk in several stages, starting with a thorough understanding of the risks in question, and their possible effects, and ending with an integrated business risk framework that provides a common language for discussing risks. McNamee defines risk as a concept used by auditors and managers to express concern about the probable effects of an uncertain environment on business goals, and suggests that risk is merely a conceptual device to help deal with the consequences of being unable to predict the future with certainty. He suggests that four types of asset should be considered: financial assets, physical assets, human assets and intangible assets. He uses the idea of risk domains in relation to ownership risk, process risk and behavioural risk.

Modelling versus heuristics

Segerstrom (2000) addresses the issue of how to handle 'model' risk. He claims that it is dangerous to assume that a computer model purchased from a vendor is complete and accurate. He links model risk to interest rate risk, price and exchange rate risk, and argues that a user must validate any model. He notes that model development is a complex and error-prone business, that some models contain fundamental errors and that the internal logic is abstract and limiting.

Jarret (2000), working in a more mathematical tradition, explores the part played by risk in business decision making. He argues that risk is an inherent component of decision making, and that managers should be prepared to address it effectively. He notes that risk can be modelled using anchored scales and probabilistic analysis. He also suggests a heuristic approach in which there are three general types of risk:

- High risk: risk must be reduced before going ahead.
- Medium risk: risk can be accepted but the means of mitigation must be understood.
- Low risk: risk is not a significant factor.

Jarret suggests that managers should know the difference between risk characterization, anchored scales and probabilistic analysis (subverted by the extreme subjectivity of the estimates), noting that real world decisions in a risky environment require trust in those who provide the analysis. He commends the tactic of portfolio diversification but notes that risk and funding is problematic; risk should be encountered, assimilated, mitigated and ultimately embraced.

Zolkos (2000) offers insights into the problem of setting an acceptable level of risk; that is the amount of unexpected loss that would be tolerated by an entity's stakeholders. He raises the idea of a risk retention capacity, and (somewhat bravely) puts this at 2 per cent of net worth or 3 per cent of operating cash flow.

Interestingly, these authors demonstrate that the creation of a common language for risk management is a piece of social construction by individuals and communities of practice, such as trade associations, professional bodies and consultants.

Corporate governance

The risks inherent in corporate governance have been a central concern of policy makers on both sides of the Atlantic. Building on the Cadbury report on corporate governance, which emphasized the duty of care held by boards of directors, the Turnbull Report (1999) made recommendations that have since been rigorously enforced by the London Stock Exchange. All listed companies are required to have an internal control system to monitor significant threats. Risks are defined as any events that may affect a listed company's performance, including environmental, ethical and social risks. For each risk, boards must consider the extent to which it is acceptable, the likelihood of it materializing and the ability of the organization to reduce its incidence and impact (Brown, 2000).

The International Federation of Accountants (IFAC, 1999) defines risks as uncertain future events that could affect the achievement of strategic, operational and financial objectives. The IFAC report is biased towards shareholder value, and suggests that risk management 'establishes, calibrates and realigns the relationship between risk, growth and return' (ibid., p. 4). The report suggests that risk should be viewed as an opportunity rather than a threat. It suggests a risk management architecture comprising a structure of corporate governance and a risk management group to oversee policy and 'the transition to risk ownership by line managers' (ibid., p. 27). This risk architecture also involves establishing a culture of risk awareness and a reporting and monitoring system to ensure that risk is responsed to effectively and that resource allocation responds to the continuum of risks (the risk profile) faced by the organization. The risk profile should be based on an assessment of systemic risks (political, economic, social and financial) over which the organization has very little control, risks that cannot be controlled but could be influenced (for example competitive, reputational and regulatory risks), and risks that are industry-specific and can be influenced by individual organizations. The report refers to a natural progression in risk management: managing risks associated with compliance and prevention, minimizing the risks of uncertainty, and moving to a higher level of managing opportunity risks. In so doing, the report clearly identifies the need to shift risk management to the business unit level.

Organizational design for uncertainty

Various reports on corporate governance put stress on organizational structures and procedures for managing the risks and uncertainties that arise in the external (and to some extent the internal) world of an organization. Galbraith (1977, p. 5) defines uncertainty as 'the difference between the amount of information required to perform the task and the amount of information already possessed by the organization'. He argues that the success of goals and rules depends on the frequency of exceptions and the capacity of the hierarchy to handle those exceptions. Galbraith proposes four organizational strategies to use when uncertainty increases:

- The creation of slack resources: minimizing exceptions by relaxing budget targets, creating longer delivery lead times and 'buffer' inventories.
- The creation of self-contained tasks: changing the division of labour by allocating resources to an output-focused product group structure instead of a skills-based functional structure. Creating slack resources and self-contained tasks reduces action arising from lower performance standards, fewer exceptions are likely to occur and fewer factors will affect the interdependence between business units.
- Investing in vertical information systems: this permits the information to be analysed as a result of task performance, without overloading the managerial hierarchy. Galbraith argues that unanticipated events create exceptions that lead to incremental updating of the plan or, if they occur in sufficient quantity, to a new plan. This is the approach used in most risk management reports.

■ Creating lateral relations: shifting decision making to the location of information but without creating self-contained groups. Lateral relations can be achieved through direct contact between managers or through liaison roles, task forces, teams and integrating roles. Investing in vertical information systems and creating lateral relations increase the organization's capacity to process information. Supply chain management is a typical example of the creation of lateral relations.

Galbraith argues that the amount of information processing increases as uncertainty increases, or as higher performance expectations are imposed. He suggests that failure to adopt one of the four organizational strategies will result in reduced performance standards.

There is a distinction between event uncertainty, which is commonly viewed as risk, and Galbraith's information uncertainty. This distinction is important, not least because organizations have little or no control over external events, merely their response to those events. Organizations' response to event risk involves rational practice of assigning probabilities, either on an interval or an ordinal scale. By contrast organizations can decide what measures to take in the face of information uncertainty.

Despite organizational differences, all organizations establish processes to help manage risk. Many forms of risk have been identified. The notions of bias and risk transfer (in the form of redistribution) were noted in early research into budgeting (Box 16.1). The distinction between event risk and information uncertainty is also important when organizational design responses to uncertainty are considered. However Galbraith's 'rationalist' model contrasts Preston's (1995) 'social constructionist' model, which has more of a behavioural emphasis.

BOX 16.1

Risk and management accounting

In the management accounting literature, risk has been given an implicit rather than explicit profile. Budgeting is undertaken in a context of uncertain outcomes, but little emphasis has been placed on the effect on budgets of managerial perceptions of risk, risk management and tolerance of errors over time and at different organizational levels.

Early research was carried out by Lowe and Shaw (1968) into sales budgeting in a retail chain, in which the annual budgeting process was an 'internal market by which resources are allocated' (ibid., p. 304) and managers had to

▶

▶

compete. Budgeting identified three sources of forecasting error: unpredicted changes in the environment, inaccurate assessment of the effects of predicted changes, and forecasting bias. Lowe and Shaw examined possible sources of the bias and found they emanated from the reward system, the influence of recent practices and norms, the insecurity of managers and 'the desire to please superiors in a competitive managerial hierarchy' (ibid., p. 312). They explain counterbias as 'the attempt by other managers to eliminate that part of a forecast which stemmed from the personal interest of the forecaster' (ibid., p. 312). They conclude that there was a need for information that was independent of interested parties and for a reward system that would minimize managerial conflicts of interest.

Berry and Otley (1975) explored the estimation of outcomes made by individuals at one hierarchical level in an organization and the coupling of their estimates to ones made at a higher level. They describe the means of estimating, communicating estimates to superiors, combining estimates and bias in estimating. Risk was redistributed in the organization during the budgetary process, usually downwards. They conclude that subordinates bore a greater risk of not achieving budgeted outcomes than the superiors, suggesting that the budget process should be adjusted to the desired pattern of risk, and that concentration on single-point estimates ignored the need for flexibility.

Otley and Berry (1979) argue that the difficulty of achieving budget targets varies between managers. In practice budgets are not static models of expectations but are subject to upward or downward bias by subordinates. Otley and Berry also argued that quite minor deviations from the 'expectation budgets' at the unit level can produce severe distortions when budgets are aggregated at the organizational level. They conclude that insisting on arithmetic additivity is likely to produce a number of undesirable consequences, including the inequitable treatment of entities and the demotivation of managers.

Faced with differences between information held at different levels, the compounding of bias when preparing estimates and the aggregation of budget estimates, it is little wonder that budget estimates can be error-prone, even before the effects of unpredictable environmental change and inaccurate predictions of the effects of known environmental change are considered.

It is by no means clear whether the often recommended internal control procedures can effectively control the risks an organization faces, for recognizing and assessing risks is by no means simple. Moreover risks are not static, rather they emerge and change over time. The next section will explore how organizations and managers perceive risk.

Perceptions of risk

The *Concise Oxford Dictionary* defines risk as 'a chance or possibility of danger, loss, injury, or other adverse consequences'. However there is a general lack of consensus on the definition of risk in the management literature, and numerous definitions have been proposed (see Baird and Thomas, 1990; Bettis and Thomas, 1990). At the beginning of the chapter we noted that in the early 1990s researchers had very little knowledge of how managers in organizations perceived risks, or of the commonalities or differences between individual risk taking and risk taking by managers in the organizational context. As will be shown, not all researchers take this view.

March and Shapira (1987) explore the relationship between theoretical conceptions of risk and those held by managers, arguing that managers are insensitive to probabilities and focus on critical performance targets. They identify three reasons for risk taking by managers. First, managers see risk taking as essential to successful decision making. Second, they associate risk taking with the expectations of their jobs rather than having any personal predilection for risk. Third, they recognize the 'emotional pleasures and pains' of risk taking (ibid., p. 1409). Hence both individual and institutionalized risk preferences are important in understanding organizational responses to risk management. March and Shapira concluded that:

> Managers look for alternatives that can be managed to meet targets, rather than assess or accept risks. Although they undoubtedly vary in their individual propensities to take risks, those variations are obscured by processes of selection that reduce the heterogeneity among managers and encourage them to believe in their ability to control the odds, by systems of organizational controls and incentives that dictate risk taking behavior in significant ways, and by variations in the demand for risk taking produced by the context within which choice takes place (ibid., p. 1414).

Weber and Milliman (1997) describe responses to risk as traits on a continuum, ranging from risk avoidance to risk taking, with two risk factors being taken into account: the magnitude of potential losses and their chance of occurring. They conclude that risk taking is a stable personality trait, and that the effect that situational variables have on choice might be related to changes in risk perception.

In a study of national cultural differences amongst IBM employees, Hofstede (1980) classifies differences along four dimensions, one of which is uncertainty avoidance. This refers to the extent to which a society feels threatened by uncertainty and ambiguity. It is associated with seeing uncertainty as a threat, but is compensated for by hard work, written rules and a belief in experts. In a comparative investigation of attitudes in four cultures (American, German, Polish and Chinese), Weber and Hsee (1998) found that the majority of respondents in all four cultures were risk averse. The authors' 'cushion hypothesis' proposes that a culture's position on the individualism–collectivism continuum determines objective risk, for example collectivism cushions members against the consequences of negative outcomes, which affects subjective perceptions of the riskiness of options.

Measuring perceptions of risk

The question arises of whether and how an individual perceives risk. Mitchell (1999) provides an extensive review of 30 years of treatises on risk in the consumer marketing literature. In his study of consumer decision making perceived risk has two components: uncertainty and consequences. consumers' responses are collapsed into a three-point scale, to which a numeric value is assigned. These are multiplied and weighted in order to rank products along a risk continuum, but Mitchell notes that high or low perceived risk might be a generalized tendency. This suggests that perceived risk is both product specific and unique to individuals. The ranking, however, assumes that consequences and certainty are equally weighted and that gradations are equally spaced along the scales. Mitchell's analysis of usability, practical implications, prediction, reliability and validity testing, and the development of understanding suggest that a two-component model of perceived risk is very serviceable. However Mitchell argues that these components ought to be combined additively rather than multiplicatively. This model appears acceptable because it is likely to be a suitable predictor and should be simple to use because of the small scale involved.

Helliar *et al.* (2001) found that the managers in their study were sometimes unable to distinguish between risks they were taking in their personal capacity and risks they were taking on behalf of their organizations. Managers in failing firms often focused on just one or two issues and were sometimes unable to separate personal risks from business risks. They were willing to take risks that might save their business from insolvency, although when threatened they became more risk averse. Managers in turnaround activities tended to ask for help sooner and recognized the need for action, demonstrating a more secure personal position.

Cognitive psychology theory and risk

Several factors may influence managers' approach to risk. The fact that individuals are averse to making a loss (Kahneman and Tversky, 1979) manifests itself in regret when a wrong decision is taken. This suggests that decision makers tend to follow simple heuristics, or rules of thumb, when evaluating risky situations, which can result in biased decision making and run counter to the practice in economics of using variance or standard deviation to assess risk. March and Shapira (1987) found that executives did not consider uncertainty about positive outcomes as risky; 80 per cent of the respondents associated risk only with negative outcomes. Risk was not strongly related to the probability of different outcomes. Instead 54 per cent of the interviewees considered that risk was associated with the magnitude of any possible negative outcomes rather than the dispersion of possible outcomes. These managers would have been likely to reject a risky project – even if it had a positive expected net present value (NPV) – if there was a tiny chance of there being a negative outcome that would threaten the survival of the firm. (They appeared to accept the power law approach rather than the variability approach in respect of the likelihood of detrimental outcomes.) Forty-two per cent of the managers viewed risk as a multifaceted concept encompassing various types of risk and suggested that such complexity could not be usefully condensed into a single probability distribution of the NPV of future cash flows.

In line with these US findings, Helliar et al. (2001) found that managers thought that four perceived factors would affect their assessment of risk.

- The magnitude of a loss associated with a decision.
- The possibility that a project might incur losses in the future.
- The range of outcomes from a decision.
- The ability of competitors to react.

Helliar et al. note that the third factor accords with the textbook views of probability, that the first two (and more important) factors are consistent with the notion of loss-aversion, and that the fourth suggests a more strategic approach to risk and its consequences. However the managers in their study tended to ignore past losses when making subsequent decisions and did not attempt to recoup the losses by seeking extra profits. They were likely to choose an option with a lower expected value but no losses rather than one with a higher expected NPV but the probability of a large loss, or one with a choice that had a relatively high probability (25 per cent) of making a very small loss. These findings are consistent with those of March and Shapira (1987), and with Alderfer and Bierman's (1970) finding that business students show a strong preference for a lower mean, a larger variance, a large positive skewness and no chance of loss.

Preference reversal

Research indicates that managers may uncouple probabilities and monetary values when defining risk, and therefore give too much importance to monetary values (Tversky and Thaler, 1990; Tversky *et al.*, 1990). This suggests that there may be a reversal of preferences when managers overvalue decision outcomes that have a low probability of occurring but have a high payoff (Helliar *et al.*, 2001). This preference reversal may also occur when framing a decision. A decision framed in terms of losses will be different from one framed in terms of gains (ibid.; Kahneman and Tversky, 1979). Decision makers often avoid extreme outcomes and tend not to choose options with the largest or the smallest expected value. The availability of new and riskier options might result in managers selecting an intermediate option that is different from their previous choice (Simonson and Tversky, 1992), which reflects a tendency to opt for the 'prudent middle ground'.

The effect of personal and organizational factors on risk

Attitudes towards risk differ within organizations and appear to be strongly related to position in the organizational hierarchy (March, 1988a). As an individual's age and seniority rise, so does the tendency to take risks. Both the scale and the frequency of risk taking increases up the hierarchy, and it appears that senior executives accept that risk taking is an integral part of their job (Helliar *et al.*, 2001). Many junior managers believe that they have neither the authority nor the duty to take major risks on behalf of the organization.

As Lowe and Shaw (1968) have observed, problems with meeting budgets can lead to the taking of risky decisions, a finding supported by Laughhunn *et al.* (1980). Risk-taking propensity increases as an individual's wealth and fortune increases (March, 1988; May, 1995), and this also happens when a company is successful, dynamic and not in a business cycle trough (Ghemawat, 1993). It has also been observed that managers in larger firms are less risk-averse than those in small firms (Helliar *et al.*, 2001).

Risk taking can be influenced by the incentives contained in managerial contracts (Hoskisson *et al.*, 1993; Lypny, 1993; Ouchi, 1977; Palley, 1995). If managers have a generous equity or bonus incentive scheme, riskier decisions will be taken (May, 1995). However when decisions are reached after group discussion, in the context of formal monitoring and evaluation, with the aid of expert knowledge or if the organization is a follower, then less risky decisions will be taken (Heath and Tversky, 1991).

The assertion that there are national and cultural differences in risk taking (Hofstede, 1980) is supported by Laughhunn *et al.* (1980), who note that Dutch managers pay greater attention to potentially ruinous losses than do their German counterparts. There are also differences between industrial sectors (Bussard and Doyle, 1996) and historical and cultural settings (Baum *et al.*, 1993). Organizational culture was believed by 88 per cent of those surveyed by Helliar *et al.* (2001) to have a crucial bearing on the size of risks that managers were prepared to take. Project champions with a good track record tend to be chosen to manage unusually risky ventures (Lonie *et al.*, 1993).

Constructing risk

The theoretical discussion so far has focused on risk management as part of corporate governance (in a functionalist manner), concentrating on rational ideas of risk. Another view is that risk is socially constructed. Beck (1986, 1992) argues that we live in a 'risk society', asserting that while natural hazards exist, much risk is socially constructed by humans and the use or misuse of technology. In order to develop our theoretical understanding we shall consider how perceptions of risk are formulated.

Spira and Page (2003) note that ideas about risk have changed greatly, as illustrated in Table 16.1. With regard to risk management in organizations,

Table 16.1 Evolution of attitudes towards risk

	Conceptualization of risk	Response to risk	Accountability for risk
Premodern	Fate, superstition, sin	Acceptance, blame	Expiation, punishment, vengeance, retribution
Modern	Calculable, quantifiable	Avoidance, protection	Compensation, e.g. financial
Risk society	Manageable	Control and regulation via systems, based on expert advice. Systems for response and blame avoidance	System amendment, extended control

Source: Adapted from Spira and Page (2003), p. 645.

one implication of the assertion that risk is socially constructed is that the homogeneity of the management team's perception of risk will prevail as the recruitment process will filter out those whose risk preference is incompatible. Simultaneously, socialization processes will serve to normalize perceptions of risk in the organization's environment. In line with this perspective, Douglas and Wildavsky (1983) see risk as a joint product of knowledge about the future and agreement about the most desirable outcomes. They comment that 'each culture, each set of shared values and supporting social institutions is biased toward highlighting certain risks and downplaying others' (ibid., p. 14). They argue that the construction of risk is based on degree of equality (how choice is negotiated or constrained) and degree of individualism/ collectivism. Their model is shown in Figure 16.1.

Following Adams (1995, pp. 57–9), the figures can be interpreted as follows:

- Individualists are enterprising, self-made people who are willing to bargain with fate in order to achieve higher returns. They prefer to increase their skills in order to take risks rather than seeking to reduce the probability of the event occurring.
- Hierarchists inhabit strong groups and strictly follow rules. They assume that people accept too much risk and often expose themselves to risk

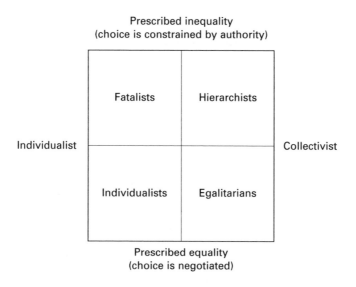

Figure 16.1   Basic constructions of risk

through ignorance. They use procedures and business analysis to reduce both the variance of risk (the influence of mistakes and chance) and the distribution of risks (the number of risks identified).

- Fatalists accept they have little control over their lives. They accept that risks are a fact of life about which they can do very little. Context risks are capricious, and the best response is indifference.
- Egalitarians have strong group bonds but resist externally imposed rules. They work in accordance with strongly held values rather than explicit procedures. They tend to be risk averse, and believe that risk should be eliminated through consensus and precautionary approaches.

One implication of this is that managers and organizations (or organized collectivities) will take very different stances on what they perceive as risk, and will adopt different risk management processes.

Adams (1995) builds on this construction to develop a model of risk compensation based on the balance between people's propensity to take risks, the expected rewards from risk taking and the perceived dangers. He uses this to explain that road accidents are more serious in sparsely populated areas because people risk driving faster. In a similar vein, boards of directors may install a risk management procedure, and because they now feel safer they take decisions with higher risks. This might not lead to perverse outcomes but it is likely to produce a peculiar state: organizations with good risk management procedures may end up as riskier organizations.

Risk management, uncertainty, decision and judgement

Consider a manager faced with a decision related to market growth. The manager can, from experience or with the help of a predictive model, estimate the probable growth rate of the market and make the decision on the basis of that estimate. Table 16.2 shows the three possible outcomes.

Managers strive to avoid making bad decisions and type I errors (not reject reliable estimates) and type II errors (reject unreliable estimates) and having to solve subsequent problems caused by making errors. Once the risks are analyzed, managers can use avoidance, transfer (insurance, outsourcing),

Table 16.2 State of market growth

	Is as estimated	Is not as estimated
Accept estimate	Good decision	Type II error
Reject estimate	Type I error	Good decision

mitigation (hedging, pooling) and acceptance (gather more information on risks) to reduce unmanaged risk to a residual core (Hutter and Power, 2000; Klein, 1997; Miller and Lessard, 2001; Muelbroek, 2001). By concentrating on avoiding Type I and Type II errors, or managing the consequences of their being made, risk managers may fail to recognize many of the uncertainties that organizations experience. The use of probability captures the pervasiveness of uncertainty. Risk management is defined by the ability to work with the connection between the judgement needed to assess risks and the probability of these happening, however the judgement may be difficult to understand. Uncertainty pertains when the probability is either difficult to estimate or is just a guess, and when observation fails to yield sufficiently similar states of affairs for classification and the assignment of probability. Indeed complexity and policy theorists (for example Stacey *et al.*, 2000) argue that historical events follow the power law, which gives quite a different picture, compared with Gaussian distributions, of the small probability of extreme events occurring.

Shotter (1993) explains how managers invoke socially constructed decision-making structures informed by prevailing and emerging values that allow them to make heuristic judgements about the ways in which analyses of risk probabilities should be used. For example instead of cost–benefit decisions based on lexical weightings of risk incidence and impact, risk managers have been found to use threshold rules, whereby if a risk threatens an organization's survival it is deemed 'urgent', and if the organization can afford to avoid or mitigate the risk it will do so, purely on the grounds of a precautionary heuristic linked to a psychological desire for safety (Meszaros, 1999). There is little attempt to convert uncertainties into groups of Type I and II errors against which a series of weighted, problem-solving actions can be taken. There can also be risk escalation, as suggested by Adams' (1995) observation that the greater the limits on liability via insurance, shared risks and public safety nets, the more managers will avoid the opportunity cost of taking risky decisions and become less responsible for the whole decision, and the greater will be their propensity to conceal mistakes and increase commitments to poor strategic decisions, devoid of organizational reason (see also Drummond, 1998).

So risk management involves addressing not only type I and II errors but also type III errors: incorrectly judging the nature and scope of problems. Where type I and II errors assume structures of risk, type III errors immerse risk management in what Wenger (2000) calls local communities of practice. Type III errors occur when risks stem from the inability to make accurate estimates in the first place. As a consequence risk management is also about using of rules of thumb to remain accountable and seek higher-level ratification of decisions, and to avoid threats to survival if transfer or mitigation policies are affordable. These may remain hidden as organizational defences (Argyris, 1990) or tacit knowledge (Nonaka and Takeuchi, 1995). This constrains an organization's ability to assess threats and opportunities because technical modelling will only be possible for some situations, and managers' emotional influences on decision making will be underconsidered or hidden. If type III errors were included in the risk management procedures, these managers would become open, in a self-reflexive way to the motivations that inform organizational strategy.

As noted earlier, Beck (2000) calls today's society the 'risk society', where risk is all pervasive and cannot be contained by the rational assignment of probabilistic estimates. Beck thus attends to type III problems, where there is little expectation of finding a solution, let alone producing a controlled, tidy outcome. Examples of approaches to risk are diverse and two examples are provided in Boxes 16.2 and 16.3.

BOX 16.2

An example of risk in action

'Here it is not only expert opinions on probability, impact and possible remedial measures that are under challenge, but the relevance of even trying. Probability is only one type or description of uncertainty and the event and fault tree analysis of risks only one method of recognising it. Other uncertainties include: opportunism; fashions and feelings of alienation, all of which resist any thorough investigation from the means-end, causal analyses favoured by typical risk management practices. In the advent of the UK foot and mouth epidemic, for example, the centralising institution (the as was Ministry of Agriculture, Fisheries and Food (MAFF)) were no longer agents of controlled response to threats, and at best could make only unfounded re-assurances whilst acknowledging their responsibilities both in terms of offering advice and critically reflecting upon the content of that advice and the values and vested interests informing it. The expert-sanctioned unilateral closure of the countryside enforced through legal sanction did little to explain the risks to either the business community or the wider public – the technological solution creating more risks (business failure; public anxiety; animal distress) than, arguably, it solved. The breakdown of shared practices and institutional stability elicited in people an individualized identity prone to examine its own perceptions and experiences as the arbiters of meaning rather than that of the experts, making for a fragmented recognition and contested conceptualization of risks (Ungar, 2002)); further eroding the already contested ability of people to negotiate their public experiences, so creating a vicious circle of ever increasing risk (Kopp *et al.*, 2000).'

Source: Holt *et al.* (2003)

BOX 16.3

Some evidence from small businesses

As entrepreneurial organizations grow they often adjust their behaviour. According to McCarthy (2000), as managers gain experience they involve their peers and confirm their intuition by using systematic analysis and management control. Das and Teng (1998) have found that when adopting transfer and mitigation risk management strategies by using partners to expand a business, a new raft of risks arise from misaligned interests and asymmetric information, requiring consultation, contractual management and caution when formalizing rules.

The participants in a study by Holt *et al.* (2003) were aware of the importance of having explicit management processes, if only in self-reflection, yet they were reluctant to lay down rigid procedures. A crisis made them become more cautious, but they retained an entrepreneurial edge. They became more critical of emotional responses to risk, preferring to act within individualistic decision-making frameworks. This blend of individualist and hierarchist world views meant that the boundaries between the socially constructed categories were permeable – owner managers were capable of responding positively to both individualist and, as their business grew, hierarchist statements. From a social constructionist perspective, when agents can change their strategies in respect of shifting objectives and experiences there is no inherent contradiction (Chell *et al.*, 1991). As owner managers experience risks in increasingly reflexive ways, they appreciate the importance of rules and resources that lay outside their 'individualist' repertoire – new staff, separate premises, clear communication procedures – but retained their personal orientation towards those rules and resources. They are reluctant to use 'off the shelf' types I and II solution packages. Thus the slide towards a hierarchist perspective on risk coupled with continuing suspicion of procedure might be explained as tacit acknowledgement of a primary risk (Hirschhorn, 1999).

Understanding this primary risk is to understand the often hidden assumptions and orientations of the core decision makers as they experienced the anxiety that accompanies important strategic decisions. Despite the varied communities of practice of participants, they shared concerns in reconciling their experiences of market isolation and connection with the prospect of bureaucratic weight. This suggests that primary risk is rooted in the possibility that inflexible procedures emerged to 'shadow' and 'counter' the owner-manager's individualist tendencies (Stein, 2000). For managers in small communities of practice the primary risk of inflexibility is a lack of the self-reflexivity needed not only examines the efficacy of instrumental control, but also questions its universal relevance and sense (Beck, 1986).

The risk of control

Earlier in the chapter, in the discussions found in the IFAC and Turnbull reports, we addressed the control of risk and the trade-off between return and risk. IFAC (1999) contrasts 'risk as hazard' with 'risk as opportunity', in which risk should not to be avoided but managed through a 'risk architecture'. The Turnbull report (Institute of Chartered Accountants in England and Wales, 1999) suggests that profits are the reward for successful risk taking, and that risks should be managed and controlled rather than attempting to eliminate them. This can be achieved through a 'risk-based approach to establishing a sound system of internal control' (ibid., p. 4).

There is an implicit assumption in these corporate governance approaches that the higher the risk (in terms of its likelihood and adverse consequences), the greater the control of that risk should be. However this is a circular argument. Risk is deemed to be high because something is uncertain or has significant consequences, or both. If the likelihood and consequence of a risk can be controlled, then by definition it is not a risk. While risk management techniques may be effective in the case of risks over which the organization has control, external risks are a different matter. Organizations can develop methods of anticipation, contingency plans and flexible practices, but control can impede or prevent anticipation, contingency and flexibility. That is the risk of control.

Control theorists deal with risk as a variable to be incorporated into a static cybernetic control model in which inputs are converted into outputs and compared with a target, which may result in corrective action, guided by a predictive model (Otley and Berry, 1980; see also Chapter 1). In this model risk is indeterminate in relation to inputs (resources), processes (behaviours) and outputs (results). This relatively closed system model takes little account of the external environment. Risk is most likely to be assessed by means of probabilities, standard deviations or portfolio analysis, or techniques such as sensitivity analysis and decision trees. Information systems such as EWRM may be used and give the appearance that they manage risk effectively. Budgeting, particularly flexible budgeting, can be seen as an attempt to counter risk.

Many risk theorists deal with control in a different way from that outlined above. Weber and Hsee (1998) state that differences in risk preference, ranging from risk avoidance to risk taking, are due to differences in the perception of risk or differences in the risk–value trade-off. In the extreme case, controls may be implemented (following the Turnbull report's recommendation for a 'risk-based approach' to internal control – Institute of Chartered Accountants in England and Wales, 1999) to prevent worst-case scenarios, but this also prevents opportunities from being grasped. There may be a temptation to establish a range of prescriptive controls that serve to constrain organizational actions.

Adams (1995) argues that in practice risk management is more concerned with reducing risk than with balancing risks and rewards. In particular there is no common denominator for risk and reward and risk perceptions vary enormously between individuals. Neither Douglas and Wildavsky (1983) nor Adams (1995) believe that it is possible to manage risk because it is socially or culturally constructed. For example March and Shapira (1987) conclude that managers look for alternatives that can be managed in order to meet targets, rather than assessing or accepting risks. They argue that both controls and rewards dictate risk-taking behaviour in significant ways, as does the context in which decisions and choices are made.

Although the Otley and Berry's (1980) framework allows for the predictive model to be amended on the basis of experience and learning, in practice the predictive models used by organizations are rarely altered to any significant degree. This was evident in the four organizations studied by Collier and Berry (2002), in which employees considered risk less in financial terms than in terms of operational, political and personal domains, which reinforces the social construction perspective. By excluding some risks and considering others the budget process was different from, and had to be interpreted separately from, the content of the budget, in which there was little evidence of risk modelling or the use of probabilities.

According to Wallander (1999), if business continues as usual, previous experience can be used as the basis of future activity and therefore budgeting is pointless. If business does not continue as usual there is nothing that can be done in advance as there is no ability to foresee something of which there is no prior experience. Therefore Wallander disputes the value of budgeting.

As risk increases, controls should (according to corporate governance guidelines) be increased to offset the risk. As this happens, controls become more prescriptive and more dependent on the predictive model used. Consequently organizational participants may have less room to manoeuvre, and in a turbulent environment this may result in an increase rather than a decrease in risk as policies, plans and budgets do not have the flexibility to cope with the unexpected.

As pointed out above, excessive control can result in opportunities being missed. This is not an argument for a lack of control, but for the application of sensible controls that permit a flexible response to emerging trends and unexpected environmental changes. By applying the Galbraith (1977) model described earlier, we can see that as uncertainty increases performance standards will fall unless one of Galbraith's strategies is adopted. However there are dysfunctional consequences. Excessive control leads to slack resources, which may not be available to respond to changing circumstances. Self-contained tasks and lateral relations may enable flexible responses, but they may also transfer risk both within and outside the organization, sometimes in inappropriate ways.

A further example of the risk of control is provided by this notion of risk transfer. Collier and Berry (2002) discuss examples of risk transfer between and within organizations. Risk transfer may be a response by managers to avoid the problems inherent in separating budget performance targets, which exclude a consideration of risk, from the process of meeting those targets, which include explicit or implicit considerations of risk based on the risk perceptions of managers and employees. The Collier and Berry case studies show that risk can be transferred along the supply chain to different departments or individual managers, which can have significant negative effects.

Applying the typology by Adams (1995) described earlier, we can identify a risk of control in control systems that have unreliable predictive models (defeating the hierarchists) or are dependent on differing perceptions among individuals (defeating the egalitarians). The risk of control can constrain individuals' ability to cope (defeating the individualists) or cause them to think that risk cannot be managed or controlled at all (satisfying the fatalists). This dichotomy presents a dilemma for those who seek to manage and control risk.

Organizational controllers must be able to demonstrate effective risk management and internal control policies and practices in order to obtain institutional legitimacy. However while (hierarchical) systems and processes need to be in place to ensure that gaps or overlaps in risk management are avoided, the (egalitarian) cultural approach demands recognition of the socially constructed nature of risk propensity and risk perception, while the (individualist) perspective requires encouragement of a spirit of anticipation, contingency and flexibility, whereby controls encourage and empower rather than constrain behaviour that is sensitive to the risk–return trade-off.

Conclusion

This chapter has explored an interesting paradox in the notions of risk and control. If control and risk are considered from a positivist and realist standpoint, then the proponents of enterprise-wide risk management by means of a wide array of rational approaches are making a useful contribution to the management of risk, and perhaps uncertainty. However as we have seen, there are problems with the idea that the best or only way that risk can be managed is by a system of well considered and operated internal controls. The risk of control is that unconsidered risks may cause fundamental problems.

If a social constructionist stance is taken on understanding how risk is perceived and how risk management is conceived then, it can be seen why procedure-driven approaches may mask or render invisible some of the very problems they are expected to solve. The role of the managers who must deal with risks that change over time in organizations with different cultural characteristics, sizes and maturity, is crucial in the practice of management.

17 Ethics, organization and control

Ken McPhail

Introduction

Much of the conventional literature on managerial control, along with the burgeoning systems perspective, has tended to present organization in an abstract, technical and apolitical way (Morgan, 1986; Puxty, 1998). For example Willmott (1998) comments that 'in the majority of mainstream texts on organisations, these organisations are seen as morally and politically neutral . . . they are characterised as impersonal and goal oriented.' While some textbooks do consider behavioural issues, the analysis is generally limited to the impact on managerial control and organizational goals. Ethical perspectives on organization thus seem to be markedly absent from the majority of mainstream management control texts. This is a somewhat surprising omission. The paucity of ethical analysis seems to be out of line both with developments in the business environment and public opinion in general. The increased complexity of business – globalization, environmental degradation and heightened public expectation – means that the management and control of business organizations has become not just more technically difficult, but also more ethically complex (Bauman, 1998). Faced with these changes, management might be tempted to view them as technical or contingent factors that need to be accommodated within organizational control systems and to overlook the ethical challenges they represent. For example, while the new spatial configurations of the globalized economy present management with new organizational and control problems, they also correspond to seismic changes in the nature of ethical relationships (ibid.). Of course organization and management control have always been about ethics (Willmott, 1998), but the ubiquity, size and power of modern-day multinationals gives this oversight added significance.

The omission of ethics from many management control texts also ignores the growing awareness within organizations of the value of values. According to Parker (1998) for example, many businesses are now moving away from a dehumanized bureaucratic conception of organization towards viewing (the construction of) values as an organizational asset. Yet the language in which this discussion is often couched, for example 'values engineering', seems to indicate that rather than being superseded, the bureaucratic conception has simply been expanded to subsume a very narrow and instrumental view of ethics (ibid.: see also Willmott, 1998). There is, however, a potentially more challenging, paradigm-threatening perspective that can be taken. If we were to take ethics seriously then we would be confronted with a host of interesting and disruptive questions. How does organization affect the way in which individual members think ethically? In what sense is organization ethical? Is control ethical? Are some forms of organization more ethical than others? The objective of this chapter is not to answer these questions. This would be neither possible nor appropriate for a single chapter. The aim is much more modest: it is to provide an introduction to some ethical concepts that might encourage us to begin to think about management control and organization in an ethical way, so that you can ask your own questions and develop your own answers.

This chapter, then, presents an ethical perspective of organization and control. It would be helpful to pause here and try to place this kind of analysis within the context of the broader literature. Puxty (1998) provides a useful taxonomy of approaches that have been taken in the study of management accounting and control. He sites one main theoretical perspective, a second prominent position and three further peripheral perspectives. According to Puxty the traditional approach to thinking about management accounting and control is technical, apolitical, ahistorical, functionalist and rationalistic. In short it is scientific. Systems theory provides the grounding for the second major perspective, and the remaining three peripheral perspectives are hermenutic/interpretative, critical/marxist and poststructuralist. This chapter introduces the beginnings of an ethical analysis. Of course these divisions are somewhat arbitrary and partial. All of the positions outlined above are based on some set of implied values and are therefore to some extent ethical. However what is proposed here is a more explicit ethical analysis based on common ethical concepts and drawing on a broad range of moral philosophy and ethical theory.

Gareth Morgan, in his innovative and stimulating book *Images of Organization* (1986), promotes a metaphorical reading method for expanding our understanding of organizations and diagnosing their problems, for example the organization as a machine, organism, brain or instrument of domination. He comments:

theories and explanations of organization are based on metaphors that lead us to see and understand organization in distinctive yet partial ways. ... By using different metaphors to understand the complex and paradoxical character of organizational life, we are able to manage and design organisations in ways that we may not have thought possible before (ibid., p. 12–13).

The proliferation of organizational metaphors is undoubtedly important for developing new ways of thinking about organization and new organizational forms. However what is proposed here is not another metaphor but a form of analysis that recognizes that corporate organization is intrinsically about ethics. This perspective construes managers not only as readers but also as public actors who are ethically responsible for the way in which they control and organize.

Effective management and control systems in economic organizations have to deal with many different kinds of ethical issue: employee safety and equal opportunities, advertising issues, environmental pollution, fraud, information ethics and so on (see McEwan, 2001, for a more detailed discussion). This chapter will not focus on these dilemmas, rather it will study two more fundamental ethical questions: the ethics of organization, and how organization might have an impact on the way in which individuals experience ethical dilemmas. The remainder of the chapter is structured as follows. The next section provides a brief introduction to some ethical questions, concepts and theory. The subsequent section considers the ethical nature of organization and control. The third section studies some of the issues, identified in the ethics literature, that contribute to our understanding of how individuals experience and resolve ethical dilemmas within an organizational setting. The final section provides a summary and some concluding remarks.

Concepts and definitions

This section provides a brief introduction to some ethical questions, concepts and theories (see MacIntyre, 1998, for a comprehensive history of ethical perspectives). It introduces a few of the major debates and strands of moral philosophy that will be discussed later in the chapter.

Ethical questions

This chapter advocates taking an ethical view of organization. But what does an ethical perspective involve? What kinds of question should we be asking when we adopt an ethical perspective? Different scholars have focused on different questions. Socrates, for example, was concerned with right or appropriate action and the questions 'how should I live?' and 'how should I act?' The Swiss philosopher Jean-Jacques Rousseau changed the focus of ethical analysis. For Rousseau the most important question in ethics was not 'what should I do?' but 'who am I?' Rousseau contended that the answer to this question would place the individual within society, and therefore within a complex of relationships with other human beings. A third important strand of ethical questioning is associated with the German philosopher Fredrich Nietzsche. Nietzsche changed the orientation of ethical analysis again by arguing that it was morality itself – that is, the very idea that there is a right and wrong way to behave – that should be opened up to analysis. He posed the question 'how do individuals use moral norms to control others?' (MacIntyre, 1998). The suggestion that morality – that is, notions of what is good and bad – may be used to control and dominate was developed through poststructuralist analysis. Poststructuralists argue that the answer to Socrates' question of how one should act has proved too difficult to answer. They propose a move away from the question of how an individual should behave and towards the way in which notions of good and bad are developed, sustained and used. The work of the French historian of thought, Michel Foucault, is quite important here (McPhail, 1999). In his later work Foucault posed the question 'how do individuals become ethical subjects?' How does 'ethical self understanding' develop (see Hoy, 1994; Hacking, 1994). His kind of ethical analysis was therefore at a level below that of conventional moral philosophy (MacIntyre, 1998). The focus changed from moral codes to the underlying ethical substance that allows these moral codes to function (Hoy, 1994).

From this brief introduction it is obvious that the kinds of question that have concerned moral philosophers have a particular application to the study of organization and management control. How do organizations affect the way in which individuals respond to the question 'what should I do?' How does the issue of organizational identity affect the answer to the question 'who am I?' How are concepts of good and bad, created, sustained and employed within organizational settings? How is control exercised through concepts of good and bad, right and wrong?

Let us return to the traditional question with which moral philosophers have grappled: 'what should I do?' There is a debate within the ethics literature over how this question should be answered, and different theoretical perspectives propose different ways of addressing it. Emmanuel Kant provided one of the most prominent perspectives. According to MacIntyre (1998), Kant's work is so important that it represents a major division in the historical development of ethical analysis. Kant believed that the answer to the question of how one should act could be found in the power of reason.

Taking moral consciousness as a given, he set out to establish universal principles, or laws, of moral reasoning (ibid.; see also McNaughton, 1988). John
Locke similarly contended that morality could be demonstrated in the same
way as one might prove a mathematical formula. Bauman (1993) comments
on the consequence of this perspective: 'Morality was cast fairly and squarely
in the unfeeling domination of reason. Appointing reason as the sole faculty
relevant to the moral evaluation of action pre-empted the questions of morality as rule governed and rules as heteronomous.'

The historical division to which MacIntyre (1998) refers relates to two
distinct schools of thought. The first, which is generally called the
rational/cognitive school, assumes that reason can be used to solve ethical
dilemmas. The debate is over how reason should be used. The second school
questions whether reason on its own can solve ethical dilemmas, and the
debate focuses on the role of emotion in ethical decision making. Each debate
will be considered in turn.

The rational/cognitive perspective is based on the assumption that the
correct response to an ethical dilemma can be established through the application of reason. Two distinct strands of thought have developed from this
assumption. Kant provides the basis for the first position. He argued that it is
possible to use reason to identify universally acceptable rules of behaviour.
The first principle that Kant suggested could be deduced by applying our
reasoning capabilities is what he called the categorical imperative. This rule is
summed up as follows: 'Act only on the maxim through which you can at the
same time will that it be a universal law.' In other words we can determine
whether a particular action is ethical by considering the logic of the action
itself. Kant described those who adhere to rational, universalizable principles
as acting out of duty. This kind of duty-based ethic is generally referred to as
deontological ethics (from the Greek *deon*, meaning duty). According to Kant,
acting ethically involves acting out of a duty to the principles that reason has
established. From a deontological perspective a particular action is therefore
ethical because the action itself satisfies a certain ethical logic. The second
strand of rational/cognitive ethics is generally called teleological ethics (from
the greek *telos*, meaning goal). In contrast to deontological theories, according to the teleological position the rightness or wrongness of an action is
determined by the nature of its consequences, rather than the nature of the
action itself. In order to understand this consequentialist position we need to
distinguish between good and right. Within the teleological framework, right
refers to the action whereas good refers to the goal. Consequentialism is
primarily concerned with the process of determining whether an action is
right with reference to a given goal rather than with establishing what that
gaol should be (see Chryssides and Kaler, 2001, for a detailed discussion of
teleological and deontological perspectives).

While both deontological and teleological theories are based primarily on the application of reason, a contrasting position is provided by the 'moral sense' theorists. The Scottish philosopher Francis Hutcheson (1999), the English politician Lord Shaftesbury and more recently Zygmunt Bauman (1993, 1996, 1997) all suggested that some emotional or more innate moral sense is involved in determining the most appropriate response to ethical dilemmas (MacIntyre, 1998; Broadbent, 1998). Shaftesbury argued that moral distinctions are made by a moral sense rather than by reason. He conceptualized this idea in terms of an inner eye that was able to distinguish between ethical and unethical actions. 'A moral judgement is thus the expression of a response of feeling to some property of an action . . . just as an aesthetic judgement is the expression of just such a response to the properties of shapes and figures' (MacIntyre, 1998). David Hume followed Shaftesbury in his rejection of rationalist ethics. He argued that reason is simply concerned with establishing matters of fact. Moral judgements, according to Hume, cannot be based on reason because reason does not lead us to act. It is emotion and not reason that is the motivating factor in moral judgements (MacIntyre, 1998).

This brief resume of some of the main ethical debates in the literature provides a base for exploring organization and managerial control from an ethical perspective. It serves two functions in particular. First, it helps us to understand and label the kind of ethical thinking that is deeply embedded in much of the mainstream management control and performance measurement literature. Accounting and managerial decision making, or at least as it is taught by many textbooks, is based on a narrow form of consequentialist ethic called financial utilitarianism. In the fields of financial and management accounting, many students are implicitly or explicitly taught to respond to the question 'what should I do?' by reasoning out the financial consequences of an action rather than referring to any emotional or empathetic feeling (Gray *et al.*, 1994). Second, this review also helps to clarify that this perspective is only one of many different ethical perspectives that can be adopted.

This section has provided a brief overview of the kinds of question and position that have shaped the development of different strands of ethical theory. It has supplied an insight into some forms of ethical analysis that provide a useful background against which to discuss the ethics of organization and control in more detail.

Ethics and organization

This section focuses on the ethics of organization and control. Despite the fact that organizations are often presented as instrumental and goal orientated, they are undeniably ethical. They have to be. For example Willmott (1998, p. 84) states that 'organisations are irredeemably moral orders where ethical as well as performative criteria are widely applied to the assessment of conduct'. This section will pick up on two issues in particular. First, the kinds of question introduced above suggest that the question of ethics has traditionally been applied to individual action. This is not necessarily the case, and this section explores the idea that organizational structures can also be subjected to ethical analysis and evaluation. Second, the section picks up on the rather obvious but fundamentally important point that organization is about people.

The ethics of organization

Moral philosophy has long made a connection between ethics and organization, specifically at the societal level. This is particularly the case in the work of Thomas Hobbes. It might seem quite obvious but it is a point that is often overlooked: our civil forms of organization represent a particular set of ethical ideals and values, although they do change over time.

Hobbes contended that any reasonable human being will conclude that in order to live together in relative peace each person must respect the other members of the community. However he also suggested that this 'moral law' cannot on its own secure a peaceful and safe society – there is always the possibility that some members of the group will acquiesce to the moral law in order to lull the others into a false sense of security. Therefore morality cannot rely on common sense, rather it depends on a more fundamental 'social contract'. He suggested that this contract, to which individuals implicitly subscribe when they become members of a society, must be enforced by the state, for example through the legal system, the police, the army and so on. Thus the members of society should organize themselves in a particular way, that is, hand over power to the state to enforce the social contract. Hobbes contended that the members of society subsequently obey the moral rules of the social contract not only because they are enforced by the state, but also because they would rather obey than suffer the consequences of not obeying: imprisonment, or ultimately disorganization and anarchy if everyone behaved in the same way.

Hobbes' arguments were based on the assumption that all individuals are equally vulnerable. Although he did not claim that everyone is actually equal in terms of power, he did suggest that moral constraints arise when individuals are more equal in power. The function of the state is therefore to equalize power amongst its constituents.

John Locke drew on Hobbes' idea of the social contract and suggested that individuals should hand over authority and power to legislative and administrative bodies provided there are laws to protect natural rights. However the state's legitimacy rests on the proviso that only those laws which are passed by a majority vote are valid. The arguments of both Hobbes and Locke are therefore precursors to liberal democracy (see MacIntyre, 1998). It is important to remember that it is within this broader context of social organization that corporate organization takes place. The majority of mainstream texts fail to situate management control within this broader political economy.

A more contemporary form of organizational ethic is found in the work of the German social commentator Jürgen Habermas. While Kant promoted the use of reason to discover immutable objective moral principles, Habermas advocates a morality based on consensus. The crucial aspect of his argument is the way in which this consensus is negotiated. In its ideal form, this would be a process in which all modes of power and influence have been removed, such that all the participants in the debate are equal (Rossouw, 1994). He coins the phrase 'ideal speech situation' to refer to all the characteristics that should pertain to this process. Habermas thus promotes a specific form of social organization that will facilitate ideal speech (see Outhwaite, 1996).

Both these examples indicate that ethics is not just a characteristic of individual action, it is also a property of systems and organizational structures. This observation is important because it prompts us ask different questions from those normally posed within mainstream managerial control texts. In addition to investigating what is the most efficient kind of organization, or the most economical or effective, it is also important to ask what is the most ethical organizational form? Are hierarchical organizational forms more or less ethical than participatory forms? Willmott (1998) suggests that the prevailing forms of organizational control are unethical. For example he likens modern corporations to fascist organizations, condemning their structures as 'the institutionalised silencing of dissent' (ibid.). Certainly few commercial organizational structures could be construed as being democratic or displaying the characteristics of an ideal speech situation.

Management is about people

The task of management and control is fundamentally about people. Fisher and Lovell (2003) remind us that organizations are *'configurations of people* established to co-ordinate a series of work activities with a specific goal or set of goals in view'. Chryssides and Kaler (1996) similarly comment that 'executive power primarily relates to *power over people.* Executives control the companies resources and assets but it is primarily a matter of controlling people.' This may seem a rather banal observation, but it is quite fundamental from an ethical perspective. Management control and performance measurement are about relationships between human beings. This point can be easily lost in the abstraction that takes place within much organizational literature.

Traditionally the main issues of ethics have been associated with the fact that we live with other people. As Bauman (1993) puts it, 'that to live is to live with others is obvious to the point of banality'. As noted earlier, one of the main questions that ethical theorists have grappled with is 'what should I do?', that is, how ought I to behave? This question is important because our actions impinge on other people. However it has also been studied in a more abstract way in relation to Rousseau's question 'who am I?' For example Nielsen (1991) suggests that 'the I is part of a prior and much more foundational we'. Bauman (1993) similarly contends that 'the other' opens the venue for ethics. It is the place where ethical existence originates. At one level Bauman is advocating an emotional approach to ethics (Broadbent, 1998; McPhail, 2001). He conceptualizes ethical behaviour in terms of emotional and empathetic commitment to other people. However he also contends that modern bureaucratic forms of organization impede the development of these types of relationship. He argues that the holocaust is crucial to understanding the negative potential of modern, managerialist forms of organization. According to Bauman (1996) the success of the 'final solution' depended on the capacity of managerial techniques to denude individuals of their dignity and deprive them of their humanity (Fahy *et al.*, 1999; Funnell, 1998):

> [Auschwitz] was . . . a mundane extension of the modern factory system. Rather than producing goods, the raw material was human beings and the end product was death, so many units per day marked carefully on the manager's production charts. The chimneys, the very symbol of the modern factory system, poured forth acrid smoke produced by burning human flesh. The brilliantly organised railroad grid of modern Europe carried a new kind of raw material to factories. It did so in the same manner as with other cargo. In the gas chambers the victims inhaled noxious gas generated by prussic acid pellets which were produced by the advanced chemical industry of Germany. Engineers designed the crematoria; managers designed the system of bureaucracy that worked with a zest and efficiency more backward nations would envy (Feingold, quoted in Bauman, 1996, p. 9).

According to Bauman the two key characteristics of modern organizational structures that contribute to the process of dehumanization are distantiation and categorization. These concepts are briefly discussed below.

A series of famous experiments by the American sociologist Stanley Milgram (1974) suggest that there is an inverse correlation between individuals' willingness to be cruel to someone else and their proximity to their victim. For example Milgram argued that while it may be difficult to harm a person we can see hear and touch, it becomes progressively easier to inflict pain on them the greater the distance we are from them. Bauman (1998) contends that modern bureaucratic forms of organization and control facilitate distantiation in two ways. First, in a very literal sense the multinational nature of business means that there is very often a huge gap between the centralized decision-making function and the individuals who will be affected by its decisions. There is a danger that ethical obligation to individuals – employees, customers and suppliers – is reduced because they exist only at a distance and as grossly simplistic categories and typifications.

Second, the problem of distance relates not just to the increasingly multinational nature of business and the physical distance between individuals. Bauman (1993) also contends that bureaucratic organization increases the moral distance between individuals who are spatially close. Bauman applies Milgram's (1974) work to modern managerial techniques and contends that distantiation and then dehumanization are achieved by representing individuals as objects in technical and ethically neutral terms (Bauman, 1996). Representing people in quantitative terms quashes the moral significance of managerial decisions and consequently suppresses the potential moral conflict of knowing how one's actions can adversely affect another human being (Donaldson, 1988).

In classical ethical theory, relationships between individuals have traditionally been explored through the concept of justice. While there are different kinds of justice, for example procedural, retributive and distributional, they all incorporate an idea of what people have a right to. Justice is therefore related to rights and duties. A right is a moral entitlement. For example workers might have a right to a minimum wage whereas employers have a duty to provide it. A right is what I can expect from others, a duty is what others can expect from me. An appreciation of this opens up the discussion to include issues such as employment rights, equal opportunities and so on (McEwan, 2001). This rights-based perspective is certainly one way of beginning to explore the relationship between individuals in an organizational context. However Bauman's argument is much more radical than this. He contends that most forms of proceduralized ethical thinking, of which the concept of right is an example, are actually detrimental to ethical development because they base ethics on rule following. F. W. Taylor once said, 'in the past the man has been first. In the future, the system must be first' (quoted in McEwan, 2001). It certainly seems that the majority of organizational studies texts have tended to prioritize systems over their impact on sentient human beings. One of the objectives of the kind of ethical analysis proposed in this chapter is to promote a continuing reorientation on human beings as well as organizational systems.

This section has presented two ways of beginning to think ethically about organization and management control. Firstly, it has suggested that particular modes of organization, as opposed to individual action, can be subjected to ethical analysis and appraisal. Second, it has highlighted the rather obvious point that organization and managerial control are fundamentally about human relationships, and as such are inherently ethical endeavours.

Ethical thinking in an organizational setting

In the organizational and management control literature there is a general awareness that despite the programmed way in which control is often discussed, business decisions do not follow the mechanistic patterns laid down in textbooks. Behavioural factors influence organizational control and are also important for understanding ethical practice in an organizational context. This section focuses on some issues that might contribute to our understanding of how individuals experience and respond to ethical dilemmas within organizations.

An individual's response to an ethical dilemma is generally determined by issue-related and context-related factors. Issue-related factors include social consensus, how sure the individual is of the consequences of his or her actions, the number of people affected by the actions and the proximity of individuals affected by the actions (Jones, 1991). Context-related factors include reward systems, authority structures, the level of bureaucracy, work roles, organizational culture and so on. How an issue is experienced in the context of an organization therefore has a significant effect on how it is conceptualized and whether or not it is construed as an ethical issue. People experience issues in different ways in different organizational settings. This section introduces what has been termed the moral psychology of organization. What happens to ethics when people are organized? The discussion covers two areas: the relationship between social forms of organization and the organization of cognitive memory structures; and the impact of organizational characteristics on ethical dispositions.

Organizing work and memory

Many studies suggest that ethical dilemmas are experienced differently depending on the setting in which they are encountered. The fields of learning theory and cognitive psychology are concerned with the way in which information is encoded in the memory (Tajfel and Fraser, 1990). This process has been conceptualized in both cases using the notion of categorization (ibid.; Cole and Scribner, 1974; Hewstone *et al.*, 1993). According to learning theory, the process of categorization involves learning to ascribe specific properties to particular groups of objects. Learning theorists suggest that the resulting connections are organized and stored in cognitive memory structures called schema[1] (Choo, 1989; Fiske and Taylor, 1984; Markus, 1977). These schema direct attention to relevant information and guide its interpretation and evaluation. Categorizations are thus seen to play a primary role in individuals' understanding of the world and their choice of an appropriate course of action within it (see Fogarty, 1992).

In the cognitive psychology literature the notion of scripts has been developed to reflect the part that sequences of actions play in forming the basis of different behavioural roles, for example visiting a doctor or attending a lecture. It is argued that 'scriptal' knowledge structures[2] retain knowledge of expected sequences of behaviours, actions and events. Cognitive psychologists therefore suggest that practice plays a defining role in the development of cognitive categories, and the psychology literature thus infers that different forms of organization may influence the development of cognitive categories. The literature also suggests that categorizations may be associated with different ethical values. Ponemon (1990; see also Ponemon, 1992) contends that different roles may engender different ethical proclivities and may also engender different ethical attitudes towards similar attitudinal objects. Philips (1991) likewise argues that ethical knowledge is role dependent: 'what activities are correct depends on the role being played at a particular time'. Liedtka (1991) argues that fulfilling a role not only requires an appreciation of appropriate behaviour but also an awareness of the 'environment of values' in which the role is played, or to put it more simply, an appreciation of what is generally perceived by the members of the group to be ethically acceptable behaviour. He contends that while personal values may provide the underpinnings for ethical decisions in private life, in work life it may be that personal values are mediated by institutional structures and forms of organization. These different spheres are often referred to as public and private ethics (Fritzsche, 1991). Cultural anthropologists suggest that if individuals play different roles in their lives, this may result in different values, norms and behaviours in different 'life domains' (Trevino, 1992). A study by Weber (1990), for example, found that managers' power of moral reasoning appears to be lower in work-related situations than in non-work-related ones, and Liedtka (1991) has found that managers employ differing modes of analysis when making choices in different areas of their lives.

Hence there is quite a significant amount of research evidence to support the contention that organization and work roles are two quite fundamental contextual factors that influence an individual's experience of ethical issues. This contention is based on the relationship between modes of social organization and forms of cognitive organization. However the literature also points but that other organizational characteristics – such as reward systems, authority structures, the level of bureaucracy and organizational culture – may also be influential factors. The next subsection briefly looks at five such issues: ignoring, indifference, incentive schemes, peer pressure and the problem of authority.

Organizational characteristics and ethical dispositions

Intentionally ignoring an ethical dilemma that occurs in another part of the organization and guarding one's own interests is common in organizations and relates to individuals' conception of their role in the organization. The concern here is that individuals might respond to an ethical dilemma by turning a blind eye because it is not happening in their department or sphere of organizational responsibility. It is related to their sense of accountability to the organization and the response they are likely to receive if they blow the whistle.

A second issue is indifference, which is related to the sense of impotence that an organization can often engender. Individuals often feel that if everyone else is going to carry on in the same way, then their solitary stance is not likely to make any difference. This kind of attitude is often termed 'justification via inefficacy' and is an example of consequentialist thinking on ethical dilemmas.

Incentive schemes are also extensively discussed in the literature. A common concern is that performance appraisal systems tend to focus individuals' attention only on those aspects of a decision that can be measured. This also reflects the kind of consequentialist ethic discussed above. There is a danger with most forms of incentive scheme that employees will end up doing something not for its own sake, not for deontological reasons, but because of the consequences of the action.

Another important factor in understanding ethical issues within an organizational setting is peer pressure. This refers to overt or subtle pressure from peers to compromise standards and conform to group norms. Some studies have identified peer pressure as a significant motivational factor in managerial decisions. Less scrupulous organizational members can become annoyed by what they perceive as the pious actions of others.

A fifth important organizational tendency is that individuals often do things simply because management tells them to – they uncritically submit to authority. One of the problems that Bauman (1996) identified in his analysis of the holocaust was that many individuals viewed themselves as simply following orders. Bauman explains, 'what we do know for sure, thanks to Milgram, is that the subjects of his experiments went on committing deeds which they recognised as cruel solely because they were commanded to do so by the authority they accepted and vested with the ultimate responsibility for their actions' (ibid., p. 162).

This section has briefly explored two areas. First, it introduced the idea that social forms of organization may be related to the way in which cognitive memory structures are organized. It was suggested that the way in which ethical issues are experienced might subsequently be influenced by the resulting memory structures. Second, the section has briefly introduced some characteristics of organizational behavioural that may impinge on ethical dispositions.

Conclusion

The history, breadth and complexity of the discipline of moral philosophy are vast and somewhat daunting. This chapter has attempted to convey some of this richness in order to combat the rather narrow focus on codes of ethical conduct that characterises much of the business ethics literature (Parker, 1998; Willmott, 1998). The chapter has picked up on some of the themes of this rich philosophical tradition and applied them to the study of organization and control. It has also briefly explored the ethics of organization and control, and the ways in which organization can affect how individuals experience particular ethical dilemmas. The objective of the chapter has been to pose rather than answer questions in the hope they might stimulate further ethical thinking and an exploration of organization and control from an ethical perspective.

Discussion questions

1. What questions have ethical theorists historically asked, and what insights and challenges do they present for the study of organization and control?
2. What are the main ethical challenges facing organizations today?
3. Are some forms of organization more ethical than others? How can we decide which organizational types are more or less ethical?
4. In what ways does organization affect an individual's experience of ethical dilemmas?

Notes

1. A schema is an abstract notion that refers to the knowledge structures that individuals may unconsciously employ in order to organize and make sense of social and organizational situations.
2. The metaphor of the actor's/actresses's script may be helpful in explaining this argument. Schemas may be thought of as a script that an actor follows in a film. The script provides the actor with an understanding of the situation and an idea of what she or he is expected to say and how she or he is expected to act.

18 Sustainability and management control

Amanda Ball and Markus J. Milne

Introduction

Picture this: just as you are about to board an aeroplane, you see a man busily prying rivets from one of the wings. As you rush in panic down the steps he calls out, 'Don't worry, I've taken a lot of rivets out already and the wing hasn't fallen off.' Are you reassured? This scenario comes from the cover of Anne and Paul Ehrlich's book *Earth* (1987). They go on to state:

> No sane person would want to travel on a plane whose airline did not have a 'progressive maintenance' programme . . . and only a lunatic would want to ride on Spaceship Earth if the components of its ecosystems were being dismantled so fast that maintenance could not begin to keep up with repairs. Yet here we are – and we have no other spaceline offering transport.
>
> The free services which Earth provides to civilisation – the air we breathe, the climates in which we live, fresh water, waste disposal, recycling of nutrients, control of potential pests and disease carriers, provision of food – are rapidly being eroded by man's destructive impact on the complex biological network of the planet. Humanity is living on its capital, while rapidly destroying the natural systems that are its principal source of income (ibid.).

The book provides numerous examples of destruction and destructive forces, but it also notes there are some hopeful signs that recovery and transition to a sustainable society might be possible, if only the Earth's 'opponent', Homo sapiens, would cease its relentless battering.

In 1987 the concept of sustainability moved centre stage politically, and somewhat more recently onto the agendas of business leaders and managers. With the release of *Our Common Future* (WECD, 1987), sustainable development and the oft-quoted 'Meeting the needs of the current generation without compromising the ability of future generations to meet their own needs' have become the catchwords of many politicians and business leaders.

Using Otley's management performance framework (Chapter 6), this chapter explores how management control systems might be adapted to ensure that businesses contribute to sustainability rather than unsustainability. That is, it investigates whether and to what extent Otley's framework can help to get business managers to stop prying rivets out of the wings of our only aircraft – planet Earth – and perhaps even replace them. First, however, it considers the term 'sustainability' and what is meant by an ecologically sustainable economy.

What sustainability is and what it is not

The concept of sustainability is contested and ambiguous (Barbier, 1987, 1989; Bishop, 1993; Dixon and Fallon, 1989; Milne, 1996; Norgaard, 1989, 1992; Pearce, 1988; Redclift, 1987; Sadler, 1988; Toman, 1992; Turner, 1993; WECD, 1987; Zorvanyi, 1998), and our understanding of the concept is far from universally accepted. Echoing the remarks made by Ehrlich and Ehrlich (1987), Wackernagel and Rees (1996, p. 32–40) argue that sustainability is a simple concept that means 'living in material comfort and peacefully within the means of nature':

> Imagine a bucket being filled with water at a fixed rate. The water in the bucket is a capital stock that can be drawn upon only as rapidly as the bucket is being refilled. This balanced withdrawal rate is a form of sustainable income. Similarly, nature is a 'bucket' that is continuously replenished by the sun: photosynthesis produces plant matter, the basis of all biological capital and most other life, and climatic, hydrological, and other biophysical cycles are solar powered too.
>
> Sustainability implies that nature's capital should be used no more rapidly than it can be replenished. However, trade and technology have enabled human-kind progressively to exploit nature far beyond sustainable levels so that present consumption exceeds natural income (the 'interest' on our capital). This leaves the next generation with depleted capital and less productive potential even as the population and material expectations increase.

The idea that sustainability is about maintaining natural capital or critical natural capital and learning to live off natural income is held by many commentators who subscribe to what has now been termed 'strong sustainability' (for example Daly, 1973; Ehrlich and Ehrlich, 1987; Gray, 1992; Dobson, 1998). Such commentators are clear that something needs to be sustained or maintained. For example the International Union for the Conservation of Nature (1980) is clear about what it wishes to be sustained, and claims a necessary condition for achieving sustainability is the maintenance of 'essential ecological processes and life support systems' and the preservation of genetic diversity.

Strong or constraints-based definitions of sustainability emphasize not just efficient allocation of resources over time, but also a fair distribution of resources and opportunities between the current generation and between present and future generations, plus a scale of economic activity that does not exceed its ecological life support systems (Daly and Cobb, 1989; Daly, 1992; Dobson, 1998; Low and Gleeson, 1998; Noble and Costa, 1999). For example Daly (1992), in defining sustainability, specifies that (1) the rate of use of renewable resources should not exceed their regeneration rate, (2) the rate of use of non-renewable resources should not exceed the rate at which sustainable renewable substitutes are developed, and (3) the rate of pollution emission should not exceed the assimilative capacity of the environment. To these three the OECD (2001) adds a fourth: avoiding the irreversible impact of human activities on ecosystems.

Such definitions suggest a broader ecosystem-based approach that requires an understanding of cumulative environmental change (Canter, 1999; Costanza and Folke, 1994; Odum, 1982; Piper, 2002), and new or alternative decision-making arrangements and institutions (Bryant, 1995; Young, 1992). To give effect to sustainability, there have been calls for cumulative effects assessments of economic activity based on regional ecological criteria (Canter, 1999; Piper, 2002; Rees, 1988), for ecological footprint analyses (Wackernagel and Rees, 1996), for precautionary decision-making principles (O'Riordan and Cameron, 1994), for bioregionalism (Sale, 1980, 1985; Welford, 1995; Harrill, 1999) and for more just, democratic and participatory decision-making forums (Bryant, 1995; Low and Gleeson, 1998; Young, 1992).

Other definitions and commentators tend to be far more ambiguous about what it is that is to be sustained. As a consequence sustainability is often confused with managing the social and environmental impact of businesses and other organizations. *Our Common Future* (WECD, 1987) contains references to sustainability but couples sustainability with development, and this seems to have caused much confusion about and debate on what sustainability is and what it is not. Whether biophysical thresholds or environmental bottom lines should act as constraints on social and economic matters or be balanced or traded off against them, has been widely debated in the legal, planning, geography, ethics, economics and environmental literatures (for example Buckingham-Hatfield and Evans, 1996; Johnson, 1996; Norton, 1989; O'Riordan, 1993; Sagoff, 1988; Turner, 1993). Of course notions of sustainability that permit the balancing or trading off of environmental values for social and economic values are far more consistent with existing business and economic activities. Those who accept that trade-offs are acceptable and/or inevitable, and this includes a great many business commentators (including the World Business Council on Sustainable Development, and the New Zealand Business Council on Sustainable Development), tend to subscribe to 'weak sustainability'. This version of sustainability tends to downplay questions of equity and social justice, absolute levels of material resources and energy use and the scale of developments relative to the resource base, while playing up the gains to be made by more efficient use of materials and energy relative to the outputs being produced.

Sustainability at any level poses a number of challenges to businesses and their decision makers, but with constraints-based definitions the traditional measures of business success and sustainability, namely profit and efficiency, also come under scrutiny. As Milne (1996, pp. 151–2) notes:

> Sustainable outcomes require the rationing of scarce ecosystem capacities, and the presumption of such an approach is that the ecosystems are the going concerns, not the economic project. To recognise the limits of ecosystems, it seems appropriate to develop regionally-based initiatives in which the entity and going concern concepts are applied, not to companies, but to natural entities – to rivers, lakes and forests.

For practical and ethical reasons, sustainability implies and requires collective decision making for the common good. It suggests that one of our greatest problems – in terms of control, accountability and reporting for sustainability – is the organizational entity concept, and all the traditional paraphernalia of success that goes along with it. Defining sustainability as being about continual maintenance of the life-supporting capacities of the planet's ecosystems requires the subordination of traditional economic criteria to criteria based on social and ecological values, and this begs the question of whether business decision makers operating within the constraints of a capitalist system are capable of sacrificing profits in the interest of future generations and other species (Gray, 1992; Gray and Bebbington, 2000; Milne, 1996). It also begs the question of whether it is even fair to suggest they should do so, or that there is any credence whatsoever in their claim that they are able to do so (Gray and Milne, 2004). Moreoever it raises the question of whether capitalist societies it is possible or sensible to suggest adaptations to organizations' management control systems that could lead to something remotely resembling a contribution to an ecologically sustainable society.

Sustainability and management control

In seeking to determine the effectiveness or otherwise of an organization's management performance framework, Otley (Chapter 6 of this volume) asks researchers, managers and others to consider the following questions:

- What factors does an organization see as crucial to its continued success, and how does it measure and monitor its performance: each of these areas?
- What level of performance does the organization wish to achieve in each of these areas, and how does it go about setting appropriate performance targets?
- What rewards (both monetary and non-monetary) will managers gain by achieving these performance targets (or conversely, what penalties will they suffer by failing to achieve them)?
- What information flows are necessary for the organization to be able to monitor its performance on these dimensions, to learn from its past experiences and to adapt its behaviour in the light of those experiences?

While this framework was never intended to be used to analyze how management control systems should be adapted in order for organizations to contribute to a sustainable economy, such an analysis can indicate the limitations and boundaries of the framework. However it could equally reveal that it is not Otley's framework that is limited, but rather that the real problem lies with the way in which business school professors, consultants and management decision makers choose to interpret its questions. As the discussion progresses we shall consider the extent to which business decision makers are able to make claims relating to sustainability, and, more importantly, the question of how much further organizations could take their initiatives in the pursuit of sustainability. Accordingly we are interested in new dimensions, elements and interpretations of organizational control that emerge when we move beyond outmoded and unhelpful ideas about economic growth, human progress and attendant ideas about what constitutes management control in business organizations.

Performance management and the sustainability agenda

The first of the questions listed above focuses on key success factors, how they might be achieved and what measures should be used to assess performance.

There are two conceptual problems that need to be overcome in the transition to sustainability. First, there is a need to develop a coherent alternative to the current notion of the discrete, tightly bounded 'economic organization'. Second, ideas about what constitutes success or otherwise in the context of economic activity need to develop exogenously, within a social and economic framework informed by new values and ideas on sustainability.

Success and the business entity

It can be claimed that the current indicators of success show we are moving away from rather than towards a sustainable future. It is not necessarily that profit is bad, but rather that the predominant means by which it is generated and accumulated, and at what or whose expense, is bad. The conventional measures of performance (GDP, financial profit and so on) and the activities they give rise to are part of the problem. Not only do they fail to capture the realities of environmental damage and the quality of many people's lives, in many cases they positively encourage destructive acts against nature and people. Conventional ideas on wealth, profit making and economic entities provide us with no system for understanding our cumulative impact and the enormously wasteful throughput of materials and resources. As Hawken *et al.* (2002, p. 14) explain:

> the present industrial system is, practically speaking, a couch potato: It eats too much junk food and gets insufficient exercise. In its late maturity, industrial society runs on life-support systems that require enormous heat and pressure, are petrochemically dependent and materials intensive, and require large flows of toxic and hazardous chemicals. These industrial 'empty calories' end up as pollution, acid rain, and greenhouse gases, harming environmental, social and financial systems. Even though all the reengineering and downsizing trends of the past decade were supposed to sweep away corporate inefficiency, the U.S. economy remains astoundingly inefficient: It has been estimated that only 6 percent of its vast flow of materials actually end up in products. . . . Overall, the ratio of waste to the durable products that constitute material wealth may be closer to one hundred. The whole economy is less than 10 percent – probably only a few percent – as energy-efficient as the laws of physics permits.

Questions about organizational success, the means to pursue it and how to measure it, then, need extending and rethinking because they do not easily accommodate the idea of economic activity being in harmony with nature. The notion of an organization or an entity is a legal and accounting fiction that prevents us from understanding that most human and economic activity is intimately bound up in (usually hostile) relationships with the environment (Shrivastava, 1994).

To date, one of the main changes in business organizations that are grappling with sustainability has been to take up the practice of social and environmental reporting, with the Global Reporting Initiative (GRI, 2000, 2002) emerging as something of a standard (Bebbington *et al.*, 2003; Moneva *et al.* 2003).[1] In the most genuine cases, such reporting is being used as a means to drive internal changes to organizational practices, most notably with regard to energy and waste management. While this does constitute a first step, this new element of control system thinking at best reflects an end-of-the-pipe approach focused on eco-efficiency (cf. Bebbington *et al.*, 2003; Stone, 1995) and the prevailing attitude that organizations have the right to make increasing financial profits, mediated only by relatively weak legislative and market drivers (cf. Gray and Milne, 2004; Howes, 2002; Schaefer *et al.*, 2003, p. 225). Indeed if we reflect on our earlier discussion on sustainability, renewable and non-renewable resource use, pollution emissions and irreversible impacts, we can see the limited nature of these first steps. As Hawken *et al.* (2002, p. x) explain:

> Eco-efficiency . . . is only one small part of a richer and more complex web of ideas and solutions. Without a fundamental rethinking of the structure and the reward system of commerce, narrowly focused eco-efficiency could be a disaster for the environment by overwhelming resource savings with even larger growth in the production of the wrong products, produced by the wrong processes, from the wrong materials, in the wrong place, at the wrong scale, and delivered using the wrong business models.

This questions the sense of producing an account of performance recording finite and integrally valuable natural capital and environmental services that is produced by the ecologically illiterate for the purposes of stakeholder management (cf. Gray, 2001; O'Dwyer *et al.*, 2003). This can be seen as an attempt to sustain the organization at all costs, and makes no sense except in a world on a road to nowhere. Such a conception of the organization, with the right (as opposed to responsibility) to define what success is, is arguably implicit in Otley's first question on performance management.

What emerges from this brief analysis is that the current environmental or sustainability reports are woefully inadequate means on which to form ideas about success as seen in terms of the ecological logic needed to reorganize and control economic activity. Multi-lead analysis of long-term thinking, cumulative environmental impacts, multilevel analysis and a proper understanding of the economic organization, as located in wider ecological and cultural systems, suggests we need radically different notions of success. This will provide an important step towards what we might term 'control for sustainability'.

Rethinking fundamentals

In a society that has already decided to move towards sustainability, the focus will have shifted to understanding current problems and formulating a way forward (cf. Hawken *et al.*, 2002, p. 149). The corollary is that Otley's framework must (again) be extended and problematized to enable organizational thinking to encompass human institutional, cultural and ecological systems, and in order to rethink what is meant by success. Bebbington *et al.* (2003) illustrate the importance of this level of analysis by placing the development of environmental reporting in the context of regime change. They state that 'A regime involves much more than *practice* – it also involves *beliefs* and the presence or otherwise of *formal legal* requirements' (ibid., p. 11).

Ideas about what constitutes business success would still prevail, but from an organizational perspective the concern might strategies (which might be more appropriately termed principles and obligations) for a sustainable future. Such strategies would have to draw on a wider analysis and understanding to enable organizations to behave as though natural capital were valued. As Hawken *et al.* (2002, p. 321) put it:

> Today, the central issues for thoughtful and successful industries – the two being increasingly identical – relate not to how best to produce the goods and services needed for a satisfying life – that's now pretty well worked out – but rather to what is worth producing, what will make us better human beings, how we can stop trying to meet non-material needs, and how much is enough.

The central strand of a shared social and ecological framework will be the articulation of new values, reflected in a new entrepreneurial culture. Some researchers have suggested that as organizations move away from the (nominally) value-free assumptions of conventional economics and take on value commitments linked to sustainability, business culture may shift, providing an important context for reform (see Ball, 2003; Birkin 2000; Hayward, 1994, p. 97; cf. Schaefer *et al.*, 2003). Hayward (1994, p. 88) argues that reform is a necessary first step towards seeing 'just how far existing economic practices might be pushed in an ecological direction'. Ball's (2003) study of a Canadian city council, for example, shows how a gradual rise in the household waste recycling rate to around 70 per cent led to organizational life taking on a schizophrenic quality characterized by conflicting (economic versus ecological) value systems. This shift at the City Council was both commensurate with its traditional business values and provided pressure for reform:

> a significant drive . . . had been going on for some years in the city to recy-
> cle and reduce the amount of garbage that we had, and had been actively
> embraced by citizens for some years, and the notion of burning garbage
> was just anathema to citizens . . . [who] would have had no part in it.
> Anyway . . . once we decided, or it became evident that landfill was almost
> impossible, we were forced to look at what else . . . we could do then as a
> local solution to it. . . . [T]he pieces started to come forward as kind of a
> comprehensive program, and we realized the magnitude of what we meant
> by comprehensive programming. It really was going to change everything;
> . . . how we collected [rubbish] and where, and what we did with it, and
> . . . the costs (city councillor).

Yet the first steps taken by some organizations in the last two or three decades have done nothing to reverse the destruction of natural systems, and, in general little progress has been made in determining the order of change required to move towards a sustainable economy. As Schaefer *et al.* (2003, p. 211) note, much of the 'greening' advocated in the management and practitioner literatures is only likely to results in change if it does not question the assumptions on which business organizations operate. For example well-intentioned advocates of environmental accounting attempt to balance their recommendations for radical change with an appeal to the (orthodox) business case (see for example Gray, 2002; Howes, 2002). In short, many advocates of sustainability are in fact the courtiers of business, speaking to a business agenda of 'weak sustainability', as business moves to capture and appropriate the agenda (Welford, 1997). By failing to talk about how to revive our planet, we fail both ourselves and future generations.

We envision 'control for sustainability' in other areas as well, including industrial production. Hawken *et al.* (2002, ch. 2) argue that current innovations in the automotive industry could lead to a fundamental shift in what we drive and a massive upheaval in the car, oil, steel, aluminium, electricity and coal industries: 'materials would flow in closed loops, with toxicity carefully confined or designed out and longevity designed in' (ibid., p. 27). Ideally we should strive to 'extend . . . gains in resource productivity by making any kind of car less necessary' (ibid., p. 40).

> With or without Hypercars, the problem of excessive automobility is
> pervasive. . . . Congestion is smothering mobility, and mobility is corrod-
> ing community. People demand a lot of travel and have few non-automo-
> tive ways to do it. This effectively immobilizes everyone too old, young,

infirm, or poor to drive – a group that includes one-third of all Americans, and whose numbers are rising. Street life and the public realm are sacrificed as we meet our neighbors only through windshields. As architect Andres Duany puts it, this stratification 'reduces social interactions to aggressive competition for square feet of asphalt' (ibid.)

According to Jacobs (2000, p. 100), addiction to car travel and the mistaken idea that the volume of road (and other) traffic can continue to grow indefinitely has caused an economic vicious circle:

> Economic vicious circles are intended to solve problems, but they don't. The problems they're meant to solve persist; as solutions recede, the costs of temporizing continue to rise. We should become suspicious of activities displaying these characteristics and seek to cut vicious circles instead of indulging them – essentially the same advice given to drug abusers, compulsive gamblers, smokers, or other addicts. Economic vicious circles are economic and political addictions. The most effective ways to cut them are with bifurcations instead of continuing as is.

Both analyses point to the need for radical changes in how economic organizations address key objectives, strategies and success the pursuit of success. The meaning and measurement of success should be reconsidered so that fundamental business, community and personal goals can be re-evaluated. We need to find more meaningful measures of economic activity than highly abstract accounting measures such as profit, loss, GDP and so on. As members of economic organizations, communities and biosystems we should ask how much we really need, how much is enough?

In the context of Otley's framework and the definition of business success, there has been a failure by many of us at many levels to articulate the problems interest in the dominant understanding of human progress, and to offer alternatives. Human development, as Hayward (1994, p. 87) explains, has become almost inseparable from the now almost global conception of economic growth that 'is in many respects the antithesis of ecological ends'. Arguably, the mindset of the current capitalist system provides no proper basis for even the most conscientious businessperson to make reasonable decisions about success. For the state of sustainability we must re-examine the conventional understanding of growth (as reflected in the usual measures of economic success), admit to our addiction to economic success, and reject maximizing behaviour in respect of the production of material goods, the overuse of natural resources, the destruction of habitats and ecosystems, and so on. Thus the required order of change can only be apprehended by questioning with the most fundamental basics by which we live (Singer, 1997).

Organizational performance and target setting

Apart from our belief that most conventional indicators of organizational performance and target setting are contrary to sustainability, our concern here is with business organizations' perceptions of appropriate standards of performance and future targets for sustainability. We suggest that the change encouraged by the targets implied in the current generation of corporate accounting and reporting developments is unhelpful. It is disproportionate to the necessary sense of urgency and scale of action required to address the risks associated with ongoing environmental exploitation. While organizations seeking change for sustainability have to start somewhere, we are concerned that these approaches should ensure there is a rapid speeding up of the transformation required rather than provide excuses for slowing it down.

Beyond 'exemptionalism' and eco-efficiency

When taking stock of adaptations that businesses have made so far in terms of taking up the sustainability agenda, our general conclusion is that the only value provided by the new accounting, reporting and control frameworks (although these are largely positive developments) is that they have encouraged organizations and those who work in them to think about what they are doing (see Gray, 2001, 2002). According to Howes[2] (2002, p. 18; see Birkin, 2000, for a fuller discussion):

> For a company committed to moving towards environmental sustainability, the challenge is to try and determine/estimate what its environmentally-sustainable profits may be and hence to gauge to what extent it is really adding value and making the transition to becoming a more environmentally-sustainable enterprise. The development of a more complete, transparent and integrated accounts/accounting systems – systems that specifically take into account the most significant external environmental impacts resulting from a company's operations – is a prerequisite . . . [for] this.

While new ideas and management control tools, are essential to the shift towards sustainability (Hawken *et al.*, 2002; Tylecote, 1992), the new accounting and reporting approaches are being managed in such a way as to improve financial rather than environmental or social results. For example environmental accounting and performance reporting permit businesses to tackle the environment in the context of a win–win scenario, focusing on incremental improvements in material use and carrying on regardless of the scale of their overall environmental impact, and/or the postconsumer impact of their products. That major car manufacturers claim to embrace sustainability and eco-efficiency and yet continue to produce energy-inefficient vehicles suggests they have a warped understanding of eco-efficiency.

Cairns (2001, p. 148) argues that a great many of what he labels 'exemptionalists' either believe or behave as if they believe that:

> human ingenuity, technology, and creativity free humans from the laws of nature that limit and control other species . . . [and] that resources are infinitely substitutable and exhaustion of one will ultimately lead to the appearance of a substitute when there is enough economic incentive to do so. Thus, humans are the ultimate resource and the species is not limited by finite natural resources.

Sustainability requires us to move beyond such beliefs and assumptions. Similarly, thinking that 'win–win' eco-efficiency can control environmental impacts and problems is fallacious as it encourages greater material and energy use and does little to change beliefs about what constitutes success. Eco-efficiency, as McDonough and Braungart (1998, p. 4) note:

> . . . works within the same system that caused the problem in the first place . . . It presents little more than an illusion of change. Relying on eco-efficiency to save the environment will in fact do the opposite – it will let industry finish off everything quietly, persistently, and completely.

In order for businesses to pursue sustainability initiatives further, management control systems should be adapted to include measures to counter the growing human pressure on the environment.

Emerging concepts for a sustainable future

Getting us beyond the 'change but no change' approach to environmental sustainability are new ideas and tools for understanding 'the entity' and its relationship with nature. The value of these 'ecological accounting' tools lies in bridging the gap between conventional economism and ecological thinking. Birkin (1996, pp. 247–9) develops the notion of 'burden to base' as a key relationship:

> the word 'capital' could be substituted by the word 'burden'. . . . This substitution acknowledges fundamental ecosystem dependence. . . . To support the burden, a base is required within the ecosystem . . . following on from the burden to base relationship, wealth can no longer just be

mystically 'created', it will have to be appropriated. . . . Representations of the four categories of burden to base could then be incorporated in a 'balance sheet'. This balance sheet would include scientific assessments, social reports and aesthetic judgements as well as economic measures. Such an account would seek to explain critical issues as fully as possible.

A more practical concept that is gaining some currency is the 'ecological footprint' (Wackernagel and Rees, 1996). This is based on the idea of 'Earthshare' or people's share of the total amount of productive land on the planet divided by the total global population. Estimates of the footprints of average citizens of Western countries reveal they require vastly greater areas of land to support their lifestyles (and therefore have vastly greater footprints) than those in Asia and Africa. Such footprints are useful indicators of inequality as well as giving some idea of human pressure on nature, but they do not provide direct indicators of the deteriorating state of the environment.[3] The idea is that reducing the size of footprints leads to improvements in environmental quality, or at least to reduced levels of degradation. Some adaptations of the footprint concept have been made in New Zealand, where several organizations have calculated their carbon footprints (using imputed carbon dioxide metrics) in respect of travel, electricity consumption and so on.[4] Again the idea is to reduce the size of their footprints, although for organizations that are seeking to grow this is somewhat of a challenge. A related notion is that carbon footprints can be offset by investment in forestation or the regeneration of vegetation.[5]

Associated with footprints is the concept of material inputs (including energy) per unit of service (MIPS), and the 'ecological rucksacks' to which it gives rise: surface area per unit of service (FIPS) and ecotoxic exposure equivalent per unit of service (TOPS) (Factor 10 Club, 1999; Schmidt-Bleek, 1993). These concepts are intended to foster dematerialization, and provide a way of understanding that damage to the environment comes not just from pollution but also from resource extraction and usage, since ultimately all resources end up as pollution or waste.

MIPS and TOPS are calculated for consumer products, and assess the amount of raw materials used (including energy) in producing, transporting, consuming and disposing of a product, minus the weight of that product. For example it has been calculated that a 1 kg personal computer carries an ecological rucksack of 200 kg of materials. Rucksacks can also be calculated for base materials, for example metals, plastics, glass and cement. MIPS calculations relate material inputs to 'service' outputs, and improvements can come from either fewer material inputs or improved services from given inputs. Related to MIPS and rucksacks are the notions of 'products as services' and 'divorcing use from ownership' (see www.product-life.org). The idea here is that if producers do not sell final products but merely rent them out, they have a continuing incentive to design products that will minimize material waste streams, are long or lasting and/or can be easily recycled. An example of this kind of practice is provided by Interface – a US manufacturer that leases floor coverings (see www.interfaceinc.com).

The aim is to lower MIPS and rucksacks, and the goal of the Factor 10 Club, as its name implies, is to lower their value by a factor of 10. Importantly, though, improvements must be at the level of economies and ultimately the planet, and not simply on the basis of individual products – a tenfold reduction in material inputs per computer is of little use if it is accompanied by a greater than tenfold increase in the consumption of the product. This problem of 'rebound' or 'boomerang' (see for example Factor 10 Club, 1999; Hukkinen, 2003; McDonough and Braungart, 1998) is encouraged by gains in resource productivity, because efficiency gains tend to create competitive advantages that in turn lead to greater investment and expansion.

Even if the problem of rebound is avoided, some believe that dematerialization is not sufficient because although it reduces absolute levels of resource use, it still involves waste and toxic emissions, albeit to a lesser extent. For McDonough and Braungart (1998), what is required is nothing short of an industrial revolution, in which product life cycles are not simply slowed down but products designed to continue indefinitely in one form or other:

> If people are to prosper within the natural world, all the products and materials manufactured by industry must after each useful life provide nourishment for something new. Since many of the things people make are not natural, they are not safe 'food' for biological systems. Products composed of materials that do not biodegrade should be designed as technical nutrients that continually circulate within closed-loop industrial cycles – the technical metabolism (ibid., p. 2).

For McDonough and Braungart, success means no longer producing 'unmarketables' – products that pose hazards or cannot safely or economically be recycled – and keeping products of consumption separate from products of service. The former consist of organic nutrients that can safely be returned to nature, while the latter are made from 'technical nutrients' that circulate in industrial cycles forever.

Social accounting targets: beyond stakeholder management

More meaningful and realistic analyses of entrepreneurial activity and the belief that many more people should have a say in whether or not organizational responses are proportionate to sustainability gaps are embodied in the ideal of social accounting. Social accounting involves the 'creation of . . . social visibilities and exposure of values and priorities that become inputs to wider democratic processes of discourse and decision-making' (Boyce, 2000, p. 53). Or as Gray (2001, p. 11) puts it in the context of capitalist mind-sets, 'social accounting should hurt. If it doesn't raise difficulties, cause unwelcome re-examinations of the organisation and so on, then it is probably not good social accounting.' However the adaptations businesses have made to date with reference to wider (anthropocentric and ecological) interests than their own have tended to focus on 'stakeholder management' (see for example, Gray, 2001, 2002; O'Dwyer *et al.*, 2003; Owen and Swift, 2001).

It should be acknowledged that any business involvement in the development of social accounting and reporting represents a significant advance on the view that the only responsibility of the firm is to maximize shareholder profit (Friedman, 1970) or 'shareholder value' (Mintzberg *et al.*, 2002). Nonetheless change is only happening at the margins. Companies are generally striving for early closure of any engagement with questions that challenge basic assumptions about 'how much performance' or the targets for what they do, and in whose interests they do it (cf. Gray 2001; Neu *et al.*, 1998; Owen and Swift, 2001; Schaefer *et al.*, 2003). While eco-efficiency has gained some acceptance in the business community, eco-justice seems a bridge too far, and some of the new environmental and sustainability reporting schemes allow companies to side-step consideration of social strategies or obligations (cf. Ball *et al.*, 2003; Howes, 2002; Moneva *et al.*, 2003).

O'Dwyer *et al.*'s (2003) study of less economically powerful' stakeholders' attitudes towards corporate social disclosure (CSD) revealed strong demand for regular, regulated, standardized, audited and accountable CSD. Currently however, CSD, is 'widely perceived as little more than an untrustworthy symbolic stakeholder management exercise with little concern for "true" accountability. They note that amongst the interviewees '[t]here was . . . a clear consensus that current CSD was motivated by corporate self-interest and stakeholder management rather than a genuine interest on the part of companies to account to less powerful stakeholders' (ibid., p. 17). In short, based on prevailing ideas about their responsibilities towards the wider community, companies continue to exploit the absence of systems to regulate their social and environmental performance. Indeed, considering the magnitude of the social problems with which many business organizations are inextricably linked, their failure to report properly on their social impact amounts to abuse of their substantial power:

> For the poorer two thirds of humanity living in the South, nature's capital is their source of sustenance and livelihood. The destruction, diversion and takeover of their eco-system in order to extract natural resources or dump

waste generates a disproportionate burden for the poor. In a world of globalised, deregulated commerce in which everything is tradable and economic strength is the only determinate of power and control, resources move from the poor to the rich, and pollution moves from the rich to the poor. The result is global environmental apartheid. . . . (Shiva, 2001, p. 112).

Notwithstanding the need for political action on the development gap between the world's nations and the poverty gap that is still pervasive in the developed world, if corporate attempts to measure, control and report on social performance is to have any meaning beyond public relations puffery, organizations must seriously engage with the social ramifications of their inputs, processes and outputs. When conducted with genuine concern for stakeholders, stakeholder dialogue is a valuable element of the organization's control system and of quite a different order from stakeholder management.

Social wounds cannot be salved nor the environment 'saved' as long as people cling to the outdated assumption of classical industrialism that the summum bonum of commercial enterprise is to use more natural capital and fewer people. . . . The true bottom line is this: A society that wastes its resources wastes its people and vice versa. And both kinds of waste are expensive (Hawken *et al.*, 2002, p. 55).

Rewards for achieving targets

For Otley (ch 6 of this volume), motivation is a key issue in the design and operation of management control systems. In the current capitalist mind-set, economic conceptions of success dominate organizational life and individual behaviour. Economic considerations will continue to be important in the transition to sustainability, but as noted in Chapter 6, the reality is that people in organizations have complex motivations. The transition to sustainability implies attention to how people are motivated at work, deriving from changing financial considerations for individual enterprises and linked to wider debates stimulated by socially unsustainable trends.

Financial motivation

Transition requires changes to be made to economic framework, and regimes (cf. Bebbington *et al.*, 2003), with business behaviours being rewarded or penalized differently. Sustainability is arguably beginning to guide public governance (and business strategy), and the need for economic regime change is beginning to be recognized, or at least in Europe. In the UK, for example, the introduction of ecological taxes has attached a price to environmental damage (examples include the climate change levy and landfill tax). With regard to organizations' control systems, there is a need for accounting tools and methods that pay 'due attention to the environmental inputs and outputs of economic systems' (Hayward,1994, p. 90) and take fuller account of ecological factors.

It is also necessary to re-examine ecologically damaging financial incentives, such as 'subsidies doled out to the fossil-fuel industry, ranging from cheap access to oil on government land to the ongoing American military presence in the Middle East' (*Economist*, 25 October 2003, p. 11). More generally:

> Hundreds of billions of dollars of taxpayers' money are annually diverted to promote inefficient and unproductive material and energy use. These include subsidies to mining, oil, coal, fishing, and forest industries as well as agricultural practices that degrade soil fertility and use wasteful amounts of water and chemicals. Many of these subsidies are vestigial, some dating as far back as the eighteenth century (Hawken *et al.*, 2002, p. 13).

Similarly Jacobs (2000, p. 100) points out that subsidies exacerbate vicious circles:

> the cod fishery and its workers were subsidized . . . in Canada, ever more heavily during the years cod were declining. Had it been possible to add subsidy costs into cod prices, cod would have been priced out of the market before cod stocks collapsed. Subsidies were intended to support the industry and its workers, and they did. The price of automobiles doesn't begin to pay for their many indirect costs: waste of land and energy, loss of amenities, and the expenses of traffic enforcement, pollution, and accidents caused by uninsured drivers.

Paradoxically, but perhaps unsurprisingly in the context of stakeholder management (see the earlier discussion), certain clear laggards (those who are not prepared to make radical changes) in the transition to sustainability regularly emerge as leaders in environmental or sustainability accounting and reporting.[6]

It is to be hoped that governments will soon begin to understand the need to give financial rewards to companies that opt for new technologies aimed at environmental sustainability, and recognize the need to modernize the economy to meet the challenge of sustainability (cf. Christie and Warburton, 2001; Hawken *et al.*, 2002; Murray, 1999). What constitutes success for individual enterprises should therefore be linked to their capacity to exploit environ-mentally friendly markets and technologies, for example renewable energy, organic and low-impact farming, public transport, waste recycling and the repair and reuse of products. Notable losers would include the fossil-fuel energy industry and producers of cars, which will have to restructure radically (see Hawken *et al.*, 2002, for a discussion). With regard to organizational control systems, ideas about the changing economic future and organiza-tions' place in should inform their definition of success.

Beyond exceptionalism and redefining rewards

Whilst economic incentives and penalties will be important in the transition to sustainability, the current capitalist mind-set thinking will also have to undergo transformation. A factor in this will be growing pressure on the socially unsustainable Western economic growth model. As already noted, companies are implicated in the poverty gap that is increasingly characteriz-ing the economically developed countries. In the words of Christie and Warburton (2001, p. 6), who write on behalf of the Real World Coalition (a coalition of UK not-for-profit organizations campaigning on what they see as causally linked but distinct policy constituencies),[7] 'for the last two decades, economic change in the industrialized world has, in many cases, widened the gap between the richest and the poorest groups, compounding the disadvan-tages suffered by people on low incomes and leading to growth of a "super-class" . . . of hyper-affluent people'. Similarly, and perhaps surprisingly as this comes from the mainstream management literature:

> In 1989, the United States had 66 billionaires and 31.5 million people living below the official poverty line. A decade later, the number of billion-aires had increased to 268, whereas the number of people below the poverty line had increased to 34.5 million . . . the United States [ranks] highest both in gross domestic product and poverty rates . . . (Mintzberg *et al.*, 2002, p. 72).

Both of these sets of commentators are concerned with the creation of a 'superwealthy' class that claims a disproportionate share of the Earth's resources. (Cairns, 2001, uses the term 'exceptionalism' to connote belief in such an entitlement.)[8] For example:

> In March 2000, Barclay's Bank [UK] announced thousands of job cuts along with closure of hundreds of bank branches, leaving many commu-nities without access to banking services. This sounds like the behaviour of a firm in deep trouble. But, far from being in crisis, it was at the same time

posting record profits, and announced also that its Chairman's salary had quadrupled to £1.75 million in the previous year (Christie and Warburton, 2001, p. 14).

Similarly Mintzberg *et al.* (2002 p. 72) point out that the much heralded trickle-down effect of the US neoliberal economics of recent decades has failed to materialize, thus widening the gap between rich and poor. They argue that it is time to stop relying on this particular idea to appease our consciences.

> In the past 15 years, we in North America have experienced a glorification of self-interest perhaps unequalled since the 1930s. It is as if, in denying much of the social progress since then, we have reverted to an earlier and darker age. Greed has been raised to some sort of high calling; corporations have been urged to ignore broader social responsibilities in favor of narrow shareholder value; chief executives have been regarded as if they alone create economic performance. Meanwhile, concern for the disadvantaged – simple, old-fashioned generosity – has somehow been lost (ibid., p. 67).

Arguably, at a number of levels their is a perverse relationship between social (and environmental) well-being and the crude economic incentives that are used to motivate managers to accumulate far more economic capital than they could ever reasonably need.

If we view the issue of motivating people in organizations through the prism of sustainability, in contrast with the morally and spiritually unambitious economism of the last few decades (cf. Hayward, 1994; Shearer, 2002), we can ask rather more creative questions about what we do at work, how we do it, and the possibility of intrinsic (in addition to financial) rewards. For example, linked to acknowledgement of 'the deep dissatisfaction with the "stress and spend" culture of Millennial Britain' (Christie and Warburton, 2001, p. 2), we might ask how the demands of work can be reconciled with the knowledge that community life, families and individuals are being damaged by the way in which economic activity is organized. A much-needed antidote to the idea of 'continuous (economic) improvement', we suggest, is the idea of 'enough performance'.

> Like the other easy assumptions of this syndrome of selfishness, lean and mean is supposed to offer it all: lower costs, higher productivity, flatter and more flexible structures, more empowered workers (with their bosses gone) and happier customers. . . . Sure all this can happen, but once again it is a half-truth. The other half comprises burned-out managers, angry workers, quality losses in the guise of productivity gains and disgruntled customers.

. . . Maybe it is time to develop healthier organizations by cleaning up our attitudes. We need economic sustainability too, in addition to social and environmental sustainability (Mintzberg *et al.*, 2002, p. 72).

If we are going to have a socially sustainable future, and work in socially and environmentally sustainable economic organizations, control systems must include a reward system that reflects the long-term interests of the environment and society and provides practical alternatives to 'stress and spend'. This would emphasize individual and collective potentialities and welfare, and would, heed natural limits. We might want what we do at work to be driven, for example, by a vision of prosperous, safe and supportive communities and a healthy environment for all of us. Of course this raises the question of how long-term thinking can be fostered in communities, particularly in the context of a business culture based on short-term thinking and a polity/citizenry that failing to (or prefers not to) face up to the consequences of its present consumption habits. Yet recent interest in 'work–life balance' (see for example Nord *et al.*, 2002) and the rewards paid to the superaffluent class reflect growing concern about the paradoxes of Western organizational life. Christie and Warburton (2001, p. 3) note that:

> Repeatedly, researchers have identified a tension between the demands of work and the claims of family life, a growing divide between official yardsticks or progress and citizens' anxieties and priorities and a search for more meaning in life than 'consumer choice' can provide. At the same time, there is no doubt that we live in historically exceptional times of good fortune and plenty.

Indeed it might be something of a relief if our potential were measured in terms other than the quantity of goods our income allows us to consume or how productive we are (cf. Hayward, 1994, p. 92).

Information flows for sustainability

This final section focuses on what we see as the most outstanding defect in organizational control systems: ecological illiteracy (see Orr, 1992). Ecological literacy is organizations' capacity to comprehend environmental matters, recognize the damage their individual and collective economic and industrial activities are causing, and appreciate that such damage is putting everyone's our survival at risk.[9] At one level, the information flows that might feed into organizational control systems in the context of ecological literacy are already apparent. As Jacobs (2000, p. 94) puts it: 'These days, ecological loops and intersecting loops are constantly being identified and measured. But there's a sad and desperate reason for so much interest. We're cutting such loops at a terrible rate. Well, at least knowing what we're doing is one prerequisite to doing better.' Yet such knowledge is not captured (in Otley's, terms as described in Chapter 6) in arrangements for performance monitoring, let alone being treated as the basis for learning and change. In spite of attempts by organizations to take up the sustainability agenda via initiatives such as environmental, social or sustainability reporting, there has been no real attempt to develop ecological literacy.[10]

An important step in this direction would be for individuals to relate environmental (and attendant moral) issues that arise in their roles as private citizens or parents to their work contexts. However Schaefer *et al.*, 2003 (p. 212) suggest that because of the current capitalist mindset, managers are more likely to wait for specific legislation before they relate issues such as ozone depletion and climate change to their work context. Such duplicity is practically and ethically unacceptable. Ecological literacy may develop as organizational discourse is given new meaning by stakeholder dialogue. A further possibility, as indicated by studies of environmental accounting in action, is that social or political groups within organizations will champion the 'greening' of the organization (cf. Ball, 2003; Dey, 2002; Larrinaga-Gonzalez and Bebbington, 2001; see also Schaefer *et al.*, 2003).

The implementation of better accounting and control tools for sustainability, such as the ecological footprint, could also be used to develop ecological literacy (see the earlier discussion on this subject). Some initiatives to develop 'control for sustainability' are emerging beyond the defined boundaries of corporate activities and operations, partially reflecting Milne's (1996) ideas on regionally based initiatives, and switching the entity and going-concern concepts from companies to natural entities. The Cities for Climate Protection campaign by the International Council for Local Environmental Initiatives (*ICLEI*), for example, has drawn about 500 local governments in various countries into a common performance initiative to reduce ozone-depleting and air polluting emissions, with the aims of improving community 'livability'.[11] The initiative involves the entire community, with coordinated action by households and enterprises as well as the local government. In New Zealand, concern for the long-term ecological health of such entities as lakes and rivers has prompted several community initiatives to stop certain land uses and family practices.[12] As people in organizations begin to use better tools and engage in issues of sustainability at other levels, their ecological literacy should develop.

A further driver of ecological literacy is the re-evaluation in technical terms of organizational activities and operations, linked to a better understanding of the present environmental crisis and various legislative or regulatory pressures.

The waste management industry is a good example of this (see for example, Ball *et al.*, 2003; Murray, 1999). Existing ideas on the instrumental value of some core business functions are being challenged (for example conventional accounting) and there is a requirement for people to combine areas of functional expertise. Murray (1999, p. 130) suggests that in the waste management business, obtaining accurate environmental data requires as much attention as financial accounting. However the Forum for the Future pointed out that the current capacity of organizations to respond to the demands of sustainability is limited:

> Few work-forces have encountered even the most basic scientific principles that underpin environmental sustainability at any stage of their education or training, and many organisations are structured so as to prevent the integrated, cross-disciplinary approach that is at the heart of identifying and implementing sustainability solutions (Forum for the Future, quoted in Christie and Warburton, 2001, p. 33).

Of course precisely the same comments may be applied to the vast majority of people working in business schools around the world. Not only do the educators of tomorrow's business managers fail to engage with their peers in the sciences and humanities, they rarely read the literature or consider the ideas of these disciplines. This is in part due to the increasingly stringent and narrow performance management frameworks to which academics are subjected. Ecological literacy is perhaps the most important dimension of adapting control systems in the transition to sustainability.

Conclusions

For those who are still imprisoned by the mind-set of late industrial capitalism, this chapter's attempt to reconcile management control with the pursuit of sustainability will seem like an engagement in fantasy. For orthodox economists and accountants who view the business world as largely devoid of environmental and social stresses, the abstract concepts of profit, growth and development are just plain common sense. The challenge for us is to make those in the business and business school communities understand that their concepts serve as institutional, cultural and personal barriers to the addressing of sustainability.

We know that social structures depend on attitude and belief systems. Economic conceptions of human existence are not unassailable beliefs. The stumbling attempts by businesses to address sustainability (discussed in this chapter in terms of the developments in the new accounting for the environment or sustainability) show that sustainability campaigners have been able to import some alternative values and beliefs. Environmental and social stresses will continue to manifest themselves, but governments will regulate and things could change for the better.

It remains essential to strip away the rhetoric of 'business as usual', and to present coherent alternatives to systems driven by the economic self-interest of the relatively few at the potentially staggering (if not fatal) cost of the many. Whilst some aspects of the sustainability agenda are now being reflected in institutional practices, these only constitute a tiny step towards the introduction of systems of control for sustainability. Ignoring the issue of how business should change is perhaps emotionally comforting, but we have a practical and ethical duty to apprehend the world and the place of individual and collective enterprise within it in ways that do not exclude the precious natural and cultural systems on which we all rely.

The next logical step is to set up a business teaching, learning and practice agenda that takes as its starting point some of the principles outlined in this chapter. In particular businesses must respond adequately to the social and environmentally unsustainable trends in which they are implicated, and rid themselves of their propensity for incrementalism and short-termism. They must develop more ecologically and socially sophisticated management control systems and approaches, and set their sights higher than the remedial class for ecological literacy.

Otley's framework in Chapter 6 of this book has been helpful to us in setting out a range of questions about the complexity of the sustainability agenda and what it means for business. But we are not confident that the questions included in the framework would, outside the context we have been at pains to establish in this chapter, challenge basic assumptions about what business does, and in whose interests. Instead, what is needed is an ongoing debate within the business and business school communities on the development of a common framework for sustainability.

Notes

1. The Global Reporting Initiative scheme (GRI, 2000, 2002), which claims to provide the basis for standardized global reporting on the sustainability of business organizations, has gained some momentum (ACCA, 2001; Adams, 2003; Gervais, 2002; Moneva *et al.*, 2003; NEF, 2000).

2. Howes (2002) details a methodology for quantifying companies' environmentally sustainable profits, as developed by the sustainable development organization Forum for the Future (a UK charity) in association with the UK Chartered Institute of Management Accountants.

3. For example Best Foot Forward (BFF, undated) estimates that each of the residents on the Isle of Wight in the UK consumes about 2.5 times the sustainable average

Earthshare. It presents a detailed analysis of the 'supply–consumption–disposal' chain on the island, and offers an understanding of the collective impact of the islanders' and tourists' material consumption, as well suggesting some (albeit short-term and incremental) solutions. It notes, for example, that 13 000 of the 34 000 tonnes of milk produced on the island are consumed locally. However there is an additional 5000 tonnes of local demand, which could be satisfied by island-produced milk rather than being imported, thus reducing the environmental impact of transporting the milk. This would reduce the island's Footprint by 100 hectares)

4. See for example http://www.landcareresearch.co.nz/research/sustain_business/ EBEX21.

5. Trees and vegetation sequestrate carbon from the air, and this can counter the emission of carbon by organizations. This is reflected at the global level by the Kyoto Protocol, with nations receiving carbon credits for planting forests.

6. See for example the Association of Chartered Certified Accountants (ACCA) Sustainability Reporting Awards (http://www.acca.co.uk/sustainability/awards/ ?session=ffffffeffffffffc28288ca3f9cf7adb966ef1fd56ea99d8b36b0103e758470.

7. See http://www.realworld.org.uk/index.html.

8. According to Cairns (2001, p. 148), 'Exceptionalists believe that some humans are vastly exceptional to most humans and, as a consequence, are entitled to a markedly disproportionate share of the planet's resources. Without question the superwealthy are different from the ordinary citizen in some regard, having contributed to a sizeable technological advance or having exceptional financial acumen, or both'.

9. See also 'Moving Sustainable Development Centre Stage', speech given by Jonathan Porritt (chairman of the UK Sustainable Development Commission and programme director of the Forum for the Future), 24 May 2002 www.culture.gov.uk/PDF/sustainable_heritage_porritt_speech.pdf).

10. Indeed, one of the present authors once asked a member of a 15-strong corporate environmental management team of an organization employing 40 000 people, and a leading environmental reporter at that, how many full-time ecologists they employed. The answer, perhaps unsurprisingly, was none.

11. See http://www.iclei.org/co2/; Ball, 2003).

12. For example there is long-term plan to protect Lake Taupo, *Protecting Lake Taupo*. (See www.ew.govt.nz/policyandplans/taupo/index.htm). Community involvement in reducing nitrogen in the lake by 20 per cent over the next 10 years has resulted in the abandonment of certain farming practices. Similarly the Fiordland marine conservation strategy by the Guardians of Fiordland's Fisheries and Marine Environment is aimed at protecting the ecological, economic, spiritual and recreational basis of New Zealand's South Island sea fiords (see www.fiordland-guardians.org.nz/documents.htm).

19 Conclusion

Anthony J. Berry, Jane Broadbent and David Otley

This concluding chapter provides a brief overview of this volume and explores some of the questions and issues that have arisen. For Fayol (1949) control was one of the universal activities of organizations and of managing, with a central place in planning, leading, organizing and motivating. In this sense management control is an aspect of all domains of practical managing: marketing, production operations, personnel, purchasing, selling and so on. Figure 19.1 illustrates this. The plane created by the axis of activities and the axis of domains is the plane of practice. From an inspection of this figure you can see how it is that Fayol and others could conceive of universal activities, and in a straightforward practical sense they were right.

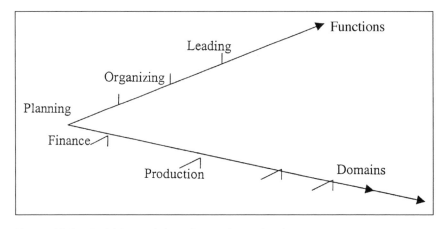

Figure 19.1 Activities and domains: a plane of action

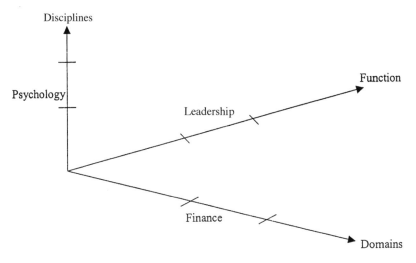

Figure 19.2   Activities, domains and disciplines

Figure 19.2 contains a third axis, that of academic disciplines. This represents the numerous disciplines through which students can try to understand activities and their interactions (for example planning can be examined by means of mathematical modelling) and domains and their interrelationships; for example they can explore marketing through the discipline of linguistics. In combination the three axes of activities, domains and disciplines show that the control of production can be studied using social psychology, the control of personnel using psychoanalytic theory, and so on.

Clearly management control can be studied from the standpoint of any number of disciplines. For example economic theory led Williamson (1973, 1975) to explore control from the standpoint of markets as a counterpoint to hierarchies. The discourse of accounting has provided concepts such as cost absorption to enable the flow of resources to be traced through to products, and shown how the budget model can be used to understand the relationship of inputs to outputs. Anthropology, the study of human societies, has provided the cultural concepts that enabled Ouchi (1980) extend to Williamson's framework. And of course sociology and psychology have underpinned much of the behavioural analysis of control processes. Whilst this is not primarily a research text, research literature from these disciplines has informed our understanding of management control and shaped some of the contributions in this volume (for a broader discussion the reader is referred to Chua *et al.*, 1989).

This volume has explored control from a variety of approaches. It has not been our intention to provide an integrating framework, but the simple framework of managerial activities, managerial domains and disciplines provides a very rich potential map of the field. It also provides a rationale for including issues that at first sight may seem to be somewhat unrelated.

Part I reviewed how different authors and theorists have approached management control. Chapter 1 was concerned with control in purposive organizations. From that standpoint, management control was explored through the domains in which control is encountered. This was followed by a discussion of the way in which control is described and understood in the literature on organization theory. Structures and procedures for control were examined prior to a discussion of the context of control.

Although we did not set out to provide an overarching theory, we did seek to provide a reasonably coherent picture of some basic approaches to management control. The aim was to broaden the view of management control from that found in the standard texts. The material is complex, mainly because the practical world of organizations is complex, and we cannot give a normative answer to the question of how we should control. However we have endeavoured to indicate the limits of rational approaches by addressing the problems of uncertainty, ambiguity and multiple and differentiated values. These explain the multiple theoretical approaches put forward in this volume and our unwillingness to offer clear prescriptions. We have sought to present our views in a manner that is complementary to those in standard accounting and control texts. Our text can be seen as an attempt to broaden the theoretical perspectives traditionally used to analyze the design and operation of management control systems.

In Part II the focus was on management control systems and the numerous ways in which control has been understood in relation to particular issues. The chapters examined the issues of accounting, divisional management, strategy, risk, operations management and performance measurement. Based on differing of approaches, the chapters explored some of the familiar problems of organizations. This was complemented by discussions of control from the standpoint of the discipline of economics and the influence of culture.

Some final comments to students and managers

For students of management we have been concerned to provide a counterpoint to the prescriptive and technical material found in the standard texts on management control, which tend to equate control with accounting. We do not in any way dismiss this approach, and its very ubiquity indicates that accounting is of central importance. It has provided a transorganizational language to describe some aspects of organizational activity, including notions of value expressed in monetary terms. It is a vehicle for control that appears to be growing in importance as its logic is being applied in more and more situations. However what is clear from the considerations in this volume is that the lack of social and cultural factors in the accounting discourse means that great care must be taken when applying accounting concepts to organizations that are not predicated on liberal market economics. The notions of value that exist in a wide range of organizations are not readily comparable, and it would be a serious mistake to assume that they are just because it is possible to record some interactions or transactions in accounting terms. Moreover accounting reduces complex systems to one dimension, and therefore oversimplifies many factors that are essential to effective management control.

The quantification of activities wrongly supposes that all organizational matters of interest can be quantified and that quantification is adequate in itself. For example it is possible to produce quantified management accounts for the process of control in schools, churches, professions and hospitals. However to assume that the activities and outputs (and the social significance) of such organizations are measured by such statements is to be misled as to the limitations of management accounting. Hence to base decisions about such organizations upon the information provided by existing management accounts would be a grave mistake.

For managers, the variety of approaches to understanding control presented in this volume provides examples to help them reflect on the context of different organizational settings. Some scholars see organizational analysis as the process of understanding technical systems for resource acquisition, production and distribution. Others see organizations as primarily social structures. What we seek to encourage is connecting these technical and social structures and processes in order to explore the significance of the issues raised and develop a rich understanding of managerial control in your organization.

If you are currently managing in an organization we hope that the material in this book will help you to build on your own experiences. Again we make no apologies for our discursive rather than prescriptive approach. The literature on managing democratic organizations, empowered organizations, creative organizations and efficient and resourceful organizations has led scholars away from mostly technical prescriptions. We set out with an underlying approach that rejects the idea that simple technical prescription is sufficient for effective management. It seems to us that control systems must take account of external and internal social structures and processes, and we encourage the reader to understand the significance and utility of processual approaches to management control.

This might seem to be an obvious point but in practice managers do tend to take a reductionist approach to information, as demonstrated by the widespread use of targets and budgets as benchmarks for plans and action. It seems that financial goals, because they are readily quantifiable, even if there is considerable slippage between what is known and what is represented, are commonly used as ends to dictate present behaviour. It is unusual to find commercial organizations in the West that focus on management control of process beyond the operational sphere.

During the privatization movement there has been a tendency to apply technical management accounting to organizations that can in no sense be comprehended by such a limited calculus. Yet the assumption of privatization is that such a calculus is not only universal but also morally and politico-economically more effective and efficient than the more subtle, insightful processes it replaces. Indeed there are always political processes in organizations and between organizations and their environments, and choosing not to recognize them does mean that they will be removed. The ideas presented in this volume provide a foundation for understanding how management control can be developed in disparate organizations.

You will have noticed that we have avoided the question of power in organizations and instead looked at the issue of authority, its legitimacy and its explication in various social and cultural contexts. Power presents particular problems for academic theorists and writers. Central among these is the problem that control can reduce one to doing what one is ordered to do. Closed systems of power regress to coercion as a mode of control. Even some apparently normative organizations regress to power modes in which adherence to norms is demanded under considerable duress.

Conflict, however, is one of our concerns. A further problem with technical management accounting as a basis for management control is the assumption that all conflict is dealt with prior to the recording and measuring of transactions. This is unlikely. There is plenty of evidence that the processes of management control provide organizations with some of the necessary systems of conflict suppression and provide means of quasiresolution or actual resolution of conflict.

Almost all accounting procedures bear the risk of objectifying the experiencing self, as though human experience can be set aside by some or other calculation. Hence there is a risk of reducing our human concerns both for our work, for each other, for our organizations and for the society in which we live to abstractions and pretending that such abstractions are the stuff of intelligent management. This is to mistake the model for the substance, a common enough occurrence when one group is seeking dominance over another.

Whatever our views, and whatever yours are, the study and implementation of control systems remain both fascinating and inevitable. We hope that our thoughts have stimulated your interest and encouraged reflection.

Bibliography

ACCA (2001) *UK Environmental Reporting Awards 2000: Report of the Judges* (London: ACCA, March 2001).

Ackoff, R. (1974) *Redesigning the Future* (New York: John Wiley).

Adams J. (1995). *Risk* (London: UCL Press).

Adams, R. (2003) 'The Global Reporting Initiative', in ACCA *The Big Picture: How the Environment Influences Corporate Profit* (London: ACCA).

Adler, P. S. (2001) 'Market hierarchy and trust: the knowledge economy and the future of capitalism', *Organisational Science*, vol. 12, pp. 215–34.

Agrizzi, D. A. (2003) 'Steering the NHS', unpublished PhD thesis, Royal Holloway, University of London.

Ahrens, T. (1996) 'Styles of Accountability', *Accounting, Organizations and Society*, vol. 21, pp. 139–73.

Ahrens, T. (1997) 'Talking Accounting: an Ethnography of Management Knowledge in British and German Brewers', *Accounting, Organizations and Society*, vol. 22, pp. 617–37.

Ahrens, T. and J. Dent (1998) 'Accounting and Organizations: Realizing the Richness of Field Research', *Journal of Management Accounting Research*, vol. 10, pp. 1–39.

Akoi, M. (1988) *Information, Incentives and Bargaining in the Japanese Economy* (New York: Cambridge University Press).

Alderfer, C. P. and H. Bierman (1970) 'Choices with risk: beyond the mean and variance', *Journal of Business*, pp. 341–53.

Aldrich, H. E. (1979) *Organisations and Environments* (London: Prentice-Hall).

Allaire, Y. and M. E. Firsirotu (1984) 'Theories of Organizational Culture', *Organization Studies*, vol. 5, no. 3, pp. 193–226.

Alvesson, M. (1994) *Cultural Perspectives on Organizations* (Cambridge: Cambridge University Press).

343

Alvesson, M. (2002) *Understanding Organizational Culture* (London: Sage).

Alvesson, M. and O. Berg (1992) *Corporate Culture and Organizational Symbolism: an Overview* (Berlin: de Gruyter).

Alvesson, M. and K. Skoldberg (2000) *Reflexive Methodology: New Vistas for Aualitative* (London: Sage).

Alvesson, M. and H. Willmott (2002) 'Identity Regulation as Organizational Control: Producing the Appropriate Individual', *Journal of Management Studies*, vol. 39, pp. 619–44.

Amey, L. R. (1969) 'Divisional Performance Measurement and Interest on Capital', *Journal of Business Finance*, vol. 1, Spring, pp. 1–7.

Amey, L. R. (1979) *Budget Planning and Control Systems* (London: Pitman).

Andrews, K. (1971) *The Concept of Corporate Strategy* (Homewood, Ill.: Dow Jones/Irwin).

Ansoff, H. I. (1965) *Corporate Strategy* (New York: McGraw-Hill).

Ansoff, H. I. (1979) *Strategic Management* (London: Macmillan).

Anthony, R. N. (1965) *Planning and Control Systems: A Framework for Analysis* (Cambridge, Mass.: Harvard University Press).

Anthony, R.N. (1970) *Management Accounting Principles*, 2nd edn (Homewood, Ill.: Richard D. Irwin).

Anthony, R. N., J. Dearden and N. Bedford (1989) *Management Control Systems*, 6th edn (Homewood, Ill.: Irwin).

Anthony, R. and V. Govindarajan (2004) *Management Control Systems*, 11th edn (Singapore: Irwin).

Aoki, M. (1990a) 'The Participatory Generation of Information Rents and the Theory of the Firm', in M. Aoki, B. Gustaffson and O. E. Williamson (eds), *The Firm as a Nexus of Treaties* (London: Sage).

Aoki, M. (1990a) 'The Participatory Generation of Information Rents and the Theory of the Firm' in M. Aoki, B. Gustaffson and O. E. Williamson (eds), *The Firm as a Nexus of Treaties* (London: Sage).

Aoki, M. (1990b) 'Towards a Theory of the Japanese Firm', *Journal of Economic Literature*, vol. 27, March, pp. 1–27.

Argyris, C. (1952) *The Impact of Budgets on People* Ithaca, NY: The Controllership Foundation.

Argyris, C. (1990) *Overcoming Organisational Defences: Facilitating Organisational Learning* (Boston, Mass.: Allyn and Bacon/Prentice-Hall).

Argyris, C. and D. Schön (1978) *Organisational Learning: A Theory of Action Perspective* (Reading, Mass.: Addison-Wesley).

Arnold, R. (1999) *Education Development Plans: Meeting Targets and Improving Schools*, (EMIE Report no. 51) (Slough: NFER).

Arnold, T. W. (1937) *The Folklore of Capitalism* (New Haven, CT: Yale University Press).

Ashby, E. (1956) *An Introduction to Cybernetics* (London: Chapman and Hall).

Astley, W. G. and C. J. Fombrun (1983) 'Collective Strategy: Social Ecology of Organisational Environments', *Academy of Management Review*, vol. 8, no. 4, pp. 476–587.

Atkinson, P. (1992) 'The Ethnography of a Medical Setting: Readings, Writing and Rhetoric', *Qualitative Health Research*, vol. 2, no. 4, pp. 451–74.

Audit Commission (2000) *Money Matters: School Funding and Resource Management* (Audit Commission).

Austin, P. and P. Larkey (2002) 'The Future of Performance Measurement: Measuring Knowledge Work', in A. Neely (ed.), *Business Performance Measurement, Theory and Practice* (Cambridge: Cambridge University Press).

Baiman, S. (1982) 'Agency Research in Management Accounting: a Survey', *Journal of Accounting Literature*, Spring, pp. 154–213.

Baiman, S. (1990) 'Agency Research in Managerial Accounting: a Second Look', *Accounting, Organizations and Society*, vol. 15, no. 4, pp. 341–71.

Baird, I. S. and Thomas, H. (1990) 'What is Risk Anyway? Using and Measuring Risk in Strategic Management', in R. A. Bettis and H. Thomas, (eds), *Risk, Strategy and Management* (Greenwich, CT: JAI Press).

Ball, A. (2003) 'Environmental accounting as activism? A social ecology perspective on environmental accounting, values and change in a Canadian City Council', paper presented at the 7th Interdisciplinary Perspectives on Accounting (IPA) conference, Universidad Carlos III de Madrid, Madrid.

Ball, A., J. Broadbent and T. Jarvis (2003) 'Waste management, the Challenges of the PFI and "Sustainability Reporting" ', working paper (London: Royal Holloway, University of London).

Barbier, E. B., (1987) 'The Concept of Sustainable Economic Development', *Environmental Conservation*, vol. 14, pp. 101–10.

Barbier, E. B. (1989) 'The Contribution of Environmental and Resource Economics to an Economics of Sustainable Development', *Development and Change*, vol. 20, pp. 429–59.

Barnard, C. (1938) *The Functions of the Executive* (Cambridge, Mass.: Harvard University Press).

Batonda, G. and Perry, C. (2003) 'Approaches to relationship development process in inter-firm networks', *European Journal of Marketing*, vol. 37, pp. 1457–84.

Baum, J. R., J. D. Olian, M. Erez, E. R. Schnell, K. G. Smith, H. P. Sims, J. S. Scully and K. A. Smith (1993) 'Nationality and work role interactions: A cultural contrast of Israeli and US entrepreneurs' versus managers' needs', *Journal of Business Venturing*, vol. 8, pp. 499–512.

Bauman, Z. (1993), *Postmodern Ethics* (Oxford: Blackwell).

Bauman, Z. (1996), *Modernity and The Holocaust* (Oxford: Blackwell).

Bauman, Z. (1997), *Life In Fragments* (Oxford: Blackwell).

Bauman, Z. (1998), *Globalisation, The Human Consequences* (Oxford: Blackwell).

Bebbington, J., E. Kirk and C. Larrinaga-Gonzalez (2003) 'Building regimes for effective regulation: the example of environmental reporting in the electricity sector in Spain and the United Kingdom', paper presented at the 7th Interdisciplinary Perspectives on Accounting (IPA) conference, Universidad Carlos III de Madrid, Madrid.

Beck, U.(2000) *What is Globalization* (Malden, Mass: Polity Press).

Beck, U. (1986, 1992 in translation) *Risk Society* (London: Sage).

Beer, S. (1966) *Decision and Control* (New York: John Wiley).

Beer, S. (1972) *Brain of the Firm* (Harmondsworth: Allen Lane).

Benbassat, I. and A. S. Dexter (1979) 'Value and Events Approaches to Accounting: An Experimental Evaluation', *The Accounting Review*, vol. 54, no. 4, pp. 735–49.

Bernon, M. P. and J. Cullen (2004) *The Efficiency of Reverse Logistics* (London: Department of Transport).

Berry, A. J. (1983) 'Management Control and Methodology', in E. A. Lowe, and J. L. Machin (eds), *New Perspectives in Management Control* (London: Macmillan).

Berry, A. J., M. Ahmed, J. Cullen, A. Dunlop and W. Seal (2000) *The Consequences of Inter-firm Supply Chains for Management Accounting* (London: CIMA).

Berry, A. J., T. Capps, T. Cooper, P. Ferguson, T. Hopper and T. Lowe (1985) 'Management Control in an Area of the National Coal Board', *Accounting, Organizations and Society*, vol. 10, pp. 3–28.

Berry, A. J. and D. T. Otley (1975) 'The Aggregation of Estimates in Hierarchical Organisations.' *Journal of Management Studies* (May 1975).

Berry, A. J. and D. T. Otley (1986) 'The Aggregation of Estimates in Hierarchical Organisations', *Journal of Management Studies*, vol. 12, pp. 175–93.

Best Foot Forward (BFF) (undated) *Island State: An ecological footprint analysis of the Isle of Wight* (Oxford: Best Foot Forward).

Bettis, R. A. and H. Thomas (1990) *Risk, Strategy and Management* (Greenwich, CT: JAI Press).

Bhimani, A. (1996) *Management Accounting: European Perspectives* (Oxford: Oxford University Press).

Birkin, F. (1996) 'The Ecological Accountant: From the Cogito to Thinking like a Mountain', *Critical Perspectives on Accounting*, vol. 7, pp. 231–57.

Birkin, F. (2000) 'The Art of Accounting for Science: A Prerequisite for Sustainable Development?', *Critical Perspectives on Accounting*, vol. 11, pp. 289–309.

Birkin, F., P. Edwards and C. Larrinaga (2003) 'New Essentialism and the Foundations of Accounting Realism', paper presented at the 7th

Interdisciplinary Perspectives on Accounting (IPA) Conference, Universidad Carlos III de Madrid, Madrid.

Birnberg, J. G. (1998) 'Control in inter-firm cooperative relationships', *Journal of Management Studies*, vol. 35, pp. 421–8.

Bishop, R. C. (1993) 'Economic Efficiency, Sustainability and Biodiversity', *Ambio*, vol. 22, pp. 69–73.

Bolman, L. G. and T. Deal (1997) *Reframing Organizations: Artistry, Choice and Leadership*, 2nd Edn (San Francisco: Jossey-Bass).

Boulding, K. E. (1956) 'General Systems Theory – the skeleton of a science', *Management Science*, vol. 2, pp. 197–208.

Bourn, M. and M. Ezzamel (1986) 'Organisational Culture in Hospitals in the NHS, *Financial Accountability and Management*, vol. 2, no. 3, pp. 203–25.

Bower, J. L. (1986) *Managing the Resource Allocation Process: A Study of Corporate Planning and Investment* (Boston, Mass.: Harvard Business School Press).

Boyce, G. (2000) 'Public discourse and decision-making: Exploring possibilities for financial, social and environmental accounting', *Accounting, Auditing and Accountability Journal*, vol. 13, no. 1, pp. 27–64.

Braybrooke, D. and C. E. Lindblom (1963) *A Strategy for Decision* (London: Macmillan).

Broadbent, J. (1995) 'The Values of Accounting and Education: Some Implications of the Creation of Visibilities and Invisibilities in Schools', *Advances in Public Interest Accounting*, vol. 6, pp. 35–67.

Broadbent, J. (1998) 'The Gendered Nature of Accounting Logic: Pointers to an Accounting That Encompasses Multiple Values', *Critical Perspectives on Accounting*, vol. 9, pp. 267–97.

Broadbent, J., K. Jacobs and R. Laughlin (2001) 'Organisational Responses to Unwanted Accounting and Finance Changes with Specific Reference to General Medical Practice in the UK and New Zealand' *Accounting Auditing and Accountability Journal*, vol.14, no.5, pp. 565–86.

Broadbent, J. and R. Laughlin (2003) 'Control and Legitimation in Government Accountability Processes: The Private Finance Initiative in the UK'. *Critical Perspectives on Accounting*, vol. 14, nos. 1–2, pp. 23–48.

Broadbent, J. and R. Laughlin (2004). 'The Role of PFI in the UK Government's Modernisation Agenda'. *Financial Accountability and Management* (forthcoming).

Broadbent, J., R. Laughlin and K. Jacobs (1999) 'Performance Evoluation in Schools: The Individualising and Socialising Tendencies of Accountability Changes and some Implications for Management Control', *Management Accounting Research*, vol. 10, no. 4, pp. 339–46.

Broadbent, J., R. Laughlin and S. Read (1991) 'Recent Financial and Administrative Changes in the NHS: A Critical Theory Analysis', *Critical Perspectives on Accounting*, vol. 2, no. 1, pp. 1–29.

Broadbent, J., R. C. Laughlin, D. Shearn and N. Dandy (1993) 'Implementing Local Management of Schools: A theoretical and empirical analysis', *Research Papers in Education*, vol. 8, no. 2, pp. 149–76.

Bromwich, M. (1990) 'The Case for Strategic Management Accounting: The Role of Accounting Information for Strategy in Competitive Markets', *Accounting, Organizations and Society*, vol. 15, no. ½ pp. 27–46.

Bromwich, M. (1991) 'Accounting for strategic excellence', in *Okonomistyring OG strategic – nyeideer nye erfarinjer* (Denmark: Pub. Systeime).

Bromwich, M. (2001) 'Thoughts on Management Accounting and Strategy', *Pacific Accounting Review* (January) pp. 41–8.

Bromwich, M. and A. Bhimani (1989) *Management Accounting: Evolution not Revolution* (London: CIMA).

Brooke, P. (2000) 'How much risk is too much?' *Information Week*.

Brown, K. (2000) 'Playing by the Rules', *Director*, vol. 53, pp. 32–4.

Brownell, P. (1981) 'Participation in Budgeting, Locus of Control and Organisational Effectiveness', *Accounting Review*, vol. 56, pp. 844–60.

Bruns, W. J. and R. S. Kaplan (eds) (1987) *Accounting and Management – Field Study Perspectives* (Boston, Mass.: Harvard Business School Press).

Bruns, W. J. and J. H. Waterhouse (1975) 'Budgetary Control and Organizational Structure', *Journal of Accounting Research*, vol. 13, pp. 177–203.

Brunsson, N. (1985) *The Irrational Organisation* (Chichester: John Wiley).

Bryant, B. (ed.) (1995) *Environmental Justice: Issues, Policies and Solutions* (Washington, DC: Island Press).

Buckingham-Hatfield, S. and B. Evans (eds) (1996) *Environmental Planning and Sustainability* (New York: John Wiley).

Buckley, W. (1968) *Modern Systems Research for the Behavioural Scientist* (Chicago, Ill.: Aldine).

Burns, T. and G. Stalker (1961) *The Management of Innovation* (London: Tavistock).

Burrell, G. and G. Morgan (1979) *Sociological Paradigms and Organisational Analysis* (London: Heinemann).

Bussard, D. and J. Doyle (1996) 'A comparative study of managerial perception of strategic and financial risk', paper presented at the International Trade and Finance Conference, San Diego.

Cadbury (1992) *Report of the Committee on the Financial Aspects of Corporate Governance: The Code of Best Practice* (London: Professional Publishing).

Cairns, J. Jr (2001) 'Sustainability, Exceptionalism, and Exemptionalism', *Ecosystem Health*, vol. 7, no. 3, pp. 147–54.

Canter, L. (1999) 'Cumulative Effects Assessment', in J. Petts (ed.) *A Handbook of Environmental Impact Assessment* (Oxford: Blackwell) pp. 405–40.

Capps, T., T. Hopper, J. Mouritsen, D. Cooper and T. Lowe (1989) 'Accounting in the Production and Reproduction of Culture', in W. F. Chua, T. Lowe, and A. G. Puxty (eds), *Critical Perspectives on Management Control* (London: Macmillan).

Carr, C. and J. Ng (1995) 'Total cost control: Nisan and its UK supplier partnerships', *Management Accounting Research*, vol. 6, pp. 347–65.

Carter, N. (1989) 'Performance indicators: "backseat driving" or "hands-off" control', *Policy and Politics*, vol. 17, pp. 131–3.

Castells, M. (1996) *The Rise of the Network Society* (Oxford: Blackwell).

Chandler, A. D. (1962) *Strategy and Structure: Chapters in the History of the American Industrial Enterprise* (Cambridge, Mass.: MIT Press).

Chandler, A. D. (1977) *The Visible Hand: The Managerial Revolution in American Business* (Cambridge, Mass.: Harvard University Press).

Checkland, P. (1981) *Systems Thinking, Systems Practice* (Chichester: John Wiley).

Checkland, P. B. (1972) 'Towards a Systems-Based Methodology for Real-World Problem Solving', *Journal Of Systems Engineering*, vol. 3, no. 2, Winter 1972.

Chell, E., J. Haworth and S. Brearley (1991) *The Entrepreneurial Personality: Concepts, Cases and Categories* (London: Routledge).

Choo, F. (1989) 'Cognitive Scripts in Auditing and Accounting Behavior', *Accounting Organizations and Society*, vol. 14, nos. 5/6, pp. 481–93.

Christensen, P. R., H. Eskelnen, L. Forsstron, B. Lindmak and E. Vatne, (1990) 'Firms in Networks: Concepts, spatial impacts and policy implications.' In Illeris, S. and L. Jakobson (eds), *Networks and Regional Development* (Copenhagen: NordREFO/Akademisk Forlag), pp. 11–58.

Christie, I. and G. Warburton, The Real World Coalition (2001) *From Here to Sustainability: Politics in the Real World* (London: Earthscan).

Chryssides, G. and J. Kaler (1996) *Essentials of Business Ethics* (Maidenhead: McGraw-Hill)

Chryssides, G. and J. Kaler (2001), *An Introduction to Business Ethics* (London: Thomson).

Chua, W. F., T. Lowe and T. Puxty (1989) *Critical Perspectives in Management Control* (London: Macmillan).

Coad, A. (1995) 'Strategic Control', in A. J. Berry, J. Broadbent and D. Otley (eds) *Management Control: Theories, Issues and Practices* (London: Macmillan).

Coase, R. (1937) 'The Nature of the Firm', *Economica*, vol. 4, pp. 386–405.

Cole, M. and S. Scribner: (1974) *Culture and Thought: A Psychological Introduction* (New York: John Wiley).

Collier, P. M. (2003) *Accounting for Managers* (Chichester: John Wiley).

Collier, P. M. and A. J. Berry (2002) 'Risk in the process of budgeting', *Management Accounting Research*, vol. 13, pp. 273–97.

Committee of Sponsoring Organizations of the Treadway Commission (COSO) (1992), *Internal Control – Integrated Framework*. http://www.coso.org

Conrad, L. (2004 forthcoming), 'A Structuration Analysis of Accounting Systems and Systems of Accountability in the Privatised Gas Industry', *Critical Perspectives on Accounting*.

Cooper, R. and R. Slagmulder (2004) 'Inter-organisational cost management and relational context', *Accounting Organizations and Society*, vol. 29, pp. 1–26.

Cooper, S., D. Crowther, M. Davies and E. W. Davis (2001) *Shareholder or stakeholder value: The development of indicators for the control and measurement of performance*. (London: CIMA).

COSO (1992) *Internal Control – Integrated Framework* (New York American Institute Certified Public Accounts).

Costanza, R. and C. Folke (1994) 'Ecological Economics and Sustainable Development', International Experts Meeting for the Operationalisation of the Economics of Sustainability, Manilla, Philippines, 28–30 July.

Covaleski, M. A., M. W. Dirsmith and C. E. White (1987) 'Economic Consequences: The Relationship between Financial Reporting and Strategic Planning, Management and Operating Control Decision', *Contemporary Accounting Research*, vol. 3, no. 2, pp. 408–29.

Crockett, F., 'Revitalizing Executive Information Systems', *Sloan Management Review*, Summer 1992.

Cullen, J., T. Berry and W. Seal (2001) 'Supply Chain and Management Accounting', in J. Innes (ed.) *Handbook of Management Accounting Supplement 5* (London: Gee).

Cullen, J., Joyce, J., Hassall, T. and Broadbent, M. (2003) 'Quality in Higher Education: from monitoring to management', *Quality Assurance in Education*, vol. 11, no. 1, pp. 5–14.

Cullen, J. and M. Mather (2003) 'Supply Chain Re-engineering at School Trends Ltd', paper presented at the Supply Chain and E-Business Conference, Sheffield Hallam University, 8 July.

Cyert, R. M. and J. G. March (1963) *A Behavioural Theory of the Firm* (Hemel Hempstead: Prentice-Hall).

Cyert, R. M., J. G. March and W. H. Starbuck (1961) 'Two Experiments on Risk and Conflict in Organizational Estimation', *Management Science*, vol. 7, pp. 254–64.

Czarniawska, B. (1992) *Exploring Complex Organizations: A Cultural Perspective* (London: Sage).

Daly, H. and J. B. Cobb (1989) *For the Common Good* (Boston: Beacon).

Daly, H. E. (ed.) (1973) *Towards a Steady State Economy*, (San Francisco, CA: W. H. Freeman).

Daly, H. E. (1992) 'Allocation, Distribution and Scale: Towards an Economics that is Efficient, Just and Sustainable', *Ecological Economics*, vol. 6, pp. 185–94.

Das, T. K. and B. S. Teng (1998) 'Between trust and control: developing confidence in partner cooperation alliances', *Academy of Management Review*, vol. 23, pp. 491–512.

Deal, T. E. and A. A. Kennedy (1982) *Corporate Cultures: The Rites and Rituals of Corporate Life* (Reading, Mass.: Addison-Wesley).

Dearden, J. (1962) 'Limits on Decentralized Profit Responsibility', *Harvard Business Review*, July/August, pp. 89–90.

Dearden, J. (1968) 'Time span in management control', in W. E. Thomas (ed.), *Readings in Cost Accounting, Budgeting and Control*, 4th edn (Cincinnati: South Western Publishing), pp. 340–54.

Dekker, H. C. (2003) 'Value Chain Analysis in Interfirm Relationships: A Field Study', *Management Accounting Research*, vol. 14, pp. 1–23.

Dekker, H. C. (2004) 'Control of inter-organisational relationships: evidence on appropriation concerns and coordination requirements', *Accounting Organizations and Society*, vol. 29, pp. 27–49.

Dent, J. F. (1987) 'Tension in the Design of Formal Control Systems: A Field Study in a Computer Company', in W. J. Bruns and R. S. Kaplan (eds), *Accounting and Management – Field Study Perspectives* (Boston, Mass.: Harvard Business School Press), pp. 119–45.

Dent, J. F. (1990) 'Process model of relationship between business strategy and management control systems: Strategy, Organisation and Control: Some possibilities for accounting research', *Accounting, Organizations and Society*, vol. 15, no. ½, pp. 3–25.

Dent, J. F. (1991) 'Accounting and Organisational Cultures: A Field Study of the Emergency of a New Organisational Reality', *Accounting, Organizations and Society*, vol. 16, no. 8, pp. 705–32.

Department of Trade and Industry/Supply Chain Networks Group (1997), 'Supply Chain Management Attitude Survey', *Report of the Supply Chain Working Group*, April 1997 (London: DTI).

Dermer, J. (1977) *Management Planning and Control Systems* (Homewood, Ill.: Richard D. Irwin).

Dermer, J. (1988) 'Control and Organisational Order', *Accounting Organizations and Society*, vol. 13, no. 1, pp. 25–36.

Dermer, J. (1990) 'The Strategic Agenda: Accounting for Issues and Support', *Accounting, Organizations and Society*, vol. 15, no. ½, pp. 67–76.

Dermer, J. D. and R. G. Lucas (1986) 'The Illusion of Managerial Control', *Accounting, Organizations and Society*, vol. 11, no. 6, pp. 471–82.

Derrington, C. (2000) *The LEA Contribution to School Improvement – a Role Worth Fighting For* (Slough: National Foundation for Educational Research).

Dess, G. G. and A. Miller (1997) *Strategic Management* (New York: McGraw-Hill).

Dey, C. (2002) 'The use of critical ethnography as an active research methodology', *Accounting Auditing and Accountability Journal*, vol. 15, no, 1, pp. 106–21.

DfEE (1998) *Fair Funding: Improving delegation to schools*, consultation paper (London: DfEE).

DfEE (1999) *Code of Practice: LEA-School Relations* (London: DfEE).

DfEE (2000) *The Role of the Local Education Authority in School Education* (London: DfEE).

DfES (2001) *Schools Building on Success; Raising Standards, Promoting diversity, Achieving Results*, Cmnd 5050 (London: HMSO).

Dixon, J. A. and L. A. Fallon (1989) 'The Concept of Sustainability: Origins, Extensions and Usefulness for Policy', *Society and Natural Resources*, vol. 2, pp. 73–84.

Dixon, R. (1998) 'Accounting for Strategic Management: A Practical Application', *Long Range Planning*, vol. 31, no. 2, pp. 272–9.

Dobson, A. (1998) *Justice and the Environment: Conceptions of Environmental Sustainability and Theories of Distributive Justice* (Oxford: Oxford University Press).

Donaldson, J. (1988) *Key Issues in Business Ethics* (London: Academic Press).

Douglas, M (1969) *Man in Africa*, London, Tavistock.

Douglas, M.(1986) *How Institutions Think*, Syracuse: Syracuse University Press.

Douglas, M. and A. Wildavsky (1983) *Risk and Culture: An Essay on the Selection of Technological and Environmental Dangers* (Berkclay, CA: University of California Press).

Drucker, P (1964) 'Control, Controls and Management', in C. P. Bonini, R. K. Jaedicke and H. M. Wagner (eds), *Management Control: New Directions in Basic Research* (New York, John Wiley), pp. 286–96.

Drummond, H. (1998) 'Is escalation always irrational?', *Organisation Studies*, vol. 19, no. 6, pp. 911–30.

Drury, C. (1985) *Management and Cost Accounting* (London: Van Nostrand Reinhold).

Drury, C. (2000) *Management and Cost Accounting*, 5th edn. (London: Thompson).

Dyer, J. H. and W. G. Ouchi (1993) 'Japanese-style partnerships: Giving companies a competitive edge', *Sloan Management Review*, Fall, pp. 51–62.

Edvinsson, L. and M. S. Malone (1997) *Intellectual Capital* (London: Piatkus).

Ehrbar, A. (1998) EVA: the real key to creating wealth (New York: John Wiley).

Ehrlich, A. and P. Ehrlich (1987) *Earth* (New York: Franklin Watts).

Emmanuel, C. R. and D. T. Otley (1985) *Accounting for Management Control* (London: Chapman and Hall).

Emmanuel, C. R., D. T. Otley and K. Merchant (1990) *Accounting for Management Control*, 2nd edn (London: Chapman and Hall).

Enthoven, A. C. (1985) *Reflections on the Management of the NHS: an American looks at incentives to efficiency in health services management in the UK* (London: Nuffield Provincial Hospitals Trust).

Etzioni, A. (1961) *A Comparative Analysis of Complex Organizations* (New York: Free Press).

Etzioni, A. (1988) *The Moral Dimension: Towards a New Economics* (New York: Free Press).

European Foundation for Quality Management (EFQM) (1999) *The EFQM Excellence Model – Public and Voluntary Sector* (Brussels: EFQM).

Ezzamel, M. (1992) *Business Unit and Divisional Performance Measurement* (London: Academic Press in association with CIMA).

Ezzamel, M. (1994) 'Organizational Change and Accounting: Understanding the Budgeting System in its Organizational Context', *Organization Studies*, vol. 15, pp. 213–40.

Ezzamel, M. and H. Hart (1987) *Advanced Management Accounting: An Organisational Emphasis* (London: Cassell).

Ezzamel, M. and K. Hilton (1980a) 'Divisionalization in British Industry: A Preliminary Study', *Accounting and Business Research*, vol. 10, no.1, Spring, pp. 197–214.

Ezzamel, M. and K. Hilton (1980b) 'Can Divisional Discretion be Measured?', *Journal of Business Finance and Accounting*, Summer, pp. 311–29.

Ezzamel, M., K. Hoskin and R. Macve (1990) 'Managing it all by Numbers: A Review of Kaplan and Johnson's Relevance Lost', *Accounting and Business Research*, vol. 20, no. 7, pp. 153–66.

Ezzamel, M., H. Willmott and F. Worthington (2001) 'Power, Control and Resistance in "The Factory that time Forgot" ', *Journal of Management Studies*, vol. 38, no. 8, pp. 1053–79.

Ezzamel, M., H. Willmott and F. Worthington (2004) 'Accounting and Management–Labour Relations: the Politics of Production in the "Factory with a Problem" ', *Accounting, Organizations and Society*, vol. 29, pp. 269–302.

Factor 10 Club (1999) *Factor 10: Making Sustainability Accountable – Putting Resource Productivity into Praxis* (http://www.factor10-institute.org/Pdf-Files.htm).

Fahy, J. M., C. J. Mitchell and S. M. Cacciaguidi (1999), 'Accounting, Accountability and the Holocaust: The Search for the Missing Millions', paper presented at the Scottish BAA, University of Glasgow.

Farris, M. T. and P. D. Hutchinson (2002) 'Cash to Cash: the new supply chain management metric', *International Journal of Distribution and Logistics Management*, vol. 30, pp. 500–14.

Fayol, H. (1949) *General and Industrial Management* (London: Pitman).

Ferreira, A. and D. Otley (2004) 'The design and use of management control systems: an extended framework for analysis', unpublished paper.

Financial Reporting Council (2003) *The Combined Code on Corporate Governance*, (London: FRC).

Fisher, C. and A. Lovell. (2003) *Business Ethics and Values* (Harlow: Pearson).

Fiske, S. T. and S. E. Taylor: (1984) *Social Cognition* (New York: Random House).

Fitzgerald, L., R. Johnston, S. Brignall, R. Silvestro and C. Voss (1991) *Performance Measurement in Service Businesses* (London: CIMA).

Fitzgerald, L. and P. Moon (1996) 'Performance Measurement: Case Study Evidence from the UK.' *Management Accounting Annual Conference. University of Aston*, September 1996.

Fogarty, T. J. (1992), 'Organisational Socialisation In Accounting Firms: A Theoretical Framework and Agenda for Future Research', *Accounting Organisations and Society*, vol. 17, no. 2, pp. 129–49.

Forester, J. (1961) *Industrial Dynamics* (Cambridge, Mass.: MIT Press).

Frances, J. and E. Garnsey (1996) 'Supermarkets and suppliers in the United Kingdom: System integration, information and control', *Accounting, Organisations and Society*, vol. 21, no. 6, pp. 591–610.

Francis, G. and C. Minchington (2000) 'Value-based metrics as divisional performance measures', in G. Arnold and M. Davies (eds), *Value Based Management Context and Application* (Chichester: Wiley) pp. 151–62.

Fraser, R. and J. Hope (2003) *Beyond Budgeting*, (Boston, Mass.: Harvard Business School Press).

Freeman, R. E. (1984) *Strategic Management: A Stakeholder Approach* (London: Pitman).

Friedman, M. (1970) 'The Social Responsibility of Business is to Increase its Profits', *New York Times Magazine*, 13 September, pp. 32–33, 122–6.

Fritzsche, D. J. (1991), 'A Model of Decision Making Incorporating Ethical Values', *Journal of Business Ethics*, vol. 10, pp. 841–52.

Frost, P., L. F. Moore, M. R. Louis, C. C. Lundberg and J. Martin, Editors, (1985) *Organizational Culture* (Beverly Hills, CA: Sage).

Froud, J. (2003) 'The Private Finance Initiative: risk, uncertainty and the state', *Accounting, Organizations and Society*, vol. 28, no.6, pp. 567–89.

Funnell, W. (1998), 'Accounting in the Service of the Holocaust', *Critical Perspectives on Accounting*, vol. 8, no. 4, pp. 435–64.

Galbraith, J. (1977) *Designing Complex Organizations* (Reading, Mass.: Addison-Wesley).

Geertz, C. (1973) *The Interpretation of Cultures* (New York: Basic Books).

Gerth, H. H. and C. W. Mills (1948) (eds) *From Max Weber* (London: Routledge and Keegan Paul).

Gervais, C. (2002) *An Overview of UK Waste and Resource Management Policy* (London: Forum for the Future).

Ghemewat, P. (1993) 'The risk of not investing in a recession', *Sloan Management Review*, Winter, pp. 51–8.

Giddens (1998) 'Risk Society: The Context of British Politics', in J.Franklin (ed.) *The Politics of Risk Society* (Cambridge: Polity Press).

Gietzmann, M. B. (1996) 'Incomplete contracts and the make or buy decision: Governance design and attainable flexibility', *Accounting, organisations and society*, vol. 21, no. 6, pp. 611–26.

Glaister, K. and D. Thwaites (1993) 'Managerial Perception and Organisational Strategy', *Journal of General Management*, vol. 18, no. 4, pp. 15–33.

Global Reporting Initiative (GRI) (2000) *Sustainability Reporting Guidelines on Economic, Environmental and Social Performance* (Boston, Mass: Global Reporting Initiative, June).

Global Reporting Initiative (GRI) (2002) *Sustainability Reporting Guidelines* (Amsterdam: Global Reporting Initiative, October).

Goffman, E. (1959) *The Presentation of Self in Everyday Life* (Garden City, NY: Doubleday Anchor).

Goldratt, E. (1984) *The Goal* (London: Gower).

Goldsby, T. J. and D. J. Closs (2000) 'Using activity-based costing to re-engineer the reverse logistics channel', *International Journal of Physical Distribution and Logistics Management*, vol. 30, pp. 500–14.

Goleman, D. (1998) *Emotional Intelligence: Why It Can Matter More Than IQ*. Bloomsbury Press.

Goold, M. (1991) 'Strategic Control in the Decentralised Firm', *Sloan Management Review*, Winter, pp. 69–81.

Goold, M. and A. Campbell (1987a) 'Managing diversity: Strategy and control in diversified British companies', *Long Range Planning*, vol. 20, no. 5, pp. 42–52.

Goold, M. and A. Campbell (1987b) *Strategies and Styles: The Role of the Centre in Managing Diversified Corporations* (Oxford: Basil Blackwell).

Goold, M. and A. Campbell (2002) 'Parenting in Complex Structures', *Long Range Planning*, vol. 35, pp. 219–43.

Goold, M. and A. Campbell (2003) 'Structured Networks: Towards the well designed matrix', *Long Range Planning*, vol. 36, pp. 427–39.

Goold, M., A. Campbell and M. Alexander (1998) 'Corporate Strategy and Parenting Theory', *Long Range Planning*, vol. 31, no. 2, pp. 308–14.

Goold, M. and J. J. Quinn (1990a) *Strategic Control: Milestones for Long Term Performance* (London: Hutchinson).

Goold, M. and J. J. Quinn (1990b) 'The Paradox of Strategic Controls', *Strategic Management Journal*, vol. 11, no. 1, pp. 43–57.

Gorz, A. (1989) *A Critique of Economic Reason* (London: Verso).

Govindarajan, V. (1984) 'Appropriateness of Accounting Data in Performance Evaluation: An Empirical Examination of Environmental Uncertainty as an Intervening Variable', *Accounting, Organizations and Society*, vol. 9, no. 2, pp. 125–35.

Govindarajan, V. and A. K. Gupta (1985) 'Linking Control Systems to Business Unit Strategy: Impact on Performance', *Accounting, Organizations and Society*, vol. 10, no. 1, pp. 51–66.

Grabner, P. (1993) *The Embedded Firm* (London: Routledge).

Granovetter, M. S. (1985) 'Economic action and social structure: The problem of embeddedness', *American Journal of Sociology*, vol. 91, no. 3, pp. 481–510.

Grant, R. (1998) *Contemporary Strategy Analysis – concerns, techniques, applications*. (Malden, Mass.: Blackwell).

Gray, R. (1992) 'Accounting and Environmentalism: An exploration of the challenge of gently accounting for accountability, transparency and sustainability', *Accounting, Organizations and Society*, vol. 17, no. 5, pp. 399–425.

Gray, R. (2001) 'Thirty years of social accounting, reporting and auditing: what (if anything) have we learnt?', *Business Ethics: A European Review*, vol. 10, no. 1, pp. 9–15.

Gray, R. (2002) 'The social accounting project and *Accounting, Organizations and Society*, privileging engagement, imaginings, new accountings and pragmatism over critique', *Accounting, Organizations and Society*, vol. 27, no. 7, pp. 687–708.

Gray, R. and Bebbington, J. (2000) 'Environmental Accounting, Managerialism and Sustainability', *Advances in Environmental Accounting and Management*, vol. 1, pp. 1–44.

Gray, R., J. Bebbington and K. J. McPhail: (1994) 'Teaching Ethics and the Ethics of Teaching: Educating for Immorality and a Possible Case for Social and Environmental Accounting', *Accounting Education*, vol. 3, pp. 51–75.

Gray, R. and M. J. Milne (2004) 'Towards Reporting on the Triple Bottom Line: Mirages, Methods and Myths', in A. Henriques and J. Richardson (eds), *The Triple Bottom Line: Does it All Add Up?* (London: Earthscan).

Griffin, D., P. Shaw and R. Stacey (1999) 'Knowing and acting in conditions of uncertainty: a complexity perspective', *Systemic Practice and Action Research*, vol. 12, no. 3, p. 295.

Grinyer, J. (1986) 'An alternative to maximisation of shareholders' wealth in capital budgeting', *Accounting and Business Research*, Autumn, pp. 319–26.

Groot, T. and K. Lukka (2000), *Cases in Management Accounting: Current Practices in European Companies* (Harlow: Financial Times/Prentice Hall).

Gulati, R. and H. Singh (1998) 'The architecture of cooperation: managing coordination costs and appropriation concerns in strategic alliances', *Administrative Science Quarterly*, vol. 43, pp. 781–814.

Habermas, J. (1984) *The Theory of Communicative Action: Volume 1 Reason and the Rationalization of Society* (London: Heinemann).

Habermas, J. (1987) *The Theory of Communicative Action: Volume 2 The Critique of Functionalist Reason* (London: Heinemann).

Hacking, I. (1994), 'Self Improvement', in C. D. Hoy (ed.), *Foucault A Critical Reader* (Oxford: Blackwell).

Haka, S., L. Gordon and G. Pinches (1985) 'Sophisticated Capital Budgeting Selection Techniques and Firm Performance', *The Accounting Review*, vol. 9, no. 4, pp. 651–69.

Hakansson, H. and Lind, J. (2004) 'Accounting and network coordination', *Accounting Organization and Society*, vol. 29, pp. 51–72.

Hall, W. K. (1978) 'SBU's: Hot New Topic in the Management of Diversification Business Horizons', in D. J. McCarthy, R. J. Minichiello and J. R. Curran (eds), *Business Policy Strategy* (Homewood, Ill.: Richard D. Irwin).

Hamel, G. (1996) 'Strategy as Revolution', *Harvard Business Review*, July–August, pp. 69–82.

Hamel, G. (1997) 'Killer Strategies That Make Shareholders Rich', *Fortune*, 23 June, pp. 70–88.

Hannan, M. T. and J. H. Freeman (1977) 'The Population Ecology of Organisations', *American Journal of Sociology*, vol. 82, pp. 929–64.

Hannon, V. (1999) 'On the receiving end: New Labour and the LEAs', *Cambridge Journal of Education*, vol. 29, no. 2, pp. 207–17.

Hansen, S. C., D. T. Otley and W. A. Van der Stede (2003) 'Practice Developments in Budgeting: An Overview and Research Perspective', *Journal of Management Accounting Research*, vol. 15, pp. 95–116.

Harland, C. M. (1996) 'Supply chain management: Relationships, chains and networks', *British Journal of Management*, vol. 7, Special Issue, pp. s63–80.

Harrill, R. (1999) 'Beyond Sustainability: Bioregionalism and Bioregional Planning', in A. G. Nobel and F. J. Costa (eds) *Preserving the Legacy: Concepts in Support of Sustainability* (New York: Lexington Books).

Harrison, G. L. and J. L. McKinnon (1999) 'Cross-Cultural Research in Management Control Systems Design: A Review of the Current State', *Accounting, Organizations and Society*, vol. 24, pp. 483–506.

Harrison, R. (1972) 'Understanding your organisational character', *Harvard Business Review*, May/June, pp. 119–28.

Hawken, P., A. B. Lovins and L. H. Lovins (2002) *Natural Capitalism: the next industrial revolution* (London: Earthscan).

Hayward, T. (1994) *Ecological Thought: An Introduction* (Cambridge: Polity Press).

Heath, C. and Tversky, A. (1991) 'Preference and belief: ambiguity and competence in choice under uncertainty', *Journal of Risk and Uncertainty*, vol. 4, pp. 5–28.

Helliar, C. V., A. A. Lonie, D. M. Power and C. D. Sinclair (2001) *Managerial Attitudes to Risk*, Institute of Chartered Accountants of Scotland Research Monograph Series. Edinburgh ICAS, p. 98.

Helper, S. R. and M. Sako (1995) 'Supplier relations in Japan and the United States: Are they converging?', *Sloan Management Review*, Spring, pp. 77–84.

Henderson, B. D. (1979) *Henderson on Corporate Strategy* (Cambridge, Mass.: ABT Books).

Hergert, M. and D. I. Morris (1989) 'Accounting data for value chain analysis', *Strategic Management Journal*, vol. 10.

Herman, J. (2003) 'The New Science of Networks', *Business Communication Review*, vol. 33, pp. 22–7.

Heskett, J. L., W. E. Sasser Jr. and L. A. Schlesinger (1997) *The Service Profit Chain: How leading companies link profit and growth to loyalty, satisfaction and value*, (New York: Free Press).

Hewstone, M., W. Struebe, J. Codol and G. M. Stephenson (1993) *Introduction to Social Psychology* (Oxford: Blackwell).

Hirschhorn, L (1999) 'The Primary Risk', *Human Relations*, vol. 52, no.1.

Hirst, M. K. (1981) 'Accounting Information and the Evaluation of Subordinate Performance', *The Accounting Review*, vol. 56, pp. 771–84.

HMSO (1998) CM 4181 'Public Services for the Future: Modernisation, Reform and Accountability. Comprehensive spending Review: Public service agreements 1999–2000' (London: HMSO).

Hofer, C. W. and D. Schendel (1978) *Strategy Formulation: Analytical Concepts* (St Paul, Minn.: West).

Hofstede, G. (1968) *The Game of Budget Control* (London: Tavistock).

Hofstede, G. (1980) *Culture's Consequences: International Differences in Work Related Values* (Beverly Hills: Sage).

Hofstede, G., 'The Poverty of Management Control Philosophy', *Academy of Management Review*, vol. 3, no. 3, July 1978, 450–61.

Holt, R., A. J. Berry and R. Sweeting (2003) 'Small Firms in the Risk Society', working paper, Centre for Professional Accounting, Manchester Metropolitan University.

Hood, C. (1991) 'A Public Management for All Seasons?', *Public Administration*, vol. 69, pp. 3–19.

Hood, C. (1995) 'The New Public Management in the 1980s: Variations on a Theme', *Accounting, Organizations and Society*, vol. 20, no. 3, pp. 93–109.

Hope, T. and J. Hope (1995) *Transforming the Bottom Line: Managing Performance with the Real Numbers* (London: Nicholas Brealey).

Hopper, T. (1988) 'Social Transformation and Management Accounting', in *Proceedings of the Second Interdisciplinary Perspective in Accounting Conference* (University of Manchester).

Hopper, T. and P. Armstrong (1991) 'Cost Accounting, Controlling Labour and the Rise of the Conglomerates', *Accounting, Organizations and Society*, vol. 16, no. 5–6, pp. 405–38.

Hopper, T., J. Storey and H. C. Willmott (1987) 'Accounting for Accounting: Towards the Development of a Dialectical View', *Accounting, Organizations and Society*, vol. 12, no. 5, pp. 437–56.

Hopwood, A. (1972) 'An Empirical Study of the Role of Accounting Data in Performance Evaluation', *Empirical Research in Accounting*, Supplement to *Journal of Accounting Research*, vol. 10, pp. 156–82.

Hopwood, A. G. (1973) *An Accounting System and Managerial Behaviour* (Farnborough: Saxon House).

Hopwood, A. G. (1974) *Accounting and Human Behavior* (Englewood Cliffs, NJ: Prentice-Hall).

Hopwood, A. G. (1987) 'The Archaeology of Accounting Systems', *Accounting, Organizations and Society*, vol. 12, no. 3, pp. 207–34.

Horngren, C. T. (1962) *Cost Accounting: A Managerial Emphasis* (London: Prentice-Hall).

Hoskin, K. and R. Macve (1986) 'Accounting and the Examination: a Genealogy of Disciplinary Power', *Accounting, Organizations and Society*, vol. 11, pp. 105–36.

Hoskisson, R. E., M. A. Hitt and C. W. L. Hill (1993) 'Managerial Incentives and Investment in R&D in Large Multiproduct Firms', *Organization Science*, vol. 4, no. 2, pp. 325–41.

Howes, R. (2002) *Environmental Cost Accounting: An Introduction and Practical Guide* (London: CIMA).

Hoy, D. C. (1994) 'Power, Repression, Progress: Foucault. Lukes, and The Frankfurt School', in C. D. Hoy (ed.) *Foucault: A Critical Reader* (Oxford: Blackwell).

Hrebiniak, L. G. and W. F. Joyce (1986) 'The Strategic Importance of Managing Myopia', *Sloan Management Review*, Fall, pp. 5–14.

Hukkinen, J. (2003) 'From Groundless Universalism to Grounded Generalism: Improving Ecological Economic Indicators of Human–Environmental Interaction', *Ecological Economics*, vol. 44, pp. 11–27.

Hurst, E. G. (1982) 'Controlling Strategic Plans', in P. Lorange (ed.), *Implementation of Strategy Planning* (Englewood Cliffs, NJ: Prentice-Hall).

Hutcheson F. (1999) *On the nature and Conduct of the Passions* (Manchester: Clinamen Press)

Hutter, Bridget and M. K. Power (2000) 'Risk Management and Business Regulation', in Pickford (ed.), J. *Mastering Risk* (London: Pearson Education).

Huxham, C. and S. Vangen (1996) *Creating Collaborative Advantage* (London: Sage).

Imai, K. and H. Itami (1984) 'Interpenetration of Organization and Market', *International Journal of Industrial Organization*, vol. 2, pp. 285–310.

Institute of Chartered Accountants in England and Wales (1999) *Internal Control: Guidance for Directors on the Combined Code* (Turnbull Report) (London: ICAEW).

International Federation of Accountants (IFAC) (1999) *Enhancing Shareholder Wealth by Better Managing Business Risk*, International Management Accounting Study no. 9.1 (New York: IFAC).

International Union for the Conservation of Nature (IUCN) (1980) *World Conservation Strategy* (Gland, Switzerland: IUCN).

Ittner, C. D. and D. F. Larcker (2001) 'Assessing empirical research in management accounting: a value based management perspective', *Journal of Accounting and Economics*, vol. 32, pp. 349–410.

Ivanevitch, J. (1976) 'Effects of Goal Setting on Performance and Job Satisfaction', *Journal of Applied Psychology*, vol. 61, pp. 605–12.

Jacobs, J. (2000) *The Nature of Economies* (Canada: Random House/Vintage).

Jalland, R. M. (1989) 'Plan-Making in Multi-divisional Companies' unpublished PhD thesis, University of Manchester.

Jarret, E. L. (2000) 'The role of risk in business decision making', *Research Technology Management*, Industrial Research Institute Inc. vol. 43, no. 6, pp. 44–6.

Jensen, M. (2001) 'Corporate Budgeting is Broken – Let's Fix It', *Harvard Business Review*, vol. 70, no. 10, pp. 95–101.

Johnson, G. (1987) *Strategic Change and the Management Process* (Oxford: Basil Blackwell).

Johnson, G. and R. Greenwood (2002) 'Institutional Theory Perspectives', in M. Jenkins and V. Ambsrosini (eds), *Strategic Management: A Multi-perspective Approach* (Basingstoke: Palgrave), pp. 39–61.

Johnson, G. and K. Scholes (1993) *Exploring Corporate Strategy* (Hemel Hempstead: Prentice-Hall).

Johnson, G. and K. Scholes (2003) *Exploring Corporate Strategy* (London: Financial Times/Prentice-Hall).

Johnson, H. T. and R. S. Kaplan (1987) *Relevance Lost: The Rise and Fall of Management Accounting* (Cambridge, Mass.: Harvard Business School Press).

Johnson, H. and R. Kaplan (1991) *Relevance Lost: The Rise and Fall of Management Accounting* (Cambridge, Mass.: Harvard Business School Press).

Johnson, R. H. (1996) *Nature, State and Economy* (London: J. Wiley & Sons).

Johnston, R. and P. R. Lawrence (1988) 'Beyond vertical integration – the rise of the value-adding partnership', *Harvard Business Review*, July–August, pp. 94–101.

Jones, T. M. (1991), 'Ethical Decision Making by Individuals in Organisations: An Issue-Contingent Model', *Academy of Management Review*, vol.16, no. 2, pp. 366–96.

Jopeck, E. J. (2000) 'Five steps to risk reduction', *Security Management*, vol 44, no. 8, pp. 97–102

Kahneman, D. and A. Tversky (1979) 'Prospect theory: an analysis of decision under risk', *Econometrica*, vol. 47, pp. 262–91.

Kanter, R. M. (1994) 'Collaborative advantage: The art of alliances', *Harvard Business Review*, July–August, pp. 96–108.

Kaplan, R. S. (1984) 'Yesterday's Accounting Undermines Production', *Harvard Business Review*, July–August, pp. 95–101.

Kaplan, R. S. and D. P. Norton (1992) 'The balanced scorecard – measures that drive performance', *Harvard Business Review*, vol. 70, no. 1, pp. 71–9.

Kaplan, R. S. and D. P. Norton (1993) 'Putting the Balanced Scorecard to Work', *Harvard Business Review*, September–October, pp. 134–47.

Kaplan, R. S. and D. P. Norton (1996a) *The Balanced Scorecard* (Boston, Mass.: Harvard Business School Press).

Kaplan, R. S. and D. P. Norton (1996b) 'Using the balanced scorecard as a strategic management system', *Harvard Business Review*, January–February, pp. 75–85.

Kaplan, R. S. and D. P. Norton (1996c) *Translating Strategy Into Action – The Balanced Scorecard* (Boston, Mass.: Harvard Business School Press).

Kaplan, R. S. and D. P. Norton (2000) 'Having trouble with your strategy? Then map it', *Harvard Business Review*, September–October, pp. 167–76.

Kaplan, R. S. and D. P. Norton (2001a) *The Strategy Focused Organization* (Boston, Mass.: Harvard Business School).

Kaplan, R. S. and Norton, D. P. (2001b) 'Transforming the Balanced Scorecard from performance measurement to strategic management accounting', *Horizons*, vol. 15, no. 1, pp. 87–104, no. 2, pp. 147–60.

Katz, D. and R. L. Khan (1978) *The Social Psychology of Organizations* (New York: John Wiley).

Kay, J. (1993) *Foundations of Corporate Success* (Oxford: Oxford University Press).

Kenis, I. (1979) 'Effects of Budgetary Goal Characteristics on Managerial Attitudes on Performance', *The Accounting Review*, vol. 4, no. 4, pp. 707–21.

Kerr, S. 'On the Folly of Rewarding A While Hoping for B', *Academy of .Management.Journal*, no.18, 1975, pp. 769–83.

King, P. (1975) 'Is the Emphasis of Capital Budgeting Theory Misplaced? *Journal of Business Finance and Accounting*, Spring, vol. 2, no.1 pp. 69–82.

Klein, M. (1997) 'The risk premium for evaluating public project', *Oxford Review of Economic Policy*, vol. 13, no. 4, pp. 29–42.

Knights, D. and G. Morgan (1991) 'Strategic Discourse and Subjectivity: Towards a Critical Analysis of Corporate Strategy in Organizations', *Organizational Studies*, vol. 12, no. 2, pp. 251–73.

Kopp, S. W. and H. Bang (2000) 'Benefit and Risk in Prescription Drug Advertising', *Health Marketing quarterly*, vol. 17, no. 3, p. 39.

Kunda, G. (1992) *Engineering Culture: Control and Commitment in a High-Tech Corporation* (Philadelphia: Temple University Press).

Lamming, R. (1993) *Beyond Partnership: Strategies for Innovation and Lean Supply* (New York: Prentice-Hall).

Langfield-Smith, K. (1995) 'Organisational Culture and Control', in A. J. Berry, J. Broadbent and D. Otley (eds), *Management Control: Theories, Issues and Practices* (London: Macmillan), pp. 179–200.

Larrinaga-Gonzalez, C. and J. Bebbington (2001) 'Accounting change or institutional appropriation? A case study of the implementation of environmental accounting', *Critical Perspectives on Accounting*, vol. 12, pp. 269–92.

Laughhunn, D. J., J. W. Payne and R. Crum (1980) 'Managerial Risk Preferences for Below-Target Returns', *Management Science*, vol. 26, pp. 1238–49.

Laughlin, R. C. (1987) 'Accounting Systems in Organisational Contexts: A Case for Critical Theory', *Accounting, Organizations and Society*, vol. 12, no. 5, pp. 479–502.

Laughlin, R. C. (1991) 'Environmental Disturbances and Organisational Transitions and Transformations: Some Alternative Models', *Organisation Studies*, vol. 12, no. 2.

Laughlin, R. (1995) 'Empirical Research in Accounting: Alternative Approaches and a Case for "Middle Range" Thinking', *Accounting, Auditing and Accountability Journal*, vol. 8, no. 1, pp. 63–87.

Laughlin, R. and J. Broadbent (1997) 'Evaluating the "New Public Management" Reforms in the UK: A Constitutional Possibility?', *Public Administration*, vol. 75, no. 3, pp. 487–507.

Laughlin, R. and R. Gray (1988) *Financial Accounting: Method and Meaning* (London: VNR).

Lawrence, S., M. Alam and T. Lowe (1994) 'The Great Experiment:Financial Management Reform in the NZ Health Sector', *Accounting Auditing and Accountability Journal*, vol. 7, no. 3, pp. 68–95.

Learned, E. P., C. R. Christensen, K. R. Andrews and W. D. Guth (1965) *Business Policy: Text and Cases* (Homewood, Ill.: Irwin).

Lebas, M. and A. Weigenstein (1986) 'Management Control: The Roles of Rules, Markets and Culture', *Journal of Management Studies*, vol. 23, pp. 259–72.

Lee, J. and J. Seraph (1995) 'Activity Based Costing for Purchasing Managers' Cost and Pricing Determinations', *International Journal of Purchasing and Materials Management*, Fall, pp. 25–31.

Lev, B. (2001) *Intangibles: Management, Measurement and Reporting* (New York: The Brookings Institution).

Liedtka, J. (1991) 'Organisational Value Contention and Management Mindsets', *Journal of Business Ethics*, vol. 10, no. 7.

Lilienfeld, R. (1978) *The Rise of Systems Theory* (New York and Chichester: John Wiley).

Lillis, A. M. (1992) 'Sources of influence on capital expenditure decisions: a contextual study of accounting measurement', *Management Accounting Research*, vol. 3, no. 3, pp. 213–27.

Lindblom, C. E. (1959) 'The Science of Muddling Through', *Public Administration Review*, vol. 19, no. 2, pp. 79–88.

Lindenblom, C. E. (1977) *Politics and Markets* (New York: Basic Books).

Llewellyn, S. (1998) 'Boundary Work: Costing and Caring in the Social Services', *Accounting, Organisations and Society*, vol. 23, no. 1, pp. 23–47.

Locke, E. A. (1968) 'Towards a Theory of Risk Motivations and Incentives', *Organizational Behaviour and Human Performance*, vol. 3, pp. 157–89.

Loft, A. (1991) 'The History of Management Accounting: Relevance Found', in D. Ashton, T. Hopper and R. W. Scapens (eds), *Issues in Management Accounting* (Englewood Cliffs, NJ: Prentice-Hall), pp. 17–38.

Lonie, A. A., W. A. Nixon and D. J. Collison (1993) 'Internal and External Constraints on the Financing of New Technology' in Swann, P. (ed.), *New Technologies and the Firm* (London: Routledge).

Lord, B. (1996) 'Strategic Management Accounting: the emperor's new clothes?', *Management Accounting Research*, vol. 7, no. 3, pp. 347–66.

Lorsch, J. W. and S. A. Allen (1973) *Managing Diversity and Interdependence Division of Research* (Cambridge, Mass.: Graduate School of Business Administration, Harvard University).

Low, N. and B. Gleeson (1998) *Justice, Society and Nature: An Exploration of Political Ecology* (London: Routledge).

Lowe E. A. (1970) 'The Information Content of Financial Statements, Financial Planning and Management Control: Towards an Integration.' *Journal of Business Finance*, no 2, vol. 2, Summer 1970, pp. 3–11.

Lowe, E. A. (2000) 'The Construction of a Network at Health Waikato', *Accounting Auditing and Accountability Journal*, vol. 13, no. 1, pp. 84–114.

Lowe, E. A. and W. F. Chua (1983) 'Organisational Effectiveness and Management Control', in E. A. Lowe and J. L. F. Machin (eds), *New Perspectives in Management Control* (London: Macmillan).

Lowe, E. A. and R. W. Shaw (1968) 'An Analysis of Managerial Biasing: evidence from company's budgeting process', *Journal of Management Studies*, vol. 5, pp. 304–15.

Lowe, T. and T. Puxty (1989) 'The Problems of a Paradigm: A Critique of the Prevailing Orthodoxy in Management Control', in W. F. Chua, T. Lowe and T. Puxty (eds), *Critical Perspectives in Management Control* (London: Macmillan).

Lynch, R. L. and Cross, K. F. 'Measure Up!', 2nd edition, Blackwell Publishers, Cambridge, MA., 1995.

Lypny, G. J. (1993) 'An Experimental Study of Managerial Pay and Firm Hedging Decisions', *Journal of Risk and Insurance*, vol. 60, pp. 208–29.

Macaulay, S. (1963) 'Non-contractual relations in business: a preliminary study', *American Sociological Review*, vol. 28, no. 2, pp. 55–67.

Macbeth, D. K. and N. Ferguson (1994) 'Partnership sourcing: An integrated supply chain approach' (London: Pitman and Financial Times).

Machin, J. L. (1983) 'Management Control Systems: Whence and Whither?, in E. A. Lowe and J. L. F. Machin (eds), *New Perspectives in Management Control* (London: MacMillan), pp. 22–42.

Maciariello, J. A. (1984) *Management Control Systems* (Englewood Cliffs and London: Prentice-Hall).

Macintosh, N. B. (1985) *The Social Software of Accounting and Information Systems* (Chichester: John Wiley).

Macintosh, N. B. (1994) *Management Accounting and Control Systems* (Chichester: Wiley).

MacIntyre, A. (1998) *A Short history of Ethics: A History of Moral Philosophy from the Homeric Age to the Twentieth Century* (London: Routledge).

Macneil, I. R. (1974) 'The Many Futures of Contract', *Southern California Law Review*, vol. 47, pp. 691–816.

Malmi, T. (2001) 'Balanced scorecards in Finnish companies: A research note', *Management Accounting Research*, vol. 12, pp. 207–20.

Malmi, T. and S. Ikäheimo (2003) 'Value Based Management Practices – some evidence from the field', *Management Accounting Research*, vol. 14, pp. 235–54.

March, J. G. (1988a) 'Variable Risk Preferences and Adaptive Aspirations', *Journal of Economic Behaviour and Organization*, vol. 9, pp. 5–24.

March, J. G. (1988) *Decisions and Organisations* (Oxford: Basil Blackwell).

March, J. G. and Z. Shapira (1987) 'Managerial Perspectives on Risk and Risk Taking', *Management Science*, vol. 33, pp. 1404–18.

March, J. G. and H. A. Simon (1967) *Organisations* (9th printing) (New York: John Wiley and Sons).

Markus, H. (1977) 'Self-schemata and Processing Information about the Self', *Journal of Personality and Psychology*, vol. 35, pp. 63–78.

Marshall, C., L. Prusak and D. Shpilberg (1996) 'Financial risk and the need for superior knowledge management', *California Management review*, vol. 38, no. 3 pp. 77–101.

Marson, J. and P. Massey (1999) 'The strategic use of IT in the supply chain', *Journal of Financial Information Systems*, http://www.shu.ac.uk/schools/fsl/fisjnl/.

Marx, K. (1972) *Capital* (London: Lawrence and Wishart).

May, D. O. (1995) 'Do managerial motives influence firm risk reduction strategies?', *Journal of Finance*, vol. 50, no. 4, pp. 1291–308.

McCarthy, B. (2000) 'The cult of risk taking and social learning; A Study of Irish entrepreneurs', *Management Decision*, vol. 38, no. 8, pp. 563–74

McCosh, A. (1990) 'Positive Control', *Economia Aziendale*, vol. IX, no. 3, pp. 405–27.

McDonough, W. and M. Braungart (1998) 'The Next Industrial Revolution', *The Atlantic Monthly*, digital edition (www.theatlantic.com/issues/98oct/ industry.htm).

McEwan, T. (2001) *Managing Values and Beliefs in Organisations* (Harlow: Pearson Education).

McNamee, D. 'Targeting Business Risk,' *The Internal Auditor*, October 2000, pp. 46–51.

McNaughton, D. (1988) *Moral Vision An Introduction To Ethics* (Oxford: Blackwell).

McPhail, K. J. (1999), 'The Threat of Ethical Accountants: An Application of Foucault's Concept of Ethics to Accounting Education and Some Thoughts on Ethically Educating for the Other', *Critical Perspectives on Accounting*, vol. 10, pp. 833–66.

McPhail, K. J. (2001), 'The *Other* Objective of Ethics Education, Rehumanising the Accounting Profession: A Study of Ethics Education in Law, Engineering, Medicine and Accountancy', *Journal of Business Ethics*, vol. 34, no. 3–4, pp. 279–98.

McSweeney, B. (2002) 'Hofstede's Identification of National Cultural Differences and Their Consequences: A Triumph of Faith – A Failure of Analysis, *Human Relations*, vol. 55, no. 1, pp. 89–118.

Meagher, D. and G. O'Neill (2000) 'Enterprise wide risk management', *Accountancy Ireland*, vol. 32, no. 6 (December).

Merchant, K. (1981) 'The Design of the Corporate Budgeting System: Influences on Managerial Behaviour and Performance', *The Accounting Review*, vol. 56, no. 4, pp. 813–29.

Merchant, K. (1985) *Control in Business Organizations* (London: Pitman).

Merchant, K. (1987) 'How and Why Firms Disregard the Controllability Principle.' In Bruns, W. and Kaplan, R., (eds) Accounting and Management: Field Study Perspectives. Harvard Business School Press, pp. 316–38.

Merchant, K. A., W. Van der Stede and L. Zheng (2003) 'Disciplinary constraints on the advancement of knowledge: the case of organizational incentive systems', *Accounting, Organizations and Society*, vol. 28, pp. 251–86.

Merkley, B. W. (2001) 'Does enterprise risk management count?', Risk Management: New York.

Meszaros, J. (1999) 'Preventive Choices: Organisation's heuristics, deciosn processes and catastrophic risks', *Journal of Management Studies,* vol. 36, no, 7, pp. 978–98.

Meyer, J. W. and B. Rowan (1977) 'Institutionalized Organizations: Formal Structure as Myth and Ceremony', *American Journal of Sociology*, vol. 83, pp. 340–63.

Meyer, J. W. and Rowan, B. (1983) 'The Structure of Educational Organizations' in Meyer J. W. and Scottt W. R. (eds), *Organizational Environments: Ritual and Rationality* (Beverly Hills, CA: Sage).

Michael, D. (1983) *On Learning to Plan and Planning to Learn* (Josey Bass: San Fransisco).

Milani, K. (1975) 'The Relationship of Participation in Budget Setting to Industrial Supervisor performance and Attitudes: A Field Study', *The Accounting Review* no. 1, vol. 2, pp. 274–83.

Milburn, A. (1999) 'Public Service Agreements: No room for Sir Humphrey', *Public Finance*, 21–27 May, pp. 18–22.

Miles, R. E. and C. C. Snow (1978) *Organizational Strategy, Structure and Process* (New York: McGraw-Hill).

Miles, R. E. and C. C. Snow (1986) 'Organizations: New concepts for new forms', *California Management Review*, vol. 28, no. 3, pp. 62–73.

Milgram, S. (1974) *Obedience to Authority: An Experimental View* (London: Tavistock Publications).

Miller, E. J. (1976) 'Task, Territory and Technology', in E. J. Miller, *Task and Organization* (Chichester: Wiley).

Miller, P. (1994) 'Accounting as Social and Institutional Practice: An Introduction', in A. G. Hopwood and P. Miller (eds), *Accounting as Social and Institutional Practice* (Cambridge: Cambridge University Press), pp. 1–39.

Miller, P. and T. O'Leary (1987) 'Accounting and the Construction of the Governable Person', *Accounting, Organizations and Society*, vol. 12, no. 3, pp. 235–65.

Miller, R. and D. Lessard (2001) 'Understanding and Managing Risks in Large Engineering Projects', *International Journal of Project Management*, vol. 19, no. 8, pp. 437.

Milne, M. J. (1996) 'On Sustainability, the Environment and Management Accounting', *Management Accounting Research*, vol. 7, no. 1, pp. 135–61.

Minchington, C. and G. Francis (2000) Divisional Performance Measures: EVA as a proxy for shareholder wealth', *International Journal of Business Performance Management*, vol. 2, nos, 1–3, pp. 98–108.

Mintzberg, H. (1978) 'Patterns in Strategy Formation', *Management Science*, May, vol. 24, no. 9, pp. 934–48.

Mintzberg, H. (1979) *The Structuring of Organizations* (Englewood Cliffs, NJ: Prentice-Hall).

Mintzberg, H. (1983) *Power In and Around Organizations* (Englewood Cliffs, NJ: Prentice-Hall).

Mintzberg, H. (1991) 'Five Ps for Strategy', in H. Mintzberg and J. B. Quinn (eds), *The Strategy Process: Concepts, Contexts, Cases*, 2nd edn (Englewood Cliffs, NJ: Prentice-Hall), pp. 12–19.

Mintzberg, H. (1993) *Structure in Fives: Designing Effective Organizations* (Englewood Cliffs: Prentice-Hall).

Mintzberg, H., R. Simons and K. Basu (2002) 'Beyond Selfishness', *MIT Sloan Management Review*, Fall, pp. 67–74.

Mintzberg, H. and J. Waters (1985) 'On Strategies Deliberate and Emergent', *Strategic Management Journal*, vol. 6, no. 1, pp. 25–37.

Mitchell, J. C. (1969) 'The Concept and Use of Social Networks', in J. C. Mitchell (ed.), *Social Networks in Urban Situations* (Manchester: Manchester University Press).

Mitchell, V.-W. (1999) 'Consumer Perceived Risk: Conceptualisations and Models', *European Journal of Marketing*, vol. 33, pp. 163–95.

Mohr, J. and R. Spekman (1994) 'Characteristics of Partnership Success: Partnership attributes, communication behaviour and conflict resolution techniques', *Strategic Management Journal*, vol. 15, pp. 135–52.

Moller, K. K. E. and S. Svahn (2003) 'Managing Strategic Nets; a capability perspective', *Marketing Theory*, vol. 3, pp. 209–20.

Moneva, J. M., P. Archel and C. Correa (2003) 'What is there on Sustainability in the GRI Guidelines?', paper presented at the 2003 European Accounting Association Congress, Seville, Spain, 2–4 April.

Moon, P. and L. Fitzgerald (1996) 'Delivering the Goods at TNT: the role of the performance measurement system', *Management Accounting Research*, vol. 7, pp. 431–57.

Morden, T. (1993) *Business Strategy and Planning* (London: McGraw-Hill).

Morgan, G. (1979) 'Internal Audit Role Conflict: A Pluralist View', *Managerial Finance*, vol. 5, pp. 160–70.

Morgan, G. (1986) *Images of Organization* (London: Sage).

Morgan, G. (1988) *Images of Organization*, 2nd edn (Thousand Oaks, CA: Sage).

Mouritsen, J. (1999) 'The Flexible Firm: strategies for a subcontractor's management control', *Accounting Organizations and Society*, vol. 24, no. 1, pp. 31–55.

Mouritsen, J., P. N. Bukh (2003) *Intellectual Capital Statements – The New Guideline* (Copenhagen: Ministry of Science, Innovation and Technology; www.vtu.dk/icaccounts).

Mouritsen, J., A. Hansen and C. O. Hansen (2001a) 'Inter-organizational Controls and Organizational Competencies: episodes around target cost management/financial analysis', *Management Accounting Research*, vol. 12, pp. 221–44.

Mouritsen, J., H. T. Larsen and P. N. Bukh (2001b) 'Valuing the Future: Intellectual Capital Supplements at Skandia', *Accounting, Auditing and Accountability Journal*, vol. 14, no. 14, pp. 399–422.

Muelbroek, L. (2001) 'Integrated risk management for the firm: a senior manager's guide?' *Harvard Business School Working Paper* 02-046. http://www.hbs.edu/research/facpubs/workingpapers/papers2/0102/02-046.pdf.

Muir, L. (2000) 'How do you score on managing risk?', (Sydney: Australian CPA).

Munro, R. (1999) 'The Cultural Performance of Control', *Organization Studies*, vol. 20, pp. 619–40.

Murray, R. (1999) *Creating Wealth from Waste* (London: Demos).

Neely, A., R. Sutcliff and H. R. Heyns (2001) *Driving Value through Strategic Planning and Budgeting* (New York: Accenture).

Neely, A. D. 'Measuring Business Performance', *The Economist Books*, London, 1998.

Neely, A. D., C. Adams and M. Kennerley 'The Performance Prism: The Scorecard for Measuring and Managing Stakeholder Relationships', *Financial Times* (London: Prentice Hall), 2003.

Neu, D., H. Warsame and K. Pedwell (1998) 'Managing public impressions: environmental disclosures in annual reports', *Accounting, Organizations and Society*, vol. 23, no. 3, pp. 265–82.

New Economics Foundation (NEF) (2000) *Corporate Spin – the Troubled Teenage Years of Social Reporting* (http://www.neweconomics.org/uploadstore/pubs/doc_2811200045047_New%20Eco%20Text/pdf).

Newman, J. (2001) *Modernising governance: New Labour, Policy and Society* (London: Sage).

Newman, W. H. and J. P. Logan (1971) *Strategy, Policy and Central Management* (Cincinnati: South-Western Publishing).

Nielsen, R. P. (1991), 'I Am We; Consciousness and Dialog as Organizational Ethics Method', *Journal of Business Ethics*, vol. 10, pp. 649–63.

Nilsson, F. (2000) 'Parenting styles and value creation: a management control approach', *Management Accounting Research*, vol. 11, pp. 89–112.

Noble, A. G., and F. J. Costa (eds) (1999) *Preserving the Legacy: Concepts in Support of Sustainability* (New York: Lexington Books).

Nohria, N. and R. G. Eccles (1992) *Networks and Organisations: Structure, Form and Action* (Cambridge, Mass.: Harvard Business School Press).

Nonaka, I. (1994) 'A Dynamic Theory of Organizational Knowledge Creation, *Organization Science*, vol. 5, pp. 14–37.

Nonaka, I. and H. Takeuchi (1991) 'The Knowledge-creating Company', *Harvard Business Review*, November–December, vol. 69, no. 6, pp. 96–104.

Nonaka, I. and H. Takeuchi (1995) *The Knowledge-creating Company* (Oxford: Oxford University Press).

Nord, W., S. Fox, A. Phoenix and K. Viano (2002) 'Real-world Reactions to Work–Life Balance Programmes', *Organizational Dynamics*, vol. 30, no. 3, pp. 223–38.

Norgaard, R. B. (1989) 'Three Dilemmas of Environmental Accounting', *Ecological Economics*, vol. 1, no. 4, pp. 303–14.

Norgaard, R. B. (1992) 'Sustainability as Intergenerational Equity: Economic Theory and Environmental Planning', *Environmental Impact Assessment Review*, vol. 12, pp. 85–124.

Norreklit, H. (2000) 'The balance on the balanced scorecard – a critical analysis of some of its assumptions', *Management Accounting Research*, vol. 11, pp. 65–88.

Northcott, D. (1991) 'Rationality and Decision Making in Capital Budgeting', *British Accounting Review*, vol. 23, no. 3, pp. 219–34.

Northcott, D. (1992) *Capital Investment Decision Making* (London: CIMA/Academic Press).

Norton, B. G. (1989) 'Intergenerational Equity and Environmental Decisions: A Model Using Rawls' Veil of Ignorance', *Ecological Economics*, vol. 1, pp. 137–59.

O'Donnell, A., A. Gilmore, C. Cummins and D. Carson (2001) 'The network construct in entrepreneurship research; a review and critique', *Management decision*, vol. 39, no. 9, pp. 749–61.

O'Dwyer, B., J. Unerman and J. Bradley (2003) 'Stakeholder Perceptions of Corporate Social Disclosure in Ireland: A Story of Antagonism, Powerlessness and Poor Practice', paper presented at the 26th Annual Congress of the European Accounting Association, Seville, Spain, 2–4 April.

O'Riordan, T. (1993) 'The Politics of Sustainability', in (ed.), R. Kerry Turner *Sustainable Environmental Economics and Management: Principles and Practice* (London: Belhaven Press).

O'Riordan, T. and J. Cameron (eds) (1994) *Interpreting the Precautionary Principle* (London: Earthscan).

Odum, W. (1982) 'Environmental Degradation and the Tyranny of Small Decisions', *Bioscience*, vol. 32, pp. 728–9.

Office of Public Service Reform (OPSR) (2002) *Reforming our Public Services: Principles into Practice* (London: HMSO).

Okimoto, D. I. (1986) 'Regime characteristics of Japanese industrial policy', in Hugh Patrick (ed.), *Japan's High Technology Industries* (Seattle: University of Washington Press).

Oliver, A. L. and M. Ebers (1998) 'Networking network studies: an analysis of conceptual configurations in the study of inter-organisational relationships', *Organisation Studies*, vol. 19, pp. 549–84.

Olsen, O., J. Guthrie and C. Humphrey (1998) *Global Warning: Debating International Developments in New Public Management* (Oslo: Cappelen Akademisk Ferlag).

Organisation for Economic Cooperation and Development (OECD) (2001) *OECD Environmental Strategy for the First Decade of the 21st Century* (Paris: OECD).

Orr, D. W. (1992) *Ecological Literacy: Education and the Transition to a Postmodern World* (New York: State University of New York Press).

Osborne, D. and T. Gaeble (1993) *Reinventing Government: How the Entrepreneurial Spirit is Transforming the Public Sector* (New York: Plume).

Otley, D. (1978) 'Budget Use and Managerial Performance', *Journal of Accounting Research*, vol. 1, no. 6, pp. 122–49.

Otley, D. T. (1980) 'The Contingency Theory of Management Accounting: achievement and prognosis', *Accounting, Organizations and Society*, vol. 5, no. 4, pp. 413–28.

Otley, D. (1987) *Accounting Control and Organizational Behaviour* (London: Heinemann).

Otley, D. (1990) 'Issues in Accountability and Control: some observations from a study of colliery accountability in the British Coal Corporation', *Management Accounting Research*, vol. 1, pp. 101–23.

Otley, D. (1999) 'Performance Management: a framework for management control systems research', *Management Accounting Research*, vol. 10, pp. 363–82.

Otley, D. (2001) 'Extending the Boundaries of Management Accounting Research: developing systems for performance measurement', *British Accounting Review*, vol. 33, pp. 243–61.

Otley, D. and A. J. Berry (1980) 'Control, Organization and Accounting', *Accounting Organizations and Society*, vol. 5, no. 2, pp. 231–46.

Otley, D. and A. J. Berry (1979) 'Risk Distribution in the Budgetary Process', *Accounting and Business Research* (Autumn 1979) pp. 325–37.

Ouchi, W. G. (1977) 'The Relationship between Organizational Structure and Organizational Control', *Administrative Science Quarterly*, vol. 22, pp. 95–112.

Ouchi, W. G. (1979) 'A Conceptual Framework for the Design of Organisational Control Mechanisms', *Management Science*, vol. 25, no. 9, pp. 833–49.

Ouchi, W. G. (1980) 'Markets, Bureaucracies and Clans', *Administrative Science Quarterly*, vol. 25, no. 1, pp. 129–41.

Ouchi, W. G. (1981) *Theory Z* (Reading, Mass.: Addison-Wesley).

Outhwaite, W. (1996), *Habermas: A Critical Introduction* (Oxford: Blackwell).

Owen, D. and T. Swift (2001) 'Social Accounting, Reporting and Auditing: Beyond the rhetoric', *Business Ethics: A European Review*, vol. 10, no. 1, pp. 4–8.

Palley, T. I. (1995) 'Safety in Numbers – a Model of Managerial Herd Behaviour', *Journal of Economic Behaviour and Organisation*, vol. 28, pp. 443–50.

Parker, L. D. (1979) 'Divisional Performance Measurement: Beyond an Exclusive Profit Test', *Accounting and Business Research*, vol. 9, no. 3, Autumn, pp. 309–19.

Parker, M. (1998), 'Introduction: Ethics, the Very Idea', in M. Parker (ed.), *Ethics & Organisations* (London: Sage) pp. 1–14.

Parker, M. (2000) *Organisational Culture and Identity: Unity and Division at Work* (London: Sage).

Parsons, T. (1951) *The Social System* (London: Routledge Keegan and Paul).

Partridge, M. and L. Perren (1994) 'Cost analysis of the value chain: Another role for strategic management accounting', *Management Accounting*, July–August, pp. 22–8.

Pascale, R. T. (1990) *Managing on the Edge: How Successful Companies Use Conflict to Stay Ahead* (London: Viking Penguin).

Pask, G. (1961) *An Approach to Cybernetics* (London: Hutchinson).

Pearce, D. W. (1988) 'Economics, Equity and Sustainable Development', *Futures*, vol. 20, pp. 598–605.

Perrow, C. (1967) 'A Framework for the Comparative Analysis of Organisations', *American Sociological Review 32*, April, pp. 194–208.

Perrow, C. (1970) *Organisational Analysis: A Sociological View* (London: Tavistock).

Perrow, C. (1986) *Complex Organisations*, 3rd edn (New York: Random House).

Peters, T. J. and R. H. Waterman (1982) *In Search of Excellence* (New York: Harper and Rowe).

Pettigrew, A. M. (1979) 'On Studying Organisational Cultures', *Administrative Science Quarterly*, vol. 24, pp. 570–81.

Pettigrew, A. M., L. McKee and E. Ferlie (1989) 'Hints on How to Ring the Changes', *Health Service Journal*, 16 February.

Petty, R. and J. Guthrie (2000) 'Intellectual Capital Review: Measurement, Reporting and Management', *Journal of Intellectual Capital*, vol. 1, no. 2, pp. 155–760.

Pfeffer, J. and C. R. Salanick (1977) *The External Control of Organisations: A Resource Dependent Perspective* (New York and London: Harper and Row).

Philips, N. (1991) 'The Sociology Of Knowledge: Toward an Existentialist View of Business Ethics', *Journal of Business Ethics*, vol. 10, pp. 787–95.

Pike, R. (1983) 'The Capital Budgeting Behaviour and Corporate Characteristics of Capital-Constrained Firms', *Journal of Business Finance and Accounting*, vol. 10, pp. 663–72.

Pike, R. (1988) 'An Empirical Study of the Adoption of Sophisticated Capital Budgeting Practices and Decision-Making Effectiveness', *Accounting and Business Research*, vol. 18, pp. 341–51.

Piper, J. M. (2002) 'CEA and Sustainable Development: Evidence from UK Case Studies', *Environmental Impact Assessment Review*, vol. 22, pp. 17–36.

Plato (1996) *The Collected Dialogues* (Princeton, NJ: Bollingen).

Ponemon, L. A. (1990) 'Ethical Judgements in Accounting: A Cognitive-Development Perspective', *Critical Perspectives on Accounting*, vol. 1, no. 2, pp. 191–215.

Ponemon, L. A. (1992) 'Ethical Reasoning and Selection-Socialization in Accounting', *Accounting, Organizations and Society*, vol. 17, no. 3–4, pp. 239–58.

Porter, M. E. (1980) *Competitive Strategy: Techniques for Analyzing Industries and Competitors* (New York: Free Press).

Porter, M. E. (1985) *Competitive Advantage, Creating and Sustaining Superior Performance* (New York: Free Press).

Power, M. and R. Laughlin (1992) 'Critical Theory and Accounting', in M. Alvesson and H. Willmott (eds), *Critical Management Studies* (London: Sage), pp. 113–55.

Prahalad, C. K. and G. Hamel (1990) 'The Core Competence of the Corporation', *Harvard Business Review*, vol. 68, no. 3, pp. 79–91.

Preston, A. (1995) 'Budgeting, Creativity and Culture', in D. Ashton, T. Hopper and R. W. Scapens (eds), *Issues in Management Accounting* (London: Prentice Hall).

Pruitt, D. G. (1981) *Negotiation Behaviour* (New York: Academic Press).

Purdy, D. E. (1991) 'Natural Learning in Committee B', *Management Education and Development*, vol. 22, part 1, pp. 60–70.

Purdy, D. E. (1993a) 'Accounting, Controls, Change and the Perceptions of Managers: A Longitudinal Study of Ward Units in a Teaching Hospital', *Financial Accountability and Management*, vol. 9, no. 1, pp. 45–66.

Purdy, D. E. (1993b) 'Ward Sisters and Financial Management Accounting', *Financial Accountability and Management*, vol. 9, no. 4, pp. 279–96.

Puxty, A. G. (1989). *Critical Perspectives in Management Control* (London: Macmillan)

Puxty, A. G. (1993) *The Social and Organizational Context of Management Accounting* (London: Academic Press).

Puxty A. G. (1998) *The Social and Organizational Context of Management Accounting*, 2nd edn (London: International Thomson Business Press).

Quillian, L. (1991) 'Curing "Functional Silo Syndrome" with Logistics Total Cost Management', *CMA Magazine*, June, pp. 9–14.

Quinn, J. B. (1980) *Strategies for Change: Logical Incrementalism* (Homewood, Ill.: Richard D. Irwin).

Redclift, M. (1987) *Sustainable Development: Exploring the Contradictions* (London: Methuen).

Reece, J. S. and W. R. Cool (1978) 'Measuring Investment Centre Performance', *Harvard Business Review*, May–June, pp. 29–49.

Rees, W. E. (1988) 'A Role for Environmental Assessment in Achieving Sustainable Development', *Environmental Impact Assessment Review*, vol. 8, pp. 273–91.

Richardson, G. B. (1972) 'The organisation of industry', *Economic Journal*, vol. 82, pp. 883–96.

Ring, P. S. and A. Van de Ven (1992) 'Structuring cooperative relationships between organisations', *Strategic Management Journal*, vol. 13, pp. 483–98.

Roethlisberger, F. J. and W. J. Dickson (1964) *Management and the Worker* (New York: John Wiley).

Roos, G., G. Ross, L. Edvinsson and N. C. Dragonetti (1997) *Intellectual capital: navigating in the new business landscape.* (Houndsmil: Macmillan Business).

Rose, M. (1975) *Industrial Behaviour: Theoretical Development Since Taylor* (London: Allen Lane).

Rossouw, G. J. (1994) 'Rational Interaction for Moral Sensitivity: A Postmodern Approach to Moral Decision-Making in Business', *Journal of Business Ethics*, vol. 13, pp. 11–20.

Rousseau, D. M., S. B. Sitkin, R. S. Burt and C. Camerer (1998) 'Not so different after all: a cross discipline view of trust', *Academy of Management Review*, vol. 3, pp. 393–404.

Rowlinson, M. (1997) *Organisations and Institutions* (London: Macmillan).

Sadler, B. (1988) *Natural Capital and Borrowed Time: The Global Context of Sustainable Development*, (Victoria, BC: Institute of the North American West).

Sagoff, M. (1988) 'Some Problems with Environmental Economics', *Environmental Ethics*, vol. 10, pp. 55–74.

Sako, M. (1992) *Prices, Quality and Trust: Inter-Firm Relationships in Britain and Japan* (Cambridge: Cambridge University Press).

Sale, K. (1980) *Human Scale* (New York: Coward, Cann and Geoghegen).

Sale, K. (1985) *Dwellers in the Land: The Bio-regional Vision* (San Francisco: Sierra Club).

Samuelson, L. (2000) 'The effects of increasing turbulence on organizational control: some reflections', in S.B. Dahiya (ed.), *The Current State of Business Disciplines, Management Volume 5* (Rotak, India: Spellbound).

Saunders, M. (1994) *Strategic Purchasing and Supply Chain Management* (London: Pitman for the Chartered Institute of Purchasing and Supply).

Scapens, R. W. and J. Roberts (1993) 'Accounting and Control: a case study of resistance to accounting change', *Management Accounting Research*, vol. 4 no. 1, pp. 1–32.

Schaefer, A., A. Coulson, K. Green, S. New and J. Skea (2003) 'Sustainable Business Organisations?' in F. Berkhout, M. Leach and I. Scoones (eds) *Negotiating Environmental Change: New perspectives from social science* (Cheltenham: Elgar), pp. 209–30.

Schein, E. H. (1985) *Organisational Culture and Leadership* (San Francisco, CA: Jossey-Bass).

Scheytt, T., K. Soin and T. Metz (2003) 'Exploring Notions of Control Across Cultures: A Narrative Approach', *European Accounting Review*, vol. 12, pp. 515–47.

Schiff, M. and A. Y. Lewin (1970) 'The Impact of People on Budgets', *The Accounting Review*, vol. 45, pp. 259–68.

Schmidt-Bleek, F. (1993) *The Fossil Makers*, English translation of *Wieviel Umwelt Braucht Der Mensch – MIPS, Das Mass Für Ökologisches Wirtschaften* (http://www.factor10-institute.org/Pdf-Files.htm).

Schoderbeck, P. P., C. G. Schoderbeck and A. G. Kefalas (1975) *Management Systems: Conceptual Considerations* (Dallas, Tex.: Business Publishers).

Schoeffler, S., R. D. Buzzell and D. F. Heany (1974) 'Impact of Strategic Planning on Profit Performance', *Harvard Business Review*, March–April, pp. 137–45.

Schön, D. A. (1983) *The Reflective Practitioner* (New York: Basic Books).

Schreyogg, G. and H. Steinmann (1987) 'Strategic Control: A New Perspective', *Academy of Management Review*, vol. 12, no. 1, pp. 91–103.

Scott, B. R. (1971) *Stage Four of Corporate Development – Park 1* (Cambridge, Mass.: Harvard Business School).

Scott, W. R. (1995) *Institutions and Organisations* (London: Sage).

Seal, W., A. Berry and J. Cullen, A. Dunlop and M. Ahmed (1999) 'Enacting a European supply chain: a case study on the role of management accounting', *Management Accounting Research*, vol. 10, no. 3, pp. 303–22.

Seal, W., A. Berry and J. Cullen (2004) 'Disembedding the supply chain: institutionalised reflexivity and inter-firm accounting', *Accounting, Organizations and Society*, vol. 29, pp. 73–92.

Segerstrom, J. R. (2000) *How do I handle 'model' risk?* (Sydney: Australian Bankers Association).

Selznick, P. (1957) *Leadership in Administration: A Sociological Interpretation* (White Plains: Row, Peterson).

Senge, P. M. (1990) *The Fifth Discipline: The Art and Practice of the Learning Organization* (New York: Doubleday).

Shank, J. K. (1989) 'Strategic Cost Management: New Wine, or Just New Bottles?', *Journal of Management Accounting Research*, vol. 1, Fall, pp. 47–65.

Shank, J. K. and V. Govindarajan (1992) 'Strategic Cost Management: The Value Chain Perspective', *Journal of Management Accounting Research*, vol. 4, pp. 179–98.

Shank, J. K. and V. Govindarajan (1993) 'Strategic Cost Management: The New Tool for Competitive Advantage (New York: Free Press).

Shearer, T. (2002) 'Ethics and accountability: from the for-itself to the for-the-other', *Accounting, Organisations and Society*, vol. 27, pp. 541–73.

Shillinglaw, G. D. (1982) *Cost Accounting Analysis and Control* (Homewood, Ill.: Richard D. Irwin).

Shiva, V. (2001) 'The World on the Edge', in A. Giddens and W. Hutton (eds), *On the Edge: Living with Global Capitalism* (London: Vintage), pp. 112–29.

Shotter, J. (1993) *Conversational Realities: Constructing Life Through Language* (London: Sage).

Shrivastava, P. (1994) 'Castrated environment: Greening organizational studies', *Organization Studies*, vol. 15, no. 5, pp. 705–26.

Silvestro, R. and S. Cross (2000) 'Applying the service profit chain in a retail environment: Challenging the satisfaction mirror', *International Journal of Service Industry Management*, vol. 11, no. 3, pp. 244–68.

Simmonds, K. (1981) 'Strategic Management Accounting', *Management Accounting*, April, 59 pp. 26–9.

Simon, H. (1957) *Administrative Behaviour* (New York: Free Press).

Simon, H., H. Guetzkow, G. Kozmetsky and G. Tyndall (1954) *Centralisation vs Decentralisation in the Controllers Department* (New York: Controllership Foundation).

Simons, R. (1987a) 'Planning, Control and Uncertainty: A Process View', in W. J. Bruns and R. S. Kaplan (eds), *Accounting and Management – Field Study Perspectives* (Boston, Mass: Harvard Business School Press), pp. 339–62.

Simons, R. (1987b) 'Accounting Control Systems and Business Strategy: An Empirical Analysis', *Accounting, Organisations and Society*, vol. 12, no. 4, pp. 357–74.

Simons, R. (1990) 'The Role of Management Control Systems in Creating Competitive Advantage: New Perspectives', *Accounting, Organizations and Society*, vol. 15, no. 1/2, pp. 127–43.

Simons, R. (1995a) *Levers of Control* (Cambridge, Mass.: Harvard Business School Press).

Simons, R. (1995b) 'Control in an Age of Empowerment', *Harvard Business Review*, March–April, pp. 80–8.

Simons, R. (2000) *Performance Measurement and Control Systems for Implementing Strategy* (Englewood Cliffs, NJ: Prentice-Hall).

Simonson, I. and Tversky, A. (1992) 'Choice in Context: Tradeoff Contrast and Extremeness Aversion', *Journal of Marketing Research*, vol. 129, pp. 281–95.

Singer, P. (1997) *How are we to live? Ethics in an age of self-interest* (Oxford: Oxford University Press).

Skinner, R. C. (1990) 'The role of profitability in divisional decision making and performance evaluation', *Accounting and Business Research*, vol. 20, Spring, pp. 135–41.

Smircich, L. (1983) 'Concepts of Culture and Organizational Analysis', *Administrative Science Quarterly*, vol. 28, no. 2, pp. 328–58.

Smith, A. (1937) *The Wealth of Nations* (New York: The Modern Library) (first published in 1776).

Smyth, P. S. and P. B. Checkland (1976) 'Using a Systems Approach: The structure of Root Definitions', *Journal of Applied Systems Analysis*, vol. 5, no. 1.

Society of Management Accountants in Canada (SMAC) (1997) *Measuring and Managing Shareholder Value Creation, Management Accounting Guideline, No. 44* (Mississauga Ontario: Society of Management Accountants of Canada).

Soin, K., W. Seal and J. Cullen (2002) 'ABC and Organizational Change: An Institutional Perspective', *Management Accounting Research*, vol. 13, no. 2, pp. 249–71.

Solomons, D. (1965) *Divisional Performances: Measurement and Control* (Homewood, Ill.: Irwin).

Spicer, B. H. and V. Ballew (1983) 'Management Accounting Systems and the Economics of Internal Organization', *Accounting, Organizations and Society*, vol. 8, pp. 73–96.

Spira, L. F. and M. Page (2003) 'Risk Management: The reinvention of internal control and the changing role of internal audit', *Accounting, Auditing and Accountability Journal*, vol. 16, pp. 640–61.

Stacey, R. D. (1996) *Strategic Management and Organizational Dynamics*, 2nd edn (London: Pitman).

Stacey, R. D., R. Griffin and P. Shaw (2000) *Complexity and Management: Fad or Radical Challenge to Systems Thinking?* (London: Routledge).

Starkey, K., M. Wright and S. Thompson (1991) 'Flexibility, Hierarchy and Markets', *British Journal of Management*, vol. 2, pp. 165–76.

Steers, R. M. (1975) 'Problems in the Measurement of Organizational Effectiveness', *Administrative Science Quarterly*, vol. 20, no.4, December, pp. 613–29.

Stein, M. (2000) 'The Risk Taker as Shadow: A psychoanalytic view of the collapse of Barings Bank', *Journal of Management Studies*, vol. 38, no. 8, pp. 1215–29.

Stewart, G. B. III (1994) 'EVA™ Fact and Fantasy', *Journal of Applied Corporate Finance*, vol. 7, no. 2, Summer, pp. 71–84.

Stewart, T. A. (1997) *Intellectual Capital* (London: Nicholas Brealey).

Stone, D. (1995) 'No longer at the end of the pipe, but still a long way from sustainability: a look at management accounting for the environment and sustainable development in the United States', *Accounting Forum*, vol. 19, nos. 2–3, pp. 95–110.

Stuart, F. I. and D. McCutcheon (1996) 'Sustaining Strategic Supplier Alliances', *International Journal of Operations and Production Management*, vol. 16, no. 10, pp. 5–22.

Sveiby, K. E. (1997) *The New Organizational Wealth: Managing and Measuring Knowledge-based Assets*, (San Francisco, CA: Berrett-Koehler).

Swedberg, R. and M. Granovetter (eds.) (1992) *The Sociology of Economic Life* (Boulder, Co: Westview Press).

Swieringa, R. J. and Weick, K. E. (1987) 'Management Accounting and Action', *Accounting Organisations and Society*, vol. 12, no. 3, pp. 293–308.

Tajfel, H. and C. Fraser (1990) *Introducing Social Psychology* (Harmondsworth: Penguin).

Taylor, F. W. (1911, reprinted 1947) *Scientific Management* (New York: Harper and Brothers).

Teece, D. (1996) 'Firm organisation, industrial structure, and technological innovation', *Journal of Economic Behaviour and Organisation*, vol. 31, pp. 193–224.

Teubner, G. (1983) 'Substantive and Reflexive Elements in Modern Law', *Law and Society Review*, vol. 18, no. 2, pp. 291–301.

Thode, S. F. (1986) 'The Trouble with Divisional Hurdle Rates', *Business Horizons*, Jan.–Feb., pp. 62–6.

Thomas, H. (1993) 'Perspectives on Theory Building in Strategic Management', *Journal of Management Studies*, vol. 30, no. 1, pp. 3–10.

Thompson, J. D. (1967) *Organizations in Action* (New York: McGraw-Hill).

Tocher, K. (1970) 'Control', *Operational Research Quarterly*, vol. 21., June, pp. 159–80.

Tocher, K. (1976) 'Notes for Discussion on Control', *Operational Research Quarterly*, vol. 27, June, pp. 231–9.

Toman, M. A. (1992) 'The Difficulty in Defining Sustainability', *Resources*, no. 106, (Washington, DC: Resources for the Future).

Tomkins, C. (1973) *Financial Planning in Divisional Companies* (London: Haymarket).

Tomkins, C. (2001) 'Interdependencies, trust and information in relationships, alliances and networks', *Accounting, Organizations and Society*, vol. 26, pp. 161–91.

Tosi, H. (1975) 'The Human Effects of Managerial Budgeting Systems', in J. H. Livingson (ed.), *Management Accounting: The Behavioural Foundations* (Columbus, Ohio: Grid).

Trevino, L. K. (1992) 'Moral Reasoning and Business Ethics: Implications for Research, Education and Management', *Journal of Business Ethics*, vol. 11, pp. 445–59.

Trice, H. M. and J. M. Beyer (1993) *The Cultures of Work Organizations* (Englewood Cliffs, NJ: Prentice-Hall).

Trist, E. (1976) 'A Concept of Organizational Ecology', *Australian Journal of Management*, vol. 2, no. 2, pp. 161–76.

Turnbull, P., N. Oliver and B. Wilkinson (1992) 'Buyer – supplier relations in the UK automotive industry: Strategic implications of the Japanese manufacturing model', *Strategic Management Journal*, vol. 13, pp. 1159–68.

Turnbull Report (1999) *Internal Control: Guidance for Directors on the Combined Code* (London: Institute of Chartered Accountants in England and Wales).

Turner, R. K. (ed.) (1993) *Sustainable Environmental Economics and Management: Principles and Practice* (London: Belhaven).

Tversky, A., P. Slovic and D. Kahneman (1990) 'The Causes of Preference Reversal', *The American Economic Review*, vol. 80, no. 1, pp. 204–17.

Tversky, A. and R. H. Thaler (199) 'Anomalies: Preference Reversals', *Journal of Economic Perspectives*, vol. 4, no. 2, pp. 210–11.

Tylecote, A. (1992) *The Long Wave and the World Economy: The Current Crisis in Historical Perspective* (London: Routledge).

Ungar, S. (2001) 'Moral panic versus the risk society: the implications of the changing sites of social anxiety', *The British Journal of Sociology*, vol. 52, no. 2, p. 271.

Van der Meer-Kooistra, J. and E. Vosselman (2000) 'Management control of inter-firm transactional relationships: the case of industrial renovation and maintenance', *Accounting, Organizations and Society*, vol. 25, no.1, pp. 51–77.

Van Gusteren, H. R. (1976) *The Quest for Control* (London: John Wiley).

Vancil, R. F. (1979) *Decentralisation: Ambiguity by Design* (Homewood, Ill.: Richard D. Wiley).

Vickers, G. (1965) *The Art of Judgement A Study of Policy Making* (London: Methuen).

Vickers, G. (1967) *Towards a Sociology of Management* (London: Chapman and Hall).

Wackernagel, M., and W. Rees (1996) *Our Ecological Footprint: Reducing Human Impact on the Earth* (Canada: New Society).

Wallander, Jan (1999) 'Budgeting – an unnecessary evil', *Scandinavian Journal of Management*, vol. 15, pp. 405–21.

Weber, E. U. and C. Hsee (1998) 'Cross-cultural Differences in Risk Perception, but Cross-cultural Similarities in Attitudes Towards Perceived Risk', *Management Science*, vol. 44, pp. 1205–17.

Weber, E. U. and R. A. Milliman (1997) 'Perceived Risk Attitudes: Relating Risk Perception to Risky Choice', *Management Science*, vol. 43, pp. 123–44.

Weber, J. (1990) 'Measuring the impact of Teaching Ethics to Future Managers: A Review, Assessment and Recommendations', *Journal of Business Ethics*, vol. 9, no. 3, pp. 183–90.

Weber, M. (1948) 'The Social Psychology of the World Religions', in H. H. Gerth and C. W. Mills (eds), *From Max Weber* (London: Routledge and Keegan Paul), pp. 267–301.

Weick, K. E. (1979) *The Social Psychology of Organizing*, 2nd edn (New York: Random House).

Weick, K. E. (1995) *Sensemaking in Organizations* (Thousand Oaks, CA: Sage).

Weiner, N. (1948) *Cybernetics* (Cambridge, Mass.: MIT Press).

Welch, J. B. and T. L. Kainen (1983) 'Risk Adjusted Multiple Hurdle Rates: better capital budgeting', *Financial Executive*, May.

Welford, R. (1995) *Environmental Strategy and Sustainable Development: The Challenge for the 21st Century* (London: Routledge).

Welford, R. (ed.) (1997) *Hijacking Environmentalism: Corporate Response to Sustainable Development* (London: Earthscan).

Wenger, E. (2000) 'Communities of Practice and Social Learning Systems', *Organizations*, vol. 7, no. 2, pp. 225–46.

Whitley, R. (1994) *Business Systems in East Asia; Firms, Markets and Societies* (London: Sage).

Wildavsky, A. (1975) *Budgeting: A Comparative Theory of Budgetary Processes* (Boston, Mass.: Little, Brown).

Williamson, O. E. (1970) *Corporate Control and Business Behavior* (Englewood Cliffs, NJ: Prentice-Hall).

Williamson, O. E. (1973) 'Markets and Hierarchies: Some Elementary Considerations', *American Economic Association*, vol. 63, no. 2.

Williamson, O. E. (1975) *Markets and Hierarchies: Analysis and Antitrust Implications* (New York: Free Press).

Williamson, O. E. (1979) 'Transaction-Cost Economics: the governance of contractual relations', *Journal of Law and Economics*, vol. 22, no. 2, pp. 3–61.

Williamson, O. E. (1985) *The Economic Institutions of Capitalism* (New York: Free Press).

Willmott, H. (1993) 'Strength is Ignorance; Slavery is Freedom: Managing Culture in Modern Organizations', *Journal of Management Studies*, vol. 30, pp. 515–52.

Willmott, H. (1998), 'Towards a New Ethics? The Contributions of Poststructuralism and Posthumanism', in M. Parker (ed.), *Ethics and Organisations* (London: Sage), pp. 76–121).

Wilson, R. M. S. and W. F. Chua (1992) *Managerial Accounting: Method and Meaning* (London: VNR).

Womack, J. P., D. T. Jones and D. Roos (1990) *The Machine that Changed the World* (New York: Rawson).

Woodward, J. (1958) *Management and Technology* (London: HMSO).

Woodward, J. (1965) *Industrial Organisation: Theory and Practice* (Oxford: Oxford University Press).

World Commission on Environment and Development (WECD) (1987) *Our Common Future* (Oxford: Oxford University Press).

Yeung, W. H. (1994) 'Critical reviews of geographical perspectives on business organisation and the organisation of production: towards a network approach', *Progress in Human Geography*, vol. 18, no. 4.

Young, M. D. (1992) *Sustainable Investment and Resource Use: Equity, Environmental Integrity, and Economic Efficiency*, Man and the Biosphere Series, vol. 9, (Melbourne: Parthenon).

Zheng, J., C. Harland, T. Johnsen and R. Lamming (1997) 'Features of supply networks', paper presented at the BAM conference, London.

Zolkos, R. (2000) 'Analytic methods best for setting risk retention', *Business Insurance*, vol. 34, no. 35, pp. 54–6.

Zovanyi, G. (1998) *Growth Management for a Sustainable Future: Ecological Sustainability as the New Growth Management Focus for the 21st Century* (London: Praeger).

Index

Notes: f = figure; n = note; t = table; **bold** = extended discussion or heading emphasized in main text.

381